"Effectively the first-ever modern biography of Cato. The writing is excellent, the stories unforgettable, and the lessons practical." —Tim Ferriss

"Well-crafted retelling of the life of Cato." —*The New American*

"[This] wise and lively book offers two lessons: first, knowing modern politics can yield insight into study of the ancient world; and second, Rome still has lessons to teach us today." —*City Journal*

"The authors succeed brilliantly in bringing this fascinating statesman to life." —*Kirkus Reviews*

"In a rare modern biography of Marcus Cato the Younger, a rival of both Caesar and Pompey, Goodman, formerly a Democratic speechwriter, and Soni (managing editor, *The Huffington Post*) argue that understanding Cato and the many legends surrounding him will help readers understand both the current American political climate and contemporary notions of freedom. . . . There are great moments here: Cato, struggling in Utica after the defeats at Pharsalus and Thapsus, is revealed in all his flawed humanity. Where others (e.g., Adrian Goldsworthy in *Caesar: Life of a Colossus*) are inclined to view Cato as a hypocrite, using his virture and stoicism as another tack to rise in the high-stakes world of late Republic Rome power politics, Goodman and Soni take a more nuanced approach, broaching many questions, never answering firmly. This makes for a more revealing portrait of a real man and demonstrates just how much a symbol Cato has become." —*Library Journal*

"Written in flowing, nonacademic prose, this biography suits the never-waning popular interest in the dramas of ancient Roman history." —*Booklist*

"This well-paced and dramatic book narrates the controversial life and political and moral legacy of Marcus Porcius Cato. . . . They [the authors] give their account depth by closely grounding it in the ancient sources, and their experience in and knowledge of modern politics adds special value to their assessments of Cato . . . indeed frankly describing his flaws as a politician and a man. . . . As the opening discussion shows and the main narrative confirms, there is indeed a lot worth thinking about in deciding what should be the lessons to draw from Cato's life and legacy." —*History Book Club*

"Goodman and Soni's examination of Cato the Younger—the Roman reactionary, Stoic, and enemy of Caesar—is the story of a harsh man in a violent age. With his pronounced British accent, Derek Perkins is a surprising choice for narration as this book seems directed at an American audience. But his voice is strong, and he sets the pace like someone leading a brisk, invigorating jog. The slightly cynical, skeptical edge of his tone fits the text, which refuses to take Cato at his own saintly face value or to respect the turbulent 'banana republic' of Rome. His edgy take fits both Cato's troubled republic and (despite the accent) our own, which is part of the book's point. Perkins's vigorous performance helps keep this an absorbing program." —*AudioFile* (starred review)

"When the Roman Republic finally fell, the last man standing was Cato, staunch defender of old Rome's venerable legacy and enemy of Caesar's new world order. Thanks to Goodman and Soni, this rare creature—a politician of honor willing to die for his principles—steps out of the shadows into history again. Illuminating and timely!"

—Adrienne Mayor, Stanford University,
National Book Award finalist for *The Poison King:
The Life and Legend of Mithradates, Rome's Deadliest Enemy*

"Cato, history's most famous foe of authoritarian power, was the pivotal political man of Rome; an inspiration to our Founding Fathers; and a cautionary figure for our times. He loved Roman republicanism, but saw himself as too principled for the mere politics that might have saved it. His life and lessons are urgently relevant in the harshly divided America—and world—of today. With erudition and verve, Rob Goodman and Jimmy Soni turn their life of Cato into the most modern of biographies, a blend of *The Decline and Fall of the Roman Empire* and *Game Change*."

—Howard Fineman, *New York Times* bestselling
author of *The Thirteen American Arguments*

"A truly outstanding piece of work. What most impresses me is the book's ability to reach through the confusing dynastic politics of the late Roman Republic to present social realities in a way intelligible to the modern reader. *Rome's Last Citizen* entertainingly restores to life the stoic Roman who inspired George Washington, Patrick Henry, and Nathan Hale. This is more than a biography: it is a study of how a reputation lasted through the centuries from the end of one republic to the start of another."

—David Frum, *Daily Beast* columnist, former
White House speech writer, and *New York Times*
bestselling author of *The Right Man*

"Cato's life always had epic dimensions in his own mind. His principled, gory suicide made him a symbol of liberty for two thousand years, the model for George Washington and many others. Jimmy Soni and Rob Goodman have somehow given us a life of Cato that is neither hero-worshiping nor debunking. Instead, this handsomely written biography is vividly intelligent and valuably reflective. It is a very fine treatment of a life worth knowing, and a valuable meditation on how a life becomes a myth."

—Jedediah Purdy, professor of law at Duke University,
author of *For Common Things: Irony, Trust, and
Commitment in America Today* and *Being America:
Liberty, Commerce, and Violence in an American World*

"Cato, an icon to the founding fathers, has become a neglected figure. In their spirited new biography—the first since Plutarch!—Rob Goodman and Jimmy Soni give us his story, and explain why this Roman statesman meant so much to our political forbears."

—Jacob Weisberg, chairman and editor in chief of the
Slate Group and *New York Times* bestselling
author of *The Bush Tragedy*

ROME'S LAST CITIZEN

THE LIFE AND LEGACY OF CATO,
MORTAL ENEMY OF CAESAR

ROB GOODMAN

AND

JIMMY SONI

THOMAS DUNNE BOOKS
ST. MARTIN'S GRIFFIN
NEW YORK

THOMAS DUNNE BOOKS.
An imprint of St. Martin's Press.

www.thomasdunnebooks.com
www.stmartins.com

Designed by Omar Chapa

The Library of Congress has cataloged the hardcover edition as follows:

Goodman, Rob.
    Rome's last citizen : the life and legacy of Cato, mortal enemy of Caesar / Rob Goodman and Jimmy Soni. — 1st ed.
       p. cm.
    Includes bibliographical references and index.
    ISBN 978-0-312-68123-4 (hardcover)
    ISBN 978-1-250-01358-3 (e-book)
  1. Cato, Marcus Porcius, 95–46 B.C.   2. Rome—Politics and government—265–30 B.C.
3. Rome—Senate—Biography. 4. Rome—History—Republic, 265–30 B.C. I. Soni, Jimmy. II. Title. III. Title: Life and legacy of Cato, mortal enemy of Caesar.
  DG260.C3G66 2012
  937'.05092—dc23
  [B]

2012028302

ISBN 978-1-250-04262-0 (trade paperback)

St. Martin's Griffin books may be purchased for educational, business, or promotional use. For information on bulk purchases, please contact Macmillan Corporate and Premium Sales Department at 1-800-221-7945, extension 5442, or write specialmarkets@macmillan.com.

First St. Martin's Griffin Edition: February 2014

D   20 19 18 17 16 15 14 13

For Ellen
——R. G.

For my parents, Bhupendra and Aruna
——J. S.

CONTENTS

A Note on the Text

For the sake of clarity, where Anglicized names are better known than their Latin counterparts (e.g., Pompey for Pompeius, Catiline for Catilina, Lucan for Lucanus), we have used the former. Along similar lines, we have modernized the punctuation and diction of translated quotations from ancient sources, where such changes are appropriate and helpful, but we have not changed the meaning or purpose of any quotation. Additionally, all dates in the text are BCE through chapter 14, where the transition is noted. And finally, though settling on the modern value of Roman currency has proved notoriously difficult, estimates for the equivalent of one Roman sesterce have ranged from one dollar to five dollars.

Whether these things should be set down to greatness of spirit or smallness of mind is an open question. —PLUTARCH

ROME'S LAST
CITIZEN

PROLOGUE

THE DREAM

General Washington paused and studied his boot prints in the newly thawed mud. He took a deep breath of spring air, closed his eyes, and released the breath. He was pensive; it had been a year of long marches and small success, and winter's toll on his troops had been heavy.

Food was scarce at Valley Forge. The men had to make do with a tasteless, tough, fire-baked combination of flour and water. Hundreds of horses were dead, some from sheer exhaustion, and others wasted away with hunger. The shelters the men had built could hardly handle the freezing and melting snows of the Pennsylvania winter. The entire camp seemed to be soaked and full of men yellow with jaundice, feverish with typhoid, or doubled over from diarrhea.

At the end of that bitter winter, before an audience packed into a converted bakery at the Valley Forge camp, soldiers dressed in togas mounted a rickety stage and began reciting blank verse. Washington did not have many means of inspiration at his disposal, but he did have drama. And the play he chose to stage for his officer corps was the story of a Roman senator named Marcus Porcius Cato the Younger.

For much of the captive, bone-tired audience, the story was a familiar one. Washington, along with a good part of the world's English speakers, counted Joseph Addison's *Cato: A Tragedy* as a personal favorite. By the time the play made its debut at Valley Forge, it had already been staged 234 times in England alone. With twenty-six different editions in print, it had become a mandatory text for every well-read man of the day. On the front lines of his first war, a twenty-six-year-old Washington wrote that he would rather be home, acting a part in *Cato* himself.

Washington's peers studied and memorized the tragedy. They quoted it, consciously and unconsciously, in public statements and in private correspondence. When Benjamin Franklin opened his private diary, he was greeted with lines from the play that he had chosen as a motto. When John Adams wrote love letters to his wife, Abigail, he quoted *Cato*. When Patrick Henry dared King George to give him liberty or death, he was cribbing from *Cato*. And when Nathan Hale regretted that he had only one life to give for his country—seconds before the British army hanged him for high treason—he was poaching words straight from *Cato*.

George Washington and Samuel Adams were both honored in their time as "the American Cato"—and in revolutionary America, there was little higher praise. When Washington wrote to a pre-turncoat Benedict Arnold and said, "It is not in the power of any man to command success; but you have done more—you have deserved it," he too lifted the words from Addison's *Cato*.

How did the legend of a Roman who walked the halls of his Senate eighteen hundred years before America was born speak so powerfully through the ages? And why did Washington, in the darkest moment of his career, choose *Cato* to lift the spirits of his army?

Who was Cato?

. . .

For Washington and the entire revolutionary generation, Cato was Liberty—the last man standing when Rome's Republic fell. For centuries of philosophers and theologians, Cato was the Good Suicide—the most principled, most persuasive exception to the rule against self-slaughter. For Julius Caesar, the dictator who famously pardoned every opponent, Cato was the only man he could never bring himself to forgive.

Through two millennia, Cato was mimicked, studied, despised, feared, revered. In his own day, he was a soldier and an aristocrat, a senator and a Stoic. The last in a family line of prominent statesmen, Cato spent a lifetime in the public eye as the standard-bearer of Rome's *optimates*, traditionalists who saw themselves as the defenders of Rome's ancient constitution, the preservers of the centuries-old system of government that propelled Rome's growth from muddy city to mighty empire.

Cato's world was the Roman Republic, a state at the apex of its power, able to make foreign kings tremble with a single decree, and rotting from the inside out. Cato's arena was the Senate, an awesome assemblage of gray-haired eminences, the symbol of Rome's republican heritage, and a body crippled by personality politics, rigged elections, ritualized bribery, and sex scandals. Public life in the late Republic resembled a soap opera, and if we didn't find in that fact a sharp enough reflection of our own time, we could surely find familiarity in the grave challenges that threatened Rome and its Senate. They included homegrown terrorism, a debt crisis, the management of multiple foreign wars, the fraying of conventional social bonds and mores, and a yawning gap between rich and poor.

For our time, the question that Cato most urgently poses is this: What happens when a public man, in the face of all that, treats compromise like a dirty word? Cato made a career out of purity, out of his refusal to give an inch in the face of pressure to compromise and deal. His was a powerful and lasting political type: the man who achieves and wields power by disdaining power, the politician above politics. It was an approach designed to elicit one of two things from his enemies: either total surrender or (in Cato's eyes) a kind of moral capitulation. This strategy of all-or-nothing ended in crushing defeat. No one did more than Cato to rage against his Republic's fall. Yet few did more, in the last accounting, to bring that fall to pass.

At the same time, Cato's behavior also established an enduring way of being a man in public, a style still seen in operation today. Playing up an idealized past, obstructing in the name of principle, drawing power from utter inflexibility—Cato could credibly claim to be an originator of such strategies. The history of the filibuster, for instance, essentially starts with Cato. If we notice some resemblance between Cato and present-day politicians, it might be because the patterns set by Cato's life inspire our expectations of our leaders, and perhaps even their expectations of themselves. If this is so, then we have a great deal to learn from returning to the source.

• • •

History remembers Cato as Julius Caesar's most formidable, infuriating enemy—at times the leader of the opposition, at times an opposition party unto himself, but always Caesar's equal in eloquence, in conviction, and in force of character, a man equally capable of a full-volume dawn-to-dusk speech before Rome's Senate and of a thirty-day trek through North Africa's sands, on foot.

Cato's struggle against Caesar, and against his Republic's collapse, played out across the benches of the Senate House and the battlefields of a civil war. But it was their final confrontation that turned Cato into a legend. Facing Caesar's total victory, Cato committed suicide in the North African town of Utica, choosing to take his own life rather than live a single day under Caesar's rule. His stand against tyranny and his famous suicide made Cato the icon of civic duty. They also made him the pagan saint of lost causes.

Yet for all that, Cato's name has faded in our time in a way that Caesar's has not. Perhaps that is the cost of his political defeat; perhaps his virtues are out of style. More likely, Cato is forgotten because he left behind very little that was concrete. He reached the heights of Roman politics, but he didn't pen epics celebrating his own accomplishments, as Cicero did. He was a brave, self-sacrificing, successful military commander, but he didn't send home gripping third-person histories of his exploits, as Caesar did. His name was proverbial in his own time, but he didn't engrave that name on monuments. He studied and practiced philosophy with focused intensity, turning himself into the model of the unflinching Stoic ideal, but he preferred that his philosophy be lived, not written. In fact, the only writing of Cato's that survives is a single, short letter.

Cato was certainly a self-promoter, but the only form of promotion he valued was example, the conspicuous conduct of his life—righteous in his friends' eyes, self-righteous in his enemies'. Cato's Rome teemed with imported wealth; Cato chose to wear the simple, outmoded clothing of Rome's mythical founders and to go barefoot in sun and cold. Powerful men gifted themselves villas and vineyards; Cato preferred a life of monkish frugality. Roman politics was well-oiled with bribes, strategic marriages, and under-the-table favors; Cato's vote famously had no price. These gestures were all, in their own way, a deliberate message to his fellow citizens, a warning that they had gone fatally soft. It is the kind of message that is remembered but rarely heeded.

It is also the kind of message stark enough to wipe out the memory of much that made Cato so complex and so human. He suffered from a volcanic temper. He indulged in all-night drinking bouts. He made the career-endangering choice to become the public face of Stoicism, a school widely regarded in his day as subversive and un-Roman. He collapsed in weepy, uncontrolled, un-Stoic grief at the death of his half brother. His strange and scandalous marital history remained the stuff of slander long after his death.

· · ·

As far as we know, human details such as these didn't change the founding generation's opinion of Cato. For them, Cato was the ideal man—the model of personal rectitude and public sacrifice. What is so remarkable about Washington's play at Valley Forge is not simply the display of high culture in a disgusting, diarrheal army camp—it is how the play ends. In the last act, Cato's army is crushed. His friends abandon him. The tyrant's forces are at the gates. And seeing all this plainly, Cato retires to his room (tastefully offstage) and, calmly and fatally, stabs himself in the guts. It was a play of defeat, and Washington did not stage it for an effete audience of connoisseurs. He chose it for a moment of peril, to inspire a weary army of blunt, hardened, armed men. And, by all accounts, it worked.

We profit from studying Cato because he is part of the American inheritance. Whether or not we acknowledge it, he helps illuminate the founders' understanding of liberty. But we can learn just as much from Cato the man and Cato the politician as from Cato the myth. How he lived, how he practiced politics, and how he died all raise powerful, timeless questions—and he can still give us answers, both when he is inspiring and when he is insufferable, in his moments of triumph and in his desolate end.

Above all, his life speaks to a dream as old as politics. In the dream, in whose mold politicians keep casting themselves to this day, we are on the point of disaster—of flux, venality, imminent collapse. And then, at hope's lowest ebb, there appears on the scene a remarkable man. He is a born leader, a man who effortlessly attracts power without a hint of force. He is in politics yet somehow not *of* politics. He is a man of action and a spellbinding orator, but he is also deeper; in quieter moments, he gives the impression of barely restraining the urge to retire and become a philosopher. He is the man brought into being by the crisis, and he is its solution, the mirror image of the greed and self-seeking that surround him.

Cato's life is the story of how, at the improbable height of crisis, the dream came true. And it is also the story of how the dream failed.

1

WAR GAMES

The first time we see boy Cato, in the account of his great biographer Plutarch, he is being hung by his feet from a high window.

He is four years old and already an orphan; it is the year 91. The man dangling and shaking him out over the ground, intermittently threatening to drop him, is a stranger. He is Pompaedius Silo, an Italian politician visiting from out of town, a friend of Cato's uncle and guardian. He is in Rome to plead once more for citizenship for the towns of Italy, Rome's "allies."

Pompaedius was evidently the kind of single-minded reformer who couldn't let the cause go even when playing with children. He'd asked the boys of the house, with a smile, "Come, beg your uncle to help us in our struggle." Though they barely understood the request, all of them, even Cato's half brother, had nodded yes. Cato had only stared.

There came another request for help, then a joke, then the guest's dropped smile, then threats, and still the angry stare from this four-year-old boy either dumb or self-possessed beyond his years, until he was shaken and dangled out the window—without a scream, without a cry for help, yielding just that same unblinking stare.

After Pompaedius gave up and set the boy back on his feet, he was overheard to say, "How lucky for Italy that he is a boy; if he were a man, I don't think we could get a single vote."

• • •

It is the kind of perfect story that could only come from a culture that didn't believe in childhood. The truth is that we know precious little about the boy Cato, or the boy Caesar, or the boy Cicero. Most of the details of their childhoods, or any Roman childhood, were considered too trivial to remember. And when their stories do come down to us—like the story of Cato and the window, told by Plutarch about a hundred years after the fact—they are the stories of little adults. We talk about "formative" years, but in childhood stories like this one, it is as if the Romans were born fully formed.

Whether or not there was an authentic incident of a houseguest, a political controversy, and a children's game turned violent, this is, at the very least, a projection back into boyhood of all the indelible qualities of the grown Cato: stubbornness (or obstinacy); fearlessness (or foolhardiness); traditionalist politics (or reactionary politics). The story shows Cato grabbed by an overwhelming force, facing death, and evincing utter calm in the face of it. It shows him proving so unshakable that the force, while remaining every bit as overwhelming, recognizes that it has suffered some kind of moral defeat. Plutarch was a deliberate artist: He started Cato's life with a typology of his death.

What else do we know of Cato's beginnings? We know he was born in 95 to his mother Livia Drusa and father Marcus Cato, a senator of whom little record survives. The conventions of Roman childhood and parenting are well understood in outline, though we know little unique to Cato. If the first moments of his life were at all typical, the screaming newborn Cato was placed at the feet of his father. His father raised him from the ground, held him close, inspected him for signs of strength and health—a tender gesture, but one that held the power of life and death. His father's nod made him a citizen and a son; rejected on the ground, he would have been marked a bastard and left to die. Several days' wait, and he was given the name of his family's men for at least six generations: Marcus. Then came a series of rituals. The house was swept to rid it of evil spirits. A lucky golden locket was placed around the newborn's neck. His future was divined in the flight of birds and the entrails of sacrificed animals. All this signaled Cato's entrance into his father's household and family line.

Above all, of course, we know that Cato survived his earliest days—no small feat in a culture that tested the toughness of newborns by exposing them to the elements, bathing them in ice water, and kneading the weakness out of their soft muscles. That there was not much weakness in Cato can be inferred from the simple fact that he lived.

· · ·

Whether or not an enraged houseguest nearly defenestrated the boy Cato, what is indisputably true is the grievance the guest came to Rome to press. Italy hadn't always paid tribute to Rome: Its independence had been worn down over centuries of war. Even where Rome's authority was acknowledged, it was hardly welcomed. When Hannibal had marched over the Alps in 218, intent on conquering Rome, half of Italy had sided with him; when he was driven out, Rome punished the traitor cities severely, destroying some outright.

And yet, as Rome built an overseas empire, Italian soldiers shared the burden, manning up to two-thirds of the Roman army; Italian sons died alongside Romans to secure Sicily and Carthage and Greece. Romans and Italians were interchangeable to the conquered, indistinguishable *Romaioi*. Yet the spoils went overwhelmingly to the Roman capital, and Italians were denied the vote, even as they paid men and money into the Roman machine.

The Italian question had vexed Roman politics for generations, and it was a central theme in the brief careers of Rome's greatest radicals, the brothers Tiberius and Gaius Gracchus. Their failure is often considered the beginning of the Republic's slow end.

The oldest son of an old family, already decorated in war, Tiberius Gracchus is said to have conceived his political platform while on the march. A generation before Cato's birth, he was infuriated to see firsthand an Italian countryside almost entirely given over to imported slave gangs and the massive plantations of the Roman rich. He grieved that "the Italian race . . . a people so valiant in war, and related in blood to the Romans, were declining little by little into pauperism and paucity of numbers without any hope of remedy." He also feared that Rome, with its hardy, small farmers on the decline, would grow increasingly vulnerable to its enemies.

In 133, soon after his return to Rome, Tiberius won election as tribune of the people. The Senate had set aside the office of the tribune as a pacifier for Rome's underclass, but it was rarely used for any radical purpose until Tiberius got his hands on it. He electrified Rome with his passionate words on behalf of the soldiers who fought to build an empire, even as their own small pieces of that empire were stripped away:

> It is with lying lips that their commanders exhort the soldiers in their battles to defend sepulchres and shrines from the enemy; for not a man of them has an hereditary altar, not one of all these many Romans an ancestral tomb, but they fight and die to support others in wealth and luxury, and though they are styled masters of the world, they have not a single clod of earth that is their own.

On the strength of this rallying cry, Tiberius proposed to remedy Rome's wealth gap by capping the holdings of the rich and distributing public lands to the urban poor. Ignoring the outrage of Rome's senatorial establishment, Tiberius took his bill for land redistribution directly to the people's assembly, a body with the authority to pass laws, but one that rarely dared to defy the aristocracy. The Roman masses passed the land reform by acclamation.

In the Senate, Tiberius's success was perceived not merely as the action of a radical, but as the ambition of a would-be king, an attempt to put a faction in permanent power with the backing of the poor. Not long after passage of the land bill, a senator and neighbor of the Gracchus family was brought forward to testify that Tiberius was hiding a crown in his home. The Senate's suspicions seemed all but confirmed when Tiberius broke with Roman tradition and announced his campaign for a second consecutive year in office. It was only because he wanted immunity from political prosecution, he insisted. It was the first step to declaring himself tribune-for-life, his enemies said.

It is not surprising that the fracas ended in the murder of Tiberius and the death of his followers. What is astonishing is that the party of senators who beat Tiberius to death in open daylight was led by Rome's high priest, who wore his toga pulled over his head, just as he dressed when sacrificing an animal. The assassination of Tiberius was dressed up as a religious rite, a sacrifice to the Republic's guardian gods.

●　　●　　●

Tiberius's younger brother, Gaius Gracchus, escaped the killings—and for the rest of his short life, "the grief he had suffered encouraged him to speak out fearlessly." Friends and enemies alike painted Gaius as a man on fire for revenge. Yet, elected tribune ten years after Tiberius, he brought more than anger and grief to the work of coalition building and legislating. He brought a discipline that outdid his brother's. While Tiberius reached out to the Roman poor alone, Gaius made inroads with Rome's merchant class, the *equites* (so called because they could afford to outfit themselves with a horse in times of war). And in the most critical departure from his brother's example, Gaius invited Italians into his populist coalition. For the first time, a leading Roman was offering equal citizenship, including full voting rights, to Rome's closest Italian allies.

It was Gaius's most creative act of statesmanship—but it was also the opening that allowed his conservative opponents a chance to destroy him. It took little effort to drive a wedge between Gaius's Italian and Roman backers: His opponents had only to point out that more voting power and more cheap bread for Italians meant less of both for Romans. "If you give citizenship to the Latins," said one nativist consul, one of two co-heads of the Roman state, "I suppose that you think that you will continue as now to find somewhere to stand to listen to speeches and attend games and public festivals? Surely you realize that *they* will occupy all the spaces?" Rhetoric like this helped pry away enough of Gaius's supporters to weaken him fatally.

When Gaius finally met electoral defeat, the Senate pounced, moving for the repeal of his entire agenda. What was left of the Gracchan faction took this as such a provocation that it rioted. A consul's servant was killed in the street fighting, all the cause needed for the Senate to deem Gracchus and his friends enemies of the state and call out the army against them. Though Gaius fled through the streets and "all the spectators, as at a race, urged Gaius on to greater speed, not a man came to his aid, or even consented to furnish him with a horse when he asked for one, for his pursuers were pressing close upon him." Chased over the Tiber and cornered in a sacred grove, Gaius fell on his sword. Thousands of his followers joined him in death, summarily executed in a political purge. When it was over, and the blood was washed from the streets, the Senate broke ground for a grand new temple: the Temple of Concord.

· · ·

But the prayers offered in the Temple of Concord, sincere or cynical, would be empty smoke. Concord, if it ever lived in Rome, was gone. The purge of the Gracchi might have, at least, promised peace through force, but as each side reflected on the decade that had fractured Roman consensus, it became clear that the purge had settled nothing. It hadn't satisfied the Italians, who had been promised political rights and were furious to see the pledge go unfulfilled. It hadn't resettled the countryside or calmed the poor. What Rome's conservatives took from the Gracchan years was a conviction of how easily the masses could be bribed—the revelation that their loyalty belonged not to the state, but to the highest bidder. For those who had cheered Tiberius and Gaius, the brutal lesson was that their enemies had been the first to settle arguments with clubs and knives.

Out of this violent decade were born the two factions that would define the last century of the Republic. The *populares* ("men of the people") took the Gracchi brothers as models and martyrs—often too dangerous to be spoken of directly, but an inspiration always. The *optimates* ("the best men," a bit of self-flattery) stood for the traditional power of the Senate as a bulwark against what they saw as populist tyranny.

To be sure, the Republic never saw anything that we would recognize as political parties. Roman politics rested on a ceaselessly knitted web of personal attractions, alliances, and enmities: marriages, family ties, favors done and owed, old friendships, and older grudges. And Roman politics was always a rich man's game: The average *popularis* may have played to the people more openly, but his economic interests differed little from his *optimas* neighbor's. Whether Rome's populists meant their words sincerely, or whether they merely held their well-born noses in the pursuit of selfish power, was always hotly argued—and still is. The *optimates*, on the other hand, might at least be credited with speaking up for their interests forthrightly. They were proud of selflessly swearing off pandering, of a readiness to speak hard truths to and about the people.

Though the factions had no organization, no structure, and no formal discipline, they changed the face of Rome. The stakes, as each side saw them, were life and death for the Republic itself.

"Whoever wants to save the Republic, follow me!" the priest had cried on his way to sacrifice Tiberius Gracchus. And when Gaius Gracchus heard that his followers were being killed in the streets, he took refuge in Diana's temple, where "he sank upon his knees . . . and with hands outstretched towards the goddess, prayed that the Roman people, in requital for their great ingratitude and treachery, might never cease to be enslaved."

• • •

These fractured politics were Cato's birthright—and Cato could barely walk before the war came to his home.

By 91, three decades after the death of Gaius Gracchus, the Italians' cause had gone nowhere. Yet the Italian elite continued to press for its say in the government and its share of the loot. And Roman reformers continued to see in the towns of Italy a massive, untapped source of political power.

Cato's uncle and guardian, Marcus Livius Drusus, tribune of the people, was one of those reformers. Like the Gracchi brothers, he had made his name by demanding land reform for the peasants and subsidized bread for the urban plebs. Unlike the revolutionaries, he had demonstrated enough deference to keep in healthy standing with the Senate, which accepted him as a good, moderate pressure valve for popular discontent. But when Drusus took up the cause of Italy, he went too far. His proposal to grant citizenship to all of Italy launched a panic of rumormongering. His enemies claimed that every Italian city had pledged to enter Drusus's political clientele, a bonanza of money, men, and favors that would bring him the biggest power base in the Republic. They alleged that Pompaedius had signed an agreement with Drusus and was marching on Rome at the head of ten thousand men. His enemies whispered, "A free state will become a monarchy, if a huge multitude attains citizenship by virtue of the activity of one man."

The Senate isolated Drusus and revoked his reforms. Soon after, in the house he shared with four-year-old Cato, a stranger drove a knife into Drusus's thigh. The attack left a deep enough impression on Rome to be singled out in a rhetorical handbook as a prime example of pathos: "Drusus—your blood splattered the walls of your home and your mother's face." Did Cato hear the struggle and the shouts?

Drusus bled to death, and Italy exploded.

• • •

Inconclusive battle played out up and down the Italian peninsula. A disfigured, often-drunk Roman general named Sulla made his reputation by storming and burning the allied cities, risking his neck so often and so bravely that his troops honored him with a sacred crown woven from battlefield grass. Rome triumphed as it always did, with brutality in one hand and careful conciliation in the other, turning Italy at last into one nation under Rome. But the success was illusory. The Republic was too divided and distracted to anticipate a genocidal danger building in the East.

In the spring of 88, as Rome's war with its allies drew to a negotiated close, the governors of the towns of Asia Minor received identical copies of a letter from their lord, King Mithridates. In thirty days, Mithridates ordered, they were to kill every Roman or Italian man, woman, and child they could lay hands on. On the appointed day, throughout the province, wherever the resented Roman influence extended, the command was carried out—at the cost, Appian calculated, of eighty thousand lives. Though Rome had often inflicted similar treatment in its turn, Appian was shocked to report Roman children held under the sea by rough hands until they drowned, civilians' hands chopped off as they desperately clutched sacred images, families murdered in cruel sequence before one another's eyes—children first, then wives, then husbands.

At the far end of the world, in Asia Minor, just as in Italy, Rome was hated. Its rapacious taxes, its colonists, and its occupying troops generated a seething resentment. Cicero was honest enough to acknowledge that "the Roman name is held in loathing, and Roman tributes, tithes, and taxes are instruments of death." Mithridates put it more starkly still: Rome was "the common enemy of mankind."

Who was the king who acted on that hate and gave the brutal order? Mithridates claimed descent from Alexander the Great and Darius, Persian King of Kings. On the strength of that ancestry—and of a flamboyant personality, which made him the anti-imperial standard-bearer of his day—he laid claim to Asia Minor and the Black Sea. By the time of the massacre, he had already created a counter empire in the image of Greek Alexander's—a check on Rome's regional dominance.

Mithridates was ready to lock his mother and brother in prison to safeguard his throne; he was ready to swallow poison every day, to build his immunity to assassination; he was ready to conceive and launch the greatest premeditated massacre in the history of the ancient world. The massacre turned a border skirmish into a quarter century of war. And it put the future of Rome's supremacy into grave doubt.

•   •   •

Growing up as he did in those years—a time of shaken confidence, war on his doorstep, and murder in his own home—it's not surprising that what we know of Cato's childhood and play is cast over with a sullen seriousness.

Along with the other boys, Cato played at law and at war. Playing lawyer was natural. For the adults in Cato's life, law was sport and spectacle, always the dominant conversation. For a Roman unable to win advancement under arms, the only other arena was the Forum and its courts—the place of open-air word-combat, where the prize was a bequest from the will of a wealthy client, or an office and title taken from a politician successfully convicted, or, above all, the adoring eyes of the crowd. Like Roman politics, of which it was simply another branch, Roman law had room for both remarkable flights of rhetoric and lewd personal attacks. When denouncing the wanton ex-lover of a client, Cicero, the greatest lawyer of his time, slipped in a mention of "her husband—oops, I mean her brother. I always make that mistake."

No wonder that Cato and his friends would turn a playroom into a courtroom. Left alone to amuse themselves at a grown-up party, they assigned plaintiffs, defendants, witnesses, a jury, judge, and jailers. They practiced accusations and alibis for sacrilege, vote-buying, and slander. They turned on one another those comprehensive rhetorical educations that were mandatory for Roman boys of their class, the cruelty of children standing in for the cruelty of politicians.

In the midst of one of these play-trials, when a shy boy was falsely convicted and hauled off to be shut in the closet jail, he cried for Cato to save him. "Cato, when he understood what was going on, quickly came to the door, pushed aside the boys who stood before it and tried to stop him, led forth the prisoner, and went off home with him in a passion, followed by other boys also," Plutarch writes of the incident.

A few years later, there was another solemn game—the Troy Game. It was a public game for youths on horseback, the kind of well-off young men who would soon be leading troops from the saddle. Its character was religious, its origin ascribed to the ancient games that sanctified Trojan funerals.

Its object, for once, wasn't competition, but shared perfection in horsemanship. The poet Virgil lauded its roots in the Trojans' drills:

> . . . *The column split apart*
> *As files in the three squadrons all in line*
> *Turned away, cantering left and right; recalled*
> *They wheeled and dipped their lances for a charge.*
> *They entered then on parades and counter-parades,*
> *The two detachments, matched in the arena,*
> *Winding in and out of one another, . . .*
> *So intricate the drill of Trojan boys*
> *Who wove the patterns of their prancing horses.*

But that was a pious myth. There was nothing Trojan, or even ancient, about the exhibition; it was quite new in Cato's time. Yet the patina of antiquity dignified the games—and the name of Troy was invoked for good reason. The Trojans, valiant as they were, were history's great losers. They were also, as the myth went, Rome's true ancestors, beaten in war and sea-tossed from Asia Minor to Italy, where they rebuilt at last. In their heartfelt identification with a band of refugees from a razed city, the world-beating, city-razing Romans gained something priceless: the moral assurance of the underdog. Every reenactment of the Troy Game helped to recall it.

· · ·

But in Cato's year to participate, the Troy Game entered a minor crisis. The two leaders of the boys on horseback were both nepotistic appointments chosen for their closeness to General Sulla.

Sulla had every right to choose. He had forced his way to the head of the state, and he did it with the help of the most potent weapon in Roman politics: an army of the poor. Though he used the weapon to great effect, Sulla was not its inventor. That credit belonged to his old commanding officer, a rural *popularis* named Gaius Marius, who, with a single innovation, had ended the dilemma of Roman army recruitment but created a host of new, worse dilemmas.

Since the days of the Gracchi, it had been clear that the Roman army was on a dangerously dwindling course. Only landowning Romans were allowed to fight in the Roman armed forces. Small independent farmers were held to be the hardiest soldiers the earth could produce, rough-handed men who fought for their homes and had a hearth to return to when campaigning season was done. So tightly did Romans link property and military service that the requirement remained in place for years after it became evident that the number of landowners was shrinking precariously. The Gracchi had aimed to solve the problem by expanding the base of property owners, but Marius had found far more success with the revolutionary step of simply erasing the property qualification altogether. The desperate legions that resulted from this change ended Rome's manpower worries for good. But rather than fight to protect land they already owned, the vast majority of Roman soldiers now fought to win land of their own. They were bound in loyalty to any commander who could deliver them spoils and acres when the campaign was finished—and, as Marius and Sulla demonstrated, they would follow their general-patrons into battle even when fellow Romans stood in the enemy lines.

By 88—the year that ended the war with the Italians and began the war with Mithridates—Marius was an old and sagging man, his best days as general behind him. Sulla was the natural choice to lead the new war in the East. But as soon as Sulla left the city to take up command, Marius's faction forced through a decree handing the army back to Marius. Sulla, in response, demonstrated shockingly and conclusively that his troops answered to him alone. He ordered his army into Rome itself, across the city's sacred and inviolable boundary line, proving in an afternoon the emptiness of Rome's most central taboo. Having captured the city, forcing Marius to flee, and extorting the right to command the new war, Sulla marched east. But virtually the moment Sulla was out of earshot, Marius returned to follow his example and rampaged *his* troops through the city for five days, setting himself up as Rome's first man again—until he dropped dead soon after, quite possibly of a heart attack.

Sulla was able to ignore the reports of chaos in Rome long enough to beat Mithridates out of Roman territory and force him into a wary truce. Without those reports, Sulla might have finished him, rather than leave an enemy alive and wounded. But there was no time for that. Back in Rome, there was revenge to be taken. In late 82, Sulla's army met Marius's faction in the shadow of the city's walls. The result was a slaughter—and the dictatorship of Sulla.

• • •

The cowed Senate and people had no choice but to acclaim Sulla as Dictator Legibus Faciendis et Reipublicae Constituendae Causa: "Dictator for the Purpose of Making Laws and Stabilizing the Republic." Unlike the other dictators in the venerable republican tradition—Cincinnatus, for instance, who famously fought off Rome's enemies and then returned to his plow—Sulla's term came without a limit. For the first time in memory, the Republic, that hive of ambition, had something resembling a king. Sulla was feared like a king, free to dole out spoils like a king, and, like a king, able to kill with a word.

For Sulla, rich with plunder from the East and even more bloated with the estates of his dead enemies, putting the children of his cronies at the head of the Troy Game was a very little thing. So, for the game of 81, he chose his wife's son and a boy named Sextus, nephew of his lieutenant Pompey. Evidently, and unsurprisingly, there wasn't a word of protest from the adults. But the young aristocrats responded with something unexpected, even brave: They went on strike. Sextus was disliked enough that they refused to drill under him at all; they put down their wooden weapons and called for a worthier leader. Sulla was there at the practice. He humored them, though he could have done much worse: "Who do you want to lead you?" The call went up for Cato.

So it was Cato who led the boys into mock battle and play charges under Sulla's eye—Romans playing at being Trojans, conquerors playing at being the conquered, boys who in a matter of years would be carrying real metal weapons to real war in Africa, in the Eastern deserts, in Spain, in Gaul, boys who in their lifetimes would turn their weapons on one another.

Sulla was impressed with the boy-general. And this, it seems, is how the qualities of fourteen-year-old Cato came to a dictator's attention—a promising and a dangerous thing.

• • •

Sulla's house "looked exactly like an Inferno." In came the fresh heads of Rome's leading men; out went gold. Undisturbed by screams or moans, there reclined in state the dictator with the fierce gray eyes and the blotchy red birthmark, "like a mulberry sprinkled with oatmeal"—Sulla Felix, the Fortunate; Sulla Epaphroditus, Venus's Favorite. Cato and his half brother often sat by Sulla's side, eyewitnesses to the arbitrary power of a man fond of making the Senate listen to his harangues and the cries of the executed at the same time.

In what passed for dissent in Sulla's Rome, a senator begged at last, "At least let us know whom you intend to punish." The next day, eighty names were posted on a white tablet in the Forum. The day after and the day after that, several hundred more joined the list. This was privatized justice: The head attached to any of those names brought a fat bounty. The estates of the executed were sold to the highest bidder, with Sulla himself presiding as auctioneer. And while his wish list at first had a certain brutal logic to it—a purge of *popularis* enemies and any lingering supporters of his old commanding officer Marius—it grew to include the names of the conspicuously rich, the victims of private grudges, and, in one notorious case, a man who was already dead. Having killed his own brother, a crony of Sulla's arranged to have the dead man's name added to the proscription list, blessing the fratricide after the fact.

The sacred laws against bloodshed on hearths or in temples were pronounced null and void. Slaves had license to murder their masters, and sons their fathers. Any Roman sheltering a marked man was himself marked for death. A grisly commerce in human heads, the unpredictability of the killing amplified its terror—as Sulla well grasped. "I am adding to the list all of the names I can remember," he announced with chilling nonchalance. "Those who have escaped my memory will be added sometime soon." By the end of the bloodletting, as many as nine thousand Romans were dead.

Sulla went about it with the resentment of a man reclaiming a right denied. His family was noble, illustrious, and ruined. He came of age in rented rooms in the Roman slums. A favorite of prostitutes and comedians, he was a tireless drinker and sexual omnivore, whose ruined complexion naturally sparked talk of venereal disease. At home among the plebs, he might have been a revolutionary. And yet the theme of Sulla's political career was restoration. He was another Roman in love with the sacred past, so in love that he swore to wash out with blood everything he found modern or decadent.

And so, as soon as Sulla had his say, gone was the power of the tribunes, the people's representatives. The office was an old one, but there was nothing like it in the Rome of the fathers, in the austere golden days of senatorial power—or so Sulla's argument went. There were only tribunes at all because the underclass had dared to go on strike against the patricians, leaving Rome's fields unplowed and its wars unfought until the Senate promised the poor dedicated voices of their own in the councils of state. The tribunes were ten chosen men of the people with the power of veto over the Senate, backed by the plebeians' oath to kill any man who so much as laid a hand on a tribune's body. The office was the embodiment of all that was democratic in Rome; in the hand of politicians like the Gracchi, it was the platform for working-class agitation for jobs, cheap grain, and land redistribution. By Sulla's time, the office of the tribunes was four centuries old, but for Sulla and other long-memoried patricians, it was still a foreign growth on the body politic, a deviation from the old ways, a modern imposition.

Having been voted sole power by the Senate and having asserted his power in the proscriptions, Sulla castrated the tribunate. Never again could a tribune propose a law. Never again could a tribune veto a decree of the Senate. Further, any man who had held the office of tribune would be removed from further participation in political life: Sulla forbade every other office to ex-tribunes. His aim was to cull the stock of ambitious and competent politicians willing to serve as the people's voice.

Those well-off Romans who survived the proscriptions were given a strong stake in the restored order. Sulla doubled the Senate's size from three hundred to six hundred, packing it with his partisans and with business leaders who agreed to back his program in return for an aristocratic title. To the augmented Senate, Sulla restored power over the law courts, which had belonged to the merchant-class *equites* since the Gracchi reforms.

Perhaps most important, Sulla, a general who had installed himself in power at the head of a personal army, did his best to pull the ladder up after himself. The *cursus honorum*, or "honors race," the orderly progression of a political career—which Sulla had so dramatically stepped over—was permanently fixed in place, with mandated minimum ages for each successive step. There would be no more meteoric rises. Each magistrate, no matter how popular, would face a two-year waiting period before he was allowed to run for a higher post. No one man would ever again hold perpetual power: Even the most ambitious would have to cool his heels for a decade before running again for the same office. And no general would be permitted to form a bond with his legions as tight as Sulla's had been. The two consuls, the state's highest officials, would serve their year's term in Rome, where armies were forbidden, before leading troops in the provinces—for one year only. There would be no more marches on Rome.

If there was anything new in Sulla's constitution, it was laid down in the name of what was fundamentally old, a Rome ruled by an elite collective. There was something prophetic and sincere in it: an insight that this bloody play of ambition had every reason to repeat itself, and a determination that, nevertheless, this would be the last time. It was, as Sulla imagined it, the autocracy to end all autocracies. He himself would be the last. Rome would restore its immemorial competition, but not while Sulla ruled. And even after he passed, no one would attain the unchallenged height that he had occupied. As a last, despotic act, he redrew Rome's sacred boundary line—the same line whose sanctity he had been the first to break by crossing it at the head of an army—simply because he could. Only the kings had ever done that.

• • •

Judging by the man Cato would become, he would have found much to like in that program. The reactionary spirit of Sulla's reforms would animate Cato's politics. But as a teenager watching the imposition of Sulla's platform by fiat, Cato was shocked by the blood it required—shocked not just secondhand but daily and in person, as he reclined with the dictator on his couch. Here was Cato's early education in politics: his guardian's assassination, and Sulla's government by murder. This boyhood in civil war would produce a man with an almost neurotic attachment to rules, to precedent, to propriety—to everything that was not Sulla.

One wonders how the boy Cato could have stomached the violence. "If you had put Marius himself in that place," speculated an imperial chronicler, "he would have quickly started making plans for his own escape." Coming home from the slaughter- and auction-house one day, Cato pulled aside the tutor walking with him and asked why Sulla was still alive. "Because," he answered, "men fear him more than they hate him." Cato regularly sat a mere arm's reach away from the dictator, well out of any bodyguard's range. And that, reports Plutarch, was all the plan his adolescent ambition needed: "Give me a sword, so I might kill him and set my country free from slavery."

Every day after that plea slipped from Cato's mouth, the tutor patted him down for weapons before setting out for Sulla's house.

• • •

Give me a sword, so I might kill him and set my country free from slavery. Surely he didn't say *that.* It's a line from a tragedy, or from the base of a statue, not from real life. We have good reason for skepticism. Again, this is Plutarch writing the boy Cato in light of the man. In this, and in all of his Roman and Greek *Lives,* Plutarch did not practice what we would recognize as straight history, but rather moral education, a kind of didactic drama.

Nevertheless, to write off that line as the climax of a fable is to miss the more-interesting point: Boys of Cato's class were trained to speak like that and to think like that. To our ears, it sounds stiffly strident, but the Roman education was, above all, rhetorical. It sounds uncharacteristically murderous for an elite teenager, but tyrannicide was a classical virtue.

Like much of Roman high culture, rhetorical education was an expensive Greek import. Tutors like Cato's were often high-priced Greek slaves or Greek freedmen. In the same way that a genteel Edwardian was expected to spice his speech with well-placed Gallicisms, the Roman gentleman knew that a sophisticated moment called for something more than his native tongue. So his education was bilingual from the start. No sooner had he learned to string together his Latin and Hellenic alphabets than he began committing to memory long passages of Homer or Hesiod or Euripides, declaiming them with the proscribed gestures—a clenched fist for enraged Achilles or a knitted brow for wise old Nestor—and then inscribing on wax tablets variations and glosses on the old stories.

From Athens, Rome carried home not just a literature, but a conviction that public speaking should be at the center of learning. In the words of Isocrates, a legendary Athenian orator and a founder of rhetorical education: "I do think that the study of political discourse can help more than any other thing to stimulate and form the character." But the character Roman fathers would pay to have instilled was that of the practical man, the advocate swaying a jury, the commander haranguing his troops, the man who, like Sulla, could respond to a delegation of Athenians orating at length on the glories of their city, "I didn't come here for a history lesson." The lessons Romans wanted were above all relevant ones, socializing and career-building ones.

So Cato was drilled in composing, organizing, memorizing, and reciting repeatedly two eminently useful genres of rhetoric: the *controversia* and the *suasoria*. The *controversia* was lawyer training: given the law and the facts of a case, persuade a jury of your schoolmates in both directions. A rich man claimed that his poor neighbor's bees were destroying his flowers. He dusted the flowers with poison, the bees died, and the poor man sued. Argue the rich man's side of the case. Now argue the poor man's.

The *suasoria* was senator training: imagine yourself declaiming not in front of a bored teacher and an antsy class, but at a defining moment in the councils of one of history's great men. Deliver your opinion, back it up with quotation, definition, precedent, and pathos, and do it all from memory. Should Alexander turn back at India? Should the three hundred Spartan warriors hold their ground at Thermopylae against the Persians and overwhelming odds? Should Hannibal and his elephants cross the Alps?

And what should we do with a tyrant? Roman boys were raised on stories of arrogance and its violent comeuppance. There was Hipparchus, the tyrant of Athens, slain by a pair of young lovers whose statue now stood in Rome's Capitol. There was Tarquin the Proud, Rome's last king, who demonstrated his style of rule by slicing off the heads of the tallest, most distinguished flowers in his poppy field, and who was driven out of the city when his sadistic son went too far and raped a nobleman's daughter. There was, too, a long line of would-be reformers and friends of the plebs— starting with a rich farmer in the Republic's early days who sold grain at a discount during a famine, and culminating with the Gracchi brothers— each of whom was accused in his time of coveting a crown, and each of whom was righteously killed in turn. "There can be nothing baser, fouler than a tyrant . . . for though in form a man, he surpasses the most savage monsters," writes Cicero, who would have known those stories by heart. "If anyone kills a tyrant—be he never so intimate a friend—he has not laden his soul with guilt, has he?"

There wasn't a Roman boy of such an education who hadn't imagined himself the hero of such stories, time and again. In fact, it was mandatory. "Do you teach rhetoric?" sighed one burned-out teacher:

> What iron bowels must you have when your troop of scholars
> slays the cruel tyrant, when each in turn stands up and repeats

what he has just been conning in his seat, reciting the same things in the same verses! Served up again and again, this cabbage is the death of the unhappy master.

Cato certainly would have stood up in his turn. And if he went further than his classmates—if he tried to turn from reciting these stories of tyrannicide to acting one out—then it would not be the last time that he took Rome's professed ideals further than any of his fellows were prepared to take them.

Yet those ideals, which must have proved so seductive to an unsmiling boy like Cato, were often the rhetorical gloss on an ugly reality. There can be nothing fouler than a tyrant—but who is a tyrant? Leaders of the working class were often called budding tyrants, and were killed as tyrants, whether they were dealers in discount grain, debtors' advocates, or land reformers. Cato's own uncle was killed as a tyrant. Conversely, Sulla was a liberator in his own propaganda and in his own mind—a liberator of the lands he added to the empire, the restorer of ancient *libertas* to Rome itself. For all the practical training Cato's cohort received in allusion, in memory, in voice, and in stamina, what they were not taught was a way to apply the heroic stories to a politics in which every side of every argument cast itself as the friend of liberty, in which "tyrant" was the favorite accusation of the ruling class, in which a King Tarquin was seen to be lurking in every potential enemy.

It was too much for a boy, even for a young man. And perhaps Cato, rash as he was, understood this. When his formal lessons were over, he put off his entry into politics and went looking for training in philosophy. His classmates were already seeking army appointments or rich widows to defend in court, but Cato kept quiet.

"Men find fault with you for your silence," a friend once reproached him.

Cato replied, "Only let them not blame my life. I will begin to speak when I am not going to say what was better off left unsaid."

THE PILLAR

Cato broke his early silence only once, in defense of a pillar.

The pillar stood in an old basilica, or public meeting hall, and it crowded the seats of the tribunes who conducted business there. It should have been a simple thing to have it moved in the name of convenience, but the tribunes weren't counting on the fierce opposition of an eighteen-year-old without office and without authority on any topic except that very building. It was the Basilica Porcia: It carried Cato's family name, and it had been erected, the first of its kind, by Cato's great-grandfather. To move even a single pillar from this century-old place would be to disgrace the great man's legacy—at least in the eyes of his great-grandson.

It was one thing to hold that view, petty as it sounds. It was another to convey it to a crowd of strangers for whom it was not a family matter. But Cato played upon the kind of Roman superstition so keenly felt that it led priests to repeat entire rituals if just one word of an ancient formula was misspoken—the kind of superstition that saw moving one pillar as tantamount to tearing down a whole building. Hadn't it served perfectly well, right up to the present? Hadn't it been good enough for the generation of Romans that had stood against Hannibal? Had the basilica changed, or had the Romans changed? This was more than mere remodeling. This was about the old ways, the *mos maiorum*, brought into conflict with modern comfort seeking.

There was something strange about the youth who already spoke like an old man. But austerity was a winning theme (especially when the stakes were low), and Cato was already politician enough to sell it with charm. He won his case. The pillar stayed.

· · ·

It helped immeasurably that the man whose name was on the building, Cato the Elder, embodied the old ways. His life was the model for any Roman who called himself conservative—and above all, for his great-grandson.

Cato the Elder had given his family its name. Originally just another in an interminable line of one "Marcus Porcius" after another, he came to be hailed by the cognomen "Cato," a title connoting wisdom and experience. His descendants took the title by hereditary right. The son of a farming family from the Roman countryside, Cato the Elder was well-off enough to own his own land, but not above working shirtless in the field alongside his slaves, sharing their bread and cheap wine at mealtime. When he went to war for the first time, around 217, he was still at the tail end of boyhood. He returned with a chest full of scars and a veteran's record, the indispensable foundation of a Roman political career.

At home in little Tusculum, Cato the Elder made himself into something of a country lawyer. With little hope of payment, he spent his mornings in the town market, defending his neighbors in small cases before the local judge, returning in the afternoons to the plow. That might have been all. But though the rule of the Republic passed through the same few families' hands year by year, there was still a narrow valve of Roman meritocracy: just enough room in each generation for the fresh blood of a few *novi homines*, "new men." Cicero would later be one. So was Cato the Elder.

The reason that this particular new man was plucked from arguing suits over cattle in the town square was that he was needed to make a point. Rome was enjoying its first taste of wealth, wealth that drained toward Rome from every edge of the world: wealth in tribute, wealth in plunder, wealth in gold and silver from the Spanish mines, wealth in the bodies of slaves from every conquered city and tribe, wealth in culture. Shining Greek bronzes and marbles were appearing in the city of mud huts and clay gods.

Once, defending himself against corruption charges, Cato the Elder contemptuously listed just a few of the many routes by which an enterprising Roman might enrich himself through empire:

I have never distributed my money or that of our allies in bribery. I have never placed garrison commanders in the towns of your allies, to seize their goods and families. I have never divided booty nor what had been taken from the enemy nor spoils among a few of my friends, so as to deprive those who had won it of their reward. I have never granted permits to requisition at will, so that my friends might enrich themselves by exploiting such authorization. I have never distributed the money for the soldiers' wine among my attendants and friends, nor made them rich at public expense.

Those "nevers" were only worth hammering on so vehemently because they were glaring exceptions. His colleagues had, frequently and gladly.

• • •

As the wealth of the world concentrated itself in a single city, the old, rough equality among the elite was dying. With the right foreign postings, a fortunate few among the oligarchs suddenly set themselves off spectacularly from their fellows. The new wealth could turn luxury and dining into cutthroat sports. It could buy a senator's son the best foreign education. It could, and did, buy elections.

For the first time, a select few were beginning to affect Greek learning, toying with the philosophy of Plato and the poetry of Euripides, not simply as academic pastimes, but as rich cultural capital. Such learning set the new elite apart from their uncouth countrymen who still held to Latin as a point of pride at a time when there was no Latin literature to speak of. There was even a word to express what the authentically unpolished Romans possessed, and what the elite of the elite were leaving behind: *Latinitas*, "Latin-ness." The most fruitful attack on the new elite was simply that they lacked *Latinitas*—they were decadent, cosmopolitan, un-Roman.

It was an attack launched by a competing faction of the elite, not from anywhere significantly below. But it had no better spokesman than a country boy who lived Latin-ness: a frugal farmer, a scarred soldier, a plain, loud speaker with a distinctive shock of red hair, always with a proverb at the ready. It was a neighbor who discovered Cato the Elder, a patrician senator who owned the next plot over from Cato's. And with that patrician's blessing,

27

Cato was on his way to Rome and a sparkling career speaking for the old-time, nationalist faction. Luck and talent would take him to the consulship and beyond.

In Rome, he made up for his rustic accent with an untrained eloquence and an ability to wrap any controversy in the comfortable mantle of Latin patriotism. For example, in defense of a law banning women from wearing colorful clothes or owning more than half an ounce of gold, Cato said:

> The community suffers from two opposite vices—avarice and luxury—pestilential diseases that have proved the ruin of all great empires. The brighter and better the fortunes of the Republic become day by day, and the greater the growth of its dominion . . . so much the more do I dread the prospect of these things taking us captive rather than we them. . . . I hear far too many people praising and admiring those statues that adorn Athens and Corinth and laughing at the clay images of our gods standing in front of their temples. I for my part prefer these gods who bless us.

When he represented Rome abroad, he governed provinces with the same thrift he used to manage his farm. Gone were the public banquets, retinues of attendants, and slave-toted litters that usually dignified high-ranking Roman officials. During a yearlong governorship of Nearer Spain, Cato boasted that he stormed more rebellious cities than he spent days in the country—and at the end, he proudly left his horse behind rather than ship it back to Rome at state expense.

There was little doubting that all of this fanatical economy was genuine. Cato practiced it both in public and private. In private, his extreme frugality took on a tinge of cruelty. Never own an old slave, Cato advised his fellow farmers: As soon as he's too worn-out to plow, sell him for what you can get and let someone else waste food on him. It was advice that he was unafraid to put in writing, because it was of a piece with the war record, the budget trimming, and the refusal to learn Greek, and it all played extraordinarily well. There was no better publicist of Cato's virtues, it was said, than Cato. No one was more thrilled when he learned that his name was officially becoming proverbial—as in, "What do you expect? We aren't Catos"—and no one was more eager to help the story make the rounds.

The best measure of Cato's swelling clout was his willingness to take on a man who should have been untouchable: the victor over Hannibal, and Cato's ex-superior, Scipio Africanus. Scipio was as urbane a man as his era could have produced, a Graecophile patron of foreign philosophers whose war record made him a legend in his own time. To Cato, Scipio was a disgustingly liberal spender with no concept of military discipline. To Scipio, Cato was a crabbed and cruel leader of men whose mercilessness in the provinces only sowed the seeds of more insurgency. Their rivalry, which spanned two decades, was at the heart of Rome's culture war.

By the time of its climax in 185—seventeen years after Scipio's defeat of Hannibal had brought the war to a close—Cato's traditionalist faction had chipped enough away from the hero's aura to bring a charge of corruption against him. Scipio stood accused of accepting a stupendous bribe from a foreign king. On the day of the trial, after the prosecution had laid out the accusations in exhaustive detail, Scipio rose in his own defense and spoke a single grave sentence: "Romans, this is the date on which I conquered Hannibal."

Hardly a soul in the crowd, the jury, or even the prosecution had not carried a shield, taken a wound, or lost a brother or son in that great war. Those memories were enough to see the general carried from the court with all charges dropped, to tears and cries of gratitude from the assembled. But they were not enough to save his reputation. The more perceptive members of the crowd must have realized that Scipio had offered not a word of rebuttal. Scipio himself felt that the trial had permanently shamed him. He spent the few remaining years of his life in self-exile and ordered that he be buried away from the city that had spurned him. When he died, he left on his tomb not a catalog of accomplishments, but only this inscription: UNGRATEFUL FATHERLAND, YOU WILL NOT EVEN HAVE MY BONES.

•   •   •

A year after the trial, his leading rival neutralized, Cato the Elder put himself forward for Rome's most rarified office: censor. Officially, Rome's two censors conducted the regular survey of the city's assembled manpower. But from that simple counting function flowed remarkable authority. The censors compiled the lists of the senatorial and equestrian classes and could eject any man from his class on a whim. They could expel members of the Senate, who otherwise served for life. They set the code of public morals and enforced it through the example of those demotions. And they held sweeping power over the public finances. Such was the responsibility of the censorship that only the most accomplished politicians, typically ex-consuls, were permitted to run.

In Cato's year, Scipio's old faction put up seven candidates, all running as explicit anti-Catos and pledging to wield the censorship's powers with a light hand. Cato, on the other hand, ran on a platform of unabashed traditionalism. He called out by name those he considered corrupt and luxury glutted, declared Rome in need of a great purification, and pronounced himself the severe doctor to carry it out. As it would for the length of Cato's career, that message found an eager audience among the downtrodden, even more than among the elite. Cato won convincingly, and with him, the only other candidate for censor who shared his punishing platform.

Cato was a man of his word. During the year of his census, many a Roman must have suffered cold sweats at the thought of stepping up to the inquisitor's table, declaring on oath his family, class, wealth, and landholdings, and submitting to an examination of morals. Woe betide the promising politician who kissed his wife in public, the prosperous merchant who was too fat to serve Rome in war, the senator who made a joke in Cato's presence. Scipio's own brother was singled out, ostensibly for luxurious living, but also, it was widely suspected, for spite.

Some parts of Cato's purge sound eminently sensible even now, such as the ex-consul ejected from the Senate for impressing his lover with a private execution at a banquet. But some of his platform was only conceivable in a city that knew no right to privacy in our sense. Rome, in many respects, still thought of itself as an army. The state was expected to reach behind doors and around drawn curtains. So it was within Cato's power to tax at ten times their value any expensive possessions he considered a waste of money, including fine clothing, jewels, gold and silver plate, and furniture. It was within his power, a few years later, to advocate a law that capped the number of guests at a dinner party. Cato's Rome was one in which distinction in learning, in style, in entertaining, in essentially anything except warfare was suspect. And though this cutting-down-to-size naturally made him a whole legion of senatorial enemies—not to mention the owners of the buildings he demolished because they encroached on public land, or the citizens whose water supplies he cut off because they were siphoning from the aqueducts for free—Cato's spectacle of strictness won the people's cheers. They even voted him a statue (a frowning one, no doubt), whose inscription praised him for coming to the rescue WHEN THE ROMAN STATE WAS TOTTERING TO ITS FALL.

•   •   •

In his last years, Cato turned his single-mindedness on the enemy of his boyhood: Carthage, the state that had sent Hannibal to set Italy on fire. Hadn't Carthage already been crushed? Yes, presumably: It had long since been reduced to a Roman satellite. The small army it had left was not even permitted to march past its own borders. But as the head of a delegation sent to North Africa to arbitrate a land dispute in 157, Cato was shocked to discover that the Romans hadn't been paying adequate attention. He found Carthage rich again, thriving from the Mediterranean trade, its markets stocked with fat produce, its population healthy, growing, full of resentment toward Rome—and only three days' sail away. From the moment his delegation was tersely asked to leave Carthage, the threat of renewed war—whether real or imagined—dominated Cato's mind.

"The Carthaginians are already our enemies," the old man informed the Senate on his return, luridly narrating the atrocities he had witnessed in his youth. "He who prepares everything against me, so that he can make war at whatever time he wishes—he is already my enemy, even though he is not yet using weapons."

For the rest of his life, Cato tirelessly hammered on that theme. Whether the subject was farming or religion or the number of guests allowed at a dinner party, every one of his public utterances ended in the same offhand, ferocious way: "In addition, Carthage must be destroyed." Any laughter at the non sequitur would have died away with one look at his face. It was the foresight of a statesman, or a legendary display of grudge holding, or even "the first recorded incitement to genocide." The Senate's resistance eroded bit by bit—until Rome's ships sailed for decisive, preemptive war. Eleven years after Cato took up his ruthless campaign, Carthage was destroyed utterly—though Cato did not live to see it. Perhaps he found it a satisfying end. Many years before, he had left his farm for war. Now his persistence had sent a new generation of Romans against the same enemy, this time to finish the work. Some things, then, had not changed.

. . .

But in the end, even Cato had altered with the times. Having made a career railing against the corruption from the East, Cato, at the age of eighty, gave in to the inevitable and taught himself Greek. Some sources maintain that he finally took up the kind of books that he had so begrudged Scipio. Others allege that he had to begin with the alphabet, an elderly schoolboy. A concession like that, from the most Roman man in Rome, meant that, for all of his unbroken political success, one of the great causes of his life had largely failed.

The Rome of Cato's old age was one dramatically more open to the world than the one of his childhood. The Rome of his children would be more open still. *Latinitas* would still be a fault line in Roman politics, but it would be an increasingly symbolic one: It would be preached by men who spoke Greek from childhood. Cato the Elder understood as much, and it infuriated him. One of his last writings, in a manual for his son, deplores it:

> In due course, my son Marcus, I shall explain what I found out in Athens about these Greeks, and demonstrate what advantage there may be in looking into their writings (while not taking them too seriously). They are a worthless and unruly tribe. Take this as a prophecy: when those folk give us their writings they will corrupt everything. All the more if they send their doctors here. They have sworn to kill all barbarians with medicine—and they charge a fee for doing it.

There is a surviving bust of Cato the Elder, and it looks like a man who could have written those words. The face is submerged in creases. The corners of the mouth are pulled down. The nose wrinkles up in the beginnings of a sneer, of bigotry, perhaps, or obstinate pride.

. . .

Two more generations of Marci Porcii bring us down to 95, to the birth of Cato the Younger. The younger Cato must have passed under the great frowning statue almost daily. He was the heir of a family no longer "new," one for whom the fame and even the name of their historic ancestor was a blessing and a burden. A forebear already having reached the prize of the consulship, the Catos were now and in perpetuity a "consular" family. They could expect to run for and win the offices Cato the Elder had scraped for, on the strength of name recognition and competence by association, if nothing else. But shame on any Cato who wasted such an advantage. Other Romans might use "we aren't Catos" as a flip excuse, but those attached to the name had a long way to fall.

It was presumed, in fact, that they had fallen by default. The myth of universal decline was set as deep in the ancient mind as the myth of progress is in ours. It permeated politics and religion. It was a powerful figure for poets. Virgil, writing a generation after Cato the Younger, took decline for granted in these lines on an ancient warrior from the epic *Aeneid*:

> . . . *As he looks about he sees*
> *a giant stone, an ancient giant stone*
> *that lay at hand, by chance, upon the plain,*
> *set there as boundary mark between the fields*
> *to keep the farmers free from border quarrels.*
> *And twice-six chosen men with bodies such*
> *as earth produces now could scarcely lift*
> *that stone upon their shoulders. But the hero,*
> *anxious and running headlong, snatched the boulder. . . .*

Twelve times weaker: The Romans of Cato's day felt themselves in a similar relation to their ancestors. The ancients were, almost by definition, purer, wiser, braver. In every Roman home of consequence, the faces of the fathers themselves were witness to the decay: Death masks pressed from the flesh, realer than any photograph, hung on the walls in their stern rows, eyes empty and staring.

Robbed young of a father and a guardian in turn, Cato the Younger seems to have chosen his third and most lasting father from among those death masks. He conceived of his challenge like this: to show the same qualities that were so valued in his great-grandfather, and to do so in a world grown four generations worse. The Rome of Cato the Younger was not merely feeling tremors of a cultural and political rupture; an earthquake was fully underway. Cato the Elder grew up under catastrophic, but unifying, attack from abroad. His great-grandson grew up under a homegrown reign of terror. It was in that world that Cato the Younger set himself the task of proving his great-grandfather's model still possible and still indispensable—just as the pillar in Cato the Elder's basilica, no matter how the tribunes complained, remained in exactly the right place.

An added danger dogged Cato the Younger's efforts: affectation. Both Catos, and their constituencies, celebrated the same old-Roman ideal—but Cato the Elder had lived it, and done so unselfconsciously. He had learned to speak in the town market, not a school of rhetoric. He had been a small farmer and a citizen-soldier at a time when both roles were dying out. In fact, his own life encompassed much of the change: By the end, he wasn't a plowman, but a land speculator and shrewd investor. It was for an audience that had experienced such change that he wrote his famous book, *On Agriculture*, among the oldest known ancestors of all Latin prose. It was a compendium of practical farm advice: how to run an olive press, how to treat a sick ox, which gods to sacrifice to and when. It was not, in other words, a handbook of advice for those who had grown up on the land, learning by experience. Those people had farmed for centuries without the help of books. But under the pressures of cheap, imported grain and cheap, imported slaves, the people of Rome had largely left the plow. So Cato the Elder did not write for simple farmers. He wrote instead for citified investors of the kind he himself had become, men who would run plantations with the help of dedicated managers and enslaved prisoners of the foreign wars.

If one Cato's life had spanned both worlds, the other's was firmly planted in a latter-day Rome. In imitating his ancestor so closely, Cato the Younger was setting out on a lifelong project of calculated anachronism. It might bring reverence or ridicule, with little middle ground. If it was going to work, if it was going to look like something more than pretension, the persona could not slip for a moment. Even then, there would still sometimes be laughter.

And Cato's search for a way to cope with laughter may help account for the single greatest exception to his work of imitation. Cato took up with the same people his great-grandfather had considered a dangerous foreign cult: the Stoics.

•   •   •

Cato the Elder expelled Stoicism from Rome; Cato the Younger was instrumental in replanting it. The imperial chronicler Pliny the Elder found it "a very remarkable fact that the same [Greek] language that had been proscribed by one of the Catos, was introduced among us by the other." He was exaggerating, but not wildly.

Toward the end of the elder Cato's life, in 155, Rome received a strange diplomatic delegation from Athens. It came to plead for Roman mediation of a local dispute, and, Athens being Athens, it was comprised of three philosophers: Carneades the Skeptic, Critolaus the Aristotelian, and Diogenes the Stoic. While they waited for their chance to address the Senate, the philosophers did what came naturally: They lectured. Rome had never seen a spectacle like it. The foreign stars performed for packed crowds, the city's youths abandoning all of their other pleasures to cheer wildly. It was a pop-cultural fad of the first order—a "Greek Invasion." Part of the appeal was in the near-limitless scope of philosophy. In a world without academic disciplines as we know them, philosophy was politics and logic, ethics and science. This was the first opportunity for a whole generation of young Romans to consider whether the universe would be consumed in fire, or which was the best form of government, or whether knowledge itself was possible. All at once, in the span of a few days, everything that underlay the order of their city was up for grabs. Everything that seemed solid was slipping.

That was bad enough for the censor. But his indignation reached the breaking point when Carneades played an unthinkable trick. He spoke, in Cato's presence, on two sides of the same topic on two consecutive days, just to show that he could. Having spent the first day praising his hosts' strong, unbending sense of justice, Carneades took back everything he had said. He denied that justice existed and concluded, in a double-twisting backward summersault of logic, that there was no such thing as truth, except, maybe, the proposition that there was no such thing as truth.

A matter of days later, he and the other two were sent packing on a boat for Greece—thanks to Cato.

As satisfying as their expulsion must have felt, the irritant that had been shipped off soon returned, and many times over. Cato the Elder ultimately concluded that the corrupt tide of philosophy could not be stemmed. From a city in which a live Stoic had provoked a sensation, Rome had become, by Cato the Younger's time, a city in which no leading house was considered entirely cultured if it lacked its own "tame philosopher." Philosophical study was no longer a suspect youth craze, but a finishing school. Cato the Younger was by no means unique in seeking that kind of training. He was unique in the lifelong doggedness with which he pursued it and the thoroughness with which he put his career on hold for it. And he was a true reflection of his ancestor in his disdain for philosophy as art or performance or diversion. Others were shopping for a conversation piece; Cato was seeking something deeper.

• • •

What exactly? More specifically, what about Stoicism appealed to a privileged young man who could have had his choice of competing schools? And what caused him to reject the genteel, noncommittal eclecticism affected by many of his contemporaries?

To begin with, the Stoics were as hard, as uncompromising, as Cato the Younger aspired to be. They taught: Whether you were a foot underwater or a fathom, you were still drowning. There was no more-or-less good, no more-or-less bad. All virtues were one and the same virtue; all vices were the same vice. Your lungs were either full of water or of air. In that austere scheme, the vast diversity of characters and types were reducible to two: the sage and the fool. Fools were universal. Even practicing Stoics lumped themselves in as equally foolish, equally mired in error and sin, and equally miserable. Of sages, who alone were happy, Socrates himself was perhaps the only known case.

What could such a philosophy possibly offer to the aspiring fool? At the very least, it offered the possibility of swimming toward air. The aspirant might learn to sever happiness from everything fickle and fading, and to guard it in the single place it was safe, in the practice of virtue. A Stoic trained himself for indifference to all things outside the magic circle of the conscience. The choice between comfort and pain, wealth and starvation, even life and death, was always indifferent. To be sure, it was preferable to eat rather than go hungry, but there was no real happiness in the choice. It was always secondary to maintaining the virtuous life; pain was always welcomed as a chance to grow in virtue.

And what was a virtuous life? To live "in agreement with nature." Reason was nature's best gift, so living by nature meant, first of all, living by reason. Self-seeking, cowardice, grief, and all evil emotions could only enter the mind with reason's assent. The trained Stoic was skilled at holding back. What was promised in return was no less than freedom from passion—a word that, for all of its positive connotations today, carried in the classical world nuances of suffering and passivity (meanings that are preserved in the phrase "the Passion of Christ"). Plato taught that the passions were natural, if ignoble, parts of the soul. Aristotle recommended moderating them, not stamping them out. But to the Stoics, they were alien. With enough practice, the passions could be exiled from the citadel of the self. No unhappiness could touch the well-intentioned man. Banish the passions, and you were proof against misfortune. Banish the passions, and you were independent of the world, the owner of an unshakable contentment.

Others could fight fate. The Stoic would choose to love it. And this *amor fati* was the deepest meaning of agreement with nature and the highest reward of their practice. As one Stoic taught: "If I actually knew that I was fated now to be ill, I would even have an impulse to be ill."

What the Stoics offered Cato was not idle speculation, but a way of being, a simple and ready-made life that had already been cut to fit his character. There were, in fact, highly developed Stoic metaphysics and Stoic logic; but in making the journey from Athens to Rome, "a second-rate Greek philosophy had developed into a first-rate Roman religion." Stoicism became, above all, a practical guide to life. The Stoics who flourished in Rome were the ones who set aside their more implausible doctrines and tailored their teaching to a people who loved things that worked. Similarly, what Cato took from his tutor—a Hellenized Middle Easterner named Antipater—was not first and foremost dialectics or paradoxes, but exercises that could be put to use the day they were learned. He learned how to subsist on a poor man's food or no food at all, how to go barefoot and bareheaded in rain and heat. He learned how to endure sickness in silence, how to speak bluntly and how to shut up, how to meditate on disaster and suffer the imagined loss of everything again and again.

In effect, Cato was learning how to reincarnate his holy ancestor, and to do so in the most intellectually respectable way possible. Why Stoicism? Because the values of Cato the Elder, the ones that came from Latin soil, were potent but dead. In Stoicism, Cato the Younger found them again, as part of a living tradition. The old Cato never knew how Stoic he was. It took his descendant to merge Greek philosophy and Roman patriotism, to make that foreign school fully Roman by the force of his example.

From the very beginning, Cato the Younger's example—the bare feet, the out-of-date and wrong-colored clothing, the ostentatious poverty—was derided by some as a transparent act. And part theater it may have been. Rejecting creature comforts, living the hard, soldierly life—those virtues were still every bit as publicly lauded as they were in the days of Cato the Elder, even if they were honored more in the breach than in the observance. That could hardly have been lost on the younger Cato, growing up as he did in a city obsessed with rediscovering the lost, ancient formula for the good life. Cato the Elder, it was agreed, had had it. If the great-grandson was cut from the same cloth, why not pay attention to him?

Cato was determined to wear the mask until it fit. This was the source of his commitment to a school that promised to teach him how to endure laughter and abuse, to teach him to harden himself by seeking it out—to teach him "to be ashamed only of what was really shameful." Seneca, the great imperial Stoic, relates the story of what Cato did when, visiting the baths one day, he was shoved and struck. Once the fight was broken up, he simply refused to accept an apology from the offender: "I don't even remember being hit."

3

"Slaves Tower Above Us"

Sulla Felix, meanwhile, lived long enough to enjoy one last stroke of fortune: It wasn't an assassin who killed him, but his liver.

Testing his luck and his public's love, he did everything in his power to invite death. One day in 81, he announced his resignation as dictator, disbanded his army and his thick ranks of bodyguards, and walked through the city all alone. He offered an account of his dictatorship to anyone who cared to ask, and practically offered his neck to any aggrieved Roman who cared to stab him. None dared. Whether out of habitual fear or beaten-down affection, no one touched Sulla, who took it as a sign that the people truly believed what he had been insisting on all along: It had all been for them.

Checks on power in that era rested on the strength of rivals or, failing that, a tyrannicide's knife. It was never imagined that a man like Sulla would simply lay down his power. Julius Caesar would later say that if Sulla thought a dictator was supposed to behave like that, he clearly didn't know his ABCs. And yet, as suddenly as the autocracy was imposed, it was gone, and Romans never even had the satisfaction of ending it for themselves. Soon elections for the consulship returned. Sulla ran and won, easing the city back into a chastened normality. Once his year was up, he retired, like a good elder statesman, to write his memoirs.

Dictating his life's story, lazing on couches with the actors and drag queens who were still his only true friends, and clogging his failing body with wine, Sulla lived out the months his exhausted liver had left. He died in agony, delirious from fever, hemorrhaging blood from the mouth—but he died on no one else's schedule. He maintained to the end that he had inoculated Rome from tyranny. Now came the test: Was the patient in better health than the doctor?

●　　●　　●

Cato presented himself as a young man of the most un-Sullan moderation, but he shared with Sulla a love of the drinking bowl. His tastes were cheap, his endurance legendary. Cato was well known for the habit of staying in his cups until dawn. For the Romans, drink was no vice. But as a public Stoic, any indulgence naturally opened Cato to charges of hypocrisy.

Cato had a ready answer: Drinking was an extension of his Stoic studies. As his days began to fill with politics, time around the table provided his only hours of serious talk on philosophy and literature. The weakness of this defense is evident in the portrait of Cato as a hypocritical drunk, which sprung up among his enemies and long outlived him. Was his pretext as laughable as they claimed? We do know that, in classical culture, table talk over wine was often a serious and formalized business. As a drinking philosopher, Cato could place himself in a tradition that stretched at least as far back as Plato's great *Symposium* (or "Drinking Party"). On the other hand, perhaps drink was the draw, and philosophy the excuse. Cato may have participated in the decadence he railed against, but as a devout follower of a still-somewhat-arcane school, he had access to a unique excuse for his late nights.

●　　●　　●

Just as Cato could reconcile his philosophy with his drinking, he found room for the ambition expected of a young man of his family. His first political task was to lay two required foundations for a bright career in the Forum: to acquire a good wife and a handful of good scars.

For Cato, as for any young Roman with similar aspirations, finding a bride required far more strategy than sentiment. Marriage in the Republic was politics by other means. Alliances were born and broken at the altar, and a contest over an eligible bride could be as fierce as a lawsuit. With infant mortality higher for newborn girls than for boys—not surprising at a time when many families simply left girl babies to die—the demand for marriageable women outstripped the supply.

The shortage affected Cato's wedding plans. By his early twenties, he had found a bride-to-be within the small circle of Roman aristocrats—Aemilia Lepida, a consul's daughter and his distant cousin—only because her first suitor had suddenly broken off their engagement. Otherwise, Cato would not have stood a chance. His rival was Metellus Scipio, grandson of a consul, adopted son of a consul and high priest, and descendant of the same Scipio whose career Cato's great-grandfather had ended in humiliation. The Scipios' feud with Cato the Younger would have been stronger, not weaker, for being so old. Whether Metellus Scipio was the chronically indecisive type, or whether he simply could not resist the opportunity to humiliate a Cato, he waited until days before the wedding before declaring that he wanted Aemilia back. His furious effort succeeded in winning her away, ruining Cato's wedding practically at the altar and leaving a steaming young Stoic whose self-control was not nearly as advanced as he had thought.

Convinced by his friends that his first plan—taking Metellus Scipio to court—would only bring more embarrassment, Cato did the next best thing: "He betook himself to iambic verse." Soon after his loss of Aemilia to Metellus, a poem (sadly lost) raising urgent questions about Metellus Scipio's manhood appeared on the message boards of the Forum.

Cato was no poet. But, strange as it sounds for a jilted lover to start counting syllables as soon as his eyes were dry, politely slandering Scipio in verse was really the most practical step Cato could have taken outside of the law. In a culture whose reverence for honor matched its passion for gossip, the right words had real power to wound. And Cato could draw on old precedent. The ancient Greek soldier-poet Archilochus, one of the first to compose in the first person, was the legendary inventor of the quick iambic meter, "the measure in which ruthless warfare ought to be waged." Every writer of biting and bitter verses claimed the irascible Greek as patron, and so did Cato, who mimicked his style explicitly.

They might have understood one another well: Archilochus too had felt the shame of abandonment at the altar. He fled his hometown after a painfully public breakup, in which his prospective father-in-law reneged on the deal at the last minute and called off the engagement. The stricken Archilochus reacted in the best way he knew how. He stood up at a religious festival and publicly chanted a poem that gave a full and truthful account of the family's about-face. He included enough juicy half-truths to titillate his rumor-hungry audience. Legend had it that both father and daughter responded by hanging themselves.

Cato's foray into poetry did not end so dramatically. Metellus Scipio, relatively unscathed, went on to a respectable political career, his marriage to Aemilia thrived, and Cato was left to control his temper and look for another wife. He found one in a young woman named Atilia. Though we know very little of her apart from the personal and political betrayal with which her marriage to Cato would end, we have a detailed picture of the traditional wedding rites that would have been celebrated by such a couple. Much of it would have felt familiar. Picture Atilia, accompanied by a bridesmaid, donning white clothing on her wedding day, and a veil the bright color of fire. She wears a ring on the third finger of her left hand, from which a nerve was said to run directly to the heart. There is a legal contract to witness and sign, and the families, friends, and business associates gather after the ceremony to feast and drink at the bride's family's expense.

There, though, the similarities stop. The Roman marriage, both in concept and in ceremony, reflected deeply held traditions of patriarchy—the same traditions that saw fit to preserve so much of Cato's personality and so little of his wife's. The night before the wedding, Atilia would have delivered her lucky birth-locket to her father and given away her toys to her family. By the next evening, after Cato had untied "the knot of Hercules," the belt that secured Atilia's gown, she would have been his property, handed over along with a handsome dowry from the protection of her father's household gods to Cato's. On the other hand, Cato's dominion over his wife's property and person was not absolute. By the time of their marriage, women had established a foothold of legal and social independence. A woman could own property, divorce her husband, and even sue for repayment of her dowry.

Picture again the day of their wedding—a day they would have chosen for its favorable omens, ideally in the month of June. Cato and Atilia stand before a priest. They hold hands, a sign that Atilia consents, one of the few public displays of affection the couple will ever be permitted. Atilia's chanted oath seals the union: *Quando tu Gaius, ego Gaia*—"Where you are Gaius, I am Gaia" (ancient words, their meaning obscure, but probably derived from the fact that Gaius was the auspicious and prototypical Roman male name, while Gaia was its feminine form, which made them a pledge to join as man and wife). Sitting on stools facing the altar, the couple watches the priest sacrifice a pig or a sheep to Jupiter and pronounce the entrails favorable. They symbolize their shared sustenance by breaking and eating a small wheat cake.

After the guests have stuffed themselves at Atilia's father's house, Cato mock-wrestles Atilia away from the arms of her mother—a playful custom in their time, but also a reminder of the way the first Roman men populated their new village, seizing and raping the women of a neighboring town. At last, Atilia takes up a torch lit from her father's house and joins a procession to her husband's house, followed by a band of revelers singing dirty songs. Carried over the threshold by her new husband—another old memory of marriage by capture—Atilia lights her new hearth by the flame of the old. The crowd fights to catch the extinguished torch she tosses, much as women scramble for a bride's bouquet today. The marriage is consummated in the dark.

•   •   •

Unless Atilia was hiding something—and unless the stories about Cato's sexuality were mere extrapolations from his general air of self-denial—it was the first time for both of them. Rare for a man of his time, Cato was said to be a virgin on his wedding night. His virginity was remarkable enough that it would one day be the topic of a stock *suasoria* question in the rhetoric schools of imperial Rome: "Should Cato marry?" For more typical men, there was no shame in aggressive promiscuity. It served to highlight virility and strength, or at least popularity.

For Atilia, on the other hand, virginity was not an option—it was an expectation. Because females often married at the first signs of puberty, sometimes as young as twelve, it was taken for granted that they were untouched. Female virginity was a state-sanctioned virtue. The six Vestal Virgins who served as guardians of the Temple of Vesta and tended to its eternal hearth-flame represented the highest ideals of purity and chastity. If a Vestal Virgin broke her vow of chastity even once during her thirty-year term, she was buried alive and her lover was publicly whipped to death.

It was the epitome of a sexual ethos that touched the life of every Roman woman. For all of the Republic's sexual frankness and its fascination with boudoir antics, women were expected to practice sexual diffidence. To be too forward was to set the rumor mills grinding. And these expectations extended beyond the bedroom: Come across as too witty, too polished, too political, and you practically branded yourself a whore. To be dignified and demure was the feminine ideal. Women's wits were for spinning, weaving, and, at the most, household management.

And yet a new Rome was coming into being, part and parcel of the social revolutions that both Catos made careers of denouncing. Just as women's scope for property ownership and marital freedom grew, so too did their scope for mental cultivation. In upper-crust circles, it was possible for girls to attend primary school and study with private tutors. When their husbands were away on public or military duty, it fell to women thus educated to oversee the education of their own children and to take care of increasingly complex estates and financial dealings. Of course, such work often implicated them in politics—but in hidden politics, where they could advance their husbands' agendas away from prying eyes. For the traditionalists, even that was too much. Cato the Elder's sigh speaks for every fading paternalist: "We rule the world and our wives rule us."

Women's ability to sway and seduce their way into politics was, for some, just another sign of Roman regress. And it wasn't the only one. Sons weren't as obedient as their fathers used to be. They left home before getting married, wasted inheritances at the gambling tables, and lived on the cheap. They drank and danced and, as Cicero put it, "stayed up all night to the din of loud music." From every direction, someone was tearing at the old moral fabric: wives, sons, and—soon—slaves.

•　　•　　•

In 73, several dozen enslaved gladiators, armed with stolen kitchen utensils, broke free of a gladiatorial school in Campania. Capturing a wagon of weapons that happened to have been left outside the school's gates, they went into hiding on the wooded slopes of Mount Vesuvius. Rightly fearful of a band of armed, disgruntled slaves roaming the countryside, the Senate responded with what should have been overwhelming force: some three thousand men under the command of a praetor (second in rank only to a consul), Gaius Claudius Glaber. Though his men were largely untrained conscripts rounded up for a short jaunt, Glaber was confident in his thirty-to-one advantage and in his knowledge that the slaves were living off no more than what they could forage from the side of a mountain. But he and the Senate had overlooked something crucial. The leader of the prison break, a Thracian named Spartacus, had seen battle as a mercenary with the Roman legions. Spartacus wasn't the chief of a rabble, but a military commander in his own right. He knew the Roman way of war, and its weak spots, from experience.

When Glaber finally had Spartacus pinned on top of a plateau with a sheer drop, the brief rebellion seemed all but finished. Glaber's army set camp for the night and awaited a final charge at dawn. But Spartacus, in an inspired flash of desperate opportunism, ordered his rebels to weave rope ladders out of vines and tendrils. They slid down the cliff under cover of night and attacked the Romans from the rear. Caught sleeping and totally unprepared, the Romans were routed.

What had started as a criminal nuisance now began to resemble a war. Moving south from Vesuvius unchecked, Spartacus found slaves and poor villagers eager to join the insurgency's ranks. Only fifteen years after Rome had put down Italy's rebellion, the countryside's inhabitants—"herdsman and shepherds of the region, sturdy men and swift of foot"—seized the chance to give the imperial city a taste of its own bitter medicine. From the iron of their shackles, the slave army forged swords and spears; from Campania's wild horses, they corralled a cavalry. Another praetor and his thousands of men were easily dispatched. The victorious slaves added insult to injury by killing the praetor's horse, taking his guards prisoner, and parading the commander's fasces, symbol of Rome's sacred authority, through the slave's camp, jeering. Spartacus's force swelled to as many as 120,000, a movable city threatening to march on Rome itself. The legions had met and mastered slave mutinies before, but never one so skillfully organized, and never in the heart of Italy.

Spartacus had proven himself a more capable leader than the Romans would ever have expected of a slave, even a gladiator. In all but his chains, he fit the bill of a conquering general. A descendant of warlike nomads, "in sagacity and culture superior to his fortune," Spartacus possessed the physique of a man who had worked the fields, served with the legions, and killed in the arena. Had the Romans been able to overlook the fact of his slavery, they might have realized they were fighting their own ideal. But Spartacus also cast himself and his band as the symbolic alternative to Roman greed.

Centuries later, his success at that would make him a socialist icon. He imposed a stern egalitarianism on the slave army, dividing his profits equally among the soldiers and forbidding gold and silver within the camp. All this was the object of Roman contempt. But beneath the contempt was self-doubt and even guilt, not over the institution of slavery (which went unquestioned), but over the evident superiority of freed slaves to free Romans. Somewhat later, Pliny the Elder would eloquently sum up that guilt: "How our runaway slaves tower above us in largeness of spirit!"

· · ·

It was shameful enough for Romans to lose a battle. It was humiliating to lose, repeatedly, to slaves and peasants. But it was positively ominous that the Republic was confronted with not one, but three near-simultaneous military crises—and that, across the breadth of the known world, from the Pillars of Hercules in the west to the highlands of Asia Minor, Rome was losing.

Spain had been lost. Long among the most profitable of provinces, it was now a breakaway republic under the sway of a renegade general, a *popularis* named Quintus Sertorius. He had escaped Sulla's purges and found Iberia the ideal place to keep the populist flame burning. While most Roman governors were resented by the natives, Sertorius was loved. He rallied the native tribes against Rome, inducted them into his army and his councils, and was hailed by them as "the new Hannibal." He even conceived of himself as a kind of benevolent cultural missionary, setting up schools in which the local youths learned Latin and wore Roman togas. For six years he held the Republic's legions at bay, maintaining a government-in-exile backed by the Iberian tribes—and funded by none other than Mithridates.

Mithridates, the ruthless king in the East, "like a strong wrestler who gets up to try another fall, was again endeavoring to re-establish his power in Asia." Sulla had soundly defeated him in the field, but without the time or the troops to win a more complete victory, had left him alive and on the throne. Now, with Rome distracted by Spain and Spartacus, Mithridates seized his chance. He marched almost unopposed into the Roman client state of Bithynia, in northwest Asia Minor, claiming it for himself and destroying a Roman fleet belatedly sent to resist him. The Republic would muster the strength to fight back. But for the moment, thanks to military advisors sent by Mithridates' new allies in Spain, he had legions trained in the Roman style. He had control of the strategically vital entrances to both the Aegean and the Black Seas. And, most important, he had only one fight to win.

· · ·

Rome, by contrast, feared that all of its enemies were conspiring against it. The paranoia may have been justified: There were rumors of a compact between Mithridates and Spartacus. Whether or not they were in league, Spartacus was close to striking a devastating blow on his own. All he had to do was leave, get his army over the Alps, and he'd prove that a successful slave revolt was possible, even in the heart of Italy. There's no evidence that Spartacus aimed to abolish slavery more broadly. A disciplined commander who understood how richly he was favored by luck, he simply planned to escape the peninsula and disperse his followers to their former homes in Gaul, Germany, and Thrace. But that very success would have cast grave doubt on the sustainability of a way of life built on enslaved labor.

The inglorious war against Spartacus would give Cato, at the age of twenty-three, his first taste of military service. He joined the legions out of fraternal loyalty—his beloved half brother Caepio was a military tribune—but he wasn't alone among aristocratic twentysomethings in jumping at a chance for military command. A profitable career had no better start.

For Cato, the soldier's life held an added appeal. He had spent his boyhood playing war and studying at the knees of veterans, and he understood that his family's legacy was founded on military glory. In his own way, he had been preparing for command since childhood—since at least the time he had led Rome's youth in the Troy Game. For a budding Stoic, whose self-mastery was still a work in progress, there was no better place to seek out mental and bodily hardship than in the mud of an army camp, in the long night watches, and in the fear that attended combat, even combat against inferiors.

Cato began his career as a staff officer, the equivalent of a modern-day second lieutenant. The Roman army had no military academy and offered no formal training in leadership. The staff officers were mostly young, well-connected aristocrats like Cato, who had worked their family's social circles to secure commissions. The more powerful the family network, the better the post, and the more glory to recount on the hustings in years to come.

Telling the story was as important as living it. The days when wars ended in time for the harvest were long gone. Campaigns were drawn-out affairs that might keep officers away from Rome for years. As a result, aspiring politicians were careful to send detailed letters home, not-so-subtle reminders that they were off doing the Republic's dirty work while their families and friends were free to enjoy the fruits of their sacrifice.

It is one of the ironies of Cato's life that someone so suited for the soldier's life joined the army during a campaign in which it was performing so pitifully. The failure of two successive praetors had allowed Spartacus to create a self-replenishing, self-funding insurgency within Italy. The Senate, at last beginning to comprehend the scope of the threat, chose to commit both consuls—and consul-sized forces—to put an end to it.

The elderly Lucius Gellius Publicola was one of the two consuls dispatched to confront the slaves. Cato served on his staff. In any other realm but the tightly structured military, there might have been social tension between them. Unlike Cato, Publicola was one of those rare outsiders who had summited the political mount without any ancestor to blaze his way. And yet, even after penetrating the oldest and best-guarded of the old guards, enduring years of electoral combat, and emerging to serve as the highest official in the world's largest empire near the moment of its greatest influence, what Lucius Gellius Publicola was celebrated for was a thoughtless, decades-old prank.

While serving as proconsul in Athens, Publicola had demanded the presence of all the heads of the rival schools of philosophy, many of which had existed since Plato's time. When all the philosophers were gathered before their imperial master, he threatened, "Resolve your differences. Or I'll do it for you." It was a joke repeated decades after the fact in Rome, but we can imagine that it didn't quite tickle the Greek funny bone. The mock threat was more proof to Athens that Rome was incurably arrogant, as impoverished in culture as it was invincible in combat.

Entrusted with the theoretically invincible power, Publicola the Joker enjoyed early success in the field but failed to stamp out the insurgency. Cato distinguished himself in this, his first taste of combat, demonstrating enough personal bravery to invite explicit comparisons to his illustrious great-grandfather. Publicola even awarded him a number of military accolades.

But in a move that stunned those around him, Cato rejected any and all decorations, insisting that he had done nothing worthy of them. It may have been arrogance wrapped in modesty: Cato could have attracted far less attention by quietly accepting the awards than by angrily declining them. But the gesture may also have been an unspoken protest against the conduct of the officers and men. Plutarch contrasts Cato's "discipline, self-control, courage in all emergencies, and sagacity" with the "great effeminacy and luxury" of those around him. The indolence of the Roman legions was another sign that Spartacus was still not taken seriously. It would come at a cost.

While Publicola pursued Spartacus north, the army of his consular colleague peeled off in another direction and attempted to block the Alpine exit from Italy. But the decision to divide the Roman force was another underestimation, far more serious than luxury in camp. Spartacus simply picked off the consuls one at a time, crowning his success by crushing an unsuspecting Publicola and forcing three hundred captured Romans to impersonate gladiators and fight each other to the death. Cato must have escaped this rout with the remnants of the consular army, likely convinced that the defeat was well deserved.

As 72 drew to a close, Spartacus hunkered down in southern Italy for the approaching winter. For the Senate, this was the worst of all possible outcomes: Not only had Spartacus humiliated the praetors and consuls sent to destroy him, but he had taken up residence within striking distance of Rome. But where was the escape to the north and to home? The truth is that the slave army's strategic decisions may not have rested with its general. According to Plutarch, Spartacus recommended a hasty exit, knowing that Roman power would win out in the end, but his men were more interested in bleeding the countryside for profit.

•   •   •

The Senate needed a commander who would act swiftly and without remorse. The failed consuls were relieved of their military commands, and into their place, in the early days of the new year, stepped Marcus Licinius Crassus. He was an intimate of Sulla who had fought by Sulla's side as he'd stormed Rome. He was Rome's richest man. While Cato was becoming famous for the strength of his convictions, Crassus was already notorious for his almost complete lack of them: He would back any cause and fight any foe as long as doing so grew his accounts.

Like so many who had come through the just-concluded era of proscriptions and political violence, Crassus had lost family. Marius's forces had killed both his father and brother, and Crassus himself had only survived by spending eight months hiding in a Spanish cave. But with the change in political fortune that brought Sulla's rise, Crassus had returned home and seized the chance to build a fortune of his own. In the midst of slaughter, Crassus amassed a real estate empire from the property of the freshly deceased, bought at bargain prices. He once inserted a rich innocent's name on the death lists because he couldn't resist the scale of the prize. Even after the proscriptions ended, he showed inexhaustible creativity in inventing new sources of blood money. Whenever one of Rome's shabbily built apartment complexes caught fire (in a city without police or fire services), Crassus would send his own private bucket brigade—and then refuse to douse the flames until the building's owner sold it to him for next to nothing. Years of such shrewd dealing had left Crassus wealthy enough to buy and sell armies—and to scorn as a pauper anyone who couldn't finance at least a legion out of his own pocket. The Senate understood that well when it appointed him commander.

Crassus was eager to impose his total authority on an army whose discipline was breaking down, and he had his opportunity when one of his lieutenants, Mummius, disobeyed a direct order, engaging the slave army without authorization, only to watch his men drop shields and flee as the battle turned against them. Crassus was incensed. Here was an opportunity to fashion a military record to match his outsized fortune, and he was not about to watch it slip away due to indiscipline. So Mummius was exemplified in the most brutal way imaginable—through the revival of an ancient and pitiless ritual called "the decimation." Crassus ordered the bested troops to form ranks before the entire army. And then, no matter how a man had acquitted himself in battle, every tenth one was counted off, separated from the pack, and beaten to death. Plutarch and Appian cannot agree on whether a single battalion, a handful of legions, or even the entire army was subjected to the punishment. But Crassus's message to his men was unmistakable: "He had demonstrated to them that he was more dangerous to them than the enemy."

The cowed army now marched in full force against Spartacus, who retreated deep into the south in a search for more converts and more time. Pinned at last in Italy's toe, Spartacus was forced to make an escape plan. He contracted with local pirates to deliver him and his men to Sicily, but he was betrayed. The money he had plundered from Italy was, in turn, stolen by the pirates, who simply sailed off with the payment.

As the cold winter winds kicked up, Crassus worked patiently, constructing an enormous new prison around the slaves, a ditch and barricade that ran from sea to sea. Legions and slaves alike might have settled down for a long siege, but events on both sides of the barricade were pressing toward a final confrontation. Inside the prison, Spartacus and his men were starving. Outside, all of Crassus's efforts were about to be rendered pointless.

• • •

Two more Roman forces were due back in Italy soon, a body of reinforcements sent by the Senate from Greece, and another returning, improbably victorious, from Spain.

This should have been welcome news, but it sparked a panic in Crassus, because he knew who returned at the head of the Spanish reinforcements: Gnaeus Pompeius Magnus, Pompey the Great. Every bit Crassus's equal in ruthless ambition, Pompey had inherited his father's legions at the age of nineteen and had wielded them so brutally against Sulla's enemies that he had earned the nickname Adulescentulus Carnifex, "the Teenage Butcher." Sulla could sense in the young general a potential rival, so he co-opted him by playing to his ego. The title *Magnus* was Sulla's gift (bestowed only half seriously on someone so young), and so was Sulla's stepdaughter, and so was a triumphal parade welcoming Pompey back to Rome, with Pompey decked out as a near-god in a chariot, his troops following in ordered march, the spoils of his victories pulled behind them in heaping wagons.

The laws governing triumphs were strict, and Sulla broke them by elevating a near-boy who had never been elected by the people to any office. But that hardly mattered to the dictator. He was as charmed by Pompey as he was threatened, and he wasn't the only one. With his broad, boyish face and wave-swept hair, with cheeks that blushed almost on command, Pompey was quickly adopted as the public's favorite son. He played the part with relish, affecting a modesty that softened the edges of his glittering success. When he demanded the Spanish campaign for himself, his enemies were all too happy to see him go, especially to Spain, an ulcer where Rome had been bleeding money and forces for almost a decade. Putting down the insurgency was widely expected to either bankrupt or kill Pompey. But here too he defied expectations. He survived several defeats and wore down the rebels year after grueling year.

For Rome, Pompey's success and return were good news at last. But for Crassus, they threatened imminent disaster. The race to crush Spartacus was on, and Crassus understood that credit would go to the general who managed it first, not to the one whose patience had made it possible.

• • •

Spartacus threw all of his men at a weak point in the siege line and succeeded in breaking through and racing north, with Crassus's army in fast pursuit, swallowing up stragglers. Exhaustion, defections, and indiscipline now took their toll, and as detachments of Spartacus's men melted back into the country or pursued their own private skirmishes, it became clear to the leader that his once-massive force was disintegrating with every step. At last, Spartacus learned what Crassus knew: He was about to be pinned not by one, but by three separate Roman armies. Spartacus called a halt and stepped in front of his assembled forces. Dismounting, he took his sword from its sheath and stabbed his horse to death. The message was clear. There would be no more running. The next battle would bring victory or death.

At the head of a hopeless slave army, Spartacus charged straight for Crassus's legions. "The battle was long and bloody," reports Appian, "as might have been expected with so many thousands of desperate men." Spartacus's body was never recovered. The gladiator-general was last seen in a daring attempt to cut his way through to Crassus's tent.

• • •

Along one hundred miles of Italy's busiest thoroughfare, the Appian Way, Crassus built a monument to his victory, befitting his ruthlessness. Every forty yards, a traveler could glimpse one of the half-dead remnants of Spartacus's army nailed to a cross, slowly suffocating and rotting in the sun. The crosses stood for months. By his own measure, Crassus had saved the Republic from a slave rebellion. His grisly billboards were designed to ensure that no one would forget.

The limelight was deservedly his, but at the last possible moment, just as he had feared, Pompey swept in to steal his glory. After putting down a handful of slaves who had managed to escape both death in combat and crucifixion by Crassus, Pompey told the world that he had been the one to conclusively end the rebellion. Writing to the Senate, he credited Crassus with winning a single battle but brazenly claimed that he, Pompey, had won the war. The public's love for Pompey plugged any holes in his version of the story.

What had or had not happened on the battlefields against Spartacus mattered a great deal to both men. They each wanted the consulship, and nothing was a better crowd-pleaser than heroics under arms. Yet in the case of the rebellion, both men came home to a Roman public and Senate that preferred to put the whole unfortunate mess behind them. Victory over slaves, no matter how brutal or flamboyant, would never win love.

But if the armies of Crassus and Pompey couldn't win love, they could always serve as instruments of fear. Both men marched their battle-hardened men up to the walls of Rome, just short of the sacred boundary line—and then left them there, with their tents and their cook fires, sharpening their weapons as the election approached. Each army used the existence of the other as an excuse to refuse to disband. The threat did not even need to be spoken.

Perhaps Crassus and Pompey would have been elected on their merits alone. Neither cared to find out. Crassus hardly bothered to campaign; Pompey was still legally underage. Under the armies' watchful eyes, Rome dutifully went to the polls, and the next two consuls were—to the surprise of no one—Crassus and Pompey.

• • •

Too young to play a role in the election, Cato could only watch in disgust. Perhaps Crassus's victory had saved face for Rome. Certainly his resort to antique discipline, up to and including the decimation, had held catastrophe at bay. But for any thoughtful Roman, the famous superiority of the legions,

the docility of millions of slaves, and Rome's authority in its own backyard—
let alone its empire—were all in doubt. The Romans had stretched their
imperial curtain across the world, yet holes were beginning to show.

Most ominous was the failure of Sulla's promise. All of his civil bloodshed had come with an implied bargain: that it would be the last time. At
the price of terror, Sulla was supposed to have restored the Republic. But he
had been in the ground for hardly a decade, and already his reforms were
crumbling. Pompey, for instance, had vaulted over every step on Sulla's ju-
diciously crafted *cursus honorum,* skipping all lesser offices on the way to
his election as co-head of state. He was full of promises to restore the tribunes' power and govern as a populist. Most disturbing of all, though, were
those two armies, each answering now to a consul who had good reason to
hate the other, locked in a standoff beneath the walls of an undefended
capital.

THE FIRST COMMAND

It was in that climate of insecurity that Cato, at twenty-eight, launched his first run for office—for military tribune. If successful, he would become one of two dozen military officers directly elected by the Roman people. He would command an entire legion, more than four thousand troops. Barring scandal or conspicuous failure, he would have a smooth road into the Senate once his year of service was up.

But first he had to win, and campaigning for office was unglamorous work. Like any candidate, Cato would be obliged to promise and call in favors, to rekindle old contacts and create new ones, to pay homage to power brokers whose blessings were indispensable. It was work that, by its very nature, must have humiliated him. His Stoic lessons stressed indifference to popular opinion, even hostility to it, but now, as he worked to win the good graces of strangers, that hostility would have to be swallowed.

"You must caress men," Cicero's brother once advised, "which is in truth vile and sordid at other times, but is absolutely necessary at elections." Cato must have been well aware of the challenge to his beliefs. All candidates, from first-timers seeking junior magistracies to the handpicked few competing for a consulship, submitted themselves to public judgment. A few, like Cicero, managed to wring nobility out of the effort:

> It is the privilege of a free people, and particularly of this great free people of Rome, whose conquests have established a worldwide empire, that it can give or withhold its vote for anyone, standing

for any office. Those of us who are storm-tossed on the waves of popular opinion must devote ourselves to the will of the people, massage it, nurture it, try to keep it happy when it seems to turn against us.

Yet the man who wrote those words had worked himself to a nervous break-down by the age of twenty-five. Where Cicero had punished his body and mind in politics, others exhausted their fortunes in bribery or put themselves through endless, exhausting military campaigns, fantasizing a triumph in Rome's streets and the smooth trip to political power that followed. However rough and risky the road, the reward was incalculable. To have a hand at the instruments of Roman power was to shape the direction of the known world.

Power, though, wasn't the only draw. For some, the goals were more tangible, more self-serving. Rome's elder statesmen, especially ex-consuls who had served their year at the top, came into massive wealth at the end of their terms. They were given preference for foreign land ownership, and with a foreign clientele came the best claims on taxes and profitable money-lending opportunities. No one understood this windfall better than the Roman elite, and they prepared their sons for public life with all the care and consideration of those making a sizable investment. After all, a single son elected to high office could secure the family fortune for generations.

That fact, along with the rampant bribery that was becoming electorally indispensable, helped explain why the rich ruled the ballot box. They had more than a single finger on the scales. They could afford to purchase votes and spend months campaigning. Unlike the urban plebs, they could easily sacrifice a day's wages waiting in line for the polls. Unlike the large majorities of the nominally enfranchised Italian communities, they could travel from abroad to vote in person, as the law required. And thanks to a long-standing quirk of Roman elections, the ballots of the established families simply counted for more. Though the Roman system was only partially democratic, its forms were widely revered and jealously guarded. Elections were sacrosanct. Even in Cato's day, with Rome's neighbors long since subdued, the city authorities began election day by scanning the horizon for imminent attack, just as their forefathers had done.

For those with the means and ability to compete, Rome was a meritocracy, where the achievements of one's ancestors were mere prologue, where everything could change with the next election or the next message from the Eastern front or the next son.

In Cato's lifetime, however, the meritocracy had acquired a sinister edge. Campaigning—and winning—on the honor of a military career was an old tradition. Riding an army to power, as Marius and Sulla had done, was something unprecedented. And the election-at-swordpoint of Crassus and Pompey was a frightening sign that the dominance of generals was being normalized. That the competition carried an element of actual or implied violence was a sign that things had gone too far. Whatever his feelings, twenty-eight-year-old Cato was in no position to criticize openly what Roman politics had become. But he did begin to pioneer a gestural politics of his own, a series of symbolic acts that spoke to every Roman voter who shared his unease.

As a start, Cato became the first candidate in memory to appear in public without a nomenclator. These were long-memoried slaves who acted as dedicated campaign staff, trailing behind a politician to whisper into his ear a name, connection, or favor owed or given for everyone with whom he pressed flesh in the Forum. Instead, Cato campaigned alone, relying on his memory and refusing to fake it when it failed him. At a time when the most effective campaign tools were standing armies, it was a small gesture. But as a way of generating maximal attention from minimal resources, it was a shrewd one.

Elected on the strength of his unorthodox campaign, Cato could not yet promise a different politics, but he had cast himself as a different kind of politician. Now he would have to prove himself as a commander.

$\bullet \quad \bullet \quad \bullet$

Cato's year of command—67, in Macedonia—was dominated by the threat of Mithridates. While Roman forces had recovered from the king's attack and renewed the war, the fighting had taken a toll. Discipline disintegrated in the Roman ranks. Weary, underpaid, and harassed by guerrilla attacks, the Roman army began to do the unthinkable: to refuse orders. That was all the opening the seemingly indestructible king needed to mount the last of his stunning comebacks. Mithridates cobbled together a new army and moved to fortify his kingdom for a final time.

Near the town of Zela, in Pontus, Mithridates led his soldiers into battle against two unsuspecting Roman legions—and at the age of sixty-seven, he still fought in the front lines. Bogged down in the mud of the battlefield, the Romans suffered heavy casualties: 7,000 dead, including 174 officers, the most officers Rome would ever lose in a single battle. But rather than celebrate their improbable victory, Mithridates' men pushed and fought for a glimpse of their king. A single Roman centurion had apparently broken through the king's bodyguard and plunged a sword into Mithridates' thigh. Now, unconscious and rapidly losing blood, the king lay on the field as his medics rushed to heal the wound with a tincture of snake venom.

At last, shock turned to shouts of joy as the king—alive and revived—was lifted up on the shoulders of his doctors, in sight of his whole army. It was a gesture heavy with symbolic meaning. Just so, Alexander the Great had commanded his army from the front. Just so, in India, he had taken a grave wound in the thigh. And just so had the living Alexander been lifted up to reassure his followers. Few at the scene would have missed the rich parallels, least of all Mithridates, who had lived his life in emulation of the emperor he claimed as ancestor and whose heritage he had used to cast himself as champion of the subject peoples of the Roman East, the Greeks included.

Nor would the propaganda value have been lost on Cato, as the news reached him at his post in Macedonia. Mithridates had already roused the Greeks to rebellion once, and though Sulla had brutally suppressed them, the possibility remained that they would use the king's resurgence as a chance to reassert their independence. As legionary commander, Cato's mission included standing guard against that possibility, inspiring enough fear in the locals to put another uprising out of the question.

• • •

The army Cato joined as military tribune was fully professional, its ranks dominated by full-time soldiers. They fought in hopes of plunder or of a small land grant once their years of service were up. Short of the extraordinary step of going on strike, they had no appeal against the stern discipline intended to keep them in line. Silence in the ranks was required at all times. Any soldier who fell behind on the march received a lashing. Any soldier who fell asleep on guard duty was put to death. Almost as punishing were the legions' constant exercises in formation. As one contemporary observer notes, "It would not be wrong to describe their drills as bloodless battles, and their battles as bloody drills."

What would the men of Cato's legion have made of their new commander? He approached camp not on horseback, as expected, but on foot. This was not one of the social climbers whom they had come to expect as commander. Here, it seemed, was a man ready to live as hard as the common soldiers lived and to impose on himself the same discipline he imposed on them.

Cato's discipline differed as much from the regimen of corporal punishment dealt out by the average Roman commander as from the flamboyantly bloody methods preferred by Crassus. "He thought it a trifling and useless task to make a display of his own virtue, which was that of a single man," reports Plutarch, "but was ambitious above all things to make the men under his command more like himself." To the degree possible for a Roman army officer, Cato seemed to think of himself as an educator. If his self-appointment as the model to whom the troops should aspire revealed a flare-up of his egotism, his style of leadership was nevertheless a remarkably liberal one for the time.

Rather than reach for the lash at first resort, Cato made a point of reasoning with his men. If we wonder what connection there could have possibly been between a bookish aristocrat and uneducated soldiers, it is worth recalling that the Stoic philosophy he practiced and preached was one ideally suited to military life. For the soldier, the fundamental Stoic message was indifference to all things outside the circle of his own virtue: indifference to cold, to want, to fear, and to everything else that made life on the march miserable. As a Stoic-influenced officer from our own era explained, the philosophy teaches a disciple how to draw a line between

(a) those things which are within the grasp of "his will, his free will," and
(b) those things which are beyond it. Among the relatively few things that are . . . within my will are my opinions, my aims, my aversions, my own grief, my own joy, my moral purpose or will, my attitude toward what is going on, my own good, and my own evil.

Those forces outside the will, such as fear or rage in the heat of battle, give the illusion of irresistibility, but they are only powerful insofar as the rational will chooses to welcome them. So the Stoic ethics held, teaching Cato to harden his mind along with his body.

In Plutarch's account, Cato's Stoic training methods succeeded: "It would be hard to say whether he made his men more peaceful or more warlike, more zealous or more just—to such a degree did they show themselves terrible to their enemies but gentle to their allies, without courage to do wrong, but ambitious to win praise." Perhaps more effective than any doctrine, however, was Cato's example, particularly his consistent refusal to stand on the pomp of his office. "He made himself more like a soldier than a commander," sleeping on the ground with his troops, eating the same meager food, wearing the same clothes, digging ditches beside them, and joining them on the march, always on foot.

For a senator-in-waiting, Cato's unpretentious willingness to share hardship was mildly shocking. It won his men's affection in a way that no Stoic lecture could have. From his refusal of honors in the Spartacus campaign to his conduct as a legionary commander, Cato was proving himself allergic to ceremony of all kinds. He rejected pomp precisely at the time when shrewd deployment of military spectacle constituted the heart of political power. Pompey knew how to turn the love of his troops and his public into trophies glittering with pearls and gold, into ranks of chained captives, into all the triumphal splendor that refracted and multiplied love many times over. Cato, by choice or by chance, never learned how.

· · ·

When Cato's furlough came, he sailed for Pergamum on the coast of Asia Minor, epicenter of Mithridates' Roman massacre two decades earlier and home to the greatest library in the world, after only Alexandria's. In Pergamum, Athenodorus, one of the world's most learned Stoics, presided over as many as two hundred thousand scrolls, as well as the most advanced information-storage technology of the day: parchment. The special product of the city, parchment was replacing the flimsier papyrus and inaugurating a thousand-year reign as the stuff of books. In a massive marble reading hall dominated by Athena's statue, Cato had access to those authentic original texts of Stoicism that had not yet reached Rome, treatises on the passions, on

duty, and on the divinity of the universe, texts laid down by the first thinkers who had taught in the shade of Athens' Stoa, its public porch, more than
two centuries before Cato's arrival.

Assuming, of course, that the texts were authentic—because Athenodorus,
a proud and aloof old man, had a habit of cutting out the bits that disagreed
with him. The librarian had been caught physically deleting controversial
passages from the work of Zeno, the first Stoic. In Zeno's *Republic,* a high-
minded book on the ideal state that would cause considerable embarrassment to his successors, he had allegedly advocated free love, gender-neutral
clothing, and the abolition of money. Ideas as radical as that may have been
acceptable from a street philosopher building a new movement on the
strength of converts he could round up at the marketplace. But as Stoicism
grew domesticated, respectable—and Romanized—its radical origins grew
increasingly scandalous. Further, the Stoics' more easily caricatured notions
threatened to overshadow the cosmopolitan vision at the center of their political thought. "We should look upon all people in general to be our fellow-
countryfolk and -citizens, observing one manner of living and one kind of
order, like a flock feeding together with equal right in one common pas-
ture." The Stoic ideal presented an enlightened vision of the brotherhood of
man, but it could also become, in the right Roman hands, a friendly gloss for
empire, with Rome playing the role of civilizing shepherd to a many-
tongued flock.

Athenodorus shared with Cato a devotion to Stoicism and an urge to
make it relevant—no mere relic or foreign imposition, but a functioning fixture of the Roman world. Perhaps it flattered the old man's pride to see a
Roman commander drop everything and cross the sea to beg his company.
The chronicler Diogenes Laertius also mentions, intriguingly, that because
of the discovery of his clandestine editing, Athenodorus was "placed in a
situation of great danger." Perhaps Cato was his escape plan. At any rate, to
Cato's delight, the scholar who had refused the friendship of governors and
kings sailed back with Cato to camp. Years later, he would die in Rome, in
Cato's house.

· · ·

Cato's return stay with his legion did not last long. An urgent letter reached
him in camp: His half brother, Caepio, also presumably serving in the East,

was gravely ill. Only the army had ever separated Cato from Caepio. Fatherless Cato had spent his life idolizing Caepio as only a younger brother could. And even as he outstripped Caepio in achievement, in discipline, and in public profile, Cato held his brother dear.

The road to Thrace, where Caepio lay dying, was too difficult. The sea looked impossible: A heavy storm was pouring rain on the Aegean coast, and no ship in port was large enough to brave the crossing and the squall. At last, Cato persuaded the captain of a small, one-masted merchant boat to make the passage, past the island of Thasos and through the northern Aegean. In those conditions, even with the right vessel, shipwreck was no idle threat, and Cato knew it. Yet he arrived in good time, storm-tossed and soaking, but still whole. Caepio was already dead.

> Lead me, O Master of the high heavens,
> My Father, wheresoever you wish.
> I follow readily, but if I choose not,
> Wretched though I am, I must follow still.
> Fate guides the willing, but drags the unwilling.

So the Stoic was taught to pray, taught to welcome fate in, taught to see evil in greedy attachment to the beloved, not in the death that takes him away—taught to reflect on the utter fragility of the human vessels into which we pour our love. So Cato was taught. But at this moment, the moment for which his philosophy should have prepared him above all others, it was all smoke. Only the corpse was solid. He embraced it, sobbed over it, ordered the best incense and the best clothes burned with it on a high pyre, ordered a massive marble likeness of Caepio set up in the market of the provincial Thracian town in which he had never before set foot—lavishing on the dead the luxury he railed against for the living. Cato gave himself to grief, this once, with the same fervor that had led him to preach the effeminacy of grief, the need for independence from pain in all things. For the rest of his life, friends and enemies alike would remark that this was the moment when philosophy most abandoned Cato.

Caepio had been a Roman soldier, sober and self-possessed. Yet he had often said, in a mix of brotherly admiration and envy, that Cato made him look like a drunk. Once, when Cato was a boy in Rome, someone had asked him whom he loved the most. "My brother." Second most? "My brother." Third most? "My brother."

. . .

Still grieving, Cato served out his year as military tribune. Despite Mithridates' resurgence, Macedonia remained quiet. Cato's men saw no major combat. And yet they loved Cato like a conquering general. On the day of his departure ceremony, as the tribune left on foot, soldiers threw down their cloaks for him to walk on. They reportedly wept and kissed his hands.

Cato had not delivered them spectacular victories or made them famous in war. He hadn't brought them plunder or land of their own. Those transactions cemented the bond between commander and legion. But Cato had lived like a soldier, and few Roman commanders could claim to be more loved by their men. For the rest of his life, Cato would often be admired at a distance, but he would rarely be shown such wholehearted affection. He would not find the same comfort in the give-and-take of civilian friendship or in the always-unsteady ground of politics.

. . .

The natural next step, in 66, would have been a return to Rome and a run for a junior magistracy, which would have meant a place in the Senate. But Cato had put off entrance into public life in his youth, and he could wait again. Instead of sailing for home, he set out on a walking tour of Rome's possessions in Asia Minor, the source of so much wealth for the Republic and so much bloody conflict for its armies. Cato set himself the task of investigating firsthand the military strength and way of life of each province, speaking with locals and lodging in their towns. That was his stated purpose, but as he walked the Anatolian highlands from town to town on the edge of the Roman world, completely free for a short span, with only a handful of friends and slaves for company, how far from his mind was his devastating loss? If anyone could disguise mourning as duty, it was Cato.

An innkeeper's nod, a whisper behind the hand, a narrowing of eyes in the marketplace: These were the most valuable pieces of intelligence to come from Cato's journey, because they completed a picture of Rome's reception at its empire's end. The Republic saw itself as liberator, civilizer, protector; ensconced in the armed retinue expected of a Roman official, Cato might not have seen it any differently. But now there were no bodyguards for Cato, no welcoming delegations or cringing dignitaries. He was unknown here, without office or ancestry. Entering a town, he would often send two slaves ahead to find a room and prepare a meal—and almost as often, because they had no threats to make, they'd be ignored. Cato would follow after them—and he too would receive only scorn. Sitting on his baggage like a hopeless traveler, he would wait until he attracted the attention of someone in charge. He would then explain exactly who he was. "Not all men who come to you will be Catos," he would quietly add. The next guests may "only want an excuse for taking by force what they do not get with consent." Evidently, he was under few illusions about his fellow Romans' conduct here. And as with rented rooms, so with provinces.

Only once, toward his journey's end, was Cato received with dignity. At the gates of a town, a great welcoming party appeared, young men lined up in military finery, crowned priests in white robes, citizens in their best attire—everything a Roman dignitary deserved. Cato, naturally, was furious. He had explicitly ordered his slaves to preserve his anonymity, to prevent exactly this. Marching up with the intention of calling it all off, he was buttonholed by the master of ceremonies, an old worthy holding a crown for the guest of honor. Without so much as a hello, the old man demanded of Cato, "Where did you leave Demetrius? When will he be here?" Cato's friends couldn't stop laughing. Cato failed to see the joke.

Who was Demetrius? He was Pompey's ex-slave, and the town was turning out for him. Demetrius carried only a reflected bit of his master's glory, and the power of passing along a good word. Pompey, as it happened, was in the neighborhood—and by now, with little dispute, he was the foremost man in the world.

· · ·

The consulship of Pompey and Crassus, which had begun with two armies at stalemate and the prospect of renewed civil war, had ended with a public embrace. Neither had the force to overwhelm the other, and both were shrewd enough to know it. When Pompey proposed restoring the power of the people's tribunes, reversing Sulla's most conservative reform, Crassus jumped to second him and keep pace in the public's affection. For all those who had bristled under the regime left behind by the dictator, this final breakdown of Sulla's bargain was a triumph. Among these was Marcus Tullius Cicero, the upstart orator. In the speech that would help propel him to fame, he addressed these defiant words to the old order:

> As long as it could and as long as it had to, the Republic put up
> with that monarchical domination of yours in the courts, and in
> the whole of public life. But in case you don't yet realize it, all that
> was snatched from you and taken away on the day the tribunes
> were restored to the Roman people.

An ordinary citizen, whether put up to it or not, would help bring about the consuls' reconciliation. As Pompey's and Crassus's year in office drew to a close, a citizen appeared at a meeting in the Forum to report a portentous dream. Jupiter had come to him and ordered the consuls to reconcile. Crassus let the suspense build before reaching across the rostra to his colleague and rival:

> Fellow citizens, I think there is nothing humiliating or unworthy
> in my taking the first step toward goodwill and friendship with
> Pompey, to whom you gave the title of "Great" before he had grown
> a beard, and voted him a triumph before he was a senator.

No doubt those last two barbs—together an admission that Pompey was someone entirely unique in Roman politics—were intended as much for Pompey as they were for the crowd. And we can only imagine the disgust with which Crassus must have chewed over the words "humiliating" and "unworthy." Even if not divinely inspired, the consuls' embrace saved Rome, for the moment, from a relapse into civil bloodshed.

The two left office on officially equal terms, but Pompey's unmatched charm, sparkling war record, and success in taking credit for the restored tribunate made him the people's favorite by far. Their affection paid off when the audacity of Mediterranean pirates grew too much for Rome to bear. Piracy had been a nuisance for generations, but with the Republic's forces preoccupied in the East and Rome's ever-growing economic clout uprooting coastal communities, crime at sea was reaching new heights. Heavy-laden grain ships, sparsely guarded temples with rich stores of offerings, even (in one spectacular attack) an ex-consul's daughter were all promising targets for the disciplined pirate bands. The effects of their raids were felt most painfully in the skyrocketing price of food in Rome.

When Rome demanded a commander to restore order to the sea, a grateful tribune proposed sending Pompey the Great. The people's assembly, in the face of furious conservatives who warned of anointing "a virtual monarch over the empire," overwhelmingly voted Pompey an unprecedented military command: 500 ships, 5,000 horses, 120,000 men, and authority over the entire Mediterranean and fifty miles inland on the coasts. Those forces were set against a stateless network of enemies hiding among the rocky coastal towns of the eastern Mediterranean.

It was supposed to take Pompey years to root them out. It took him just three months. It appears that his successful "war" against piracy was as much a matter of carefully negotiated settlements and hefty payoffs as of smashing victory at sea. Pompey had used his personal navy once, and he had beaten a single pirate fleet soundly. In Rome, however, his partisans credited him with a glorious, hard-fought victory over marauding hordes. Now, there was only one enemy worth their man's ambitions: Mithridates.

Conveniently enough, Rome's armies in the East were just then in need of a new general. An open revolt now consumed all of the legions sent against Mithridates: The soldiers were refusing to take another step. It couldn't have happened to a more competent general: Lucius Licinius Lucullus, a dignified old-line senator, had been on the verge of victory a number of times. He had wiped out armies in pitched battle. He had stormed and sacked enemy cities. But he had not found the one thing that would bring an unambiguous end to the war: the king himself. Exhausted by a trackless search for Mithridates through desert and mountains and furious at a conspicuous lack of plunder, Lucullus's troops had nearly abandoned his authority. The final blow to their morale was the shocking defeat at Zela, in which a wounded Mithridates had survived.

The decision to revolt was not, however, a spontaneous one. In the army's winter quarters, one Publius Clodius Pulcher had deliberately set to stirring up mutiny. *While you freeze and starve here in Asia,* he murmured to the men, *Pompey's veterans are already settled down on farms of their own.* The whisper campaign was an especially deep betrayal: Clodius was Lucullus's brother-in-law as well as an officer on the general's staff. But Clodius had been denied a promotion, a deep insult to someone of his inflated self-worth. He was also very likely in the pay of Pompey. Funded by a political rival and instigated by a relative, the revolt against Lucullus was, by 66— the same year as Pompey's victory over the pirates—impossible to ignore.

"Oh, my endless tasks!" Pompey was careful to be overheard saying. "It would be better to be an unknown man, if I can never cease from military service, and cannot lay aside this load of envy and spend my time in the country with my wife!" He knew well the role of humble Cincinnatus, lionized for repelling an invasion then refusing dictatorial powers and returning to his farm. With sighs and protests, Pompey accepted his heart's ambition, courtesy of the Senate: the largest Roman force ever sent east, along with sole power to make war and settle peace. If his last command had made him "a virtual monarch," what was Pompey now?

•   •   •

In Ephesus, an ancient city on the coast of Asia Minor lorded over by the massive Temple of Artemis, Pompey the Great gave Cato the favor of a brief meeting, the first recorded encounter between the two. Pompey well understood the value of political theater, even on small occasions like this. Rather than allow Cato humbly to approach him where he sat, Pompey sprang out of his chair and crossed the room to offer his hand—as if Cato were the eminence in the room, as if the most decorated Roman alive "must render an account of his command while Cato was there." Pompey spent the interview heaping praise on Cato's virtue. He kept up the stream to anyone within earshot, even after he had ushered Cato out with a pat on the back.

They were not fond of each other. "Everyone knew that Pompey admired him when he was present, but was glad to have him go away." Still, Pompey understood Cato's value. In a Senate that remained deeply suspicious of his irregular career and populist tendencies, Pompey would need a Cato on his side—and Pompey was prescient in understanding his dangerously exposed place in Roman politics. In Roman public life, one day's hero was the next day's tyrant. If Pompey had funded a mutiny—if he had helped to undermine a Roman army in the field, in service of his own ambition—then he was essentially guilty of treason. This was the time to embrace tradition, to persuade any doubters that, even as he was taking on vast powers, Pompey was still a man of the old ways, a man who served the

Republic's greatness, not his own. It was clear that the way to embrace tradition was to embrace Cato. Not yet a senator, not yet out of his twenties, Cato was already building a power not dependent on arms or office: He was arbiter of the *mos maiorum*, able to bestow their stamp of approval or to withhold it. But Pompey would find that securing even a part of Cato's approval would take much more than an afternoon's work.

Happy to be done with each other for the time, they went their own ways: Pompey east to glory, Cato west and home, with his tame philosopher and his brother's ashes.

5

THE SWAMP

He could have smelled it from miles away: home. Rome stank like the swamp from which it was formed, a thick, dank, unrelenting mix of cooking fires and human and animal excrement; its legendary stench, it was said, could travel for miles.

On the mornings when his friends called for him, Cato descended on foot from his house, down the Sacred Way, and into Rome's literal center, the Forum, a stretch of flat land roughly the size of two football fields, tucked into the valley formed by the Capitoline and Palatine Hills. The Forum's close-clustered, columned buildings housed the daily bustle and jostle of Roman life, a mix of commerce, ritual, and politics. Senators flaunted their entourages of favor seekers and clients. Hundred-strong throngs of attendants trailed officeholders and candidates, hoping for spoils once their friends won election.

The Forum was the permanent home of blatant favor swapping. It was also, at the same time, the most sacred acreage in the empire. Roman legend held that the state first took root in the Forum's muddy soil. On this spot, the neutral ground between twin hills, King Romulus is said to have consented to meet his rival, King Titus Tatius; on this spot, the two kings agreed to lay down arms. Standing atop a swamp, on the single solid patch of earth available to them, they chose to unite their neighboring tribes under a common banner.

It was on this shifting, uncertain ground that the early Romans set out to build a civilization firm and enduring. Here the quarreling tribesmen constructed their first state buildings: a palace for the king, temples for the gods, a plaza for the crowds. Here they showed the first signs of the dogged-ness that would serve their legions well: Each time the Tiber poured over its banks and flooded the town, the Romans refused to move to higher ground. They simply drained the water and rebuilt.

Over time, the first humble dwellings of the Forum grew in the Roman imagination, as though the secret to the empire's success lay buried some-where in the aging brick and mortar. Veneration of the old pushed Roman practicality to the brink. Generation after generation, the Romans kept up their oldest structures at any cost, even when doing so ran up against the realities of managing a swelling city—or administering an empire. In Cato's day, preservation still usually trumped utility, with predictable results. The Forum, littered with crumbling temples and run-down monuments, took on the character of a holy junkyard.

● ● ●

By 64, at the age of thirty-one, Cato had already put off entry into the Fo-rum's public life twice, once for studies and once for travels. Others seeking office could only hope for a foundation as magnificent as his: a successful military tribuneship, multiple tours of duty, a famous family name. But he remained reluctant. For Cato, it was a matter of competence. The junior-most office on the *cursus honorum*, the quaestorship, was perhaps the most tediously detailed. How could he run for it if he hadn't familiarized himself with its demands? To his friends, this was ludicrous: For most hopefuls, preparation was an afterthought. So while other candidates spent their time canvassing the Forum and buying off voters, Cato was busy memorizing constitutional law. Strange as it might have seemed, Cato was studying for the one office that would most reward diligent preparation.

In the hands of the twenty quaestors lay the convoluted finances of the entire Republic. Quaestors received and cataloged all tax revenues, managed state debts, logged each and every financial transaction in the state account book, and handled public funds for state burials, monuments, and visiting dignitaries. Even though it was a mandatory stepping-stone to bigger things, and one that guaranteed a seat in the Senate as well, we can imagine many an established senator viewing the quaestors as glorified parchment-pushers who filed orders and tidied accounts.

But from former quaestors, whom Cato took the trouble of interviewing as part of his preparation, he heard a different tale—and a warning. The quaestorship may have been the bottom rung of Roman politics, but anyone following the money trail in Rome would find his way back to the quaestors and their small army of indispensable assistants. The quaestors were the sole officials with unfettered access to the Republic's treasury. There was real power here in the honeycomb of Rome's bureaucracy: the power to overlook a personal debt, to impose a backdoor tax on a foreign conquest, to misplace the bulk of a family inheritance. The treasury's permanent, professional staff was well-off, smug, and comfortable in its work, taking just enough to satisfy itself, not enough to attract attention. Conveniently, corruption in the treasury was far easier to rage against than to repair. *Sic vivitur*, the establishment sighed. "That's life."

The collective throwing up of hands was understandable. There was, after all, no fury quite so fierce as that of the disturbed bureaucrat, whose list of friends and favors was lengthy and impressive. Tread lightly, the former quaestors advised Cato.

•   •   •

Once elected quaestor, Cato, in his first act, stabbed straight at the heart of the bureaucracy. He summarily fired all clerks and assistants whom he judged unfit for office or guilty of corruption. It was the kind of wholesale housecleaning that made headlines—and drew out the long knives of the career clerks. Who did this young man think he was? What didn't he understand about the compact between the elected and the appointed? This sort of thing was especially appalling from a son of the establishment, the same establishment that had so benefited from the energies and exertions of the bureaucracy.

Cato, though, was oblivious to any backlash. What was there to know besides the fact that the law had been broken? Still, as with his military command, he matched strictness with softness when appropriate. In the course of his audit, he found that a number of clerks had erred not willfully but out of ignorance of the law. These, he tutored in the rules and responsibilities of the treasury. If they were willing to accept his tutelage, he was ready to keep them in their jobs. If not, they would be shown a swift exit.

If the bureaucrats had missed Cato's reformist colors, then Cato too may have underestimated their power and reach. These men had made long careers by ingratiating themselves with the elite. They were not about to be thrown out by a newcomer. The harsh reality of bureaucratic infighting was about to impress itself on him. A concerted campaign of rumormongering and favor calling ensued, and at its height, the other quaestors came out publicly against Cato. It was a move calculated to demonstrate that he was the one who was out of touch and out of line. The bureaucrats also took to the courts, building a legal labyrinth that would busy Cato until the time ran out on his year in office.

One case in particular became the flashpoint for Cato's agenda. One of the chief clerks challenged his dismissal on grounds of fraud, and the suit made it to court, with Cato arguing on his own behalf and the censor Quintus Lutatius Catulus defending the outraged clerk. No choice could better illustrate the *sic vivitur* sensibility. Eighty-five-year-old Catulus was a pillar of the establishment, one of the oldest living ex-consuls, a man famous for consistency and moderation, thought to "surpass all Romans in justice and discretion." What's more, he was a friend of Cato and an admirer of his Stoicism. No other advocate was better placed to paint the thirty-year-old's latest move as childish and radical.

But Cato hadn't spent nights memorizing the law for nothing. In this instance, the law was clear: The clerk had defrauded the treasury. Cato dissected the case with clinical precision for the assembled jury, and Catulus knew almost instantly that he had been dealt a losing hand. On the merits, Cato won. But Roman justice was notoriously unpredictable, as subject to human drama as it was to legal reasoning. So Catulus chose to beg. An elderly censor, on his knees, he pled for mercy for a client victimized by a quaestor run amok. It was an inspired tactic, and Cato knew it might sway the jury if he let it go on much longer.

He interrupted Catulus's pleas with one of his own: "It would be a shameful thing, Catulus, if you, the censor, who scrutinizes our lives, were removed from the court by the bailiffs." Catulus stopped, locked eyes with

Cato, and struggled for a response. No words came. He simply stalked away in silence.

The vote was to be taken shortly thereafter, and a straw poll had Cato winning by a single ballot. But one member of the jury, a friend of Cato, was ill and absent from the courtroom. Catulus sensed an opportunity. What he had been unable to do in public, perhaps he could do in private. He arranged a quiet house call and urged the juror to do the right thing—to put justice above his friendship with Cato. Even after his public humiliation, when Catulus spoke of justice, his words carried moral force. Soon, he sent a private litter to deliver the ailing juror to court. With his vote, the jury hung, and the clerk was acquitted.

It was a painful lesson in the realities of the law—and in response, the furious quaestor chose in turn to skirt the edges of legality. Treating the extra vote as null and void, he refused to reinstate the clerk or to give him his pay. Legal or not, Cato's demonstration of ruthlessness was enough to frighten the treasury staff into submission as long as he remained in office.

•   •   •

Yet the clerks only represented the first layer of reform: However difficult to bring to heel, they were still Cato's subordinates, without the wealth or power base needed to put up an effective resistance to a determined superior. Nor, in the scheme of things, had they pocketed outrageous sums. The real hit to the treasury came from outside, from a network of senators and financiers who had turned the public coffers into a private slush fund. These were precisely the sort of men whom Cato was well advised not to challenge, the kind who could make life difficult for a young official, who could thwart an ascent still very much in progress.

Cato had enough instinct for self-preservation to avoid such a frontal assault. Taking on public employees had been painful enough; taking on Rome's wealthiest would likely mean a fatal career wound. When it came to balancing the Republic's books, he managed to soften the sharper edges of his reform agenda. As he sifted through the monies owed to the treasury by much of the governing class, he discovered that debt ran both ways, that in fact the treasury was in arrears to many of its citizens. Most had simply shrugged it off, safely assuming the money was never to be seen. But under

Cato's watch, the treasury paid up, even as it simultaneously called in its debts. This balance had the desired effect. For almost every new enemy presented with an IOU, a new friend might receive unhoped-for cash.

With this success, he was noticed more broadly than ever. He had wrung unprecedented publicity from a political backwater. It was enough to make him the symbol of all those Romans who believed that the government could be reformed without systemic changes to the Republic. It was this growing support that Cato counted on when he undertook his boldest step of all: healing the open sore of the Sullan proscriptions.

Many Roman families had fled the city as their loved ones were hacked to death. With the return of relative safety, they had filtered back. But the shadows surrounding their self-exile still loomed. In their minds, justice remained undone, the dead unavenged. Sulla, after all, had simply drunk himself into oblivion in peace, and his partisans had quickly and quietly slunk back to their homes. Some still sat in honor in the Senate. It was as if the whole episode had been some wicked nightmare from which everyone had awoken and moved on. Everyone, that is, except for the families who grieved for lost fathers and sons.

There had been no eager pursuit of the dictator, no trial for the killers who did his bidding. This hadn't been for lack of defendants. Sulla may have died, but the hatchet men were alive and well, known to all, many living in great luxury and comfort. Sulla's bloodletting had made them rich. For each body they'd brought to the dictator's feet, they'd earned as much as twelve thousand drachmas, the equivalent of some five hundred thousand dollars in today's money. Both wealth and fear made them untouchable. "All men hated them as accursed and polluted wretches, but no one had the courage to punish them."

Cato sensed the rewards in nominating himself public avenger. He saw the chance to wipe out the last remnant of the darkest years of his life, and of recent history. His pretext was a technical one, but it gave him a place to stand: Because Sulla had paid for the killings with state funds from the treasury, the killers were accountable to none other than the quaestor, who had the right to demand the money back. Cato called each one of the accused to the treasury, billed him for repayment, and treated him to a passionate harangue on his unholy crimes. After each was publicly shamed, Cato handed him over to the judges for trial on a charge of murder. Scores of perpetrators were convicted and sentenced to death. As Plutarch put it, the Romans "thought that with their deaths the tyranny of that former time was extinguished, and that Sulla himself was punished before men's eyes."

At the age of twelve, Cato had supposedly demanded a sword to free his country from the dictator's grip. Now, almost two decades later, it was his quaestor's stylus that put Sulla's ghost to a final and inglorious rest.

• • •

Cato, in his own view, had demonstrated the resilience of Rome's constitutional foundations. So long as Romans were willing to enforce the laws and abide by them, the state could prosper, with debts and taxes paid on time and corruption held in check. His critics—both those who had come to count on handouts from the treasury and those *populares* who demanded more fundamental change—could point out that Cato had conveniently sidestepped the constitution when it served his interest. Hadn't he simply ignored the jury's vote in the case against the chief clerk? But of course, they argued, we should expect such behavior from Cato. He was the model of self-control—until you gave him a glass of wine. He frowned on others' ostentatious emotional displays—but gave his own brother a funeral worthy of a satrap. His actions as quaestor were only the latest in a long line of hypocrisy.

But even Cato's sharpest detractors couldn't argue against results. He may have been egotistical, brash, and almost painfully earnest, but he had managed his office in a fair-minded and focused way, investing "the quaestorship with the dignity of the consulship." To the keen-eyed, though, the success of Cato's agenda had its limits. Just as every man who visited one of Rome's foreign holdings wouldn't be a Cato, every man elected to high office wouldn't be a Cato. His schedule would stretch any reasonable man to the breaking point. He was the first to arrive at the treasury and the very last to leave—a commitment that would likely have required him to spend far more time than the average Roman on the city's narrow, poorly lit streets after dark. He never missed assembly or Senate meetings, remaining in the crammed city any time the Senate was scheduled to meet. He commented on every remission of debt or taxes, double- and triple-checked each entry in the state's account book. His reforms were successful because he was willing to absorb the outcry, so much so that his name became a shield against the possibility of stealing from the treasury: "It is impossible—Cato will not consent."

But where Cato would not consent, others would. Without Cato's day-in, day-out supervision, the return of corrupt insiders and well-connected oligarchs was almost assured. The reversion to a pre-Cato treasury started literally the minute he left office. Departing on his final day as quaestor, he was joined by a throng of citizens who accompanied him home. The crowd gathered both to celebrate and thank him for his service, but also to pass along tips and curry favor with the young political celebrity. It was the sort of crowd on whose edges Cato himself had stood, earlier in his Forum life.

Amid the congratulations came a warning: Only moments after Cato left the treasury, a number of prominent citizens had arrived there, with the goal of extracting from another quaestor the kind of gift—a quiet remission of debts—that would have been routinely denied under Cato's watch. The quaestor in question, Marcellus, a close friend of Cato's since childhood, was the sort of public official whose ethics shifted with his surroundings. At Cato's elbow, he was upright and strict, when he was alone, he laid himself open to the influence of the powerful.

Knowing his friend's tendency to waffle, Cato returned to the treasury—where he witnessed Marcellus in the act of writing the illegal debt forgiveness into the accounts. Cato demanded the tablets and erased the fresh entry, as mortified Marcellus stood by. After he was through, Cato motioned for Marcellus to leave the treasury with him, and they set off in the direction of Cato's home. Strict though he was, Cato wasn't above playing favorites. In this case, rather than sever ties with a boyhood friend, he forgave Marcellus. Long after that disquieting incident, the two would maintain a strong bond.

It was yet another example of Cato's moralism mixing with his humanity. But more than that, it foretold the impermanence of Cato's agenda. Cato had completely missed an essential aspect of governing: He had left to the state a remarkable personal record, but a quaestor's office that remained essentially unchanged, its success or failure still subject to individual strength or weakness. If he had imagined that his own rectitude and incorruptibility in office would ignite and ennoble the hearts of other aristocrats, he was almost instantly proven wrong. It had taken mere moments for the old network of client-patron relationships to prey upon a weak-willed man like Marcellus. Such men may have understood Cato's message, even admired his example, but they knew of no other way to behave when the powerful came calling.

6

"Do You Not See a Storm Coming?"

If Cato was blind to the dangers of personality-driven reform, there were some in Rome who were all too alive to its weaknesses. These were Cato's enemies on the populist left, radicals who asked what a slightly more honest quaestor could possibly accomplish for the debt-wracked poor, what a slightly more competent civil service could possibly do to bring down rents or the price of grain, what the *mos maiorum* could possibly mean to the peasant family driven off its land before the swelling plantations of the rich. Of these radicals, the most notorious was Lucius Sergius Catilina, whom we know as Catiline. Under his erratic leadership, the campaign for root-and-branch change—stifled for so long by Cato's fellow *optimates* in the Senate—would leave the realm of politics altogether.

By biography, Catiline could have been a new Sulla. Like Sulla, he was a son of the aristocracy, and like Sulla's, his family had fallen into poverty before he was born. But instead of dedicating his life to restoration, Catiline declared himself a traitor to his class. Having drunk and gambled far beyond his means for the better part of his young adulthood, Catiline was as debt-ridden as the underclass he sought to speak for—and in speech, in mannerisms, and in political sympathies, he sought to make himself an honorary prole. We don't know the extent to which Catiline's sympathy with Rome's lower orders was authentic, but the political advantage was clear. Inside the aristocratic circle, he was scandal stained and rejected, accused of everything from killing his son to defiling a Vestal Virgin. But the scorn of the great and the good only brought him more love from those sneered at as "debauchees, adulterers, and gamblers." Among them, Catiline found a grateful political base, one that he could never have assembled by traditional means. Moving through a thick cloud of scandal with his entourage of the young and dangerous, stating his case at table-pounding political meetings that degenerated, it was said, into raucous, all-night parties, Catiline made his name with a simple, radical platform: land redistribution and a universal cancellation of debts. He sold it under the appealing slogan of *Tabulae Novae*—"Clean Slates."

Clean Slates were a direct threat to Rome's best-off, to whom much money was owed. But to many in the 60s BCE, the promise of a fresh start hit a resonant note. Years of war in the East had wreaked havoc on interests far more concrete than Roman prestige. Upheaval on the frontier had disrupted provincial tax revenues and bankrupted many of the Republic's leading land speculators, sparking an economic crisis in the city.

Not even those who had served the Republic under arms were immune from debt. Many old soldiers who had been issued their own land found the paltry plots unequal to the dream of Roman land ownership. They were angry, armed, and just a short march from Rome's city limits. One such disgruntled veteran was Gaius Manlius, an ex-centurion from Sulla's army. His words spoke for an entire dissatisfied people:

> We are poor and wretched. Thanks to the violence and cruelty of
> the moneylenders, many of us have been deprived of our native
> land, all of us of our good name and possessions. Not one of us was
> allowed the traditional protection of the law, or to keep our bodies
> free when our inheritance was lost.

At the same time, Italy's fields could no longer produce enough grain to keep pace with a swelling population. As Rome's food supply turned increasingly to imports, prices rose accordingly. And hunger wasn't the only problem for the urban poor, who were packed in filthy tenement housing and kept chronically unemployed by a slave-glutted economy. It is no surprise that citizens on the razor's edge had begun to talk openly of revolution. In the city's rougher quarters, small but growing riots had become a fact of life. Without any police force to restore order, they could only burn out as rage exhausted itself. The Senate—conservative and slow moving as usual—had little to say about any of it.

But where it had few answers, it had ample means of keeping a threat of Catiline's caliber off the ballot. No sooner had he mounted his first campaign for the consulship, in 66, than he was accused of extortion and barred from running. In response, it was alleged, he briefly considered an outrageous plot to kill off the consuls elected in his place, along with a good part of the Senate, and take office by force. Instead, he chose patience. It remains uncertain whether his first plot was abandoned or was simply a lie cooked up by his enemies, but there was not a rumor so sordid that it would fail to stick to Catiline.

. . .

Undeterred, Catiline launched a second attempt, in 64, the year of Cato's quaestorship. The establishment was out of legal recourses—and so it did the unthinkable. One by one, the senators, many of whom came from political dynasties centuries old, lined up behind a small-town lawyer from an unheard-of family.

Marcus Tullius Cicero understood Rome as only an outsider could. He was an immigrant and a child prodigy, a stunningly talented public speaker who was hungry for a seat in the inner councils of power. Lacking the fortune and family name of his contemporaries, he set out to mold himself into the kind of man they could admire, the carbon copy of the class into which he missed being born: the finest orator, the foremost constitutionalist, the most dignified aristocrat. While the stress of the effort was enough to drive him to a collapse by his midtwenties, it won him fame in the law courts and a reputation for competence in a succession of lower offices.

The unanimity with which the aristocrats threw their support to a social inferior, a *novus homo* not even born in Rome, testified to their fear. Set alongside Catiline's Clean Slates, Cicero was the least-bad option. From the conservatives' perspective, he was a shrewd choice. Yes, he had gone on record lauding the restoration of the tribunes—but the Senate could live with that, because Cicero's ruling motive, to make himself more Roman than the Romans, was well understood. While Catiline was throwing away—and stamping on, and setting fire to—his membership in the club of the elite,

Cicero wanted nothing more than to join. Once in, he would surely do little to offend the membership.

The eloquent new man performed as expected. "Catiline has fouled himself in all manner of vice and crime," Cicero thundered. "He is soaked in the blood of those he has impiously slaughtered." And so on. In the end, Cicero was elected to one of the two consulships. Gaius Antonius Hybrida, a nonentity, won the other.

Catiline came in a losing third, and the fire of his resentment only burned higher. He had promised too much. His faction was counting on a class war, and defeat, by election or not, was unimaginable. By now Catiline was on the point of insolvency, but this too he turned to his advantage. "Who is better qualified to be the standard-bearer of the desperate," he asked his followers, "than a man who is bold and desperate himself?"

It was at this moment—when Catiline's identification with the plebs was most complete—that his aristocratic legacy gnawed at him the most. For four centuries his family had served the Republic. A first-place finish in the election should have been his birthright—and it had been stolen by Cicero, a nobody. When Cicero subjected him to the indignity of public questioning before the Senate, Catiline openly taunted him: "I see two bodies, one thin and wasted, but with a head, the other headless, but big and strong. What is so dreadful if I myself become the head of the body that needs one?" It was a cryptic prediction of the power he would soon wield over the masses.

At last, it was clear that this power, if it were to come, would be realized by some means other than an election. Midway through 63 and Cicero's term, under the watchful eyes of Cicero's hired guards, Catiline made a final, desultory run for the consulship. It ended even worse than the previous one. He had reached the point at which a would-be revolutionary could tell himself that legitimate means had been exhausted, that the system had proven itself irredeemably corrupt.

• • •

If he needed any other confirmation, he might easily have found it in Cato's run, in the same election, for the office of people's tribune. Legally speaking, he had the right: Wealthy and consul-descended as he was, Cato's line was still technically plebeian, not patrician. But *morally* speaking, wasn't it an outrage? It could not escape the notice of the radicals that the office once honored by the Gracchi brothers was now, in blatant contradiction to its original spirit, up for grabs to Rome's brightest young conservative. Nor could they have missed Cato's clear intention in joining the race: to make life difficult for Pompey, the very man responsible for returning the tribunes to power.

Pompey's continued presence in the East was still the gaping vacuum in Roman politics. But already there were whispers and hints of a triumphant return. There were even suggestions, from opportunistic partisans, that only Pompey and his army could be trusted to deal with Catiline. For Cato, the warning—and the decision to run for tribune—had come one day as he left Rome for a philosophical retreat in the country. On the road, he passed an enormous baggage train heading in the opposite direction, toward the city. It was Metellus Nepos, Pompey's lieutenant and brother-in-law, on the way to Rome to claim a tribuneship for himself and—Cato surmised—to begin paving the way for his patron.

Pompey's flattery had never convinced Cato that the most beloved man in Rome, backed by an army, would be harmless. Seeing the baggage train and guessing at its meaning, Cato made up his mind to get himself elected tribune, if only to act as a check on Pompey's man. The day after passing Nepos on the road, he was back in the Forum, enveloped in his crush of supporters, hammering out the familiar themes: an end to favor trading, an end to bribery, an end to elections won at sword point.

Cato won election as tribune, along with Pompey's placeholder. The new consuls-elect—Lucius Licinius Murena, a legionary commander in the Mithridatic Wars, and Decimus Junius Silanus, Cato's brother-in-law—both wafted into office on billowing clouds of bribes.

•　•　•

They had twisted the law, they had lined up behind a nobody, they had bought power with cash: the resourcefulness of the ruling class, the dexterity with which they held him down at every step, must have seemed to Catiline to be the true conspiracy. In response, he set in motion his long-anticipated uprising. Together with Publius Cornelius Lentulus Sura—an ex-consul expelled from the Senate on a charge of immorality—he hid weapons caches at key points across the city. Meanwhile, in the Etruscan countryside near

Rome, the angry centurion Gaius Manlius declared his alliance with Catiline and, spoiling for a fight with Rome, began to raise a small army of bankrupt peasants.

When everything was in place, Catiline allegedly took a last, brutal step, sealing his conspiracy with a human sacrifice. "He sacrificed a boy and, after administering an oath over his entrails, ate them in company with the others." The story came from Cicero, a man with the means and motive to make up the most ludicrous personal attacks. Still consul for the rest of the year, Cicero understood that establishing the conspiracy as an existential threat, and then crushing it, would earn him a place in history. But Cicero was operating from at least a small grain of truth. His target was a man notorious for flourish, zeal, and excess—someone who could conceivably have thought the sacrifice of one boy an acceptable price to pay for power. Such a grisly oath would have cemented the bond between the plotters, implicating them in a ritual so shocking that no one of wavering loyalty would have the stomach for it.

Whatever sealed it, the bond was not strong enough. Catiline overestimated the strength of his supporters' loyalty and underestimated the reach of Cicero's spy network.

• • •

On the evening of October 20, 63, hardly a month after the planning for the revolution had begun, three senators climbed up the Sacred Way to Cicero's home, carrying urgent and alarming news. Earlier that evening, after dinner, they had received an anonymous delivery of letters, each addressed to a different member of the Roman elite. One of the trio of senators, Crassus, bore an unsigned letter addressed to him, detailing a plot to overthrow the government. Each senator on Catiline's enemies list would be assassinated. The nobility's sons would kill their parents. To distract the authorities and spread a general terror, twelve sections of the city would be set ablaze. Finally, armies under the command of the conspirators would march on the city, crossing its sacred boundary under arms and seizing power—the height of treason.

Almost none of this was news to Cicero. For weeks now, he had heard mutterings of Catiline's plans from well-placed sources. But Cicero's repeated warnings had only made him look like a fearmonger, sowing terror to reap political rewards. The words he used to begin each of his public threat announcements—"I have been informed that . . ."—became the subject of much parody. The fashionable suspicion was not of Catiline, but of Cicero, a social-climbing consul exaggerating the truth so as to swoop in and play savior to the Republic. So, as much as he feared Catiline, Cicero was unable entirely to stifle his joy at the delicious opportunity presented by Crassus's hard evidence that the state was under attack. He called a meeting of the Senate for the next morning.

Cato was in attendance as Cicero opened his indictment, announcing that violent revolution was finally at hand. It may have occurred to the senators who had received letters of warning the night before that they would be implicated along with the conspirators, and it may have been to ward off suspicions of guilt that the Senate overwhelmingly voted Cicero emergency powers to put down the rebellion, through a provision known as the Final Act. It is even possible that the letters' deliverer, Crassus, had indeed been in league with Catiline, or at least silently complicit. Sensing that the whole plot was doomed to fail, he may have revealed the plans to put himself above suspicion. Guilty or no, the senators swallowed their grumbles and entrusted Cicero with absolute power for as long as the crisis lasted.

And then, for days, nothing. In the Senate, the suspicion again grew that Cicero was playing up the threat for his own aggrandizement. At last, and to the consul's relief, news came from the outskirts: Gaius Manlius had taken up arms in the town of Faesulae. A rush of reports soon confirmed slave uprisings, mass meetings of the disaffected, bad omens and prodigies. Cicero posted sentries and dispatched troops to confront the rebels. Catiline, remarkably, was not among them. He had remained in Rome, the man at the center of the city's whispers and a silent challenge to the Senate.

When they met face-to-face before the assembled Senate in the Temple of Jupiter, Cicero brought to bear a lifetime of prosecutorial skill, grilling Catiline on "this lunatic criminal enterprise." Catiline only mocked Cicero as an "immigrant" and demanded a trial. But in the court of senatorial opinion, Catiline was already convicted of treason. And in truth, Catiline had no intention of waiting for an official hearing.

That very night, Catiline openly declared himself consul. Surrounded by his consul-sized bodyguard, bearing the consul's symbol of office—the twelve fasces—he fled to his waiting armies.

· · ·

That fall, in a city braced for crisis, Cicero was virtual dictator. Yet no sooner did his power become absolute than he was forced into an embarrassing compromise with corruption.

The bribery with which Murena and Silanus had won the summer's consular election was an open secret. Electoral bribery was, in fact, everyone's open secret. To run for office was to lavish free food, gifts, and shows on the public, to promise plum treatment to one's friends and supporters. The line separating mere *benignitas* ("generosity") from outright *ambitus* ("corruption") was difficult to draw with any consistency. It was a political line, and though the law clearly made *ambitus* a crime, most of the Senate rested secure in a gentleman's agreement that the law would remain, except under the most flagrant circumstances, safely unenforced. Yet in response to the demands of a loud minority, the penalties kept rising. When not consumed by Catiline's threat, Cicero—at the vociferous and repeated urging of Cato—managed to push through a bill raising the punishment for bribery to a devastating ten years' exile.

And now, just when the establishment could have been expected to rally together in the face of revolt, the new law was put to an unexpected first test. The target could not have been more conspicuous: Murena, who in a matter of months was scheduled to take over as consul. The prosecutor could not have been more aggrieved: The distinguished jurist Servius Sulpicius Rufus, the election's loser along with Catiline, who bore Murena a special hatred. Catiline, feeling himself cheated out of power, had taken to the hills. Sulpicius, feeling just as cheated, took to the courts, at the most awkward moment for everyone involved. And in the trial of the year, Cicero, who had written the law against bribery and named it after himself, announced that he would appear in court as lead attorney—for the defense.

His calculation was brutally simple. He needed two new, unsullied consuls to hold firm against Catiline. The conviction and exile of one of them would mean political chaos at the worst possible time. And so Murena was to be acquitted.

There was perhaps only one man who took the Catiline threat more seriously than Cicero: Cato, the tribune-elect. He was every bit as aware as Cicero that Murena's conviction and exile would be a gift to the conspirators. Yet Cato was trapped—by a career built on denouncing corruption and by his public promise to prosecute any politician he considered guilty of bribery. His principles left him no room for the compromise Cicero made with ease. Cato's promise to deliver the closing argument against Murena gave the prosecution team its most recognizable member—and it would give Cato the second-to-last word, followed only by Cicero's rebuttal.

Two powerful personalities, who should have been allies in a time of crisis, forced by their irreconcilable commitments into destructive conflict: It should have been the stuff of tragedy. It played out as a comedy.

• • •

Cato, in the role of straight man, was in classic moralizing form. His closing argument against Murena does not survive, but the direct quotations preserved in Cicero's rebuttal give us a flavor of his severe tone. Cato demanded of Murena:

> Shall you seek to obtain supreme power, supreme authority, and the helm of the republic, by encouraging men's sensual appetites, by soothing their minds, by tendering luxuries to them? Are you asking employment as a pimp from a band of delicate youths, or the sovereignty of the world from the Roman people?

And in case anyone on the defense wanted to counter that soft portrayal by pointing to Murena's war record against Mithridates, Cato was quick to belittle that as "a war against women." It was a shockingly dismissive turn of phrase to apply to Rome's most persistent enemy, particularly from someone who had himself served near the front. But Cato was playing on the popular image of the East, well established in the Roman mind, as the fount of all things luxurious, voluptuous, and soft.

It was Cicero's genius to turn all of this, in minutes, into a laughing matter. He was aided by the self-evident absurdity of his position. Here was an antibribery consul defending a man he knew was guilty, in front of a jury and crowd of spectators who also knew he was guilty, but who (because they now shared his estimation of the Catiline threat) also understood that the purpose of the trial was to go through the motions of letting the accused off the hook. The blatant artifice of the entire exercise clearly enraged Cato, but Cicero treated it all with an urbane shrug: *Sic vivitur*— "That's life." He understood that the purpose of his summation was not to convince the jurymen of Murena's innocence but to help them feel better about overlooking his guilt.

The greatest obstacle to their doing so was the presence of the one man who refused to get the joke. Cicero understood that Cato's mere presence on the prosecution team was enough to secure the guilty vote of much of the jury, a worry he made explicit: "I am much more afraid of the weight of his name than of his accusation. . . . I beg you not to let Cato's dignity, nor your expectation of his tribuneship, nor the high reputation and virtue of his whole life, be any injury to Lucius Murena." The polite gesture out of the way, the summation became a mocking attack on Cato, the ivory-tower Stoic.

"There once was a man of the *greatest genius*," Cicero began, "called Zeno. The imitators of his example are called Stoics." What came next was a three-minute tour of every ridiculous, paradoxical, or overthought piece of Stoic doctrine—a tour that was only possible because Cato's school was still esoteric enough to be a curiosity. While flattering the jurors that they were men of learning who would enjoy a little philosophy with their corruption trial, Cicero also correctly gambled that none of them was informed enough to call his bluff on the parody that was to follow. What, then, he asked, does this slightly odd sect believe?

> That no one is merciful except a fool and a trifler . . . that wise men, no matter how deformed, are the only beautiful men; that even if they are beggars, they are the only rich men; that even in slavery, they are kings. And all of us who are not wise men, they call slaves, exiles, enemies, lunatics. They say that all offenses are equal, that every sin is an unpardonable crime, and that it is just as much of a crime to needlessly kill a rooster as to strangle one's own father!

Was that true? It was true enough. Stoics had always been fond of just such riddles, which won them attention and opened the door to a fuller explanation of their moral doctrines. Cicero (an admirer of Stoicism when he wasn't exploiting it to win an argument) would eventually write a short book defending and explaining these same Stoic paradoxes. But stated with more smirking than context, they were enough to paint Cato as foolishly out of touch.

The problem with our distinguished prosecutor, Cicero went on, is that he takes it all so *literally*—he is a learned man, a well-intentioned man, but a man sadly lacking in common sense. As Cato glowered from the side, the consul launched into a mock dialogue in which he played both parts himself: Cicero (reasonable and slightly perplexed) and Cato (stamping his feet in a spasm of self-righteousness):

> *Do any suppliants, miserable and unhappy men, come to us?*
> **You will be a wicked and infamous man if you do anything under the influence of mercy.**
>
> *Does anyone confess that he has done wrong, and beg pardon for his error?*
> **To pardon is a crime of the deepest dye.**
>
> *But it is a trifling offence!*
> **All offences are equal!** . . . .
>
> *You're not influenced by the facts, but your own opinion.*
> **A wise man never has mere opinions!** . . . **I said in the Senate that I would prosecute.**
>
> *Oh, but you said that when you were angry.*
> **A WISE MAN IS NEVER ANGRY!**

As the jurors chuckled over this miniature play, the crimes of Lucius Murena were likely receding further and further from their minds. How much more entertaining to talk about the crimes of Cato! Just gently enough to avoid making an enemy for life, Cicero edged toward an outright charge of hypocrisy.

> By the way, why is it that you have a nomenclator with you? It's a
> trick and a deceit. If it's an honorable thing to address your fellow-
> citizens by name, it's shameful for your slave to know their names
> better than you do. . . . Why, when he has reminded you of them,
> do you salute them as if you knew them yourself?

Of course, Cicero had a nomenclator, too—the difference being that he
didn't pretend he was above it. For any juror who remembered the twenty-
something Cato who had famously attended meet-and-greets without a
memory aide, Cicero's charge carried an extra, implied sting: Mentally or
morally, the Stoic was starting to slip.

But the most devastating charge of hypocrisy went completely unspoken: Everyone knew it already. Silanus, the other consul-elect, had bribed
his way into office every bit as conspicuously as Murena had. But Cato
hadn't brought any charges against Silanus—because he was family. True, it
would have been nearly unheard-of to indict a brother-in-law for corruption, but that was exactly the sort of extraordinary action toward which
Cato's principles were supposed to impel him. Cicero's hinting at Cato's hypocrisy would likely have been reminder enough that, by favoring family
like the rest of us, Cato was again less than advertised.

This gentle skewering of his adversary's character was not simply a matter of winning the likability contest into which Roman trials predictably
degenerated. It was also a necessary step toward Cicero's most audacious
move of the entire trial. He forthrightly defended bribery (not bribery—let
us say, members of the jury, *generosity*) as part of the Roman way. Cato, the
consul claimed, is setting up an impossible, inhuman standard,

> but our habits, our way of life, our manners, and the constitution
> itself reject it. Because neither the Spartans, the originators of that
> way of living and of that sort of language, men who lie at their
> daily meals on hard oak benches, nor the Cretans, of whom no one
> ever lies down to eat at all, have preserved their political constitu-
> tions or their power better than the Romans, who set apart times
> for pleasure as well as times for labor. One of those nations was
> destroyed by a single invasion of our army, the other only pre-

serves its discipline and its laws by means of the protection afforded to it by our supremacy. . . . The Roman people disapprove of private luxury, but admire public magnificence.

With that, Cicero managed to accomplish exactly what Cato the Censor had: to paint the Stoics as Greek—as foreign. And it was a very short walk from "foreign" to "weak." Romans were world-beaters precisely because they did not follow their intellects down absurd blind alleys; because they were men of simple, hearty, manly common sense; because they did not have to contort themselves into laughable Stoic shapes to stay virtuous. And this, Cicero argued, is where our defendant comes in: because our empire is not so tottering that it will fall over just because Lucius Murena treated some friends to a meal.

Cicero's point was that he and his flexibility, not Cato, owned the *mos maiorum*. Was he right? In front of a neutral court, the argument might have been closely fought. But in front of this court, Cicero's logic was more than enough. He had acquitted the jury of any guilt they may have felt over doing the necessary. And they, in turn, acquitted his client.

It was one of Cicero's most memorable and dexterous performances. But even more remarkably, he was politic enough to beat Cato without humiliating him. For whatever turmoil was coming, the consul needed Murena—but he needed Cato just as much, if not more. So instead of attacking Cato directly, he had done his best to bring him in on the joke, mocking a version of Stoicism that both men understood was a cartoon. And he had done it all while praising Cato—and, for good measure, Cato the Elder—to the skies.

The target took defeat better than might have been expected. No one could get anything out of Cato beyond a sarcastic mutter: "What a witty consul we have!"

Perhaps he took it so well because, for one moment, toward the end of all Cicero's wit, the consul had let his mask drop—and because the fear behind the mask was identical to Cato's. Cicero pointed directly at today's opponent, tomorrow's ally:

I am talking to you—you, Cato. Do you not see a storm coming? . . .
Everything that has been plotted for the last three years, from the time when you know that the design of massacring the

Senate was first formed . . . is now breaking out on these days, in these months, at this time.

. . .

With Catiline out of the city, and Lentulus left behind to manage the revolution on the home front, the plans only continued to swell in grandiosity. Now, in addition to a coup in Rome and the peasant army behind Gaius Manlius, there would be widespread rebellion in the provinces. When one of the plot's lieutenants learned that the city was hosting a delegation from the Allobroges—a fierce Gallic tribe that had come under Rome's sway sixty years earlier—he immediately approached the visiting tribesmen with an offer: Join Catiline and free yourselves of both Rome and your debts. Their response was encouraging to the revolutionaries: "There was nothing so disagreeable or difficult that they would not most gladly perform if it would only free their country from debt."

But the risks of a failed rebellion were ruinously high. In their hesitation, the Allobroges brought word of the offer to a friendly senator—who passed the intelligence directly to Cicero. Cicero, in turn, convinced the Allobroges to accept a counteroffer: Feign interest, get Catiline's plan in writing, and—though this part was implied—Rome would forget that the thought of disloyalty had ever crossed the Allobroges' minds.

Days later, soldiers ambushed a midnight meeting between the double agents and the conspirators remaining in Rome. The sting worked to perfection. The leaders were caught with detailed plans, stores of weapons, and incriminating letters. One letter to Catiline even argued that for the plot to be consistent and complete, it would need a slave uprising: "Consider what your views demand, and seek aid from all, even the lowest."

For Lentulus and his fellow captives, there was no point in making a defense on the grounds of altruism. It is difficult even now to weigh the conspirators' crass self-interest against any genuine urge they may have felt to liberate the poor and the enslaved—but to their judges in the assembled Senate, the distinction hardly existed. Either way, they were equally traitors and equally guilty. Lentulus, in his second and last expulsion from the elect circle, was publicly stripped of his senator's purple-edged toga—and left to await his sentence.

But choosing that sentence proved painful. Even as the full breadth of the plot was revealed, the bulk of the Senate, Cicero included, was torn over the proper response "when citizens of such eminence were detected in treason so atrocious." This was no foreign invasion: Lentulus was a colleague, a friend to many. And in a different time, under different circumstances, the senators themselves—particularly the *popularis* faction—might have been won over by Catiline's promises. Those in the worst financial hardship, who would have gained the most from Catiline's debt cancellation, were likely even in on the plot, though they had managed to stay on the conspiracy's fringes and duck suspicion.

That December, with Rome still in a state of emergency, Cicero had the power to order the conspirators' executions without a trial, without even asking the Senate's permission. Even so, his own safety hung on his decision. In a matter of weeks, his consulship would be over, and any aggrieved party had the right to put Cicero himself in the dock. Justice too harsh, and he risked turning the marginal conspirators, the families of the accused, and any of their sympathizers into permanent blood enemies. But Catiline's army still waited beyond the city walls—justice too soft, and Cicero could be held accountable for failing to prevent a bloodbath. It's not surprising that he chose to put the prisoners' fate up for a vote. Any blame, then, could at least be shared.

•   •   •

Instant capital punishment—it was the Senate's first impulse, and it was ratified by the new consul-elect Silanus, who demanded, to cheers, "the extreme penalty." He was seconded by Murena, doubtless to the satisfaction of Cicero, who had climbed into the muck to defend him, in anticipation of just such rewards. And when a string of eminent speakers all consented, it looked as though the matter was closed.

Then the young senator Gaius Julius Caesar rose and coolly asked his colleagues to take a deep breath: "Their guilt should not weigh more than your dignity; your anger must not weigh more than your character."

He was not the kind of man to counsel caution; perhaps his advice won attention precisely because it was so out of character. Caesar, entering his midthirties, shared with Catiline a luster of intrigue, sex, and scandal. With his toga worn loose and flowing in the latest style and his endearing habit of scratching his head with a single nonchalant finger, Caesar was, it was said, "every woman's man and every man's woman."

Ambitious, impatient, he had recently burst onto the public scene as a soldier and a showman. As a young officer, he had been decorated for conspicuous bravery in battle. As a junior city magistrate, he had made his year of office unforgettable with magnificent shows and gladiatorial contests. Like Catiline, Caesar's political ambitions had put him deep in debt. Unlike Catiline's, they had paid off: Caesar had temporarily bankrupted himself in the election for the post of pontifex maximus, high priest of the state religion— but, of course, he had won that post, along with the plum real estate in the middle of the Forum that came with the job. As the next year's praetor, only one rung short of the consulship, he was widely considered a man on the make: courageous enough to gamble, clever enough to place good bets.

Now, Caesar showed the Senate that he was willing to run straight into the teeth of public opinion. Speaker after speaker had dilated on the evil of the conspirators; Caesar asked them to step back and consider history. He reminded the august body of their predecessors, who had "acted with wisdom and sound policy" whenever putting down a foreign rebellion. Romans fought for order, not plunder. During the Punic Wars, the Romans had refused to retaliate against their rivals in Carthage, even though they were "guilty of many acts of injustice."

Of course, Caesar had cobbled together a highly selective story. Roman atrocities in wartime were not only well documented, but were practically official policy. The truth is that Carthage was eventually leveled, and its people sold into bondage. But in his flattering history of mercy, Caesar was attempting a remarkable turnabout, counterintuitively painting the self-styled conservatives as dangerous innovators. It was the sort of daring trick that appealed to him, if only for the fun of it.

Now, Caesar argued, these so-called pillars of the establishment were considering the nearly unprecedented step of an execution without a trial— for a crime that had not yet taken place. It went without saying that the plot against the city was the highest treason—"that the utmost degree of torture is inadequate to punish their crime"—but, still, it was un-Roman to debate fellow citizens' punishments before they had been convicted in a court of law.

Rather too cleverly, Caesar added that no punishment the Senate could invent could possibly equal the enormity of the alleged crime, which was all the more reason to stick to the books. If the Senate was going to start making up punishments for the conspirators, why not scourge their skin off first? Was that too severe? Then why had Silanus demanded the most "extreme penalty"?

Besides, going beyond the law, no matter how dangerous the threat, carried its own risks. Today, Caesar courteously allowed, the Senate was full of the wise and the just—but lesser men would surely abuse their precedent, killing "the good and the bad indiscriminately." Today's national security exception would be tomorrow's wholesale slaughter, he argued, with no one to "stay its progress or moderate its fury."

Confiscate the conspirators' property, keep them in custody, disperse them across Italy, he urged—but show restraint, in the best Roman tradition. "For certainly," Caesar concluded, "there was greater merit and wisdom in those who raised so mighty an empire from humble means, than in us, who can scarcely preserve what they so honorably acquired."

As Caesar's words settled over the Senate, consul-elect Silanus could sense that the mood had shifted. Senators who minutes ago had been clamoring for death were now set on mercy. Executing a classic waffle, Silanus awkwardly rose to explain that he of course had agreed with Caesar all along. He had said the "extreme penalty" before—and what was more extreme than imprisonment?

Any skepticism in the chamber was swallowed by the applause that followed; and we can imagine many a senator bearing admiration for Silanus's well-crafted ambiguity, which had made it possible for him to tack in either direction. The man had not reached the top for nothing.

*　　*　　*

There was at least one man in the room who had nothing but scorn for such cheap tricks. Did Cato experience a moment of doubt as Caesar spoke? Perhaps: It might have occurred to Cato that, at any other time, he would have stood shoulder to shoulder with anyone, even Caesar, who defended the settled constitution and the rule of law. But this was a time set apart, a time that threatened riots, fires, slave rebellion. And Cato's words were full of contempt for anyone who failed to see the dangers as vividly as he did.

Cato, as would have been immediately clear to anyone there to observe the contrast, had none of Caesar's charm. He paid little attention to the rhetorical niceties that were so lovingly studied by his peers. He rarely rehearsed. In this, as in so much else, he could fall back instead on one of Cato the Censor's earthy maxims: *Rem tene, verba sequentur*—"Stick to the point, the words will come." And when the words came, they could continue for hours. If need be, Cato had the lungs and the endurance to hold a room's attention from sunup to sundown.

Caesar flattered the men he wanted to win over; Cato attacked their manhood. From the moment he stood to speak, he was clawing for the Senate's jugular: "You have always valued your mansions and villas, your statues and pictures, at a higher price than the welfare of your country." No one but Cato could talk like this—but the shock made him heard. Across the benches, listeners sat up a little straighter. If you want to keep wallowing in your gluttony, he cried, you had better stamp out this rebellion now. Insults had rarely been so persuasive.

The Republic had stood the test of this soft generation, Cato said, even though his warnings about "the luxury and greed of our citizens" went unheeded. But now the Senate was past morality. The question was this: Are those precious marble busts of yours, those vacation homes and fishponds, going to stay in your grubby hands, or are they going to "fall, along with ourselves, into the hands of the enemies"? Cato knew his audience, and he knew that naked self-interest would reach them where abstractions would not—and so would fear.

Indeed, he argued, this was a threat that demanded preemptive action. "Other crimes you may punish *after* they have been committed," but this was not petty theft. Those high-flown words of justice and humanity would stick in the senators' throats when the city was on fire. And furthermore . . .

In the midst of Cato's harangue, a messenger quietly entered the chamber and passed a sealed note to Caesar. Theatrically breaking off, Cato wheeled on his opponent and demanded that he read it aloud. What else could it be, at such a sensitive time as this, but a secret message from the conspirators—proof that Caesar was in league with them, that he had spoken to save not just their skins, but his own?

"Read it yourself," murmured Caesar.

It has been observed that the effectiveness of a pie-in-the-face joke is directly proportional to the self-righteous dignity of the pie-ee as he wipes the meringue from his face—which might give us some insight into the face of Cato as he read the first lines and discovered that it was not a missive from Catiline but a love note to Caesar, from Cato's own (married) half sister.

He flung it back in Caesar's face: "Take it, you drunk!" Whether the senators were too frightened to laugh is not recorded.

Gathering himself up again and picking up the thread of the argument, Cato pushed onward. Yes, Caesar had spoken in "fair and elegant language," but he was naive to suggest that a group of traitors this dangerous could be locked up for a lifetime. It was far more likely that their "mischievous and profligate friends," who could be found up and down the Italian peninsula, would spring them from captivity.

Worst of all, Caesar had made the error of speaking as if the threat were already past. It was not. At that very moment, slaves and peasants were taking up arms against Rome. Catiline was still at large. Taking a firm hand would prove to the ringleader, his army, his sympathizers, and anyone considering joining the coup that the Senate did not intend to play games. Signal weakness, on the other hand, and the enemy "will advance upon you with fury." The hand-wringing had to stop, Cato shouted. "Why do you hesitate, even in such circumstances, over how to treat armed incendiaries arrested within your walls?"

Cato was speaking to men who had seen civil war and slaughter in the streets. He had no stronger rhetorical resource than those memories. But if the physical safety of Rome was the sharpest spur to action, there was also something intangible at stake. Cato concluded by meeting Caesar on the ground that Caesar had staked out: that of the ancestors. They were fighting over no less than the character of their state.

Caesar was painting a pretty but dishonest picture, Cato argued, when he claimed that mercy was the defining quality of the ancients. *That* was not what made them Roman. Nor was prowess on the battlefield:

Do not suppose that our ancestors, from so small a beginning, raised the Republic to greatness merely by force of arms. If that had been the case, we would be safe; because allies and citizens, arms and horses, we have in more abundance than they did. There were other things that made them great, which we lack: industry at home; equitable government abroad; minds impartial in council, uninfluenced by any immoral or improper feeling.

Instead of such virtues, we have luxury and avarice, public distress and private superfluity; we extol wealth and yield to indolence; no distinction is made between good and bad men; and ambition usurps the honors due to virtue. Since each of you focuses on his individual interest and since at home you are slaves to pleasure, money, or favor, it happens that an attack is made on the defenseless state.

What did this have to do with the conspiracy? Everything. In Cato's philosophy of history, right made might. It was not physical weakness, but moral weakness, that had brought the conspiracy on. And it was the old sternness that would drive the conspiracy out. For Cato, doling out the extreme penalty—and no one doubted what he meant by that—was not simply a matter of prudence, but of principle.

Besides, what ancient mercy was Caesar talking about? In the days of the forefathers, a young soldier once returned to camp with the spoils of victory—and his father, the consul, instantly ordered him killed for fighting without orders. Yet here, with clear cause and clear evidence, the Senate could not even pass judgment on "the most inhuman of traitors."

No studied peroration for Cato: "We are completely surrounded. Catiline and his army are ready to grip us by the throat. . . . The conspirators have planned massacres, fires, horrible and cruel outrages against their fellow-citizens and their country. Punish them in the spirit of our ancestors."

Silence, and then a roar.

•   •   •

The fuming Caesar tried, in desperation, to disrupt the proceedings. The Senate bailiffs stormed the room and pointed their swords in his direction. His friends stood in his defense, placing themselves between Caesar and sword point as he continued to rage. Finally he conceded and stormed out of the hall. He would not attend Senate meetings for the rest of the year.

On the surface, Caesar seemed to have no stake in the conspirators' fate—so what was it that set him off? Some of his rage may have been coldly calculated. Catiline's success, limited though it was, demonstrated that the *populares* were a growing force. But they were aimless and leaderless; in Catiline's metaphor, the strong body still lacked a head. Caesar was deft enough to see the opportunity, and as the nephew of Marius, he had the left-wing family pedigree to make the role plausible. At the right time, Caesar himself might be the *populares'* champion. With his words in the Senate, he was staking a powerful claim. With his dramatic exit, he was demonstrating that he would fight another day.

In truth, Cato's suspicions about the love note may not have been entirely misplaced. It was rumored that Caesar too had been a conspirator—at least in the plot's early stages. Like Crassus, the whispers went, he might have concluded that Catiline was better at dreaming up revolutions than at bringing them to pass, and shrewdly limited his participation and wiped away his fingerprints. If that was the case, why had Caesar attracted attention by speaking up for the accused? Perhaps he wanted to set the precedent of a theoretical rather than a practical interest in the conspirators, in case the accusation ever fell on him. But on a more basic level, Caesar's deep reserves of loyalty were already famous, even in a culture that made the favors shared between client and patron the foundation of politics. If anyone could keep faith with his friends after they'd been exposed as traitors, Caesar could.

Loyal or no, Caesar had learned a painful lesson. He had been on the point of victory. Instead, he had learned that one could be a war hero, a political star, a religious authority, and a honeyed speaker and still fall victim to the majority's shifting whims. One could still lose to an opponent who had barely bothered to prepare a speech. Caesar had done everything right—and Cato had won the day.

• • •

An hour later, in a dank cell at the far end of the Forum, a cord tightened around the throat of Lentulus. When it was done, and each of those arrested with Lentulus strangled in turn, hundreds of Romans carrying torches came to hail Cicero and escort him home in triumph—and Cato was at their head.

"Cicero—Father of the Fatherland!" roared Cato, and the crowd took up the cry. Surrounded by his closest friends and his Senate colleagues, a full member of the club at last, Cicero basked in the attention. All his life had been ordered for precisely this moment. But beneath the thrill, Cicero could have no doubt of the debt he owed Cato. It was Cato who had forced the Senate's hand.

For the senators parading Cicero through the streets, it was a night of triumph. They had saved the Republic, and they had done it without giving up a thing. They had offered no land for veterans, no relief for debts, no change to the creaking, centuries-old political order that still struggled to govern an empire with tools designed for a city of a few thousand. The swelling movement that had so threatened them may have looked, that night, like the product of one man's fevered imagination.

But in Julius Caesar, the populists had gained a leader with a polish and shrewdness far beyond Catiline's. He was the only man, in Cato's acid phrase, who came to the revolution sober.

In fact, though no one could have known it at the time, the clash between Caesar and the conservatives—specifically, between Caesar and Cato—was Catiline's most permanent legacy. "Their birth, age, and eloquence were nearly on an equality; their greatness of mind similar, as was their reputation," the historian Sallust, their contemporary, writes of the two rising stars of the Senate. Sallust was a partisan of Caesar, but when it came to weighing the two, he could only admit that the balance was level:

Caesar grew eminent by generosity and munificence; Cato by the integrity of his life. Caesar was esteemed for his humanity and benevolence; austerity had given dignity to Cato. Caesar acquired renown by giving, relieving, and pardoning; Cato by bestowing nothing. In Caesar, there was a refuge for the unfortunate; in Cato, destruction for the bad. In Caesar, his easiness of temper was admired; in Cato, his firmness. Caesar, in sum, had applied himself to a life of energy and activity; intent upon the interests of his friends, he was neglectful of his own; he refused nothing to others that was worthy of acceptance, while for himself he desired great power, the command of an army, and a new war in which his talents might be displayed. But Cato's ambition was that of temperance, discretion, and, above all, of austerity; he did not contend in splendor with the rich or in faction with the seditious, but with the brave in fortitude, with the modest in simplicity, with the temperate in abstinence; he was more desirous to be, than to appear, virtuous; and thus, the less he courted popularity, the more it pursued him.

Whether by mastering the people-pleasing arts or by so visibly rejecting them, each had found a way to power. Their differences ran so deep that, one suspects, they were bound for enmity. And their rivalry, once sparked by Catiline's crisis, would span the collapse of the Republic and the deaths of so many of the men who had heard them measure mercy against vengeance.

7

MEN OF THE PEOPLE

The cheers for the conspirators' fall were not universal. Left out of the celebration, or left to feign interest, were the conspiracy's well-connected sympathizers, who had hoped to profit from the coup; the urban poor, for whom Catiline had represented genuine hope; and Pompey's faction, which had an even more convoluted motive for wanting Catiline alive and menacing. Cato's year as people's tribune, 62, centered on his struggle to neutralize each of those groups in the conspiracy's aftermath.

As vehemently as he had demanded the conspirators' executions, Cato was under no illusions that their deaths had put an end to Rome's turmoil. Catiline, though fatally weakened, was still alive. Worse, the conspiracy had revealed an angry and alienated underclass, one seemingly prepared to make common cause with slaves and foreigners to settle its grievances. Cato now found himself, nominally at least, that class's spokesman. But he and all Rome knew that the plebs' true sympathies lay with the successor to the Gracchi, to Marius, and to Catiline—Julius Caesar. Cato had already made his opinion unmistakably clear: Caesar was a slippery traitor. As tribune, Cato's loathing of Caesar drove him to something almost entirely out of character: a rare outburst of pragmatism.

Cato quickly moved to undercut Caesar's standing with his political base by staking a claim to leadership on one of the signature *popularis* issues: the grain dole. For centuries, the Republic had periodically provided free or subsidized grain to Rome's masses, a measure that proved especially useful when waves of displaced peasants swelled the city's population, when poor harvests threatened famine, or when bouts of speculation drove food prices unbearably high. But it was Gaius Gracchus, six decades before Cato, who had turned subsidized grain into a central populist cause by struggling to make it a permanent fixture of urban life. Gracchus's creation of a grain entitlement helped bring him the love of the plebeians—and the enmity of the conservatives who would hound him to his death. One of his senatorial opponents even staged a protest by appearing, decked out in his purple-edged toga, in the dole line with the plebs: "Gracchus," he announced, "I wouldn't want you to have the idea of dividing my possessions among everyone—but if you do it, I would like to have my part."

As the factions fought for control of the state, altering the grain laws was one of the chief ways of marking their dominance. Sulla abolished the dole; after his abdication, it was restored. Cicero worried that too much cheap food "would draw the plebeians away from work, throwing them into the arms of sloth, and . . . would exhaust the public finances." Yet Cato presided over the single greatest expansion to date of the Roman welfare rolls. When he took office, about forty thousand Romans were eligible for subsidized grain. When he left, as many as two hundred thousand were eligible, at the cost of 10 to 15 percent of the Republic's budget.

Why would the frugal Cato, of all people, propose such a thing? And how could he secure the Senate's support? The simplest answer is that, though obstinate, the *optimates* were far from stupid, and beneath their bluster was real fear. Earlier generations of aristocrats, including Cato's uncle Drusus, had reacted in the same way when they felt threatened. Putting more grain on the market was a reliable pressure valve for public discontent. This time, there would be no cancellation of debts, no redistribution of land—but, as revenues from the East began to flow again, enough could be spent on grain to convey that the elite was not entirely oblivious. Grain subsidies were enough to co-opt Caesar and to quiet the talk of revolution, for the time being. So, as distasteful as it might have been to him, Cato found himself one of the fathers of the Roman welfare state. Perhaps the satisfaction of frustrating Caesar made it worthwhile.

· · ·

What did any of this have to do with Pompey? His backers, in their own way, had retained high hopes for Catiline. They had envisioned a revolt so successful that only one man could put a stop to it: the same man who had cleaned the countryside of the slave rebellion, who had cleared the Mediterranean of pirates, and who was even then putting the finishing touches on victory over Mithridates. Winning a war and then marching back to save the city—there would have been no better way to make an entrance.

Pompey's man Nepos assumed office as one of the tribunes, alongside Cato. And just as Cato had feared, he instantly demanded the general's return. Although the conspiracy appeared to be in its death throes, Nepos announced a bill to recall Pompey and his army, empowering him to capture or kill Catiline and end the conspiracy by force. But under Rome's unwieldy constitution, any tribune could veto the action of any other. And though Cato had already demonstrated his ruthlessness toward the conspirators, he considered Pompey's army—which would do who-knew-what after it finished with Catiline—a cure worse than the disease. Cato histrionically declared that Pompey's troops would enter Rome over his dead body.

Nepos might have taken Cato up on the offer—but before he could, Catiline's force disintegrated. Cato's prediction about the demoralizing effect of the executions proved correct: The news that the lead conspirators were dead was enough to spur the desertion of fully three-quarters of Catiline's troops in the field. Those few thousand who remained were an afternoon's work for the Roman army. Catiline's body was found deep within enemy lines, his wounds all in front. In a different cause, it was observed, his death would have been the image of heroism.

"Of the many who went from the camp to view the battlefield or plunder the slain," writes Sallust, "some, in turning over the bodies of the enemy, discovered a friend, others an acquaintance, others a relative; some, too, recognized their enemies. Thus, gladness and sorrow, grief and joy were variously felt throughout the whole army."

For a few in Rome, including Nepos, there was quiet grief at the news. The threat had not proved severe enough to demand Pompey's emergency intervention. But Pompey's intentions were now clear: Emergency or no, he was coming home, and he expected a hero's welcome. He had earned one.

•   •   •

Mithridates was dead. Earlier, encamped near the head of the Euphrates, asleep in his tent, the king had dreamed of a sea voyage: He was celebrating a safe journey home, embracing his shipmates, and then, just as suddenly, the ship was falling to pieces and he was left clinging to a single plank, drowning. Shaken out of sleep, he arose to the sight of Pompey's incomparable army, advancing under cover of near-darkness with the moon at its back. In the eerie glow of the setting moon, it was impossible to gauge the size of the force or even its distance; Mithridates' men hurled their javelins at shadows and soon broke in panic under the weight of the Roman charge. For a king pushed to the limits of his resilience, it was the last rout he would ever survive.

It was not the Romans who finished Mithridates off at last, nor the poison to which he had made himself invulnerable, but "that domestic poison, always the most dangerous to kings, the treachery of army, children, and friends." Led by the king's own son, Mithridates' army and people revolted. Once the hope of the Eastern world, Mithridates was reduced to the image of a broken warmonger, the only man left who failed to accept the Roman reality. Barricaded in his tower chamber, unable even to poison himself, Mithridates begged a servant to end his life for him. When the news reached Pompey's army, it seemed to them that "in the person of Mithridates, ten thousand enemies had died."

For Pompey, everything else had proven easy. He had accepted the surrenders of Mithridates' allies, deposing some and setting others up as puppet kings. He had converted the failed state of Syria into a Roman province. He had carried the legions' eagle standard as far as Arabia. He had settled a civil war in Judea, at the price of an annual tribute to Rome. And he had stridden through the Jews' Holy of Holies, laying eyes on "all that was unlawful for any but the high priests to see." Indeed, the pliant ease with which all of this meat fell off the bone was enough to provoke grumbles that this was not conquering at all but scavenging. The deposed general Lucullus had called Pompey a "vulture," and in some quarters, the charge stuck. Just as Crassus had done the hard work of dealing with Spartacus, Lucullus's years of diligence had laid the foundation for all that Pompey had accomplished in the East. But for the large majority, that was just envious quibbling. Pompey had single-handedly remapped a great chunk of the world; he had made the East safe again for Roman tax collectors, businessmen, and land speculators; he had restored Rome's self-confidence after two and a half decades of inconclusive war. To the city buzzing with word of his return, Pompey was no vulture, but a living Alexander.

• • •

To Cato and the nervous Senate, that was exactly the problem. In their worst fears, Pompey would soon be able to demand whatever he wanted, up to and including a crown. Even Crassus called in his money and fled as Pompey approached, though this may have been less an act of genuine fear than of political theater, meant to dramatize the danger that Pompey supposedly posed to the Republic.

Pompey had not even set foot in Italy when the demands on his behalf began. Though his bill for the army's recall now looked unnecessary, Nepos put forward another proposal: that Pompey be permitted to run for the consulship in absentia. The general would likely not be in Rome in time to campaign in person for the summer's election, as the law required, but if the law could be stretched for him, his popularity would put the electoral outcome beyond doubt. As tribune, Nepos had the right to put his plan before the people's assembly for a popular vote—and the bristling violence of that assembly day would demonstrate that much more than a technical change to the election law was at stake.

Multiple consulships (this would be Pompey's second) were still feared as a dangerous accumulation of power, and the privilege of being elected without setting foot in Rome was highly irregular. Further, the current law forbade a general to cross the city's boundary line before celebrating his triumph; even if he could make it to Rome in time, Pompey would be forced into the near-impossible choice between the consulship and the spectacle to end all spectacles. Nepos's bill would allow him to enjoy both. But perhaps the greatest cause for alarm was an implicit provision: Not setting foot in Rome meant not having to disband the army. Thus, the bills for both Pompey's recall and for his election in absentia would have the same upshot. For Pompey's supporters, they would usher in a strong man to impose order, armed with the tools to do so. For Cato and his faction, they would mean one more step toward the seemingly inevitable tyranny of Pompey and the culmination of nearly a decade's dread.

As the assembly day approached, each side gathered its strength. Nepos hired a troop of armed gladiators to patrol the grounds of the Forum and keep opponents at bay. Even more important, he secured the support of Julius Caesar and his plebeian followers. Caesar, who had backed Pompey's extraordinary commands against both the pirates and Mithridates, saw the passage of Nepos's legislation as an important chance to boost the *populares* after the humiliation of the conspirators' trial and the surprise of the new grain law. It was also an opportunity to further ingratiate himself with the general. The possibility of embarrassing Cato no doubt added to the appeal.

Cato, for his part, retreated to his home for a late-night strategy session with the *optimates* (and his role as host suggests increasing recognition of his leadership of the Senate's conservative, anti-Pompey bloc). Among the senators who gathered at Cato's throughout the night, there was no disagreement that Caesar and Nepos were preparing to perpetrate an outrage, but there was no consensus on a course of action. It was far from clear that they had enough support to change the outcome, nor was it clear how Pompey would react even if the *optimates* succeeded in frustrating him. The meeting had all the trappings of a wake. According to Plutarch,

> Great dejection and fear reigned in his household, so that some of his friends took no food and watched all night with one another in futile discussions on his behalf, while his wife and sisters wailed and wept. He himself, however, conversed fearlessly and confidently with all, and comforted them.

The next morning, Cato and the few of his colleagues set on resistance marched to the Forum in a small body, where they found the assembly already under way. Caesar and Nepos were presiding together from the porch of the grand Temple of Castor and Pollux. The steps were ringed with gladiators and hired toughs. Without breaking stride and loudly enough to be heard by Caesar, Cato interrupted the proceedings. "What a bold man—and what a coward—to send a whole army against a single unarmed, defenseless person!" After a tense moment, the guards parted to allow Cato through, and just as they were insisting that no one else would be allowed to pass, Cato succeeded in pulling up his friend Marcus Minucius Thermus by the hand. Together, they took it upon themselves to prevent a vote by any means necessary.

Cato pushed through to the center of the podium and planted himself directly between Nepos and Caesar, cutting off their communication and surprising them with the announcement that he was here to use his tribune's veto. In the crowd below, Cato's supporters—and perhaps even some of Caesar's, sensing that they were about to be treated to an unexpected spectacle—surged forward and cheered. Nepos, speeding the assembly along, ordered the clerk to read the bill.

"Whereas—"

"Veto!"

"Whereas—"

"Veto!"

Nepos took the bill and began to read it himself; Cato snatched it from his hands and crumpled it up. Nepos began to recite it from memory; Thermus gagged him with his hand. The shoving on the podium spilled over into the crowd, as Nepos's force rushed to disperse Cato's partisans and reassert control. As Caesar took cover and Cato's friends were beaten back, Cato was stranded alone on the temple's top step. Rocks flew at his head from the crowd and from the more intrepid attackers who had clambered up onto the temple roof. Exposed, in danger of a public stoning or worse, and still refusing to budge, Cato was suddenly bundled up into a toga and hustled inside the temple to safety.

It was the consul Murena who, quite possibly, saved his life. Just months before, Cato had heaped the ugliest insults on Murena at his corruption trial—but in the face of the riot, the insults were forgotten. As Cato and Murena huddled in the temple (and we can easily imagine Cato being too furious—at the rout of his supporters and the identity of his savior—to say "thank you"), Nepos restored order and confidently called again for a vote.

But before he could celebrate his victory, the tables turned again. Cheering for Cato and shouting their curses at Nepos, the conservative faction had regrouped and rounded up its own reinforcements, and the rumor sped ahead of them that they were armed and set on a bloody fight. At this new show of force, the rest of the crowd fled. Whether bluffing or not, Cato's faction had found that Caesar's was not ready to shed blood on his behalf. Nothing was accomplished, and no law passed—and that made the victory Cato's.

Meeting in emergency session soon after, the Senate, still largely the preserve of Cato's *optimates,* passed its own resolution that put the aristocracy firmly on record against Pompey. It announced that it would by no means permit the law to be changed for his sake, and it put the onus for having stirred up sedition on Nepos and Caesar—not on Cato and his partisans, who had broken up the assembly by force.

All that was left for Nepos was to loudly denounce Cato as a tyrant and author of a conspiracy against Pompey, and to flee east to the army and safety. Perhaps he imagined that, soon enough, he would be returning with that army to settle scores. But Pompey, flush with success, would take the news of his failure to heart. As the classicist T. P. Wiseman writes,

> Nepos had to explain how, with much popular support, a favorable political climate and the help of a troop of gladiators, he had succeeded only in making himself a laughing stock and Cato a hero. It must have given Pompey food for deep thought on who his friends should be.

• • •

The fracas at the assembly was exactly what friends and enemies alike had come to expect from Cato: reckless physical courage, a zeal for seemingly lost causes or a refusal to admit that they were lost, and an understanding of *libertas* so inflexible that it could require everything from extrajudicial executions to the violent disruption of a lawful people's meeting. To Cato's mind, he had simply saved the people from themselves. He had saved them, successively, from the anarchy of redistribution and from voting in a tyrant—two threats that were closely bound up in the ancient mind.

But the poor voters who had swelled the assembly did not simply melt away at the sight of Cato's victory. To an extent, Cato's behavior at the assembly undermined the progress he had made by expanding the grain dole. It was possible to paint him, again, as an enemy of the plebs. And in the wake of the assembly, the plebeians fixed their hopes even more firmly on Caesar.

After the humiliating outcome, Caesar resigned his praetorship in protest, only to be woken at his house the next day (as perhaps he had calculated he would be) by an angry crowd vowing to storm the Senate and restore him by force. This was the point at which Caesar's shrewdness served him especially well. While a much rasher man might have put himself at the head of the mob then and there, Caesar thanked his supporters for their concern and politely urged them to go home. Word of his restraint soon reached the Senate, which—still vibrating with anxiety after the near-riot—thanked him profusely and reinstated the full honors of his office with no questions asked. Calming the people's passions, not exploiting them—*that* was what was expected from members of the establishment in good standing. It was a picture with perennial appeal to the elite, one that matched its best image of itself. Virgil would compare it to the elemental force of Neptune stilling a tempest:

> . . . *Just as, often, when a crowd of people*
> *is rocked by a rebellion, and the rabble*
> *rage in their minds, and firebrands and stones*
> *fly fast—for fury finds its weapons—if,*
> *by chance, they see a man remarkable*
> *for righteousness and service, they are silent*
> *and stand attentively; and he controls*
> *their passion by his words and cools their spirits:*
> *so all the clamor of the sea subsided.* . . .

But Cato did not join his colleagues in their rosy assessment of Caesar's motives. In his view, Caesar was learning to combine the legitimacy of office with the adulation of the masses—to keep one foot in the Senate and one in the street.

●　　●　　●

All of this—Cato's fear, Caesar's ambition, the people's anger, Catiline's death—was rendered insignificant the moment a ship docked in Brundisium, at the tip of Italy, in that year's winter. The ship carried Pompey the Great back from Asia. The rest of the fleet carried his victorious army. The Republic's future was decided not in the Forum or in the Senate House, but there on the cold coast.

Pompey did march on Rome—but not as Cato had feared. In all the years of Cato's warnings, he never imagined anything as joyous and full of relief as what transpired. Pompey immediately sent his troops home. And as he made his leisurely way up the Via Appia, the towns along the road emptied out to see the commander who had accepted the surrenders of kings, traveling now like a private citizen. He looked, it was noted, like nothing so much as a man returning from vacation. Having spent years playing Alexander, he was Cincinnatus again, the image of the citizen-soldier; and as the word spread, his train swelled, until he arrived at Rome escorted by a horde of well-wishers, a second army. He settled in a villa outside the city walls and set to work planning his triumph.

Did this hurt Cato's pride? He had won office as the explicitly anti-Pompey tribune, had staked a great deal of his persona and his credibility on his contention that Pompey was a monster in the making. What stepped ashore at Brundisium made a mockery of his claim. Perhaps Cato could have argued that his very firmness had frightened Pompey out of any monstrous plans. But why should Pompey be afraid of Cato? More likely, Pompey's words to Cato some four years earlier at Ephesus had, in their way, been sincere. Pompey really did covet the blessing of the establishment—and more specifically, he wanted Cato's respect, even his friendship. The failure of his handpicked tribune, Nepos, had only confirmed that Pompey's best possible future lay with the *optimates*.

So Pompey edged away from his populist past as he began to sound out the Senate for support of his three highest priorities: land for his veterans, ratification of his sweeping political changes in the East, and, perhaps nearest and dearest to his heart, the right to celebrate the massive triumph to which he felt so richly entitled. As a first sign that he was willing to consider realigning himself in pursuit of those goals, Pompey announced his divorce from his longtime wife, Mucia. Ostensibly, she had been unfaithful to him during his long years at war—but it was difficult to miss the fact that Mucia was the half sister of Nepos, the tribune, and that the breaking of their marriage bond severed the strongest thread tying Pompey to the *populares*. As a bachelor, he was also a political free agent. Events would prove that the hint of Pompey's newfound political independence was utterly lost on Cato—or deliberately ignored.

•   •   •

Early in 61, Pompey asked the Senate, in person this time, for special treatment at another election season. He sought a postponement of the vote by several months. He still wanted his consulship and his triumph, but he faced the same conundrum as Nepos had confronted the previous year.

There was no time to organize a spectacle of the necessary size before Pompey would be required to enter the city to declare his candidacy in person. But if a general prematurely crossed the city's bounds, he instantly lost his quasi-magical quality of *imperium,* the right to exercise command, and with it the right to celebrate a triumph. Arcane though it may have seemed, this shared fiction—that a general ceased to be a general the moment he crossed an imaginary line—was one of the innumerable strands of tradition that bound the Republic together. Rather than challenge it, Pompey made a more modest request: triumph first, election second.

Now that Pompey had shown his goodwill by dismissing his troops and cutting ties with Nepos and his family, the Senate seemed willing to grant him his postponement. But Cato once again proved his ability to turn senatorial opinion around with a well-placed appeal to tradition. Hadn't the Senate, only months earlier, risked a revolt to prove that no one, not even Pompey, was above the law? Did the fact that Pompey's wife had been caught cuckolding him really change the principles at stake? Pompey was not the first moderately successful general to face this small dilemma, and he certainly would not be the last. If he wanted to forgo a year of responsibility so that he could enjoy a daylong celebration of his vanity, that was his choice to make.

Cato's repeated success in swaying the Senate confirmed him in his role as de facto leader of the majority, a place he had inherited partly through respect for his example and partly by default. Among other potential claimants, old Catulus was dying, and Lucullus, since being supplanted by Pompey, had done little but mope in his villa and invent ever-more-exotic ways to gorge himself. Few of the other *optimates* had anything approaching Cato's authority.

For Pompey, his surprising rebuff was a first sign that politics would not come as easily as had war. Though he valued the triumph above the consulship (not only out of vanity, but because a well-made spectacle was an investment that would reliably pay off in power), he left the Senate feeling frustrated that he couldn't have both immediately, and more convinced than ever that winning over Cato was the key to his ambitions.

Not long after, Munatius Rufus, Cato's friend and fellow Stoic, came knocking at Cato's door with a remarkable offer from Pompey: alliance by marriage. Pompey proposed to marry Cato's daughter Porcia. To strengthen the bond further, he also asked, on his son's behalf, for Cato's young niece (the daughter of the same Servilia who had sent the love note to Caesar during the Catiline debate). The women's shouts of joy, and dreams of the grandest wedding in memory, were crushed almost immediately by Cato's brutally blunt reply: "Go, Munatius, and tell Pompey that Cato is not to be captured by way of the women's rooms."

It was among the greatest unforced errors of Cato's career. Marriage was exactly how political allies were "captured," and Cato knew it. Yet the same political autism that led him to prosecute Murena came to the fore again, at another moment of great consequence, and this time with results far more destructive. Cato could not conceive of allying himself with anyone for any reason other than a sincere and bloodless agreement on first principles. Rather than see his daughter as the means by which Pompey could be brought fully over into the *optimates'* camp, Cato refused to make Porcia a "hostage" for Pompey's good behavior. It infuriated him that something as profound as the future of the Republic could hang on something as grubby as favor swapping, as prosaic as wedding planning. What did Cato throw away with his refusal? Nothing less than the chance to integrate Rome's greatest political force, Pompey, into the senatorial order. By Cato's own terms for preserving the Republic, it was an unmatched, unmissable opportunity.

But was there more to his refusal than outrageous idealism? Cato did show a surprising capacity to forgive, as he proved when he hailed as "Father of the Fatherland" the same man who had just openly mocked him in court. What Cato lacked almost entirely, however, was an ability to admit a mistake. He had practically built a career on predicting the worst of Pompey. Now, to become Pompey's relative by marriage would be to admit that all of those predictions had been wrong—that Pompey did not want to overturn the conservative order but only to take his place in its ranks. Cato could not bring himself to admit it.

Stung twice over by the *optimates'* rejection, Pompey was left to reconsider how best to build his political future and how best to make use of his eminently eligible bachelorhood. Julius Caesar, it occurred to him, had a young daughter.

Plutarch's judgment of Cato's actions—especially for a biographer who otherwise admired him so highly—is withering:

If we are to judge by the results, it would seem that Cato was wholly wrong in not accepting the marriage connection, instead of allowing Pompey to turn to Caesar and contract a marriage that united the power of the two men, nearly overthrew the Roman state, and destroyed the constitution. None of these things might have happened, had not Cato been so afraid of the slight transgressions of Pompey as to allow him to commit the greatest of all. . . .

•   •   •

Behind chests bearing more silver than the entire empire generated in a year; behind banners declaring "one thousand strongholds overrun, nine hundred cities taken, eight hundred pirate ships captured"; behind monumental rolling paintings of sieges, charges, and a king bleeding to death in a tower; behind a prince of Armenia, a high priest of the Jews, and pirate chiefs—all in chains; behind scowling Mithridates cast in gold and his own much-larger-than-life pearl-covered head riding on a float; behind a gleaming trophy labeled THE INHABITED WORLD, triply triumphant Pompey, dressed like a king, his face painted red like a god's, rode in his gem-studded chariot with a tattered cloak hanging from his shoulders: once Mithridates' and once, it was said, Alexander's.

"How happy it would have been for him if he had died then," sighed Plutarch.

8

CREATING THE MONSTER

Cicero, in a private letter, had this to say about Cato:

> *"Dicit enim tamquam in Platonis* πολιτεία, *non tamquam in Romuli faece sententiam."*

The word "faece" has been translated, with varying degrees of gentility, as everything from "cesspool" to "mud huts." But perhaps the historian Tom Holland best captures Cicero's bracing cynicism: "He talks like he's living in Plato's *Republic*, not Romulus's shit-hole."

It was a quip that would shade perceptions of Cato for generations to come, and though it captures just a single moment in the conflicted and decades-long relationship between the two, Cicero had every reason to feel both cynical and exasperated at the time he put those words to paper: cynical because Cicero, against his own better judgment, was spending months pursuing a lucrative deal for Rome's business lobby; exasperated because Cato spent those same months reminding Cicero to be ashamed.

At issue in the months following Pompey's triumph, from late 61 through the summer of 60, were new contracts for Rome's tax farmers, or *publicani*. The Republic had no permanent bureaucracy to take in revenue. Instead, it sold the right to collect its taxes to the highest bidder. For the aspiring tax man, the reward came in setting the rate as high as a province could bear, paying the treasury an agreed-upon amount, and pocketing the difference. It was one of the most lucrative rewards the Republic had to offer the merchant-class *equites*, who most often put up the capital to back the tax-collecting enterprises. They guarded their profits jealously. When the Senate considered the faltering fight against Mithridates, the *publicani* had been among the strongest voices urging extraordinary powers for Pompey, whom they trusted to end the war and make the revenue flow again. Now that the flow was restored, the *publicani* discovered that it would take years to return to full strength: When they returned to their haunts in the East, they found provinces wrung dry by years of war and drought. Those conditions would put them in the unfamiliar position of losing money on their tax-farming contracts—unless the contracts were renegotiated to allow the *publicani* to pay the state at a drastically lower rate.

Cicero admitted to friends that he considered the demand "a scandalous affair, a disgraceful request, and a confession of foolhardiness." If the *publicani* had bid too high, that was their misfortune. Contracts were meant to be lived by and, if need be, suffered under. Yet as he considered the politics at stake, Cicero found that he had little choice but to hold his nose and allow himself to be lobbied. The merchant *equites*—who had in Cicero a rare son of their own class at the height of power—were his natural base, and he could not afford to cross them. Their case was bolstered by a powerful new ally. Crassus, who may have had money invested in the Asian ventures—and who wanted to keep pace with Pompey in the public estimation—nominated himself the merchants' new best friend. More broadly, Cicero worried that a failure to give in on the contracts would lead to a complete breakdown of the relationship between the Senate and many of Rome's wealthiest citizens, leaving the Senate isolated and weak.

This was life in the shit-hole, a life in which making such an ugly concession seemed a matter of survival. Yet if Cicero may have been ready to make the concession, he had to look across the Senate benches—with anger and, one suspects, a little envy—at the man who had loudly sworn off that life. Cicero could recognize a "disgraceful request" that nevertheless demanded to be satisfied; Cato reached the words "disgraceful request" and stopped reading. A contract was a contract. What else was there to discuss? So adamant was Cato that he declared that not only would the *publicani* get nothing, but he would shut down the entire Senate until they went away.

In that spirit of moral purism, Cato began a campaign of obstruction that would paralyze the Senate. Day after legislative day dawned and ended with Cato holding forth on the sanctity of contracts and his fellow senators nodding off on the benches. Halfway through the deadlock, Cicero complained to a friend:

> It is now three months that he has been worrying these wretched tax collectors, who used to be great friends of his, and won't let the Senate give them an answer. So we are forced to suspend all decrees on other subjects until the tax collectors have had an answer.

Even foreign ambassadors were turned away as the Senate shut its doors to new business. In the sixth month of the deadlock, the *publicani* finally gave way. But they did not go quietly. They announced that if Cato was set on holding them to an unjust bargain, they were no longer capable of holding up their end. The *publicani* simply walked away from their contracts, and Rome's ability to raise revenue from the provinces it had strained so hard to conquer was suddenly thrown into doubt. Moreover, as Cicero had predicted, the allegiance of the business class that had long backed the senatorial status quo was thrown up for grabs.

As for Crassus, who had staked his hopes for a political comeback on his ability to deliver a rich favor to those businessmen, he and Cato had never, until now, had reason to quarrel openly. By standing up to Crassus and the tax collectors, Cato embarked on a year of systematically alienating each of Rome's most powerful men in turn—without imagining, it seems, what they could do if pushed to the breaking point.

· · ·

That same summer, Cato was also busy heaping more insults on Pompey. After the magnificence of his triumph, Pompey had assumed that securing the Senate's approval for his political settlement of the East would be a formality. But stripped of his military garb, Pompey found, like many a political general before and since, that he was no longer so readily obeyed. His plan was going nowhere, as the *optimates* insisted that each new border, each alliance, each grant of tribute, and each line in each treaty be hashed over and voted on in turn. Cato was among the auditors, but so too was Lucullus, Pompey's self-exiled rival, who felt that he deserved the right to redraw the East, and who stopped his depressive binge eating long enough to enjoy one last chance to humiliate Pompey.

As Pompey's Eastern ambitions died the slow death of senatorial quibbles, the other plank in his platform collapsed in a day. This was his long-standing pledge to settle his veterans on small farms of their own, the hope they had carried with them to the desert and back. By calling them to Rome as civilians to claim what was theirs, at the moment that his Eastern settlement failed, Pompey could claim to be reminding the Senate of his magnanimity toward the Republic. These were the same men he could have kept under arms, had he so chosen.

The veterans were not the only ones with an interest in land reform. Breaking up the big estates, reversing decades of urban migration, draining the city of its impoverished "dregs"—these had been recurring themes in Roman politics since the time of the Gracchi. Though Pompey's reform plan would apply largely to his veterans, that still meant tens of thousands of new plots in place of massive slave plantations—the biggest step in years to return the Italian countryside to its smallholding roots. Pompey had no trouble finding a new tribune, Lucius Flavius, to sponsor his bill. And sensing that such a plan would be difficult to resist, especially when it could be portrayed as a just reward for the troops, Cicero also signed on, after attaching a number of moderating amendments to ensure that wealthy landholders were well compensated for their troubles.

But again, just as consensus threatened to break out, Cato froze the Senate with another filibuster, and he did so with the full backing of the *optimates*. In Cato's mind, Pompey had become such an outsized object of suspicion that to compromise with him was to compromise with tyranny—an impression that was surely strengthened by the ominous-looking return of the veterans. Other *optimates* had earthier motives. They perceived any land reform, no matter how moderate, as a first step in an attack on their estates. Short-term gamesmanship was also in play. As a later historian observed, "They were thinking in exclusively competitive terms; anything that enhanced Pompey's status would diminish theirs."

But the strongest opponent of the bill, stronger even than Cato, had a blatantly personal reason to object. Metellus Celer was one of the consuls that year and by far the dominant of the two. He had already backed Cato in the tax debate, and he shared Cato's fondness for the host of obstructionist tools scattered across the Roman constitution. His brother was Metellus Nepos, Pompey's pitched-overboard ex-tribune. And Pompey had, just months earlier, publicly suggested that their half sister, Mucia, was a whore. Pompey had expected his divorce from Mucia to win him a Senate full of allies. Now he found that, besides failing to do that, the divorce had also made him a proud and powerful enemy. With the same vehemence it had once brought to his support, the scorned Metellus family turned sharply against Pompey.

So effective was the campaign of obstruction that, in the middle of yet another pointless Senate session, Pompey's tribune, Flavius, snapped and ordered that Celer be arrested and locked up. What followed was an escalating contest of wills. Celer refused to flinch. Rather than resist arrest, he calmly sent word that the Senate would be reconvening in prison. As senators poured out to join him, Flavius raced ahead and planted himself in front of the prison door. Because it was a religious abomination to lay a violent hand on a tribune, that should have ended the spectacle. But the consul shouted for workmen—and as soon as they arrived, he ordered them to knock a hole in the wall.

Hammers and pickaxes were already swinging when an exasperated Pompey came to put an end to the farce. Once again, Pompey and his faction proved unwilling to raise the stakes of violence. Instead, he admitted defeat and backed down. The land bill was withdrawn, and Celer, Cato, and the *optimates* had another victory.

Having chosen to triumph rather than govern, Pompey could do nothing more than attempt to manage events from a distance, and once again, in the face of the Catonian resistance, his handpicked tribune had failed him. It is close to impossible to hand a head of state the opportunity to practice civil disobedience—but that is just what Flavius had accomplished. From the moment he arrested Celer, Rome's most privileged landholders could style themselves martyrs. That performance, and the success with which the *optimates* continued to cast their opponents as would-be tyrants, was enough to kill any lingering hope of passing the land bill.

The general was left to pour his energy into one thing he could unambiguously control: a vanity project. Even as his bills languished in the Senate, the Theater of Pompey was rising, a massive entertainment-shopping-and-religion complex that would be the first permanent stone theater Rome had ever seen. The theater would soon dominate the Field of Mars, the great public plain on the city's outskirts. But in the Forum, in the heart of Rome, Pompey found himself, along with Crassus, in an unaccustomed place: something almost like powerlessness.

• • •

In Spain, just as Pompey was spending his days strolling forlornly through the construction site of his monument to himself, a certain loose-belted, balding fop was proving himself a relentless general. In late 61, Caesar left Rome for his postpraetorship year as a governor with his military reputation fading and with a staggering twenty-five million sesterces in unpaid bills. And he had incurred a troubling new obligation to Rome's most fearsome debt collector, Crassus, who had done Caesar the ambiguous favor of intervening with a small army of creditors. Caesar also left, by some accounts, in a state of near depression. His friends caught him bursting into tears over a biography of Alexander the Great—sobbing that, at the same age when Alexander was already master of the world, he himself had done next to nothing.

Yet he returned, the next year, a genuine *imperator,* full of boasts about the band of brigands he had besieged by sea, the Spanish tribe that had surrendered without a fight at the sight of his fleet, the Spanish mines whose silver could now stream untroubled to Rome. Enough of that flow was diverted into Caesar's purse that his debts were, for the moment, brought under control. These were hardly accomplishments to put next to Pompey's, let alone Alexander's—but they had the considerable advantage of being more recent. Caesar too was ready for a triumph.

But here he ran into a now-familiar dilemma. He also wanted the consulship, the better to deliver on his populist promise and outdo Pompey as a land reformer. And that meant giving up his chance to triumph, unless he could persuade the Senate to grant him the exemption it had twice denied Pompey. Surprisingly, he stood a fair chance of getting his way. This was, after all, the same Senate that had restored Caesar to office after the fiasco of Nepos's assembly. Many senators had proven themselves susceptible to Caesar's charms.

But one senator's animosity was unshakable. For the third time in a year, Cato brought the Senate to a halt, seizing the floor to denounce Caesar from dawn to dusk and preventing any vote on his request. It was, conveniently, the last day on the legislative calendar on which such requests could be considered. Aching as his vocal cords must have been by day's end, Cato's mood was surely lightened by the thought that it took only a day's work to keep Caesar out of power for a year. By running out the hourglass with such determination, Cato had made certain that his enemy would receive a definitive "no" for an answer.

So Caesar was left to choose. If he had made the conventional choice, the choice Cato and his fellow senators were all confidently expecting of him, he would have enjoyed his triumph and put off his candidacy for the consulship for another year—a year in which the memory of his Spanish successes would have faded, a year in which the *optimates,* with any luck, would have been free to devise ever-more-inventive ways to keep any serious populist out of power indefinitely. Given that well-founded, well-precedented hope, it was mildly shocking to see Caesar, not long after Cato's filibuster, pass beneath a Roman gate, renounce his *imperium,* and enter the running for consul. In parallel decisions that would come to stand as shorthand for their characters, Caesar asked for power where Pompey had asked for glory.

But to a man of Caesar's healthy ego, it was merely a case of delayed gratification. The triumph was only postponed, not canceled. He was so certain of wild successes in combat to come that he declared himself willing to "let [the triumph] pass, hoping to perform many more and greater exploits and celebrate corresponding triumphs, if elected consul." Proof of that glorious destiny is said to have come from Caesar's horse: Born with the defect of cloven hooves, it supposedly bucked every rider but the *imperator.* Strategy, arrogance, and superstition all had their claim on Caesar's mind—and, combined, they had rarely led him astray.

If Caesar had his way, his would be the most leftist government the Republic had seen in a generation. The future of land reform, at the very least, hung on the election. But the vital contest was not over Caesar's seat; he was expected to coast into first place. The real race was for second, and the right to stand as Caesar's consular colleague. If Caesar could drag an ally to victory, he could govern at will for a year. But if Cato could plant a conservative next to him, it would promise another year of stalemate.

· · ·

In the race that mattered, Caesar struck a deal with Lucius Lucceius, a literary dilettante willing to endorse Caesar's platform if it meant being addressed as "consul." Lucceius agreed to finance Caesar's bribes, provided that they were doled out under both of their names—a trade of funds for name recognition. As for Cato, he would no doubt have relished a year as consul, making "Veto!" ring in Caesar's ears from close range. But, sadly, he had not yet advanced far enough on the *cursus honorum* to nominate himself. Instead, he put forward the next best candidate: his son-in-law.

Marcus Calpurnius Bibulus was the rather dull senator Cato had chosen in Pompey's place as husband for his daughter, Porcia. Bibulus had no achievements on the Pompeian scale, but, stolid as he was, he had the right politics. To match the efforts of Caesar and Lucceius, Cato's faction set up a bribery fund of its own to propel Bibulus into office. Did the incorruptible Cato, Rome's loudest voice against crooked elections, have any idea? It's hard to imagine how he could have missed illicit funds being raised by his closest associates on behalf of a member of his family, whom he himself had nominated for the consulship. None of the ancient sources accuse Cato of active participation in the effort to buy the election. But one, the imperial biographer Suetonius, claims that "even Cato did not deny that bribery under such circumstances was for the good of the commonwealth." To be fair to Cato, Suetonius was writing from nearly two centuries' distance. Yet Cato had already proved willing, in the case of his brother-in-law, Silanus, to wink at bribes when he considered the stakes high enough and when the beneficiary was family.

At any rate, the Bibulus Fund was soon overflowing, and the electorate delivered the split verdict the *optimates* had set out to win. Caesar and Bibulus would spend the next year negating each other. It was still a personal victory for Caesar, who had tasted many varieties of failure and near failure. But it was also a political disappointment. Caesar would have the consul's fasces, but he could expect to use their authority to little effect. And that made the election, in effect, another victory for Cato. Yes, his rival would sit at the head of the state—but Cato had planted his own man right beside him.

The *optimates* closed the year with one last legislative trick. Customarily, a consul was appointed to a provincial governorship at the close of his year in office. But Cato had already had to swallow the bitterness of a Caesarian consulship; he did not want to watch Caesar, at year's end, assume a lucrative governorship. With the legislative calendar running out, he urged the Senate to assign the consuls nothing more, at their terms' end, than inglorious police work. After all, Cato argued, the Italian countryside was positively infested with bandits. Where better to apply the martial talents of a general as successful as Caesar? The plan was carried to cheers from the *optimas* benches. Rather than the glory and loot of a fresh province, Caesar could look forward to a postconsular year of sleepy obscurity, with nothing to conquer but a handful of cattle thieves.

• • •

It had been an unprecedented year of obstruction and deadlock, all spearheaded by Cato. Never before had a senator brought such a range of legislation to the same dead halt in a matter of months. The tax contracts, the postwar plans for the East, the land reform, Caesar's triumph, Caesar's bid for a strong consulship and a provincial command—Cato had not stood against them alone, but he was the common thread between each filibuster and each "no." His brand of implacable resistance had become the *optimates'* signature.

The year that saw the "end of parliamentary government" in Rome had little to tie it together besides Cato's idiosyncratic mix of principle and resentment. In the case of the *publicani,* he had clung to his principles even when they risked grave financial harm to the state. In the case of the consular election, he had arguably put his anticorruption principles on hold when they risked empowering Caesar's populism. When it came to Pompey, Cato had continued to see a tyrant where others saw a fading hero. When it came to Caesar, Cato's political suspicion had mixed with the kind of personal odium that a practiced Stoic was expected to transcend.

Yet it would have been supremely difficult for any mortal to transcend the mounting frustrations of Cato's home life—the glaring contrast between Caesar the seducer and Cato the cuckold. Caesar had already been exposed—in the midst of the Senate's dramatic Catiline debate, no less—in an affair with Cato's half sister, Servilia. Sometime after that revelation, Cato became convinced that his wife, Atilia, was conducting an affair of her own. Although we don't know for certain when Cato confronted that private disgrace and divorced the mother of his children, a note of that humiliation can surely be heard creeping into his unrelenting denunciations of Caesar. How many of his colleagues heard it in his voice, a furious quaver beneath the certainty?

Cato would never command love like Caesar, who claimed his descent from Venus herself and who was notorious for cuckolding his enemies. But at least in politics, by the rules of the game Cato had learned so well, he could keep infuriating Rome's most powerful men with little consequence. As long as they were trapped in the Roman ethos of competition, as long as Caesar measured himself against Pompey, as long as Pompey and Crassus held to their decade-old hatred, Cato could continue to sting each in turn, one by one. What Cato failed to imagine was that the rules could ever change.

.   .   .

Consul-elect at last, Caesar surveyed his awkward position. Even as the titular co-head of Rome's government, he would be isolated and weak. He was not radical enough to take willingly to the streets. He was not nearly staid enough to be a friend of the Senate. Why should the coming year, 59, be any different from the last? What would keep it from being exhausted in obstruction and filibusters? If Caesar governed as a traditional consul, he could expect to fail. What he needed was a power base outside the traditional factions, allies who shared his frustration with a sclerotic Senate, men like Pompey and Crassus, each of whom had influence but craved power and were routinely denied it by a Senate hell-bent on keeping their ambitions in check.

It wasn't enough, Caesar saw, to have one of them on his side. He needed them both. As Cassius Dio observes, "If he made a friend of either one of them alone, he would by that very fact have the other as his opponent and would meet with more failures through him than successes through the support of the other." Whether cynical or shrewd, Caesar nominated himself for the job of peacemaker, not because he expected the best of the two, but because he confidently expected the worst:

> It seemed to him that all men work more zealously against their enemies than they cooperate with their friends, not merely on the principle that anger and hatred impel more earnest endeavors than any friendship, but also because, when one man is working for himself, and a second for another, success does not involve the same degree of pleasure, or failure of pain, in the two cases.

Caesar rarely failed as a judge of character. He set out to charm each in turn, arguing to each man and his backers that a simple choice faced them: cooperation or impotence. Gossip mill that the Forum was, both Crassus and Pompey surely knew that Caesar had approached the other for a potential partnership. But Caesar preferred it this way. With each aware of the offer to the other, there was more pressure to partner up or risk being left behind.

Crassus, in particular, could feel his star fading. "Crassus thought that he ought to surpass all by reason of his family as well as his wealth." He had found the limits of his vast wealth: Whatever charisma attached itself to chronically indebted Caesar and callow Pompey could not be bought. So Crassus chose to stifle his resentment and, above all, his bitterness toward Pompey, who had stolen his victory over Spartacus all those years before. Crassus, a man with little in the way of fixed convictions, needed above all to be near power; for the moment, power was near Caesar and Pompey. Besides, no alliance was forever. As Cassius Dio tells it, Crassus confidently expected to pit Caesar and Pompey against one another in a few years' time. But first, he would have to make common cause with them.

Pompey seems not to have been quite so calculating. With his magnificent triumph still fairly fresh in memory, he should have been basking in his reputation. He had, after all, accomplished a feat unprecedented in the history of the Republic: He had celebrated triumphs for victories in Africa, in Europe, and in Asia, "so that he seemed in a way to have included the whole world in his three triumphs." But now, the man who had symbolically captured the entire world was wrestling with an intense bout of self-pity.

There was no skirting the truth. The past year had been a complete political failure. Pompey's involvement in electoral politics had brought new accusations of bribery and had sullied his clean-cut image. His conquest of the East had yet to be ratified by the Senate. He had failed to deliver land for his veterans. As a public speaker, Rome discovered to much amusement that Pompey was stilted and stiff. His theater project was a pleasant-enough distraction, but it hardly carried the urgency of a battlefield command. Cicero, while a nominal ally of the general, gleefully reported that Pompey spent the better part of his days at home, staring wistfully at his purple triumphal cloak hanging limp on the wall. Invented or accurate, no image better sums up the predicament of a man who had seen the climax of his life pass, and who remained inconveniently alive.

Meditating in front of his cloak or his theater scaffolding, Pompey had come to a regrettable conclusion: Cato and his friends had ruined the year. Cato, whom he had so recently admired unreservedly, had rejected his marriage alliance, killed off his ambitions, and cut him out of the inner circle. All of Pompey's attempts to work with him or around him had failed.

Caesar's proposal, then, came as an offer of redemption. Rather than struggle to work at a distance through incompetent tribunes and consuls, Pompey could choose an ally whose eloquence, affability, and instinct for the jugular were unsurpassed. There were risks, of course. Partnering with Caesar meant lending prestige to a future rival. Pompey knew that, without his support, Caesar would most likely have to abide by the Senate's assignment of a worthless command policing sheep farms after his term as consul ended. With Pompey's backing, Caesar might be able to persuade the Senate to reverse its decision and grant him a far-more-glittering postconsular command. The stakes in men and money that might flow to Caesar the next year were high. Few understood that better than Pompey.

But what other choice did Pompey have? Where else could he turn, and who else among the powerful would advance his ends? Without Caesar, hope for the land bill was dead. And what good was a commander who could tame millions of acres of foreign lands but could scarcely scrape together a few plots close to Rome for his men?

·   ·   ·

The triumvirate, or what a later historian would dub the "Three-Headed Monster," came into being more with a whimper than a roar. Caesar urged his two new partners to keep quiet while a small cadre of advisors began studying how best to exploit the new arrangement. Leaks to the Senate or the public seem to have been kept to a disciplined minimum.

Caesar did, however, invite his two partners to a small ritual in his home, where, in the sight of images of the gods, each man pledged himself to the others. Caesar presided over the rite in his capacity as pontifex maximus, offering up prayers and pouring out wine in libation, investing the deal with a religious dignity. It wasn't a brotherhood or even quite a friendship—a thaw between Crassus and Pompey was too much to expect—but it was more than a mere exchange of promises.

Strategy, though, couldn't have been far from Caesar's mind. Even two power brokers as hardened as Crassus and Pompey understood that pledges made before an altar were more than normally binding. The ritual was one part prayer and one part insurance policy. If either Pompey or Crassus thought to turn on the triumvirate, the rite might make them think twice. It was one thing to cross a fellow politician. It was quite another to cross the gods.

• • •

Anyone who had spent a day in Rome's teeming, stinking alleyways, straining under an influx of migrants from the country, understood the case for land reform that could repopulate rural Italy. Anyone who had seen the countryside transformed in his or her lifetime—with villages and small farms giving way to relentlessly swelling slave plantations—understood the urgency, as well. "The swollen population of the city, which was chiefly responsible for the frequent rioting, would thus be turned toward labor and agriculture; and the great part of Italy, now desolate, would be colonized afresh," notes Cassius Dio.

But, since the days of the Gracchi, the issue had been tainted: Any politician who so much as raised it had been branded a radical and slapped down by the Senate. It even bedeviled Pompey, whose battle-scarred soldiers suffered when their promised land grants became stalled in the broader debate on land reform. So it took significant determination, and not a little daring, for Caesar to announce that land reform would be the first item on his consular agenda.

The failure of Pompey's effort hardly seemed to surprise Caesar. The Senate wasn't about to hand over a prize stretch of Italian soil to the battle-tested troops of a general they considered a future enemy of the state. For a land bill to go anywhere, it would have to appear to be above any one man's personal interest. That is precisely the kind of bill Caesar set out to design.

In Caesar's proposal, Rome's decommissioned veterans and many of its landless ex-peasants would be relocated to public farmland in central Italy. The most fertile lands, around Campania in the south, would remain untouched. Any extra land necessary for the resettlement would be purchased at a fair price, and only if the owners agreed to sell. A panel of Romans from different walks of life would help administer the details, and Caesar made a point of declaring himself ineligible, "a point on which he strenuously insisted at the outset, in order that he might not be thought to be proposing a measure in his own interest." The money to pay for the reforms would come from Pompey's conquests in the East. Caesar had cobbled together legislation he could present as budget neutral, politically fair, and constitutionally sanctioned.

The bill was designed to appeal to the Senate's moderates—men like Cicero, who had been prepared to compromise with Pompey and who could discuss the Republic's land issues, Caesar felt, without the usual hyperbole. Writing to his childhood friend Titus Pomponius Atticus in December, before the start of the new legislative year, Cicero mused:

> It is, indeed, a matter for profound reflection. For I must either firmly oppose the agrarian law—which will involve a certain struggle, but a struggle full of glory—or I must remain altogether passive . . . or, lastly, I must actually assist the bill, which I am told Caesar fully expects from me without any doubt. . . . In this last course there are the following advantages: a very close union with Pompey, and, if I choose, with Caesar also; a reconciliation with my political enemies, peace with the common herd, ease for my old age.

Self-interest was never far from Cicero's mind, but no amount of self-interest would lead him knowingly to put the Republic in jeopardy. That he would even consider casting a vote in the bill's favor implies that the legislation was reasonable, or at least worth a debate.

But it was too much to ask the hard-core traditionalists to see it that way. The details were irrelevant: Land reform, in whatever form, was always a dangerous redistribution of wealth. And what made this particular land reform especially threatening was its sponsor. No matter how moderate the guise in which Caesar came before them, the Senate's conservatives claimed to see through him. What genuine interest did Caesar have in cleaning up Rome's clogged streets and reestablishing the small farm—other than his interest in enriching his friends and buying the public's love? "They suspected that by this measure he would attach the multitude to him and gain fame and power over all men." Caesar was a great seducer, and his bill was simply seduction by other means: The result, however prettily packaged, would be a return to the radical days of the Gracchi.

Caesar was no amateur. He knew that the bill, carefully constructed though it was, would inevitably provoke the full fury of Cato's circle. He also knew that there was another way to pass his legislation, one that circumvented the Senate entirely. With the tribunes' help, he could take the bill directly before the people's assembly. By custom, the assembly was little more than a rubber stamp for the Senate's "advice"; the letter of the law, however, gave the assembly the authority to pass binding legislation of its own accord. And when Caesar's land reform came on the agenda, the people were sure to give their wholehearted assent.

So why go to the trouble of taking a land-reform bill to the Senate at all? Ignoring the Senate's opinion and legislating directly through the people's assembly was the mark of an unabashed *popularis*—yet, for all the rhetoric surrounding him, Caesar had yet to cast his whole lot with the people. Approaching the Senate first was a powerful signal that he wasn't the flagrant populist they feared him to be.

• • •

The year 59 seems to have begun with an ambiguous omen. As Cassius Dio describes, it was a powerful, days-long thunderstorm that

> descended upon the whole city and all the country [so] that quantities of trees were torn up by the roots, many houses were shattered, the boats moored in the Tiber both near the city and at its mouth were sunk, and the wooden bridge destroyed, and a theater built of timbers for some festival collapsed, and in the midst of all this great numbers of human beings perished.

Whether or not Cassius Dio had an accurate weather report of the time is, to some extent, immaterial. What he captured vividly was the mood of Cato and every one of his supporters, even some of the moderates. In their view,

Caesar himself was the coming storm, a force unpredictable and uncontrollable, bringer of dark, uncertain days for Rome.

Amid the gloom, however, there was still room for a wedding. After the humiliation of his divorce from Atilia, Cato seems not to have wasted time in remarrying, and he evidently planned his second marriage with an eye to avoiding the public scandal that had consumed his first. His new wife was Marcia, daughter of a praetor, "a woman of reputed excellence, about whom there was the most abundant talk." Unfortunately, no record of that talk remains, but it is fair to assume that the memory of his first wife's adultery hung over Cato's choice. Perhaps Marcia took after her father, a kindhearted *optimas* by the name of Lucius Marcius Philippus, a widower who doted on his children and stepchildren and managed the feat of consistently opposing Caesar without ever antagonizing him.

Cato was correct: Marcia never brought him a hint of disrepute. The scandal that would ultimately end his second marriage would be Cato's doing entirely.

• • •

With his first act as consul in the new legislative year, Caesar made his plans official. Arriving at the Senate House, he wasted no time, standing center stage and looking at each man as he spelled out the particulars of the reform package. He took the extraordinary step of calling the senators by name and asking for objections and revisions—but as he read down the roll of hundreds, a process that evidently took days, he was largely greeted with sullen silence. As Cassius Dio observes, "even though no one spoke against him, no one expressed approval either."

Caesar took the silence to mean grudging support. He wasn't one to dally, and he moved to call a vote as soon as his show of consultation was complete. But Cato—the one senator he had deliberately forgotten to call on—rose from the benches and cut off the vote. He then rattled off a laundry list of complaints against the legislation and its sponsor.

We have no record of Cato's criticisms, but by now the themes must have been familiar to the men in the room: The bill was a populist insult, and Caesar a power-mad tyrant. Cassius Dio records that Cato, unable to find fault in the details of the proposal, made an entirely ideological case against it. He "urged [the Senate] on general principles to abide by the existing system and to take no steps beyond it."

Caesar's patience with Cato had reached its limit. Cato hadn't bothered to offer a single improvement. Neither had his colleagues. Yet Cato was implacably opposed to allowing a vote—a vote that, judging by the Senate's favorable reaction to Cato's speech, Caesar would likely have lost anyway. The issue, as Caesar well understood, wasn't the policy but the politics. Cato's fear was "not of the distribution of land, but of the reward that would be paid for this to those who were enticing the people with such favors." If the bill passed, the people's love for Caesar would be written in ink. Cato would risk no such disaster.

The bill at the center of Caesar's agenda was only days old, and already Cato's plan was to filibuster it dead. Caesar saw what was coming, and his temper got the best of him: Fed up, he ordered his guards to seize Cato and drag him to the door. Cato, to Caesar's surprise, didn't put up any resistance, but "offered himself with the greatest readiness to be led away." It was an oddly passive moment for such an outspoken senator, but Cato's dramatic instincts were sound—his seizure served as the spark for a general walkout. Whether ashamed of their own inaction in the face of Caesar's plans, glad to see someone else taking the lead, or jealously guarding the Senate's independence from the consul, the other members rose as a body and began to file out behind Cato.

Left in an emptying, echoing chamber, Caesar yelled that the session wasn't finished. One of the exiting senators replied, "I'd rather be in prison with Cato than here with you."

The remark cut Caesar deeply. Rarely had a consular year begun in such disgrace. It had taken Caesar a lifetime of striving to obtain Rome's highest office. It had taken Cato only hours to make a mockery of him.

Unwilling to stage a repeat performance of Metellus Celer's imprisonment the previous year, Caesar relented and ordered Cato released. Caesar then headed for the exit himself, but not before sharing with the assembled establishment an ominous final thought: "I have made you judges and masters of this law, so that if anything did not suit you, it should not be brought before the people; but since you are not willing to pass a preliminary decree, they shall decide for themselves." Caesar was finished with the Senate.

• • •

Caesar now played the part of frustrated statesman to the letter. Maybe he felt a touch of genuine disappointment at being forced to abandon the Senate, to bring his bill directly before the people without the senators' imprimatur, but he hardly had time to mope. Cato's bill-killing filibuster could be turned into a great gift. Caesar could now credibly claim "that he was driven forth into the popular assembly against his wishes, and was compelled to court its favor by the insolence and obstinacy of the Senate." The reluctant populist—it was a role tailored to fit Caesar's politics as well as his present circumstances.

To Cato's mind, Caesar's final warning had told the Senate everything it needed to know. Cato began whispering to his closest colleagues about the consul's brazen courtship of the masses and the grave dangers of a general purchasing the people's love with land. It was a timely charge. Rome's political class had long considered populist flare-ups undignified, but they found them especially threatening in the wake of Catiline.

As each side prepared for Caesar's direct appeal to the people, opposition to the land bill congealed around Cato. It was his influence, after all, that had won over most of the Senate. Cicero's decision to oppose the bill, as well as his rejection of Caesar's offer of alliance, had bolstered Cato's cause. And Caesar's attempted arrest of Cato had convinced most of the rest of the fence-sitters. It hadn't taken much pushing: Cato may have been concerned about the fate of the Republic, but many of his fellow senators were more worried about their fate in the pecking order and how far they'd be knocked down if Caesar had his way. Caesar was already a beloved, uncannily lucky general with a consulship. Why would someone who had accomplished so much pursue such an ambitious agenda, if not to lay the foundation for a tyranny?

• • •

On the January morning when Caesar intended to put the bill before the people, the now-united opposition came to terms with its insignificance.

The Forum crowd that greeted them was bursting at the seams with Caesarians. While Cato had been busy building the case against Caesar in a small pocket of elites, Caesar had tapped into a deep vein of popular discontent. The landless poor, the rural displaced, the hard-bitten veterans, the triumvirate's legions of clients—Caesar had adopted them all as his own. They filled the Forum by the thousands, packed elbow to elbow. It was precisely the sort of spectacle that could intimidate a Senate of a few hundred.

The compacted crowd was an especially menacing sight for Bibulus, who had drawn the unfortunate assignment of standing next to Caesar on the rostra and resisting the bill in person. The nervous co-consul was under clear orders: Stop the bill by any means necessary, up to and including the all-powerful consul's veto. Nothing could trump the veto, which made Bibulus—once a middling senator with a limited future—the linchpin in the *optimates'* strategy of obstruction.

Caesar finished reading the bill to the feverish roar of the crowd, many of whom were likely hearing about the spoils for the first time. Then, in a calculated piece of stagecraft, he turned on Bibulus and, in a voice strong enough to carry, asked, "Will *you* support this bill?"

Caesar's question brought the crowd to an expectant quiet, and into the hush, Bibulus stammered his response. He would support no "innovations" during his year in office.

Just in case anyone had missed it, Caesar roared to the crowd: "You will have the law—but only if he wishes it!"

Bibulus retorted, "You will not have the law this year—not even if you all want it!" The deafening boos that greeted that defiant response were enough to drive Bibulus from the platform.

As his co-consul panicked and fled, Caesar called forward two familiar faces, two men who had an outsized place in the public imagination, two men who could be counted on to hold strong opinions on weighty matters of state, two men who—the audience believed—were as suspicious of Caesar as they were of each other.

This was the triumvirate's great coming out. Even for Cato, who had been warning of a hostile partnership for the past year, the appearance of Pompey and Crassus on the same stage as Caesar must have been a punch in the gut. From the beginning, he had suspected the worst of Pompey. The endorsement of Caesar only confirmed it: Not satisfied with three triumphs, Pompey remained set on dominating the Republic. But the true bombshell came in seeing Pompey and Crassus standing side by side. What could possibly have led so proud a man as Crassus to make common cause with his sworn enemy? Was Caesar that persuasive—or was Crassus that unprincipled?

Cato had no time to indulge in speculation. He tried to force his entourage into the crowd and toward the stage, but they were violently thrown back. Caesar turned the assembly over to Pompey and Crassus, who praised the bill lavishly and gave "proof" that they "were not striving for any unnatural or unjust end, but for objects that those leaders were willing both to approve and to acclaim."

Finally, Caesar put to Pompey a single question: "In case any resistance should be made to the law, will you come to the aid of the people?"

"Yes, indeed," replied Pompey. "I will come—bringing, against those who threaten swords, both sword and shield."

The presence of thousands of his troops, brought in to fatten the crowd, made the threat deadly real. It was, according to Plutarch, such "an impulsive and mad speech," and so out of character for Pompey that his friends later did their best to apologize on his behalf, claiming that the words had escaped him mistakenly, that he had simply been caught up in the moment. They understood how provocative a line it was. Not only was Pompey promising to pit Roman soldiers against Roman citizens, he was specifically targeting the Senate, the only group that had put up resistance to the bill. He was describing a coup.

Cato had put nothing past Pompey, and now his fears had a new confirmation. Pompey's words, even interpreted in the worst light, did nothing more than match Cato's long-standing opinion. Cato must have heard them as something of a confession. In truth, though, no threats were needed: The havoc these three could wreak together was obvious.

• • •

Rome, Caesar could comfortably assume, had gotten the point. The multitude supported the land bill. The veterans deserved and demanded it. Eminent men were willing to go to arms on its behalf. If there was an opposition, it was, both physically and philosophically, on the fringe. Caesar fixed the day of the final assembly vote soon after.

Bibulus made a last attempt at using his consular authority to derail Caesar's plans. He proclaimed sacred holidays of all the remaining days on which the assembly could meet, which made any public business illegal and sacrilegious. But, still recovering from his panicky display in the Forum, he issued the announcement from behind the closed doors of his home, where he had effectively taken up hiding. A Roman politician unseen was, for all intents and purposes, a politician unheard. Caesar ignored the edict and continued his preparations without an afterthought.

The day of the vote broke with Caesar standing on the steps of the Temple of Castor, reading the bill in its entirety to a thickening crowd. Bibulus, Cato, and their supporters arrived to find the path to the temple clearer than they might have expected. Rather than fight and push the opposition away, Caesar's supporters "fell back before [Bibulus], partly out of respect, and partly because they thought he would not actually oppose them." Their confidence was misplaced. The very moment Bibulus reached the rostra, he and the opposition tried to shout down Caesar.

The next recorded moments show the Republic at its ugliest. Caesar's docile supporters turned violent, grabbed Bibulus, and hurled him down the stone steps. Rocks came flying from all directions. Bibulus's lictors, his official bodyguards, were set upon by the crowd, and two tribunes escorting him were wounded. His fasces were ripped from the lictors' hands and shattered. As Bibulus dodged rocks and blows, a member of the crowd, as a final insult, dumped a bucket of feces over his head.

Bruised and stinking, Bibulus retreated from the Forum once again, and all those who had accompanied him scattered. Cato, who had been by Bibulus's side in the melee, left the Forum in a markedly different fashion from that of his fellow senators. "All the other senators fled from the forum at a run, but Cato went off last of all at a walk, turning about and protesting to the citizens." It was a grand, defiant, courageous gesture—but nothing more. Shortly after Cato's exit, the bill sailed through by popular vote.

The months of backbiting and bickering should have ended there—but Caesar wasn't done. He had slipped into the bill a clause requiring each senator to "swear solemnly that he would uphold the law, and give it aid in case anyone should act contrary to it." It was valuable insurance, in case anyone attempted a fresh round of legislative trickery. It was also a deliberate insult. As Caesar knew, it would be a nuisance for most—but it would most likely send Cato over the edge.

•　•　•

No sooner had Caesar announced the oath than Cato refused to swear it. Cato was counting on the support of his colleagues, but only two senators stepped forward to follow him. One was Metellus Celer, who had been a hard-line opponent of land reform since Pompey first sponsored it. The other was a young man named Marcus Favonius, who had made himself into Cato's imitator and had taken to dressing, speaking, and voting as his hero did. He too refused to swear. It is not clear whether Cato was flattered or put off by the imitation.

Their refusal would carry a steep price: Caesar was mum about specific penalties, but the customary punishment was exile. It was a threat powerful enough to quiet most of the *optimates* for the time being, especially now that the battle was substantively lost, and now that any holdouts would be singled out by name.

There was a precedent within living memory for the treatment of a senator who declared himself a public enemy by refusing to honor a land-reform bill duly passed by the people. The story must have weighed heavily on the *optimates'* minds as their resistance broke down.

Four decades earlier, Gaius Marius—Caesar's distant relative and fellow populist consul—"came into collision with all the aristocrats." At issue was a bill similar to Caesar's, awarding veterans of the consul's army plots of conquered land in northern Italy. The effort was strongly backed by the tribunes and the "needy and noisy" urban plebeians, but it was just as steadfastly opposed by one of Cato's *optimas* forerunners, a senator named Metellus Numidicus.

Like Caesar's land bill, Marius's passed through the people's assembly over vociferous opposition from the establishment. Like Caesar's bill, it was amended to force its defeated opponents to swear an oath upholding it. At first, Marius made a great show of opposing the oath on the grounds of freedom of conscience—but it was a setup. Marius hoped to goad Numidicus into making a similar public pledge: "He therefore wished to bind him beforehand by a statement to the Senate that he would not take the oath, and then have his refusal to do so plunge him into a hatred on the part of the people that could never be removed." The aging conservative stepped right into the trap and loudly seconded the consul.

On the day set for the oath, senators filed behind one another to sign their assent. Marius and Numidicus stood to one side. When everyone had finished, Marius dramatically announced a change of heart: The oath was fair and just after all. All eyes turned to Numidicus, who announced that he was unchanging. "He left the Forum, saying to those about him that to do a wrong thing was mean, and to do the right thing when there was no danger was any man's way, but that to act honorably when it involved dangers was peculiarly the part of a good and true man."

That very day, Numidicus packed for exile. To the friends attempting to hold him back, he insisted that he could no longer live honorably in Rome. While he would ultimately return under more favorable consuls, his career was finished. Driven from politics, he passed his few remaining years in public silence.

Now, with his power on the wane, it looked as though Cato was preparing himself to reenact Numidicus's fall. It's possible that he considered banishment a respite from his increasingly futile work—an opportunity, perhaps, to turn back to the studies for which he lately had found so little time. More likely, he looked at the prospect with bitterness, as one more sign of Caesar's victory. Either way, Cato kept up his unwavering front. He would not, he declared, swear an oath to Caesar under any circumstances. The center of attention even in defeat, he shut his ears to the tears of his family, to the friends and clients parading to his house to plead that he stay, to the senators urging him to swear and fight another day.

Ultimately, it was Cicero who reached him where others couldn't—perhaps because Cicero, of all Cato's friends and allies, needed Cato most. Cicero felt least capable of standing up to the triumvirs without Cato's support. He held nothing back. He bluntly labeled Cato's conduct "senseless and mad." Cato wasn't alone in hating Caesar's bill—but he was alone in refusing to sign the oath. Didn't that say something?

Finally, playing to his audience, Cicero arrived at his most convincing plea. As Plutarch records it: "It would be the greatest of evils if [Cato] should abandon the city in behalf of which all his efforts had been made, hand her over to her enemies, and so, apparently with pleasure, get rid of his struggles in her defense. For even if Cato did not need Rome, still, Rome needed Cato."

In public and in private, Rome's best lawyer pressed his tireless case, by turns appealing to Cato's duty and to his vanity. At last, Cato gave in. He would sign the oath.

• • •

When the news of his total victory arrived, Caesar was "elated by this success." He would have had equal reason to celebrate whether the oath controversy had ended in Cato's humiliation or in his capitulation. Still, Cato's signature on the land bill was a powerful symbol. On the most controversial legislation Rome had seen in decades, Caesar and Cato had stood eyeball to eyeball. And Cato had blinked.

Now that his power had passed its first and most difficult test to date, Caesar wasted little time in putting it to profitable use. As soon as the Senate swore to uphold the land legislation, Caesar moved to undo one of its key, moderating provisions. The once-untouchable Campanian land—the lushest and most fruitful Italian soil, belonging almost entirely to the rich—was to be broken up, he announced, and parceled out to the poor.

For the first time since Caesar had taken office, the opposition was silent. What was the point of resistance when every key player—the consul Bibulus, the people, the tribunes, the soldiers—were, in Plutarch's words, "made submissive," either through "gratitude . . . or fear"? Of course, this was a point lost on Cato, who, when he discovered Caesar's new plans and the Senate's unwillingness to fight them, was apoplectic. For him, nothing had changed; if anything, Caesar's scheming for the Campanian land only gave further evidence of his sinister intentions. Now was just as good a time as any to stand up to them.

This time, though, Cato stood alone. In the people's assembly on the morning when Caesar introduced the Campanian legislation, the senators watched from a safe distance while Cato hurried to the rostra where Caesar was speaking, shoved his way onto the platform, and berated the consul for his duplicity. Caesar, accustomed to beaten enemies staying down, wasn't amused. He quickly called over his guards and directed them to escort Cato to prison.

For a moment, it looked like a repeat of the script that had been playing out during the prior weeks: Caesar had moved, Cato overreacted, and Caesar pointed to Cato's heated response as evidence that he, not Cato, was the level-headed one. But this time, Cato returned to his successful, passive tactic of the Senate House. He gave himself up with barely a protest. When Caesar's men reached him, he quieted down and allowed himself to be led away to prison. The *optimas* senators, out of confusion or commiseration, decided to follow their leader, marching behind him in silence, with heads down. A handful of the crowd did the same.

In sole possession of the rostra and the initiative, it suddenly struck Caesar that he may have gone too far. According to Plutarch, he "was overcome by the shame and infamy of his course, and by his own secret persuasions induced one of the tribunes of the people to rescue Cato." But guilt could not freeze his agenda. He pushed forward with the new law, and the people passed it resoundingly. Caesar scored his second legislative victory in short succession; Cato, his second loss.

And yet, Cato won a significant success of his own by discovering, for a moment, the right tone in which to oppose Caesar: not as a raving zealot, but as a humble civil disobedient. Even the most committed Caesarians were disturbed at the sight of the great Cato being carted away like a petty criminal—not simply before the Senate's eyes this time, but in broad daylight before the public. There were whispers now that perhaps Caesar had gotten caught up in the hysteria of his efforts, that maybe land reform and all that came with it was too much to entrust to one man.

Given a choice between losing on the field of battle or on the plane of politics, we can make a safe guess that Caesar would have preferred the former. At least in combat, the shame of defeat could be shared. At this moment, having lost face to Cato, he had no one to blame but himself. For someone who derived so much of his self-confidence from his preternatural political skill, it must have played on his insecurities. Was he as good as everyone thought he was? More urgently: Was he as good as he believed himself to be?

Politics, then as now, was equal parts substance and stagecraft. Caesar was, more than any of his contemporaries, hyperconscious of both—but his real skill lay in theatrics. He was the master of keeping up appearances. He went to great lengths to present himself as a benevolent warrior, ferocious in battle but forgiving in its aftermath. In speech, in dress, in bearing, he carried himself like a practiced, polished actor. He even perfected his comb-over, a valiant attempt to cover up his baldness. And that may have been why—in the face of total legislative success, with his clients and friends overjoyed, the poor and powerless slightly richer, and the Senate reduced to passive resistance—the victory still felt less than whole. Caesar may have won, but Cato had upstaged him with a moment of well-placed submission.

• • •

For the rest of the year, the ability to miff and mock Caesar was the only relief available to Cato and his allies. Cato was made to watch as Caesar passed bill after bill to his and his supporters' liking. The people and their tribunes followed him in lockstep, "although Cato warned the people that they themselves by their own votes were establishing a tyrant in their citadel." Pompey secured his political settlement of the East. Crassus's tax collectors had their long-sought relief. Most ominously of all, Caesar played on Rome's ancestral fear of an invasion from the tribal north to award himself a plum governorship. He granted himself five full years in Gaul, and a four-legion army to take with him. There was no doubt that Caesar would find the fight he wanted; yet there was still no inkling of the monumental war that he had in mind.

Through it all, Bibulus stayed shuttered away in his home, watching the heavens for evil omens, complaining of the business that was taking place on holy days, safely ignored. The running joke was that this was the year of the "Consulship of Julius and Caesar." Cato continued to warn and obstruct from the sidelines to the best of his abilities. The pressure he exerted was enough to keep himself in the public eye but not to accomplish much. The record shows him making life as difficult as possible for his enemies: "Even when they did prevail against him, it was with difficulty and toil and not without the shame of exposure that they forced their measures through at last, and this was annoying and vexatious to them." But aside from their angry stares, Cato had little to show for it.

We can guess that there were moments during this year when Cato might have preferred banishment. He was, in his opinion, watching the destruction of his life's work, a brick-by-brick dismantling of the traditions that had kept the Republic's worst passions in check. Cicero had insisted that his presence was still required in Rome—whether the city knew it or not. But Rome was proving its indifference. Cato could be a gawker and a gadfly, but what else?

By spring, Caesar and Pompey were not merely allies, but family: The marriage of Pompey to Caesar's daughter, Julia, cemented their bond. Further, they fixed the coming election seamlessly. Next year's consuls were to be Caesar's own father-in-law and one Aulus Gabinius, "a man from the lap of Pompey."

Was this, then, all Cato had to look forward to—another year of rearguard actions and fruitless protests? He could have been forgiven for wanting to leave the city in the face of it. And, unknown to him, he was about to have his chance.

Cicero had kept his friend in the city with the vow that Rome needed Cato, even if Cato could do without Rome. Those words were about to be tested.

9

ALMOST EXILE

If Cato had ever retraced the steps that led him into exile in 58, he would have found the origin of his predicament in a night of ill-advised cross-dressing four years earlier.

The culprit was Publius Clodius. In the winter of 62, Clodius had launched the implausible scheme of dressing in drag as a lute player, infiltrating the all-female religious ceremony of the Good Goddess, and seducing the hostess, Pompeia, Caesar's wife and Clodius's hopeless crush (but no relation to Pompey). Before he could lay a hand on Pompeia, a maid discovered Clodius wandering Caesar's house and asked if he needed help finding his way back to the service—and when she heard his baritone voice, she screamed for the other ladies. Clodius was found hiding under a bed.

In the aftermath, Caesar divorced Pompeia (giving rise to the famous epigram that "Caesar's wife must be above suspicion"), and Clodius was almost immediately hauled in for trial. Titillating as the incident was, it was no mere scandal: The crimes were sacrilege and sexual immorality. Rome knew few graver accusations.

Cicero's involvement compounded the strangeness of that summer's trial: His wife, Terentia, suspected him of an affair with Clodius's sister, the notoriously promiscuous Clodia. ("It is hard to imagine a more implausible romance," notes a later historian.) To stop his wife's accusations, Cicero was forced to take the stand against Clodius and testify that he had seen the accused in the city on the day of his alleged festival-crashing. It would sink

Clodius's alibi. In his version of the story, he couldn't have been the costumed intruder because he had passed the day in a nearby Etruscan town.

As a witness, Cicero was every bit his persuasive self—but this time, it wasn't enough. With the jury on the brink of conviction, Clodius's powerful friends, including Crassus, stepped in to save him. They quietly cleaned up the debts of several jurors, promised rent boys and slave girls to others, and bought Clodius an acquittal. Even the testimony of Caesar's mother, Aurelia—who had unmasked Clodius when he emerged from under the bed—couldn't outweigh the bribes. By a vote of 31 to 25, Clodius was found not guilty.

The establishment thundered its outrage: Flouting the Good Goddess—in drag, no less—threatened the safety of the city. Buying a jury deepened the disgrace. However much Clodius played the part of the bewildered innocent, nothing could shake the rumors of his sacrilege. His reputation within the small cluster of Rome's top men was ruined, and any hope of a conventional political career was finished.

And, from then on, perhaps as a means of distracting himself from his own foolishness, Clodius fixed blame on one person: Cicero. Cicero hadn't been anywhere near the house. He had no inside knowledge of the case. He had virtually nothing at stake in the trial's outcome. And yet he had testified anyway. He had put his considerable credibility on the side of the scandalmongers. He had killed Clodius's reputation. But for the timely bribes, he had come close to killing Clodius altogether.

.   .   .

If Clodius was shockingly impulsive in short bursts, he also had deep reserves of cunning. The scandal may have meant an endless stream of gossip, but it had a silver lining: The exposure burnished his emerging profile as one of Rome's brash, young hell-raisers, an image he increasingly embraced and nurtured. This was the same man, after all, who had had the gall to organize a mutiny against his commanding officer—Lucullus—in the middle of a war. In the intervening years, he had been accused of intimacy with each of his three sisters, as well as a number of male pirates. Clodius may not have done half of what he was accused of, but he was shrewd enough to realize the value in all of the talk, culminating in the untoppable Good Goddess scandal. Together, the stories secured his position as the outrageous head of Rome's party set, a large and leaderless constituency, which, as Catiline had revealed, had the energy to reshape the landscape of Roman politics if properly marshaled.

For Cicero, the jury's failure to convict had no bright side. From the beginning, his testimony had been a calculated gamble, one in which the usually cautious Cicero seems to have overestimated the winnings and discounted the risk. By placing himself so publicly at odds with Clodius, Cicero had hoped to do more than simply assuage his wife's jealousy. His testimony was another chance to cement his bond with Rome's conservatives, who shared his fear of a Catilinian relapse. Once again, it could be argued, one of Rome's young, restive aristocrats had made a mockery of the sacred traditions and openly affronted the gods. The superficial resemblance between Clodius and Catiline helped convince prideful Cicero that the city demanded a man of his ability to step forward once more. The chants of "Father of the Fatherland" still echoed loudly in his mind. All the remaining days of his career would be spent in the shadow of that bright moment—unless he could relive it.

But he did not stop to consider the high cost of failure. Clodius may have been a lush, but he was a vengeful, resourceful lush, the kind of man that even Caesar avoided crossing. He would bring to his feud with Cicero the anger of a scorned friend: Not only had Clodius joined Cicero's campaign entourage during Cicero's bid for the consulship, but the two shared next-door plots on the exclusive Palatine Hill. All his life, Cicero had coveted a house like this, a private monument to his ambitions—but now, he could barely step out the front door without being confronted with his new enemy neighbor.

Clodius may have edged away from his aristocratic origins (he even changed the spelling of his name to reflect the lower-class pronunciation), but he still came from the Claudii, one of Rome's oldest families, with generations of inherited wealth and inherited favors at the ready. He now set out to deploy those considerable means in the pursuit of one goal: making Cicero's life hell.

At first, the feud expressed itself in jokes. At one meeting of the Senate, Clodius chided Cicero for buying an opulent home, to which Cicero snorted: "One might think he was saying I had bought a jury." Cicero smiled at his own quick wit. The senators chuckled. Clodius stayed dead silent.

. . .

Cato too had tussled with Clodius. Shortly after the trial, Clodius attempted to regain some initiative by staging a public campaign against religious hypocrisy. His targets were allegedly corrupt priests and priestesses, but it came as little surprise that the bulk of them were also close friends or family of his accusers and adversaries. Among them was Cicero's sister-in-law, a Vestal Virgin. Yet Cato, volunteering to lead the defense, demolished the case against her chastity—another embarrassment for Clodius.

While Clodius nursed his wounds, Cato and Cicero celebrated. Cicero was grateful for Cato's intervention, without which his sister-in-law would have faced banishment, removal from the priesthood, or worse. He sang Cato's praises in public; Cato replied that Cicero ought to be thankful to the city, for it was in her name that he had acted.

The city's name was unlikely to suffer from Clodius's half-serious prosecutions, but Cato had a more practical cause for resisting him. Damaged goods though he appeared to be, Clodius was beginning to pose a serious threat not just to Cicero, but to the *optimates* as a whole.

Clodius had never been a comfortable patrician, and his successive humiliations in court functioned as an informal expulsion from the upper crust. If he was still to pursue his vendetta against Cicero and at the same time push the populist policies to which he was increasingly drawn, he needed a political home, a constituency so hungry for leadership that it would accept a scandal-stained swinger. Like Catiline, he found his following among the *populares,* and he took up their cause with even more fire than Caesar. In 59, Clodius cut himself off from his ancient family by arranging for his farcical adoption by a plebeian barely old enough to shave. Caesar himself presided over the public ceremony—legally dubious and unprecedented—that made Clodius an official pleb.

With his conversion complete, Clodius won election as tribune. And he seized on the power of the office—and the legal and physical untouchability it guaranteed—to make himself into Rome's most volatile political force. When Caesar secured his prize appointment to Gaul, it had been with the adamant backing of Clodius and his following. Most radically of all, by a direct vote of the people, Clodius won passage of a grain law that made the dole, for the first time, entirely free of charge.

"Your fury threatens the goods and fortunes of us all," cried Cicero—but his position was weakening by the day.

Nearly everything was in place for a frontal assault against Cicero. But even with Caesar's gratitude and the masses on his side, Clodius knew that Cato could fatally complicate an attack on Cicero. Clodius could not harm Cicero without seriously testing the limits of the law, and he knew that the response from Cato, Rome's most credible voice on the constitution's sanctity, would be swift and strong. Although Cato liked to deny that affection had any role to play in his political judgments, the truth is that he and Cicero, as much as they exasperated each other, had also built a friendship.

As Cicero's would-be defender, and as leader of the opposing faction, Cato was the most formidable man left in Clodius's way. Cato had to go.

• • •

Foreign postings were the political class's gift to itself. But the gift, in order to keep giving, required an expanding empire. Once abroad, the virtues of thrift and self-restraint so loudly praised by Rome's elite often suffocated under the weight of a province's gold. New provinces were best; otherwise, a foreign posting meant scraping at the previous governor's leftovers.

For foreign kings who managed to keep their thrones in exchange for tribute, such diminishing returns to the Romans were a serious worry. Their kingdoms—whose independence they had so carefully fought, bought, or bargained for—might receive a closer look from a poorer Senate. Two such kings who had paid mightily to remain atop their respective thrones were the Ptolemy brothers, kings of Egypt and Cyprus. Famous for lavish living and a tendency toward incest, they spent prodigious sums to remain, essentially, Roman tax administrators. They soaked their subjects to pay off the Romans, but they held on to their crowns. One such ruler was the chubby Egyptian king Ptolemy Auletes (the nickname Auletes, "the flute player," was apparently a reference to his pudgy cheeks). He owed 17.5 million drachmas to Caesar alone, a cost of the "alliance" that kept Rome out of Egypt's internal affairs. The Ptolemy brothers were largely distinguished from the other kings in Rome's orbit by their willingness, in a later historian's words, "to swallow any indignity and perpetrate any outrage to keep hold on power."

The indignities served their purpose. Caesar, during his consulship, took special pains to make sure that Auletes was recognized as a favored friend of the Romans. As long as the Ptolemies made the requisite offerings to Rome, they could cling to their nervous independence—until Clodius, as part of his plan to do away with Cato, chose to change the bargain.

. . .

Clodius had a history with the king of Cyprus. Captured by Mediterranean pirates on his way home from the war against Mithridates, Clodius had allegedly allowed himself to be ravished in return for his release. True story or malicious insult, it was not enough to secure freedom for Clodius: His captors demanded ransom money from the nearest Roman ally at hand, who happened to be Ptolemy of Cyprus.

The king chuckled when he saw the over-the-top sum of money being demanded for the freedom of a middling Roman, and he offered what he considered a more appropriate figure. It was so pitifully small (and plunder was generally so easy to come by) that the pirates had a good laugh and finally let Clodius go free. But the humor was lost on Clodius, who—rather than bless his good fortune—decided that Ptolemy had mortally insulted him. At last, as tribune, he was in a position to do something about it.

Cyprus's independence had run its course, announced Clodius. Legally, he argued, both Egypt and Cyprus were Roman property already; and here he pointed to an earlier Ptolemeian ancestor, who had supposedly bequeathed both kingdoms to Rome in his will. While the king of Egypt had paid for his independence, the king of Cyprus had not. Thus, making Cyprus the newest province was simply a matter of reclaiming what was already Rome's. It was, as Clodius knew, a weak case for annexation. So he leveled an additional charge against the Cypriot king: He was a state sponsor of piracy, which was (despite Pompey's claims to the contrary) still potent enough to inspire fear in any Roman who traveled by sea or relied on Mediterranean shipping lanes.

Declaring Cyprus annexed was one thing—but who would go and carry it out? As Clodius cleverly put it, there was only one man Rome could trust to inform the Cypriots personally that their independence was over and to take possession of the king's treasury with a minimum of graft. Clodius declared that "he regarded Cato as the purest man of all the Romans. . . . Though many were soliciting the commission to Cyprus and the court of Ptolemy and begging to be sent upon it, he thought Cato alone worthy of it and gladly offered him this favor." It would have been a masterstroke, had the intended target been gullible enough or greedy enough. Cato, though, had seen plenty of Clodius's antics and knew his true intentions. He called the commission to Cyprus a candy-coated exile, "a snare and an insult, not a favor," and flatly refused it.

Clodius was undeterred. His response to Cato was quick and to the point: "Well, then, if you don't think it's a favor, you shall make the voyage as a punishment!" He immediately won a vote in the people's assembly naming Cato the sole commissioner responsible for the annexation. To ensure that the new commissioner would spend as much time away from Rome as possible, Clodius ordered that Cato be given no ships, no assistants, and no clerks to help administer the province—only two attendants, one of them a spy planted by Clodius.

It would have been hard to construct a more plainly personal attack than the one the tribune had just pulled off. But it had deeper political overtones, as well. Clodius wasn't the only one who stood to benefit from Cato's departure. With Cato gone, Caesar, Pompey, and Crassus could each breathe a sigh of relief. Clodius shared their opposition to the *optimas* agenda. And his close relationship with the triumvirs suggests that he might have been acting as much in their stead as his own.

The hope of a Cato-free Rome may have been the spur that encouraged Clodius and the triumvirate to send Cato to Cyprus, but the real satisfaction came from finally putting a chink in the Stoic's flawless moral armor. At last, Cato would have his own morally dubious mission—and it further opened him to the charges of hypocrisy that were gaining volume as resistance to him and to the *optimates* grew. The Cyprus commission gave Clodius and the triumvirate much-needed insurance: Upon his return, Cato would have to think twice before indulging his habit of questioning the legality of provincial campaigns.

The Republic would also profit from the addition of Cyprus to its collection. The island was rich in minerals and bountiful crops, and it was a valuable strategic asset in the eastern Mediterranean. Rome had already paid a high price to conquer, under Pompey, its newest Eastern provinces; any clear-eyed strategist could see that Cyprus would be an effective perch from which to safeguard those newest holdings.

Still, Cato could have said no. Not by the furthest stretch of the imagination (and Cato was in no mood to stretch his very far) could Rome portray the annexation as self-defense, as service to its vital interests, or as anything but the most naked imperialism, which the Republic still loudly claimed to shun. Cato was particularly alive to the distinction between protection and profit: Romans, he had once muttered to the Asian provincials, "only want an excuse for taking by force what they do not get with consent." At the time, during that free year in his twenties, he had reassured them, and himself, that he was uniquely above that kind of avarice: "Not all men who come to you will be Catos." Now he was ordered, like any greedy proconsul, to go East and take. Further, Cato's commission, which was taken directly to the people and skirted constitutional procedure, was no different in form from the extraordinary, politically motivated commands that had been handed out to Pompey and others. For years, Cato had railed against those commands as magnets for corruption—and now he was asked to immerse himself in the same sins. To Clodius, of course, that was part of the appeal. Altogether, as the historian Muriel Jaeger conjectures, "It must have given Cato, the ideal Cato, who was so intimately also the real Cato, the worst moral wound he ever received."

Yet against all that was the law. The decree sending Cato to Cyprus may have been unorthodox, but it was legal. The orders may have been unjust, but they were the orders of the Roman people. What would Cato be if he unilaterally chose which laws to obey and which to ignore? The worse the law, the more conspicuous his virtue in obeying it. The more the Forum seemed to spin out of control, the more Cato clung to his faith in legalities—a shallow faith, it might seem to us, but Cato's one constant.

Stoicism did not dwell on what we might call the morally tragic, the choice in which a deep principle is broken on either side. Stoics recognized the unitary good, the unitary bad, and the natural reason that steered a man between them—but there was no readying Cato for a choice so carefully built to shame him either way. We don't know what finally swayed him to set sail, but his parting advice to Cicero sounds like the exhaustion

of a defeated man. Be your country's savior again, he told Cicero. When Clodius comes for you, don't put up a fight.

* * *

Cicero mourned the loss of a friend and protector, leaving for who knew
how many years, taking with him an irreplaceable piece of Rome's moral
authority. No one drank the Roman myth more deeply than Cicero, who
came to it by choice, not birth. Always Cincinnatus: always patriots leaving
their farms and plows with reluctance, out for neither plunder nor profit,
but only when their hands were forced, and always to return. King Ptolemy
of Cyprus was an awkward partner for this myth, and Cicero knew it. But
his lines on the king are the words of a true believer:

> He—who was always an ally, was always a friend, against whom
> there was never so much as the least suspicion expressed against
> him, either to the Senate or to our generals—lives (as they say) to
> see himself in a situation where even his food and his clothes have
> been confiscated. Behold, why should other kings think that their
> fortune is secure, when by this wicked example of that regrettable
> year, they may see themselves stripped of all their fortunes and all
> their kingdom by one tribune . . . ?

If there was a touch of exaggerated pity in Cicero's words, he might be forgiven for it: There was self-pity just beneath the surface. Cato's departure
also meant that Cicero's fortune, food, and clothing—his life as he had known
it—were imperiled.

* * *

Cicero didn't mean to go quietly. He was one of Rome's elder statesmen, after all, and a lifetime in politics had left him with a strong cadre of followers
who still deeply admired him and respected his gifts. Accordingly, he found
a sympathetic tribune and pressed him to veto any new proposals from Clodius. Suddenly frustrated after a string of unbroken success, Clodius reached
out to Cicero with a deal: If Cicero agreed to hold back his tribune friend
and release the vetoes, Clodius would promise to take no legal action against

Cicero. He even hinted at a full reconciliation and magnanimously agreed to blame the entire feud on Cicero's wife. Cicero, enormously relieved, took the outstretched hand. Letters to his friend Atticus from this time are full of praise for bright, young Clodius.

The hatchet, however, was barely buried before Clodius exhumed it. Cravenly, though not unexpectedly, he broke the bargain he had offered. With Cicero's tribune on the sidelines, Clodius passed a law exiling anyone who executed a citizen without a trial—or anyone who had ever done so. He had one unmistakable target in mind: Clodius meant to turn Cicero's proudest moment—his handling of Catiline's conspiracy—into the end of his career. It would be revenge for Catiline and Clodius both, in one act.

With passage of the retroactive exile law, Cicero could see that Clodius very nearly had him. Caesar was well known to be Clodius's sponsor, quietly egging him on. The Senate, in the face of the triumvirs and Clodius's urban following, was too scared to act. So Cicero did the only thing he could do: He called in all the favors he could find and he begged for pity.

He took on the clothing and manner of a man in mourning, wearing tattered garments and growing out his hair and beard. The *equites*, Cicero's base of support, did the same in a show of sympathy. The Senate passed a resolution declaring it a time of mourning for all Romans—but the senators would go no further. Even the toothless resolution brought a Clodian mob to the Senate House, and the meeting broke up as senators shoved and scurried their way out of the surrounded hall.

Cicero, finally and begrudgingly, turned to Caesar for help. But the best an apologetic Caesar could offer was a post on his campaign in Gaul. For Cicero, that was far too slender an offer—it was an insult, especially from his tormentor, the man ultimately behind his troubles.

Pompey was more accommodating. He told Cicero exactly what he wanted to hear: To leave Rome now was to admit defeat. If he chose to stay and fight, Pompey would back him. Yet having silently approved Cicero's exile, and lacking Caesar's stomach for hypocrisy, Pompey could hardly bear to look Cicero in the eye. Before Cicero could come visit to plot a defense strategy, Pompey took off for his country villa in the Alban Hills. Cicero pursued him, and the general, cornered in his home, ached with regret. He owed Cicero a great deal: The orator had been a steadfast friend, had defended him at great length to the Roman crowds and even to Cato. But Pompey was also

Caesar's son-in-law, and he was too shrewd to risk that connection in return for an alliance with an all-but-finished man. The choice was as clear as it
was mortifying. With Cicero waiting at his door, Pompey slipped out a side
entrance, too embarrassed to show his face. Cicero would surely have enjoyed
the farce, had the victim been someone other than himself.

With Pompey's escape, Cicero had exhausted every possibility, every
fair-weather friend. Rome was unsafe for him: There was no showing his
face in public without being surrounded and harassed by Clodius's thugs,
who were hoping to save the trouble of a trial and goad Cicero into exiling
himself. On one of his last emergences from his house, Cicero carried with
him a small statute of Minerva, goddess of wisdom. He brought it to the
summit of the Capitol and left it where its inscription would be visible to all:
TO MINERVA, GUARDIAN OF ROME. It was a public request of the goddess:
Protect Rome, now that I am gone. With that gesture of conspicuous and sad
pride, the former consul and "Father of the Fatherland" slipped quietly out
of Rome on foot in the middle of the night.

Cicero's midnight escape stunned the city. Clodius himself was
surprised—but not satisfied. He issued an edict of formal banishment, along
with a law that made it a crime to offer shelter to Cicero within five hundred
miles of Rome. He directed his followers to loot and burn Cicero's vacation
villas. They ransacked his homes, kept his possessions to one side for future
sale, and torched the mansion on the Palatine Hill, the physical symbol of
Cicero's ascent. As a final coup de grâce, Clodius placed a bronze tablet on
the Capitol, beside the statue of Minerva. It cataloged Cicero's crimes, permanent testimony to the guilt of an exiled man.

Though it would have offered him little comfort as he fled in the night,
it might have pleased Cicero to know that no one purchased a single item of
his that Clodius brought to auction, though he tried to sell each one at an
embarrassingly low price. It was a modest moral victory in the face of Clodius's stunning success.

Three years after crossing Clodius, Cicero was gone, with no expectation that he would ever return.

•   •   •

Cato was in Rome to witness Cicero's fall, and he knew that his own days in
the city were numbered. Shortly after Cicero's escape, Cato sailed from

Italy—but instead of moving on Ptolemy, he delayed his mission and spent time stewing on the island of Rhodes. While there, he had an unexpected visitor: the other Ptolemy brother, Auletes, the Egyptian king.

The people of Egypt, oppressed by Auletes' high taxes and disgusted by his silence at the annexation of his brother's kingdom, had risen up in rebellion. Fleeing to Rome for safety, Auletes made a pointed detour to lobby Cato for support. Egypt's king sailed west with the hope that the Romans who had been the beneficiaries of his outrageous payments would now repay the favor and restore his kingdom by force; his hopes were especially fixed on Pompey and Caesar. However—whether with an eye to building as diverse a base of support as possible, or whether out of ignorance of Rome's internal politics—Auletes was also determined to court the triumvirs' most dedicated enemy. So set was he on pressing his case to Cato in person that, when Cato insisted that he was sick and unable to visit the king, Auletes changed course and headed for Rhodes to visit him.

When he arrived at Cato's chambers, Cato didn't budge. He didn't lift himself up from his seat or offer a bow or even a handshake. He simply asked the king to take a seat, like any errand boy. Initially, Ptolemy was stunned by the cold and undignified reception—but then Cato began to speak to him warmly, exiled leader to exiled leader, and apparently persuaded him to give up on his effort to seek Roman intervention. Yes, Cato granted, Pompey or Caesar would probably move if paid enough—but accepting their help would only put Egypt further in hock to Rome. Another bribe would whet the Republic's appetite, not sate it. Even if Auletes was restored to the throne, he would find himself less a king than a slave.

It was a moral lecture as much as a political one—and a lecture that seemed to directly undermine the Republic's interests. Perhaps shocked to see a Roman official rail against Rome so openly, "the king, as if brought to his senses by Cato's words after a fit of madness or delirium, and recognizing the sincerity and sagacity of the speaker, determined to adopt his counsels." Cato advised Auletes to return to Alexandria and appeal to his people directly.

But as soon as he left the conference with Cato, Auletes was back among his Egyptian entourage, friends who had a keener sense than Cato of the king's weak willpower. As the impact of Cato's words faded, Auletes agreed to continue on to Rome to seek out second opinions. In Plutarch's account, the king is last seen halfheartedly knocking on the door of a Roman magistrate, frustrated that he didn't return to Egypt and face his people, "convinced that he had slighted, not the words of a good man, but the prophetic warning of a god."

What's most noteworthy about the tale of Auletes, however, is not what he and Cato discussed—but what they didn't. Nowhere in Plutarch's rendering of the king's visit to Cato does he mention any request on behalf of the other Ptolemy, the Cypriot brother, the king whom Cato was about to overthrow. It seems like a glaring oversight. Couldn't the king have appealed to Cato on his brother's behalf as well as his own? Wouldn't the attempt have renewed his people's confidence in his kingship, and perhaps saved his brother's skin?

In the end, however, Auletes showed himself primarily concerned about himself. What he found in Rome was a war-weary Senate unwilling to put Roman boys in harm's way to support a hated king, no matter the rewards for Rome's coffers. The Egyptian people too were happier with Auletes gone. They intended to send a delegation urging Rome to stay out, but Auletes intercepted the news "and sent men out in various directions to lie in wait for the envoys before they could arrive. Thus he caused the majority of them to perish by the way, while of the survivors he had some slain in the city itself."

After three years of trying—and after mounting pressure from Rome's bankers, who feared that the king would never pay off his debts unless restored to the throne—Auletes succeeded in purchasing a Roman army. Under Pompey's friend, Aulus Gabinius, the army marched on Alexandria, reinstated the king, and left two thousand soldiers garrisoned in the capital for the duration of his reign, keeping one watchful eye fixed on the monarch, the other on the ships heaped with gold and silver heading back to Rome.

*   *   *

At the time, Auletes' problems were of little concern to Cato, who still had a legal if distasteful task to accomplish in Cyprus. Whether to use his paltry resources to maximum effect, or because he wanted to spare himself the ugliness of dispossessing the king in person, Cato sent an envoy in his place. His friend Canidius brought a simple message to the Cypriot court: Give up. If the king relinquished his rule without a struggle, Cato could offer him dignified retirement as a temple priest in the city of Paphos, on Cyprus—not exactly a throne, but not a terrible offer either, considering that monarchs who lost their kingdoms to Rome often lost their lives as well.

Ptolemy of Cyprus heard Canidius out. He considered the offer. And then he poisoned himself.

•   •   •

News of the king's death reached Cato in Rhodes. All that was left was to confiscate and sell off the king's property, a trivial job, even a degrading one, and one that Cato wasn't yet ready to take up. Clodius had taken the opportunity of Cato's assignment to Cyprus to send him on an entirely unrelated task, as long as he was in the neighborhood. He was to settle things in the Bosporus town of Byzantium, which had erupted in civil conflict. It was minor business, hardly worth the intervention of someone of Cato's stature, but Clodius knew that it would delay Cato's return to Rome and buy the triumvirate more time.

While Cato busied himself as arbitrator in the backwater that would one day head the empire, he also kept a wary eye on Cyprus. Canidius, it seems, had never earned Cato's full trust. With little else to occupy him, Cato let his suspicion of his friend grow: Perhaps Canidius was taking advantage of the king's suicide by helping himself to the splendor of the court. Such behavior, after all, was second nature to Romans abroad.

Cato called on his bookish half-nephew Brutus, Servilia's son, to leave his studies and report to Cyprus to act as a check on Canidius. It was his first taste of public life. But Cato's trust, which had brought Brutus to Cyprus, was misplaced. In Cyprus, Brutus discovered a remarkable talent for loan-sharking, lending on terms he could never have gotten away with in Rome, charging interest rates as high as 48 percent a year. While Brutus was officially attending to his uncle's books, he made such an extracurricular fortune that he was long afterward called "a man of high principles, and even higher interest."

As he had demonstrated at the treasury, Cato had only one response in the presence of corruption: He centralized as much power and responsibility as possible in his immaculate self. With his work in Byzantium done, Cato stormed into the court at Cyprus and put himself personally in charge of cataloging, pricing, and taking bids for each of the dead king's possessions. Unwilling to trust even the capital's professional market criers, Cato went as far as to conduct his own private auctions in the palace. If the image of a senior Roman statesman pondering the value of Babylonian dining-room furniture or aphrodisiac oils seems amusing to us, it was shocking to the Romans who accompanied Cato. Another senator in his place would have left this labor to others while enjoying the fruits of a kingdom without its king—but not Cato.

. . .

So exhaustive was his assessment, so exacting his standards, that even his friends were driven away. It was one of those closest to him, his loyal, Stoic army comrade Munatius, who took the greatest offense at Cato's style. Traveling all the way from Rome to lend a hand and be with his friend in his trying time, Munatius expected the welcome due to an honored guest. A banquet would have been customary after a long journey, along with suitable entertainment. But Munatius arrived to an empty shore and, more troubling, a cold shoulder from his friend. Cato, he was informed, was too busy for formalities. Even when he arrived at Cato's personal tent, he was told to sit outside while Cato finished his business with Canidius. When Munatius was finally called in for a brisk audience, he couldn't conceal his anger at his ungrateful friend—or his bitterness at being made to wait like any other supplicant.

But Cato made no apology. Instead he treated Munatius to a lecture on the Stoic virtue of indifference. Munatius's anger, Cato said, was simply the natural by-product of misplaced and excessive love, which he encouraged Munatius to tamp down before their next meeting. His obvious jealousy toward Canidius, the homily went on, was equally un-Stoic. Munatius was deeply stung—but the worst insult had yet to come. No sooner was the one-sided conversation over than Cato reported the details to Canidius—who naturally carried them straight back to his rival for Cato's affection.

Cato had found the outer limits of Munatius's patience: Fearing betrayal on all sides, he had betrayed his friend's trust. Munatius couldn't bear the insult lightly, and perhaps taking Cato's advice on excessive affection, he responded in kind. He stopped obeying the commissioner's orders. Refused to attend meetings even when his presence was requested.

He rebuffed repeated invitations to official dinners. Cato could see his authority slipping with each slight, so he took measures to ensure that the private mutiny of Munatius didn't turn into anything more: He threatened to slap Munatius with a charge of disobedience and to strip him of his goods.

Munatius had had enough. The two had been through their share of trials. They had shared a cramped army tent in Macedonia, after Munatius had personally promised Cato's wife that he would watch over Cato on his first command. Pompey had come to Munatius, and him alone, when he wanted Cato's daughter in marriage. But even such a tested bond had its breaking point.

Munatius, perhaps more than any of Cato's contemporaries, had seen his friend in those moments when his self-discipline failed him, such as when he stayed up all night in drink and talk. Now, showing pettiness and high-handedness at a low point of his life, Cato was confirming the common Roman whisper: that he was not the man of moderation he styled himself but essentially a man of excess who struggled, with varying success, to hold himself in check from day to day. Munatius had seen him deep in his cups; now he seemed drunk on power or paranoia or simply boiling resentment. Cato wouldn't have been the first Roman to shed his pieties once he was safely away from the city—but Munatius had had reason to expect better.

The sea slapped his ship as he sailed for Rome, his visit aborted, his pride wounded, his friendship with Cato all but dead.

. . .

Only years later, back in Rome, would the two reconcile. It was Cato's wife, Marcia, who would bring them together, pressuring Cato to attend a dinner where she knew Munatius would be a guest. When Cato arrived—late—he picked the seat next to Munatius, and though the two men sat in silence through the whole meal, the simple gesture of sitting close by was the beginning of a thaw. Further prodding from Marcia led to a note inviting Munatius to Cato's home to talk business. As on most days in the home of a Roman public man, visitors and clients streamed in and out all morning; Marcia held Munatius back until all the rest had gone and sent him alone into the atrium. Letting their years of silence go at last, Cato threw his arms around his friend and "lavished kindness on him." It was enough to repair what he had broken in Cyprus. Munatius would ultimately write one of the first biographies of Cato, an admiring account that cast him as a Stoic hero. Through his recollections, preserved by Plutarch, we have a firsthand memory of much that would otherwise have been lost. Though neither of them could have known it, the reward for their reunion was a deeper, richer historical afterlife for both.

•　•　•

For the moment, however, Cato was left alone in Cyprus with his contempt. Abandoned by his friend, marginalized from politics, and left with a nephew sinking ever deeper into moneymaking schemes, Cato clung compulsively to the mission that was poisoning him. Outside, all might be disorder; but in the shrinking sphere left to him, in liquidating a government and whispering higher prices into bidders' ears, he could still perform flawlessly.

At the end, when the last wagon was hauled away and the last line entered in the books, Cato beheld an empty palace—and a stunning success. In a matter of months, he had netted some seven thousand silver talents for Rome's treasury. It was less than a conquering general's haul but hugely impressive for its source, a single king's estate in a middling kingdom, extracted by a lone commissioner and a handful of assistants. Cato would boast that his winnings were greater than any Pompey ever managed, and in his pedantic way he had a point. While Pompey's most recent campaign had brought home almost twenty-two thousand talents, he had had the whole of the Near East to work over. Wringing nearly a third of that sum from a little island, Cato had squeezed out far more money per inch.

The fleecing complete, Cato took great care in making sure the money came back to Rome in its totality. He stored the silver in specially constructed boxes, each one trailing a long rope and a block of cork. In case of a shipwreck, the cork would mark where the boxes had sunk, easing the recovery of the loot. The silver made its way safely to Rome and into the treasury—but Cato had far less luck with his financial records, the registers in which he had personally noted the details of each item and its selling price.

Such catalogs were more than an administrative nicety. They were proof that Cato would need in case anyone brought him up on charges of corruption—a not inconsiderable possibility, especially given Cato's affinity for accusing others. Cato ordered an exact duplicate of the record and sent it home separately with a servant—whose ship capsized. He kept the other copy safe among his possessions on the return journey—until it too was lost when, at a stop on the Greek island of Corcyra, his crew of sailors lost control of their campfire and burned down Cato's tent.

Naturally, Cato was furious. Aides from the trip could testify to the integrity of the auction. They could silence any critics. But that wasn't the point. His own integrity—in his mind—was already established as unassailable. The objective was to set an example for other Romans abroad, one in which the only acceptable greed was indulged on the treasury's behalf. The micromanaging, the exactitude, the cork-fitted boxes—it was all intended to set the gold standard for provincial administration. With the loss of the books, however, the perfect picture was lacking.

While his rivals couldn't resist casting suspicion on the loss of the books, their charges—whether of negligence or deliberately concealed corruption—were too far out of keeping with Cato's record and reputation to do serious damage. But did his critics, however crassly motivated, have a point? Could the Cyprus records have been lost or destroyed intentionally? There is at least a circumstantial reason to suspect that they were.

A law passed under Caesar's consulship required all Roman provincial administrators to leave behind two copies of their financial records, in two separate cities of the province, and to send a third copy to Rome. It was a means of guarding against precisely the situation in which Cato now found himself. Cato may have loathed Caesar, but the law was reasonable. Even if he had objected to the law, he might, as seen in his agreement to sail for Cyprus in the first place, have been expected to follow it. Evidently, he did not.

The ancient accounts offer little explanation for the missing records. But the writers of those accounts—Cicero, Plutarch, Cassius Dio, and others—would probably have assumed what most Romans of Cato's day had assumed: that Cato, of all people, would have had nothing to hide. What might have been lost in the Cyprus records? Perhaps nothing more than administrative tedium. Perhaps, though, Brutus's hand had found its way into the books. He had already proven himself financially unscrupulous, and he would only have been playing the role of the typical provincial aide had he managed to skim from Ptolemy's estate. Wouldn't Cato have stopped him? Twice before, though—for Silanus and for Bibulus—Cato had overlooked in kin the same behavior he condemned in others.

There is no conclusive evidence against the story of shipwreck and fire. We have no answer to the riddle of the Cyprus books, the failure to keep a record on the island, and the question of why there were only two sets rather than three. Whatever else the Cyprus mission was, it ended, whether by will or by accident, with less scrupulous respect for the law than it began.

•   •   •

The assembled Roman state, from consuls to tribunes, crowded the edge of the Tiber as the galleys approached. Magistrates mingled with priests, chattering over politics with the full membership of the Senate, as a mass of spectators fought for position. A triumph-sized crowd thronged both of the Tiber's banks.

Cato was finally coming home. What would happen to Clodius and, for that matter, to Caesar? What had become of Cyprus and its king? And what of Cato: Had the virtual exile humbled him? None of those questions would be answered in a day, but the crowd was charged with expectation.

The murmurs and cheers grew louder as Cato's six-oared galley drew closer to the riverbank. The dignitaries began to clap, even if some of them, like Clodius, would have preferred to stay silent. They waited for the boats to halt, for Cato and his retinue to receive the applause accorded to a returning statesman.

The noise built, and those farthest from the water surged forward, pressing up against the banks for a glimpse of Cato and his silver. Cato came into view, and the applause quickened. And then almost as suddenly it died.

He hadn't stopped. He hadn't tied up at the feet of the gathered dignitaries. Cato kept the galley rowing down the river, past the Senate and the people, past the consuls and Clodius, and the standard he flew might as well have been painted GO TO HELL!

He didn't stop until he reached the river dock, far past the assembly, where, without a word of hello or even a wave, he set straight to unloading his cargo. He left behind him a gravely insulted Senate and a buzzing crowd. What did such a calculated snub mean? If Cato couldn't acknowledge them, what could they expect when he was back in the Forum?

The dignitaries clucked with frustration as they trooped back to the city. Iconoclasm was one thing, but this was a gratuitous insult. How dare

Cato fail to show his respect—to consuls, no less? Even from someone of his stature, it was unexpected, stubborn, and galling.

He had done the work, he seemed to say to those assembled on the bank, as he was duty bound to do. But celebrate, he couldn't. Pleased though he might have been to come home, he ruined his homecoming to make that point.

The elite was now on guard. Cato was back.

10

CATO THE PROPHET

Back to the familiar Senate House, back to the milling Forum—but it had all turned strangely hollow. The reliable forms were there where Cato had left them, from the packed assemblies to the favor-hunting pack trailing each senator. But even before he reached home, the center of the Roman world had migrated some two hundred miles to the north, to the town of Luca on the Gallic frontier.

Caesar—fresh from a spectacular battle against a tribe of hairy Germanic "heroes," who had come close to encircling his legions before he took up a shield and personally intervened to stave off disaster (or so his breathless dispatch home claimed)—was now attempting a similar feat in the realm of politics. More and more, it was clear that the triumvirate and the Gallic command, for all the glory they made possible, were also acting as the proverbial wolf held by the ears. The moment Caesar let them go, he could expect to be mauled. He had bent the law with abandon during his radical consulship of 59, and now his enemies were lining up for a chance to prosecute him. There was Cato, who couldn't be sidelined forever. There was Cato's brother-in-law, Lucius Domitius Ahenobarbus: son, grandson, great-grandson, and great-great-grandson of consuls, proposing to claim the family job in his turn and immediately strip Caesar of his troops. There was even a worrisome threat to Caesar's left flank. Clodius, whose armed gangs had the run of many a Roman street, had declared himself virtually an independent power and added his voice to those baying for Caesar's comeuppance.

As long as he held *imperium* in Gaul, Caesar remained untouchable, immune from prosecution. But as soon as that command expired—or as soon as Cato or Ahenobarbus wrenched it away—he would be a mere private citizen, and in a matter of days, he would be in the dock fighting for his life. Pompey and Crassus could still protect Caesar, if they chose—but what good now was the alliance to them? It had long since delivered them everything it had promised, from land for Pompey's troops to new contracts for Crassus's tax men. In Caesar's absence, the two were either squabbling or casting their envious eyes to the north.

Caesar needed Pompey and Crassus—which meant convincing them that they still needed each other. In Luca, where the Italian homeland met southern Gaul, he called them to a summit. There, appealing to each in turn, he hammered home his pragmatic case:

> He tried to reconcile them by persistently showing them that their mutual ruin would only increase the power of such men as Cicero, Catulus, and Cato, men whose influence would be nothing if Crassus and Pompey would only unite their friends and adherents, and with one might and one purpose direct the affairs of the city.

Soon, the whispered arrangement edged toward a more open secrecy. As the three principals conferred, as many as two hundred senators, with their own entourages, hovered at the edges, hashing out subdeals among themselves—a shadow government making its way out of the shadows. At last, after negotiating for days, Caesar won his reconciliation. The price was the consulship, again, for Pompey and Crassus—sealed by Caesar's spare troops, who would be sent on leave with instructions to vote the right way. More important, after serving as consul, Pompey and Crassus would each have a command of his own and five years to equal Caesar, if he could. Pompey would have Spain, and Crassus, Syria, where Pompey had left off years before. And when Caesar's original term as commander ended in 55, the deal would allow him five more years to put off his day of reckoning.

Cato, needless to say, was not on the guest list. Even as he was rowed down the Tiber, even as he delivered his majestic snub to Clodius and the rest, all had been settled. He and Ahenobarbus and any other friend or ally he could name were free to put themselves forward for any office they chose, in an election whose outcome had already been decided.

. . .

The triumvirs, at such a delicate time, were careful to undermine any coalition that could plausibly stand in opposition. Caesar understood that the greatest danger would still come from Cato, Cicero, and the *optimates* acting in concert. There would be no winning over Cato, who had come back from exile full of defiance. But Cicero was an altogether more pliable man. End his exile, and he would come back full of useful gratitude.

By the time of Cato's return, Cicero's silence had been securely won. Pompey had lobbied the Senate for a recall, and Caesar had nodded his assent from Gaul. An outraged Clodius had been bloodied and momentarily silenced by a new rival gang, quietly backed by Pompey and led by the brawling aristocrat Titus Annius Milo. Cicero, with the consent of all the leading powers, was restored to "a sort of second life." Now the bill was due.

In the Senate, Cicero now heaped praise on Pompey, "the greatest man of all living, or who ever have lived, or who ever shall live, for virtue, and wisdom, and true glory." In the Forum, he held his tongue whenever an old colleague broached the repeal of Caesar's hated land bills. And in the law courts, he had a new roster of clients, largely drawn from the ranks of Caesar's and Pompey's hangers-on.

There were times, Cicero confessed to his friend Atticus, when this new life in Rome drove him to self-hatred. But he was deep in the triumvirs' debt, and the alternative to paying up was the one thing that Cicero feared above all: irrelevance. In a letter to Atticus, he made the case for self-preservation, as only one who had briefly lost everything could make it:

> Since those who have no power refuse me their affection, let us take care to secure the affection of those who have power. You will say, "I could have wished that you had done so before." I know you did wish it, and that I have made a real ass of myself. But now the time has come to show a little affection for myself. . . .

A boyhood friend like Atticus could be trusted to let such self-justifying talk pass without criticism. But it was at precisely such trying times as these that a far-more-demanding friend, Cato, normally appointed himself Cicero's angry conscience. Where was he?

There is no record of a happy reunion between Cato and Cicero, no warm greeting or exchange of stories from the fringes of the Roman world. Rather, they seem to have returned instantly to their old sparring in the Senate, as if hardly a day had passed. The triumvirs, following Caesar's advice, drove a wedge between the two by buying Cicero's complicity. Cato finished the work for them.

•　•　•

The cause of this foolishly timed break was a man who ought to have united them: their common enemy, Clodius. In the midst of the other favors Cicero guiltily performed for the triumvirs, he revenged himself on Clodius with relish. At a meeting of the Senate in April of 56, Cicero demanded that every action Clodius had taken as tribune—from the expanded grain dole to the decree of banishment against Cicero himself—be declared null and void and that Clodius be utterly stricken from the records of the Republic. Beyond personal animus, Cicero had a believable legal case: Clodius had never been a tribune, because he had never been a plebeian, because his "adoption" had been an obvious farce. Yet Cato, wasting little time in reacquainting the Senate with his irascible presence, would not even let Cicero finish. He pelted Cicero with objections from the benches and, given the floor at last, shocked even his close allies by coming out for Clodius.

Cato conceded that he was no fonder of Clodius than any right-thinking Roman was: Clodius was a demagogue, a scoundrel, and an embarrassment of a tribune, but he had good company in all of those qualities. He had duly renounced his patrician heritage and duly won election—and if the Senate started wiping out election results it disliked, where would it stop? As for Cicero's banishment: "It was a funeral of the Republic, but a funeral performed with all the regular solemnity."

So argued Cato the constitutionalist—as he might have argued if he'd had no interest in the case. But Cato did have an interest. Outlaw Clodius, he charged the senators, and you outlaw the annexation of Cyprus. Outlaw the annexation of Cyprus, and you outlaw everything I did there in your name.

To Cicero's advantage, there was widespread elite hatred for Clodius, who had disowned his class and brought new heights of mob violence to the streets. To Cato's advantage, there were seven thousand silver talents sitting in the Roman treasury, about to be stripped of any legal pretext for sitting there at all. To outlaw Clodius would be a collective admission of theft. Cicero would have to go without his revenge.

Cato and Cicero had once stood together as fellow victims of Clodius. Now Cato had taken their tormentor's side. For a man who had once spoken of the Cyprus mission as a curse, Cato suddenly sounded as if he were proud of it. Maybe there was philosophy in that approach, a healthy Stoic love of fate—but more fundamentally, Cato couldn't bring himself to think of nearly two years of his life as a waste. If Cicero had had his way, everything Cato had suffered—the humiliation of being outmaneuvered, the complicity in corruption, the trivial work, the sacrificed friendships—would all have been rendered pointless. If Cyprus had been a mistake, it was a mistake Cato would never admit. As personally as Cicero had taken the question, he hadn't imagined how deeply personal it was for Cato, as well.

But there was no explaining those subtleties to the incredulous Cicero, who considered himself betrayed without even the courtesy of a warning. His friendship with Cato would not recover for years—years during which the triumvirs would tighten their hold on power. Neither Cato nor Cicero saw fit to take their falling-out public, but it would nonetheless have a quietly powerful impact on the life of the Republic. Few had more authority than those two to make the constitutional case against the triumvirate and against the public corruption and violence that made the triumvirate appear so reasonable by contrast. In the estimation of historian Muriel Jaeger, they were "the only two men who had a fighting chance." But now, if there had ever been a chance that Cato could guilt Cicero out of the prestigious cover he provided to the triumvirate, it was gone.

That June, Cicero gave his most important policy address since his recall. In the name of Rome's security and its civilizing mission, he demanded that Caesar's Gallic command be extended:

> We shall only see the war actually terminated successfully if the man who began it remains to follow it up to the last. . . . As for Caesar himself, what reason can there be why he should wish any longer to remain in the province . . . ? I suppose it's the delightful nature of the country, the splendor of the cities, the civilized state

and accomplished habits of those nations and natives? No! It is a desire for victory, it is a wish to extend the boundaries of our empire, that keeps him there!

Shortly after, Cicero wrote to Atticus to apologize that he had not, as usual, mailed him an advance draft of the speech. Pompey, he explained, had been vetting the only copy.

• • •

If Cato needed further proof of his growing isolation, it was not long in coming.

Exactly what Caesar, Pompey, and Crassus had been doing at Luca with two hundred senators was still not public knowledge, and there is no indication that Cato had anything more than dark suspicions about their plans. But when Pompey and Crassus at last announced their plans to seek the consulship, they set off a panic among the Senate's *optimates*. The conservative bloc boycotted the chamber, stayed indoors for all the remaining festivals on the calendar, as though in mourning, and generally "spent the rest of the year as if they were in bondage and possessed no authority to choose officials or carry on any other public business." Without a quorum to set an election date, the future of the government remained in limbo as the year slipped away into winter.

The political climate remained so chilled, and the combined power of the three so overwhelming, that only one man could be found to stand against them: Ahenobarbus. It took a determined campaign of egging on by Cato, who drilled into him that the stakes of this election, whenever it happened, were not mere offices but liberty itself. Many Romans, Ahenobarbus was counseled, were holding their tongues out of fear—but when the vote came, enough of them would understand that Crassus and Pompey could not be allowed to rule unchecked.

Faced with the possibility of beginning the year with no government, the *optimates* backed down from their boycott and scheduled a vote for consul on the last day of the year 56, with the other offices to be filled later. And it was on that last cold day of the year, when Cato and his brother-in-law were up before dawn and traveling with their entourage by torchlight down to the polling place in the Field of Mars, that they were ambushed.

The torchbearer at the head of the party collapsed with a groan—stabbed to death. The light clattered to the pavement, and they were surrounded by shadows swinging swords. The assailants wounded each member of the party until all had fled but Ahenobarbus and Cato. These two held their ground, Cato clutching a wound that poured blood from his arm.

But their attackers were under orders to maim and frighten them, not to kill. The message sent, the armed men fled through the streets, and the two stood alone in the dark.

Who could they have been but Pompey's men? The injury aside, nothing could have been more gratifying to Cato. Whatever was intended, the message he took was that he was still threatening enough to the powerful to warrant a physical assault. The message was that all his convictions on the tyranny of Pompey and Crassus were proven—because if they perpetrated such crimes on the way to power, one could only imagine what they would do once arrived. Ahenobarbus may have been relieved to be alive; Cato, it seems, was relieved to be stabbed. What began the day as a desultory campaign was, before the sun was fully up, a chance for Stoic victory over pain and fear, the kind of stark moral drama on which Cato thrived, the kind that flattened all else by comparison. Now they would march to the polls unattended and unarmed. They would show off their wounds to the crowd and announce that they would stand for liberty as long as they had life in them.

Or so Cato struggled to convince his brother-in-law as they caught their breath. But he and Ahenobarbus had little in common beyond their politics. The latter's heart had never been in the race—he had planned on inheriting the consulship, not dying for it. So Ahenobarbus, still fearing for his life, made whatever apologies he had in him and went to barricade himself inside his home. And Cato, presumably still bleeding, walked alone to the Field of Mars—where Pompey and Crassus, on account of their opponent's unexpected withdrawal, were elected unopposed.

•   •   •

Unable to place a watchful in-law next to his enemies, as he had done in the case of Bibulus, Cato chose to put himself forward for the office of praetor. It would make him one of Rome's second-ranking magistrates, and he would have a powerful position from which to resist the coming year's agenda—most important, the new five-year commands for each of the triumvirs. Any doubts about running must have been drowned in his fury over the attack and Ahenobarbus's desertion. According to Plutarch, his mind was made up by the time Pompey and Crassus were hailed as the winners.

Plutarch reported that the new consuls opened the floodgates of bribery against Cato, lavishly financing their own handpicked candidates and even rewriting the law to make any postelection corruption trial impossible. But buying the election would be more of a struggle than usual. Cato was, despite his best efforts, at the height of his personal popularity. Had he come back from Cyprus empty-handed, the arrogance of his return might have been career killing. But once Rome saw the size of his silver haul, it was written off as merely eccentric. Now, any campaign against Cato would have to grapple with his record in Cyprus—and to paint him as corrupted by the strange luxuries of the East.

It was a familiar rival who stepped up to the task. Almost twenty years before, Metellus Scipio had stolen Cato's would-be wife, Aemilia, and Cato had responded by descending to a rare if tastefully versified campaign of mockery. They had matured from rash young men to veterans of the Senate—yet Metellus Scipio still savored the chance to attack Cato when it came his way. As an opponent for the praetorship, he published a pamphlet-length attack on Cato's conduct in Cyprus—not merely an effective campaign gambit but the first entry in an influential anti-Cato literature that would ultimately be perfected by Caesar himself.

Though the pamphlet is lost, other writers reference enough of its content to give us a flavor of the charges. Metellus Scipio evidently painted a lurid picture of palace extravagance, urging his readers to imagine the austere Stoic surrounded and seduced by Eastern delicacies. Woven Babylonian couch covers, he gasped, were selling in Cyprus for eight hundred thousand sesterces apiece—and Cato surely pocketed his handful out of the outrageous sums. The island was covered with rich marble and bronze sculptures, but Cato saved his favorite from the auction block: a statue of Zeno, that strange Greek and Stoic role model. The implication was that Cato smuggled it home for himself. Metellus Scipio even accused him of profiting from the sale of excruciating poisons, found among King Ptolemy's secret stores, compounded from the flesh of foreign grubs.

Profiteering hypocrite, soft aesthete, secret dealer in potions—the picture was a garish relative of the line of attack, originated by Cicero in the

Murena trial, on Cato the Stoic Greekling. It was also a distant descendant of the boastful *Latinitas* that had brought Cato the Elder such success. It may have been laughably far-fetched—but this was a Roman election. If his opponent didn't accuse Cato of selling his body to palace eunuchs, punches were being pulled.

Clodius, too, sensed weakness and piled on. Ungrateful for Cato's lukewarm defense before the Senate the previous spring, Clodius challenged him to produce the Cyprus account books and prove that he had not embezzled. This, of course, Cato could not do. As long as one copy was ash and the other was at the bottom of the sea (by chance or by design), Cato had no defense against the charge that he was identical to virtually every other self-dealing provincial official known to Rome—no defense but his reputation, which, while formidable, was not invincible. Though the attacks of Metellus Scipio were more grotesque, those of Clodius cut closer to the bone.

· · ·

There is no telling whether, on its own, the public campaign against Cato would have succeeded in bringing him down. Pompey knew from long experience Cato's tenacity as an enemy. He would take no chances. On the election day for the lower offices, Pompey and his bodyguards entered the assembly with a flourish and stood sternly at its head as the votes were called out, making it clear to all that the consul had a personal stake in the outcome. The first votes tallied were all for Cato—and then Pompey cast a frightened face to the horizon and announced that he heard thunder. It was an omen from heaven: The gods had made their displeasure plain, and the vote must be postponed.

It was a transparent trick, and an old one; none but the most piously credulous, or piously partisan, would have believed it. But so central was such omen reading to Rome's public life that no one present was willing to take the risk of disagreeing—certainly not with Pompey himself. Cato might have fumed, but if he were honest with himself, he would have understood that he, of all people, had no standing to object. It had been no different when his ally and son-in-law Bibulus had invented false omens in the effort to thwart Caesar. This, whether or not the gods were involved, was Cato's recompense.

A few days' delay allowed the consuls to redouble their bribes and fortify their control of the polls. When the day of the vote came again, Pompey was better prepared. Cato's most visible backers were forcibly ejected from the polls on the Field of Mars, and a comfortable number of voters were, depending on their leanings, either threatened or bought. This time, Metellus Scipio was evidently among the victors, and Cato was among the losers.

It was the first time in Cato's forty years that he had lost an election—and he would not accept the loss gently. Had he been a more ordinary Roman and this an ordinary vote, it would have been a time of deep shame, a time for taking on mourning and hiding his face. But Cato's campaign did not end with the vote. The election had been so gratuitously stolen from him—with physical assault and slanderous attacks and bribes and false omens and more bribes and thugs at the polls—that Cato moved immediately to turn the theft to his advantage. He would not be praetor that year. But he could play to perfection the scorned prophet, the righteous victim. No one would ever be better cast in that role.

A knot of his angry supporters gathered in protest on the edge of the Field of Mars. Cato formed them into an assembly to hear his nonconcession, and the crowd swelled—full of his ejected partisans, those supporters who had stayed at the polls to the end, and onlookers who had found the day's best free show. Cato denounced the sham of an election and railed against Caesar and the consuls. "As if inspired from heaven, he foretold to the citizens all that would happen to their city." And he identified that fate—the fate of the Republic and its liberty—with his own. Why, he cried, have Pompey and Crassus done this to me? Because they are afraid of me.

Were they? The triumvirs were well enough attuned to public sentiment to understand the risk they ran in wronging Cato so visibly. Taken too far, their tactics might build a broad and powerful sympathy even for a politician identified closely with the upper classes. But at this moment, the public's opinion of the consuls mattered far less than the handful of votes that would give Crassus Syria, give Pompey Spain, and keep Caesar in Gaul. Secure those votes, and there would be more than enough glory and more than enough time to wash away the memory of a single dodgy election. The consuls gambled that their goal was best served by making Cato as incapable of intervening, as constitutionally irrelevant, as possible—and that doing so would be worth any short-lived harm to their popularity.

With the election stolen from him, Cato entered on what we might call the prophetic stage of his career, years in which he would cast himself more and more explicitly as Liberty embodied. It would be a stirring spectacle. But, as Pompey and Crassus and Caesar might well have asked: "How many legions does Cato have?"

• • •

Around the time of his strange loss, Cato's second marriage ended under circumstances even stranger; "and this part of Cato's life, like a drama, has given rise to dispute and is hard to explain."

Quintus Hortensius Hortalus, the man who ended Cato's marriage, was an elder statesman of the *optimates*. In his day, Hortensius had ruled the law courts in gesticulating, hyperemotional, "Asiatic" style—such a strutting, gifted performer that even professional actors would stop rehearsal and come to watch him hold an audience captive with each swish of his toga. He was the advocate of choice for every grafting governor and the target of choice for every ambitious lawyer. But his dominance came to an end when the most ambitious rival of all, Cicero, so comprehensively assassinated the character of one of his clients that Hortensius advised the client to flee Italy. From the time of that humiliation, Hortensisus's life had been a slow fade.

By the time he approached Cato for a favor, Hortensius was semiretired and pushing sixty—and yet, he confided to his friend, he wanted nothing more than a son. He wanted a son, specifically, fathered on Cato's daughter, Porcia. He confessed that he admired Cato so much that he wanted them to be kinsmen, not merely friends. Reminded that Porcia already had a husband, Bibulus, Hortensius replied that he didn't mind. Porcia had already given her husband two children, and it seemed only fair that such an obviously fertile woman should give Hortensius one, as well.

According to the opinion of men, he argued, such a course was absurd, but according to the law of nature it was honorable and good for the state that a woman in the prime of youth and beauty should neither quench her productive power and lie idle, nor yet, by bearing more offspring than enough, burden and impoverish a husband who does not want them. Moreover, community in heirs among worthy men would make virtue abundant and widely diffused in their families, and the state would be closely cemented together by family alliances.

And if Bibulus still missed his wife after it was done, Hortensius would be happy to give her back.

Cato took this unheard-of idea more calmly than might be expected. He answered that he would be honored to count Hortensius as a son-in-law, but that he simply couldn't dissolve another man's marriage.

Very well, said Hortensius; how about your wife, Marcia? I understand that she's pregnant now, but afterward, it seems she would be much more useful bearing children to me. Cato seems to have found this persuasive.

Shortly after, the two men put the plan to Marcia's father, and the divorce papers were drawn up. Shortly after that, Cato himself gave away the bride—his own wife—at the altar. Rome had never seen a wedding like it. If we have no idea what to make of it, neither did Cato's contemporaries.

How, for instance, could Marcia have taken it—to be divvied up just as Caesar and Pompey shared out provinces, to be conferred over by three aging men who negotiated her fertility but barred her from the room? Not a word of protest was recorded. But then, as a Roman wife, hardly a speck of her character was considered worth recording, other than that she was well-born and fertile and obedient. She was, even to her philosopher of a husband, a piece of "noble soil."

But given that a woman was soil, how could she be put to the most rational use? Here, Hortensius had a point that captured Cato's imagination and bolstered his self-image as a man entirely superior to public opinion—a man who would fearlessly follow a good argument down to Hades, if necessary. "Obviously," as Jaeger tries to reimagine the case, "it is rational that the best people should have as many children as possible without regard to such irrelevancies as personal predilections, egotism, or jealousy." It was a line of logic Cato likely already knew well, even if he had never before considered living by it. In Zeno's ideal republic, women were evidently to be shared in common for just that reason—and wise men would not be possessive enough to care. It was among the oldest and most shocking Stoic teachings, a relic of a radical past, that some, like Cato's house philosopher Athenodorus, had worked to strike from the record of history. Despite their best efforts, the Stoic injunction to live according to nature retained within it a powerful countercultural force. It granted permission to ignore even the most venerable convention, even traditional marriage, if it could be shown to be unnatural and unreasonable. If Cato could not conquer in the Forum, here at least was a chance to beat back his own jealousy.

As his constitutional cause was increasingly lost, Cato felt increasingly free to follow his Stoicism back to its discomfiting, untraditional roots. His quirks grew more studied, his flouting of opinion more and more brazen. It was not the behavior of a politician interested in winning and governing— but it was perfectly suited to the aura of Cato the prophet. It was behavior born of the frustration, and perhaps liberation, of loss after loss. From within that frustration, the only victory Cato could imagine dwelt in the realm of eugenic fantasy: "Community in heirs among worthy men would make virtue abundant . . . and the state would be closely cemented together." Perhaps if the best men and women simply outbred the rest of Rome, all would someday be set right. Failing that, what else was there to do?

• • •

For the moment, very little. Pompey and Crassus continued innocently to insist that they had no interest in the question of provinces, that they would go wherever the Roman people saw fit to send them, or nowhere at all, if it came to that. That no one believed them made no difference. When, in early 55, a tribune brought forward the crucial bill that would assign the consuls to Syria and to Spain, with full power over war and peace, there was no doubt who was behind it. But what remained of the senatorial opposition was too disorganized and demoralized to mount a protest. Seven years earlier, at another moment when Pompey's power was at issue, Cato had rallied enough *optimas* support to break up an assembly by force and win a public victory. Now, such a feat was out of the question, and Cato knew it. Under the circumstances, the best he could make of himself was a martyr.

Two days of public debate were announced, and then a vote of the people's assembly. Hardly a voice in opposition could be found besides Cato's. Perhaps to make the foregone conclusion appear as fair as possible, he was given a full two hours to take the rostra and state his case to the people.

But for two hours, Cato did anything but state his case. Instead, he launched into a rambling rant. He denounced the triumvirs. He lectured on the history of Roman freedom. He prophesied its end. But he uttered not a word to the issue at hand. At last, after all of these digressions had worn themselves out, he announced that he would deliver his opinion of the bill—just as the last grains fell through the hourglass. Shouted down by the tribune, Cato refused to stop talking until he was roughly pulled from the stage.

Had rage so gotten the better of him that he forgot to come to his point? On the contrary, the historian Cassius Dio concludes that it was a fully calculated performance, designed to be cut off precisely as Cato was about to urge a vote of "no." Cato timed his speech "in order that he might be silenced . . . while still appearing to have something more to say and might thus obtain this additional grievance." Nothing he could say could ever be as persuasive as the spectacle of the fearless truth teller gagged by the authorities. Never mind that the entire tableau had been engineered by Cato with just that effect in mind. His violent silencing must have looked especially compelling from farther back in the crowd, where it would not have been immediately apparent that his time had expired.

Cato continued to milk the rough treatment for all it was worth, shouting over the next speaker from the base of the rostra, bellowing as he was taken by the arm and dragged from the Forum, breaking free and darting through the crowd, climbing back onto the stage, cursing Pompey and Crassus and Caesar the whole time. Finally, he was tackled and arrested. But as Caesar had found, Cato was a hard man to arrest. He had inflamed enough of the crowd that a chanting mob followed him to prison and frightened the consuls into letting him go. None of this made the consuls' bill any less likely to pass—but it extracted the highest possible price from their victory.

The consuls were determined to make the next day run more smoothly. A dissident tribune made plans to make a Cato-like spectacle of himself, but after spending the night in the Senate House for his own safety, the tribune woke up to find that the consuls' men had barricaded him inside. Outside, the sun rose on a Forum that looked like an armed camp. Where Cato and his followers had been allowed free access in a show of fairness the day before, they were now met at the Forum's edge and barred from entering.

Up on the rostra, a parade of worthies expanded on rumblings of revolt in Spain and on the Parthian horse-archers in the East who threatened all that Rome had won there. On the ground, a handful of Cato's friends probed for an entrance into the crowd and struggled to create a disturbance. Some of his younger followers managed to edge into the press unobserved as the vote drew close. Almost simultaneously, the proceedings were brought to a halt by a roar from the periphery.

"Thunder! Thunder!"

Cato had climbed on the shoulders of a friend and, towering above the heads of the crowd, was jeering at the top of his voice as the mass swung around to face him. It could have been a desperate attempt to stop the vote with an omen; just as likely, it was a bitter parody of Pompey's false thunder at the election. Either way, it was enough to strike up a small riot. In the melee, most of the Catonians were bloodied and, according to both Plutarch and Cassius Dio, several were killed.

But "at length, by open force, they passed the law," giving Spain and Syria to the consuls. As they celebrated their victory, their incensed opponents wandered through the chaos of the Forum, exhibiting their blood-spattered togas and working to stir up knots of the crowd. Others gathered at the base of a statue of Pompey and pelted it with rocks. But when they were on the point of climbing the statue to topple it, Cato placed himself in front of the marble Pompey to hold them back.

For the first time anyone could recall, Cato was Pompey's defender—and just as abruptly as he had sparked the anti-Pompey riot, Cato called it off.

Even as he was battered out of the Forum, Cato had, it seems, come to a painful realization. He had failed in every effort to arrest the crisis. The only man who could stop it now was Pompey.

• • •

With the two consuls' futures secured, Caesar now waited in limbo, dependent on Pompey and Crassus to hold up their end of the bargain and extend his command. It was in this tense pause that Cato saw a last opportunity.

Cato and Pompey had not, as far as is recorded, had a private audience since Ephesus—when a scholarly young soldier confronted a glory-covered commander. What could they possibly say to each other now? Every time Pompey had reached out with an offer of friendship, Cato had slapped it away; he had always believed the worst of Pompey, always spoken the worst of Pompey, and bore no little responsibility for the years of frustration that at last had forced Pompey into the arms of Caesar. On the other side, Pompey's regard for Cato was very well expressed by the deep scar on Cato's arm.

They were far beyond even a false courtesy. In Ephesus, Pompey had made a great display of rising to honor Cato; now there could be none of that. Reluctantly entering Pompey's presence, Cato was brief: These words, he announced, are in your interest. But I speak them because they are in the interest of Rome.

Plutarch records his advice as follows: Pompey "was now, without knowing it, taking Caesar upon his own shoulders, and that when he began to feel the burden and to be overcome by it, he would neither have the power to put it away nor the strength to bear it longer, and would therefore precipitate himself, burden and all, upon the city." In other words: Break your agreement, Pompey, and throw Caesar away before it is too late for you and for Rome.

Cato must have swallowed a great mouthful of pride before he could make this plea. It was a concession that his power to shape the Republic, which had been waning for years, was now exhausted. All that was left was the humiliating step of asking for a change of heart and strategy from an enemy—this man who must have appeared to Cato as the embodiment of all the world's puffed-up smugness. If Cato was able to salvage any self-regard out of the meeting, it was by speaking the language not of the plotting politician but of the disinterested seer. Cato was reduced, or elevated, to speaking in fables: "The Giant and His Burden."

Pompey only dismissed him with a smile. He had no need to listen to a rival who had accomplished nothing under arms and whom he had so thoroughly beaten at the polls and in the Forum. He had no cause to think that Caesar would ever aspire to any place higher than junior partner of the three: For Pompey, Caesar's good intentions were an article of straightforward, soldierly faith. He had no reason to fear Caesar, either: The forest tribes he had bested still paled next to Pompey's trophies.

"Always secure in his own power and good fortune," smiling, untouchable Pompey thanked Cato for his visit. The grand opening of his theater was just months away, and the inventories for the inaugural spectacular were far more pressing than Cato's predictions: five hundred lions, eighteen elephants. . . .

Cato could at least leave with the satisfaction of having done his duty and made the attempt to enlighten Pompey—perhaps also with the satisfaction of being waved off. What good is a prophet, after all, if he isn't ignored?

Days later, Caesar was voted a five-year extension of his Gallic command. The deal had held in the face of all that Cato had to throw at it. The triumvirate, which Cato had done so much to unwittingly and unwillingly bring into being, had new life.

· · ·

Outmaneuvered as he was, Cato was not alone: The sources note a band of admirers and well-wishers, and even the occasional young disciple, such as his imitator Marcus Favonius. As he fought his losing campaign against the triumvirs, he never appeared in public as a lone crank, but always as a faction leader. His followers were still ready, in some cases, to die for his cause. Neither Plutarch nor Cassius Dio speculate on the size of Cato's following or ask who was drawn to it, other than the "best" citizens—that is, those who identified with the aristocracy. But the voters who turned out to back his run for praetor, the crowds who came to hear him denounce the consuls, the mob that saved him from arrest and then, a day later, rioted at the Forum upon the victory of Pompey and Crassus, all raise the question: If Cato could rally such committed support, how could he wield so little influence? How could he be so well regarded and, on the greatest issues of the day, so comparatively ineffective?

The clearest explanation is that he was simply outnumbered. The passionate *optimas* crowds may have been an extremely vocal minority, but they were a minority nonetheless. Nor did Cato take any concrete steps to build his following or, until the last moment, to exploit chinks of envy or mistrust in the solid front of the triumvirate. On the contrary, his evermore-erratic public behavior seems to have been calculated to drive away support, not attract it. Yet he was admired enough to suffer no lasting harm from the campaign of character assassination carried out by Metellus Scipio and Clodius and to have been the people's choice for praetor before Pompey intervened. The backlash he led against the outrageous election, and against the triumvirs' tactics more generally, was enough to put their overt electoral meddling on hold for a time. On the whole, however, Cato's reputation was far out of proportion to his effectiveness. It seems that it was possible, for at least some Romans, to support Cato and the triumvirate at the same time. It was possible to love Cato as a moral exemplar, to be attracted to his commanding personality, and simultaneously to thrill to Caesar's heroic bulletins from Gaul—in other words, to honor Cato as a conversation piece without falling in behind his political platform.

The chronicler Valerius Maximus relates a small anecdote that captures the Roman public's complicated, conditional embrace of Cato. It was soon after the renewal of Caesar's command, on the Roman May Day, Floralia, a weeklong festival of blooming flowers and greenery, of drink and farces, of outrageously dyed clothing, of prostitutes parading as queens. Cato sat in the wooden stands of a makeshift theater, enjoying with the rest of the city a troupe of dancing, miming girls. As raucous as it was, Cato could point out that this, like all festivals, had its solemnity: It was a nod to the deep Latin past and to the rural fertility that gave the city life. As the dancing girls leaped and twisted on the stage, a friend leaned over to Cato with a message from somewhere else in the stands: The spectators would like to encourage the girls to take off their clothes, but are embarrassed to do so with Cato watching.

Without a word, in full view of the crowd, Cato stood up and made for the exit. "As he was leaving, the crowd loudly applauded him and then went back to their usual theatrical pleasures." The spectators hooted, the dancing girls stripped, and the Floral Games went on.

That was Rome's verdict on Cato: eager to applaud him for leaving, unwilling to follow him out; glad that someone was taking the trouble of objecting; ready to both cheer and ignore his "no." It was almost as if watching Cato was all the absolution they needed. And that was the verdict Cato himself seemed to seek out. After all, he had lived through four decades of Floral Games. He had no right to be surprised by the nudity. Why go, other than to make a show of walking out?

• • •

For Caesar, at his base of operations in northern Italy, news of his five-year extension in command was quickly spoiled by a more troubling dispatch. Two warlike German tribes—in their own language, they were called the Good Riders and the Faithful—had crossed the Rhine into northeastern Gaul, near the modern border of Germany and Belgium. The two tribes were hurriedly fleeing a third and even fiercer people on the far side of the river, but Caesar had little sympathy for them. This incursion of hundreds of thousands of men, women, and children, along with their herds, threatened to destabilize the tenuous calm he had brought to Rome's new possessions. The immigrants' camps would add a wealth of potential manpower to any rebellion against Roman rule. So Caesar marched his legions to the border to order the tribes back across the river and out of Gaul. Intercepted by a delegation sent to plead the Germans' case, Caesar offered them land on the east bank of the Rhine but no shelter on the Roman-controlled side. The Germans asked for three days to chew over the offer and insisted that Caesar not, in the meantime, come any closer to their camp. It was a strange request—especially since Caesar's scouts had brought word that the Germans' horse-mounted troops were nearly in striking distance.

Caesar ignored the appeal and cautiously closed in on the German camp. He was met a day later by a second embassy announcing that the tribes were still deliberating, and begging him again to stop the Roman march. To Caesar's mind, it was a play for time. Still, he agreed to march only four more miles to water that day and sent five thousand of his cavalry ahead first. Hours later, the cavalry was ambushed. A band of German horsemen caught the Roman lines off guard and sparked a panic by dismounting to stab the Roman horses in the belly and fight on foot. As Caesar's horses were driven into retreat, the Germans remounted and escaped back to camp, leaving seventy-four Romans dead.

When the tribes' chieftains arrived the next day under a flag of truce, calling the skirmish a miscommunication and pleading for forgiveness, an enraged Caesar shut his ears. He had them stripped of weapons and held under guard as he led his troops out for revenge. He commanded the cavalry personally, he writes, to soothe their spirits after the previous day's fright.

Caesar's men fell without warning on the leaderless tribes, who were fumbling for their weapons even as the Romans beat down their stockade. Caesar narrates the massacre in his history of the Gallic Wars (speaking of himself, as usual, in the third person, to lend an air of objectivity and grandeur to the proceedings):

[The Germans'] confusion being made apparent by their noise and tumult, our soldiers, excited by the treachery of the preceding day, rushed into the camp: Those who could readily get their arms, for a short time withstood our men and gave battle among their carts and baggage wagons; but the rest of the people, boys and women (for they had left their country and crossed the Rhine with all their families), began to fly in all directions; in pursuit of whom Caesar sent the cavalry.

When the Germans heard a noise behind them and saw that their families were being slain, they fled out of the camp, throwing away their arms and abandoning their standards, and when they had arrived at the confluence of the Meuse and the Rhine, the survivors despairing of further escape, as a great number of their countrymen had been killed, threw themselves into the river and there perished, overcome by fear, fatigue, and the violence of the stream.

In Caesar's telling, the tribes were utterly wiped out. Accounts of the dead run as high as three hundred thousand, and though the figure was likely exaggerated for effect, it was certainly among the greatest slaughters of the Gallic Wars. On the Roman side, in Caesar's dubious claim, not a single man lost his life. As for Caesar's captives, they were now chieftains without a people. Caesar informed them of what had been done that day, and "granted those whom he had detained in camp the liberty of departing. But dreading revenge and torture from the Gauls, whose lands they had harassed, they said that they desired to remain with him. Caesar granted them permission."

Carried down from the Rhine and over the Alps, news of this crushing victory raised Caesar's name to new heights and set off a Roman celebration. There were demands for a festival of thanksgiving and public sacrifices in gratitude to the gods. As the Senate prepared to vote Caesar these new honors, Cato rose to announce that a public sacrifice had his full support: "Let us sacrifice to the gods—because they do not turn the punishment for the general's folly and madness upon his soldiers, but spare the city."

Was Rome really about to honor Caesar—for a war crime? Because beneath Caesar's bluster about Germanic treachery, Cato insisted, a war crime was exactly what had occurred. Envoys were sacred. Truces were sacred. Yet Caesar had violated a truce, rounded up ambassadors like common criminals, used the confusion to run down and slaughter tens of thousands of women and children—and bragged about it!

Before the Senate could vote on a thanksgiving, Cato raised an alternative proposal: Arrest Caesar and surrender him to what was left of the tribes to punish as they saw fit.

There was, of course, no chance that anyone would dump a Roman general in chains beside a German campfire any time soon. Cato's call to hand over Caesar was of a piece with his crying "Thunder!" in the crowded Forum—another one of the hopeless, exaggerated gestures that were coming to define his role in Roman politics. But it showed in addition an intriguing concern for the rights of the conquered and the barbarian, claims that most of Cato's colleagues were ready to gloss right over. Cato shared the prejudices of his time, but he also held to a philosophy that urged him, at least in theory, to "look upon all people in general to be our fellow-countryfolk and -citizens." Cato's was not the cosmopolitanism of Marcus Aurelius, a later Stoic emperor, but there are the first beginnings of that tradition in his harsh judgment of exploitative provincial governors, his reluctance to take the Cyprus mission, his subversive advice to Ptolemy Auletes, and his insistence that barbarian tribesmen had a claim of justice to make even against a Roman proconsul.

Caesar was in no serious danger on this count. If the case ever came before a court—which it wouldn't—he could always plausibly claim that the Germans had broken the truce first, however wildly disproportionate his response. But he was infuriated enough to take time out from campaigning to dictate a long and scathing letter denouncing Cato, to be read aloud before the Senate. Even when Cato's power to harm him amounted to so little, there were few men who irritated Caesar more. From his tendency to write of Cato as a miserly drunk, we can make some guess as to the nature of the insults that spilled out across the Senate House.

Far from being ashamed to be specially called out from the Gallic front, Cato was only glad to have another excuse to make the case that Caesar was hiding his designs on the Republic behind a grossly inflated foreign threat:

> Assailing Caesar's plans from the outset and revealing clearly all his purpose, as if he were his fellow conspirator and partner and not his enemy, he declared that it was not the sons of Germans or

Celts whom they must fear, but Caesar himself, if they were in their right minds.

• • •

Yet, as 55 wound down, the three strongmen of the triumvirate were all safely out of reach. Caesar, arguing that he had to expand the war to cut off foreign aid to the tribes still resisting his rule, was preparing an unprecedented propaganda coup: the invasion of far-distant, half-mythical Britain. Crassus and thirty thousand men were en route to the East and its still-untapped wealth. Pompey was basking in the afterglow of his theater's opening spectacular—"the most carefully prepared and magnificent games within the memory of man." He alone of the three remained in Italy; lieutenants handled his Spanish responsibilities for him. The general, who was already Pompey the Great before he could grow a beard, seemed at last to be settling into a comfortable middle age. He was spotted up and down Italy's scenic retreats and country estates, arm in arm with his wife, Julia, Caesar's young daughter. It dawned on the Roman elite that theirs was no longer merely a political match: The two actually appeared to be in love.

With the Luca agreement sealed and carried out, the stakes of the election for 54 were lower than usual. The triumvirs' relative disengagement, combined with lingering public resentment over their strong-arm tactics, produced a victory for the *optimates*. Ahenobarbus, without risking his neck at all, was at last elevated to his rightful place as consul. And Cato was finally praetor, a chief judge of the Republic.

Yet he was a year late—and he seemed to know it. Now that he had real power under the constitution, he refused to shed his strange, prophetic persona. Whenever a law enacted under Caesar's consulship came up before his court, he used absurd circumlocutions to avoid its proper title, which would have forced him to utter Caesar's name. He retreated further into Stoic convention flouting, appearing in the Forum and even presiding over capital trials flagrantly barefoot and with only a simple loincloth beneath his rough toga. As 54 rolled into an unusually scorching summer, some used the heat to excuse Cato's attire. But Cato only pointed out that the oldest statues on the Capitoline Hill, statues of Romulus and others of the founders, showed them dressed in the same austere way. It was as if a senator in our times came to the Capitol dressed in knee breeches and a powdered wig. At the same time,

Cato drank more openly, and it was a point of contention between his friends and enemies whether he conducted state business under the influence of his midday wine.

All of that—from a chief judge, no less—naturally distracted from the *optimates'* efforts to use the courts as a propaganda weapon against the triumvirate. Yet 54 still saw a flurry of political trials. At least half a dozen of the triumvirs' friends were hauled into the dock that year, and Cato presided over many of the highest-profile cases. His most unorthodox move, however, came not in the courts but in an attempt to work around them.

The coming elections looked to be even more money drenched than usual. By July, Cicero reported, spending on cash bribes had depleted so many of the usual lenders' accounts that the interest rate doubled. It was in this flagrantly corrupt atmosphere that a unique delegation approached Cato with a plan to take the law into private hands.

In the summer of 54, as luck would have it, every candidate for people's tribune considered himself too cash poor to afford the skyrocketing price of office. Each professed a desire to put bribes on hold for the year, but each was afraid to put himself at a unilateral disadvantage. Whichever aspiring tribune first tipped his hand to the others, the entire field soon came together around a joint solution, a contract to swear off all bribes. As a security, each candidate would pledge to forfeit five hundred sesterces of his own money if he was caught breaking the deal. And as their private judge, they unanimously chose a man of incorruptible reputation: Cato.

Cato, no doubt taking grave pleasure in his new power to wipe out bribes at a stroke, witnessed the contract and took a written pledge for each candidate's cash (though, so as not to sully himself as a banker, he refused to handle any of the money himself). This unprecedented arrangement soon became the talk of the election season. Even Cicero allowed himself to hope that Cato had stumbled on a new model for politics. "If the election proves free, as it is thought it will," he wrote to his brother Quintus, "Cato alone can do more than all the laws and all the judges." And indeed, the Roman voters made little, if any, money from the aspiring tribunes that year.

On the election day for tribunes, Cato positioned himself at the head of the assembly to monitor the vote. After all the ballots were cast, he stood before the Roman people to announce, on his authority as election judge, that one of the candidates had cheated. It is not clear whether Cato had conducted a private investigation and waited to reveal the results until the most damaging and most watched moment or whether something strange in the vote itself led him to cry foul. Either way, he demanded that the cheater (whose name is not recorded) instantly forfeit his share to his rivals.

In that moment, it indeed looked as if Cato had done what the laws and the judges could not. He had orchestrated a clean election and, with all the city's eyes on him, delivered a ringing denunciation of a corrupt politician. His accusation carried all the humiliation of a conviction in court. But even this triumph began to unravel the moment it was achieved. Perhaps Cato pushed too hard and shamed the cheater too harshly: The remaining candidates thanked him for doing his duty with his usual uprightness, then canceled the contract on the spot and insisted that their rival keep his money. The cheater, they all agreed, had suffered enough. Maybe this was mercy; but then again, maybe it was confirmation that membership in the small intermarried club of elite politics outweighed contracts, outweighed clean elections, outweighed any push against corruption that ran the risk of embarrassing anyone of note. We can't blame Cato if for an instant he returned in memory to his days as a crusading quaestor, to reforms that evaporated the minute he left the treasury. Once again, he found himself trying to effect lasting change through the loud display of his own virtue; once again, he succeeded only momentarily. He had tried to legislate by personality, and once again he had only set the shining example so honored in the breach.

Worse, where Cicero found something to admire in Cato's extralegal inventiveness, most of Rome found something to fear and suspect. "This conduct of Cato caused more vexation and odium than anything else; [the citizens] felt that he was investing himself with the powers of Senate, courts, and magistrates." It couldn't have been overlooked that the same man who railed against the triumvirs for concentrating power and overstepping laws had—however pure his motives—attempted something eerily similar.

The experiment was not repeated. And as the candidates for every other office readied their campaigns for the fall, the cash flowed as lavishly as ever.

•　•　•

Pompey, meanwhile, spent much of the year doing what he could to help his beleaguered friends fend off the *optimates'* judicial onslaught. He acted as a character witness here, bought off a juror there, but by August, his grieving mind was elsewhere. That month, his wife, Julia, died in childbirth. The frail infant, a girl, held to life for only a few days beyond her mother. Julia had not only been the unexpected love of Pompey's life, she had been the human cord binding Rome's two most ambitious men in an uneasy alliance. She had made Caesar and Pompey kinsmen for a time, and now the cord was undone.

It was not immediately clear how the two, newly liberated from each other, would respond once the mourning was over. Pompey had planned a private funeral on his country estate—but the matter was not private. The Roman people seemed to sense that something momentous had broken: The ashes were openly seized from Pompey and carried in state by a swelling mass down to the Field of Mars, in the shadow of his theater. There, over the furious objections of the consul Ahenobarbus, Julia was laid to rest in public ground. "And everywhere surging tumult and discordant speeches prevailed, since the marriage alliance which had hitherto veiled rather than restrained the ambition of the two men was now at an end."

· · ·

But even in such fearful times, the mundane business of corruption remained a constant. From late August to early September, Cato presided over the rather grubby trial of Marcus Aemilius Scaurus, another associate of Pompey, and the unimpressive son of a far more respected senatorial father. Scaurus wanted the next year's consulship, and as governor of Sardinia, he had extorted enough silver to buy it outright. There couldn't have been, it was maliciously said, more than 120 Sardinians whom he had failed to rob. A young friend of Cato came forward to prosecute him for the gross provincial theft, and not a moment could be spared. Unless Scaurus was tried and convicted almost immediately, he would be free to use the money in question to win the consulship and its immediate immunity.

Scaurus was in great fear of the presiding judge, and for good reason, but he had access to one of the most intimidating legal teams ever seen in a Roman court. Six different advocates—an almost unprecedented degree of overkill—rose to speak for Scaurus, and among them was the best of the best. Cicero was not one to waste effort in a winning cause. He simply pointed out that the case rested on the testimony of Sardinians, and that Sardinians were well-known liars: "The worthlessness of their nation is such that they think that liberty is only to be distinguished from slavery by the boundless license it gives for telling lies." Scaurus completed the show with a bravura performance in the customary defendant's rags, "and he greatly impressed the jury by his unkempt clothing, his tears, his references to his generosity . . . and particularly his appeals to his father's reputation."

The vote to acquit was overwhelming—so overwhelming that a threateningly large crowd of spectators, many drawn from the Scaurus family clientele, rallied around Cicero's instant demand that the prosecutors be put on trial for slander. Cato, in a rare moment of mob capitulation, admitted the new charge into court. The prosecution of the prosecutors ultimately went nowhere. But Cato had seen Roman justice at its ugliest, from a front-row seat on the bench.

What had saved Scaurus, more than his rags or Cicero's race-baiting, was the near-unified backing of the Roman elite. With the exception of Cato's circle and Scaurus's direct rivals for the consulship, his case uniquely cut across partisan lines: *Optimas* or *popularis,* friend or foe of the triumvirate, the right to grow rich on a province was held nearly inviolable. Had Scaurus been disqualified from running for office on the grounds of that enrichment, there were few men in public life whom the precedent would not touch.

It may have been his experience in presiding over such a dispiriting affair that shaped Cato's renewed push against public corruption. There was little realistic action to be taken against provincial extortion, which had just received a ringing vote of confidence, nor did Cato have any future as a private election monitor. But he could move against the loophole through which Scaurus had almost escaped before his trial even began. A candidate could pass nearly instantly from buying an election to enjoying the legal immunity of office. By dispensing enough bribes, he could shield himself from any charge of bribery. Cato's solution to this problem was a radical one: Treat every candidate as guilty of bribery until proven innocent. Guided by his assumption of universal bribery (which, after nearly two decades' personal experience of Roman elections, could not have appeared very far off the mark), Cato proposed a Senate decree binding on every winning candidate for every office, whether accused by a rival or not. Each magistrate-elect would submit his campaign accounts in court. If the court uncovered evidence of vote buying, the victory could be declared void.

Cato's corruption court, had it been created and its decisions enforced, could have reshaped Roman politics and stripped the triumvirate of its most entrenched advantage. It was, for a man so invested in the practice of personality-based reform, a rare attempt at systemic change. Because bribery was as widely denounced as it was practiced, a reluctant majority of senators had no choice but to line up behind Cato's law, which regarded them all as potentially corrupt.

But a popular uprising snuffed out the proposal before it could be tested. For an urban populace with little stake or voice in the debates of the Senate or the rulings of the consuls, the gifts and favors that bound them into a favorite candidate's following were the only remaining threads tying them to the political process. An election without free meals and shows, without the yearly gifts of money, would be a drab thing. Electoral bribery was one of the few means of Roman redistribution—informal, but highly reliable. *Optimates* and their sympathizers might denounce the dependency of the idle, urban multitude, but few stopped to consider the system of enslaved labor that made such dependency inevitable. The Roman people were not about to give up their bribes, and neither were the ambitious senators who tacitly encouraged them.

No sooner was Cato's Senate decree announced than it was lustily vetoed by the tribunes and the people's assembly. No sooner did Cato show his face in the Forum than he was mobbed, cursed, and stoned. Ducking those rocks that he could, Cato forced his way to the high ground of the rostra and shamed the crowd into silence; he was still respected enough and feared enough to do that. But no effort of his could persuade the Roman people to change their minds. His failed attempt at election reform, fresh on the heels of his perceived power grab at the tribunes' election, did lasting damage to his popularity.

Nor did his Senate colleagues seem to mind the outcome. Of course, at the next session, the senators roundly praised Cato for standing up to the mob, as a good *optimas* should. Cato only pointed out, with his usual tartness, that their support was entirely absent when it mattered. He had faced the angry mass alone. "I cannot praise *you* for leaving an imperiled praetor in the lurch and not coming to his aid." Evidently, he sensed that the result—which allowed them to publicly to back an election reform that would never become law—was close to ideal for most of the senators.

. . .

By now, it was clear that the *optimates'* strategy in the courts was faltering. It had been a year of acquittals—and the year's fattest target seemed ready to join in the escape. That target was one Aulus Gabinius, ex-consul, ex-governor of Syria, wealthy and influential backer of Pompey, and the man who (for the alleged fabulous sum of ten thousand talents) had led the force that placed Ptolemy Auletes back on the throne of Egypt—in sum, "a trafficker in provinces." In September, Gabinius faced a charge of treason for marching his troops into Egypt without the Senate's permission—and in defiance of an ancient prophecy forecasting disaster if Rome ever sent an army to aid an Egyptian king. The trial coincided with a disastrous flood on the Tiber. As homes and stores and crops were washed away, Gabinius's more superstitious enemies could console themselves with the thought that the gods, at least, had rendered the proper verdict on his treason. Cicero was generally a polished skeptic in such matters—but even he, in a letter to his brother, couldn't resist reaching for the appropriate lines from Homer:

> When guilty mortals break the eternal laws,
> And judges bribed betray the righteous cause,
> From their deep beds [Zeus] bids the rivers rise,
> And opens all the flood-gates of the skies.

Ever since Gabinius had lent his weighty backing to Cicero's exile, Rome's foremost lawyer had not forgiven him. It took a personal appeal from Pompey to stop Cicero from leading the treason prosecution himself. In the hands of a far-less-experienced advocate, the complex case was sufficiently botched (and the jury sufficiently bought) for Gabinius to go free.

The next month, however, the *optimates* had a second bite at him. Gabinius couldn't be retried for treason. But *profiting* from treason, in the matter of the ten thousand talents, was a separate crime—and this new charge came before Cato's court. From the lengths to which they went to protect their man, we can judge the triumvirs' apprehension that he would not escape twice. Pompey arranged a special proacquittal rally, where he read out an endorsement letter from Caesar in Gaul; he went so far as to beg the jurors directly for an acquittal. He also put extraordinary pressure on Cicero to swallow his enmity and lead the defense team.

We can only imagine Cato's disgust when Gabinius's new counsel rose to plead before his court—but no one was more disgusted than Cicero himself. His defense of Gabinius was one of the few speeches he was too embarrassed to publish. It was a halfhearted effort and a failure. The Senate hated Gabinius for flouting its authority. The merchant *equites,* who believed themselves cheated out of their tax-farming contracts during his governorship, were no friends. Even the plebeians were said to hold Gabinius accountable for the great Tiber flood. To Cato's evident pleasure, and perhaps Cicero's quiet enjoyment, Gabinius was convicted. Either unable or unwilling to pay the exorbitant fine—set to match those same ten thousand talents—Gabinius chose exile.

For Cato and his conservatives, an uneven, disappointing year had ended in a rare victory. They had for once humbled Pompey the Great. But, beyond bragging rights, did it make a difference?

Though he had suffered a direct rebuke in court, Pompey was still a giant, wealthy and well connected beyond belief, resting on a wide power base of loyal veterans and provincial clients. No single verdict could change that. But it now began to seem possible that Cato's faction could, in the words of classicist Elaine Fantham, "regain control of him and restore him to dependence on the Optimates." If they could not break Pompey's power, they might make it work for them, "adapting it to their own needs by first isolating him and then claiming alliance as the price of the political status he longed for."

This was, in other words, an attempt to undo Cato's rejection of Pompey all those years earlier, to repair the damage that rejection had done to the conservative cause. And it was the continuation of the strategy belatedly advanced by Cato himself in his meeting with Pompey the year before, when his advice—break the triumvirate and turn against Caesar—had been so coolly rejected. Then, Pompey had no good reason to listen to the *optimates'* message. Now they had his attention. And with that attention, with that powerful and needy gaze turned on him again, Cato might have his return to relevance.

• • •

The problem, of course, was that this would be relevance on someone else's terms. So, even as the *optimates* took the first, tentative steps toward co-opting Pompey, Cato took great pains to make clear that, no matter the outcome, he would remain his own man. When Pompey loaned Caesar six thousand of his troops in a show of breezy confidence, Cato protested that "armies of this great size—and arms and horses—are now the mutual gifts of private persons." When the most hard-core Pompeians began quietly pushing their man for a dictatorship—as the only one who could end the violence in the Forum and at the polls—Cato groused that Pompey was "using anarchy to win himself a monarchy." And when Cato had the right to govern a province at the end of his year in office, he chose instead to stay where he saw the greatest danger: in Rome.

It was still his highest pleasure to make a spectacle of his eccentric uprightness. In the new year, 53, the job of planning the public games happened to fall to Favonius, Cato's ardent disciple. He in turn let Cato do the honors of picking the prizes for the winning athletes and the best actors. In other years, at more lavish spectacles, the victors won gold crowns—but gold was a useless luxury. At Cato's games, the victors wore crowns of simple olive leaves and won trophies a man could put to use: a head of lettuce, a basket of radishes, a jar of wine, salt pork, an armful of figs, or a bundle of wood.

Rome loved it: In a city inured to glittering spectacle, Cato had hit on the latest novelty. As he handed out the prizes, he was even seen to crack a smile—because, Cato insisted, one was *supposed* to smile at festivals. Had the storm never come, this is the Cato who might have lived to 90: alternately laughed at and loved, and left alone, a mascot of the Roman past.

• • •

Pentheus, said the tragic poets, had been a great king, wealthy and feared and inscrutable. He was the cousin of a god, but in his great pride, he mocked the god and locked him in prison, until the god dissolved his chains and drove the king's family mad with lust and rage; and in their mad ecstasy, they ripped Pentheus limb from limb and wrenched off his head. Crassus's head was Pentheus.

Crassus's head, reduced to a theater prop, was in the banqueting hall of the Parthian king. Crassus's army was gone, led into the desert by a guide who was a planted spy, ambushed and pressed into battle already half dead of heat and thirst, wiped out by an army of Parthian horse-archers who could fire backward as they rode. Crassus was dead, betrayed and stabbed under a flag of truce. And on the night when proof of the great victory was brought before the Parthian king, his court was watching the tragedy of proud Pentheus, and the actors fought one another for the right to hold up the shocked head of Crassus while they spoke the climactic lines of the play.

In the summer of 53, the surviving fraction of Crassus's army brought word back to Rome that the triumvirate was dead.

11

ULTIMATUM

The news came to a city on the edge of anarchy. As Crassus met his disaster, Rome was entering its sixth straight month without consuls: A stalemate between Pompey and the *optimates* kept delaying the elections for 53, month after month. Not until July would the Republic have a head again.

It was anarchy in more than the constitutional sense. The campaign for the next year's offices began almost as soon as the consuls for 53 were installed, and it was the bloodiest election Rome had ever seen, an unending, rolling brawl. The violence exploded out of fear: fear of the Parthians and their revenge in the East, rumbles of a new rising in Gaul, the collapse of the triumvirate and the factions' scramble for position in the rubble. Into the compacted space of this tense, truncated election season were pressed some of Rome's most volatile personalities. One was Metellus Scipio, who had libeled his way to victory over Cato in 55. Another was an obvious stand-in for Pompey. Given those choices, Cato found himself backing the brutal Milo, the conservative-leaning gang leader whose hired gladiators had stared down Clodius for much of the 50s. And as bad luck would have it, Clodius was a candidate in the same election; though he wanted a different office—the praetorship—he gleefully singled out his old enemy, Milo, as the main competition. Clodius, who by now had been on every side and no side of Roman politics, loaned out his armed men to anyone willing to bloody Milo's face.

The Forum was the chief contested ground in the four-sided running battle. As the struggle waxed and waned, first one gang and then another

192

set up armed camp beside the Senate House and the temples, until driven out in its turn. Plutarch writes:

> The people went down into the Forum under pay, contending on behalf of their paymaster, not with votes, but with bows and arrows, swords and slings. Often, too, they would defile the rostra with blood and corpses before they separated, leaving the city to anarchy like a ship drifting about without a steersman.

With no authority on hand to restore order or call a vote, the drift continued through the winter and into the new year.

For the second consecutive year, the calendar turned without consuls. "The Romans," writes Cassius Dio, "were absolutely without a government." The explosion that brought the anarchy to a climax was officially an accident— but even the least-observant Roman could have seen it coming from many months' distance.

• • •

January 20, 52, was supposed to be a pause in the unending campaign. Milo was traveling to his hometown, just south of Rome on the Appian Way, to preside over the installation of a new priest. Slaves and gladiators made up the entourage trailing his private coach, including the famous Eudamas and Birria, who served as Milo's most trusted enforcers when they weren't slaughtering beasts in the arena. Trotting in the opposite direction, back toward Rome, came a man on horseback: Clodius. In his escort were thirty mounted slaves with swords, "as was the custom at the time for people making a trip," according to an offhand remark in a commentary on Cicero's speeches, which reflects sharply on the violence of those days.

Only hoofbeats and footsteps sounded as the heads of the columns met and passed; a glare between the two rivals, and otherwise silence.

But Eudamas and Birria were trained killers and couldn't help themselves. Tangling and shoving between the gladiators and Clodius's slaves, then curses, then weapons drawn. An enraged Clodius wheeled on his horse and in the process made the mistake of looking at Birria the wrong way, and before Clodius could defend himself, the gladiator fell on him, stabbing him deep in the shoulder, and the rout was on. In minutes, the road was Milo's.

Of Clodius's thirty-slave train, some lay dead in the mud; some hid and bled. A small handful escaped with their wounded master slung on a horse, running for the safety of a tavern they knew in the next town. Milo, even as he caught his breath, followed the consequences to their end. He knew his enemy: If this did not end in the death of Clodius, it would end in his own.

• • •

Weak and bleeding, Clodius was dragged from a poor bed by rough hands. He seemed to have been too proud to beg for his life. It was hours before his body was found, dumped like refuse in the road, not far from a roadside shrine of the implacable Good Goddess.

• • •

For a decade, Rome's poorest had come to the house of Clodius to beg favors and spill grievances and offer their votes and line up behind the rich man's son they took as their own. Now they came to moan over his corpse. In the packed atrium of Clodius's house, the voice of his wife was heard above them all, wailing and numbering the wounds.

The wake lasted through the night. In the morning the crowd swelled farther, and now, among the rags of the poor were seen the scattered togas of gentlemen. Not a day had passed before Milo's rivals for the consulship moved to turn the death to their advantage. Just as it was, not even wrapped for burial, the body of Clodius was carried down to the Forum, and the morning rang with hateful speeches against Milo and his allies. But most persuasive of all was Clodius, naked and barefoot, lying dead on the rostra, rallying the crowd for the last time. They were too furious for distinctions. Try as the speakers might to channel their anger toward Milo, the rage overflowed its banks. At the urging of a Senate scribe who had served and loved Clodius, the people laid him on the Senate floor and made the whole Senate House his pyre. Benches and tables, state papers and records of debates fed the flames.

As Clodius and the Senate burned, sparks flew and caught on the timbers of a neighbor: the Basilica Porcia, the grand old meeting hall of Cato the

Elder, the first of its kind. It was the one public building over which Cato claimed a special ownership and took special care. At eighteen, he had fought to see that not a single pillar was moved from its ancestral place. Now, word came to him that the pillars were practically all that remained of the husk.

* * *

From the burning Forum, the crowd turned to the house of Pompey. Soon they were trampling down his gardens and waving the consuls' fasces, which they had snatched from their resting place and presented at his door, as if it were enough for the great man simply to emerge and take hold of the axes and rods. Clodius, in the last years of his life, had been no friend of Pompey—but his desperate and leaderless crowd saw no one else strong enough to avenge his death. The cries went up: "Consul! Dictator!" In other words, he could take his pick.

The Senate's response, though more restrained, was similar in substance. As their home smoldered that afternoon, Cato and his fellow senators met in an emergency session at a temple to pass the Final Act, vesting temporary power to restore order in the few magistrates still in office, and in Pompey—who was granted authority to levy the troops he needed to quiet the Forum and the streets. The senators and the Clodians may have despised one another, but neither side saw an alternative.

Ever since his return from the East, Pompey had been after one prize above all: the establishment's ungrudging approval. Now he almost had it—though the Senate had preferred to see its house burn down first. Still, Pompey, who had perfected his pose of reluctance during decades of practice, remained outwardly blasé and said nothing but the right things. He respected the Senate fathers and would always follow their advice. He had no desire to offend Caesar and would ask his advice, too. "He did not authorize anybody either to seek the [consulship] or to quit seeking it, and he had no intention of interfering with the power of the Roman people."

While Pompey demurred, there were no elections, no consuls, no revenge for Clodius. The Senate stewed, unable to impose a solution. Pompey, while beginning to raise a new army, waited to give his final answer. Whenever he showed his face in public, there was always someone to hail him as dictator.

• • •

With the ashes cooling in the Forum, it became clear that the Clodians' rampage had sparked its own backlash. Clodius, after all, was rich in enemies—and it began to look as if the destruction of the Senate House had angered more Romans than the murder that provoked it. This was very good news for Milo. He had washed himself off and slunk back to Rome on the night of the inferno. Once it was evident that Clodius's crowd had gone too far and that he would see no immediate punishment, Milo edged back into the public light. Soon, he was in full campaign mode again, shaking hands for the consulship, rallying his gang of backers, and handing coins to voters by the sackful. Pompey was still mulling the Senate's offer.

It was not long before the murder became one more political shibboleth to divide the *populares* and the *optimates*, with an Appian Way party line for each side. Clodius had only had twenty-six slaves, and Milo had chased him down with more than three hundred. He hadn't even regained consciousness when Milo finished him off—and then pried the ring off his finger for good measure.

No—the entire incident had been a setup, a clear ambush staged by Clodius, and he had paid for it with his life. Milo, acting in self-defense, had done Rome a favor—and he deserved to be rewarded.

That line had a number of powerful backers. Chief among them was Cicero, who considered both himself and the state freed at last of a dangerous enemy. He celebrated the "battle" that cost Clodius his life, and when Cato announced that he shared the same position on the killing, Cicero thanked him effusively. In a letter written two years later, Cicero still recalled with gratitude Cato's willingness to lend his moral authority to Milo's defense:

> I pass over your having shared the hatred I excited, the dangers I ran, all the storms that I have encountered, and your having been entirely ready to have shared them much more fully if I had allowed it; and finally your having regarded my enemy as your own; you even manifested your approval of his death—thus showing me clearly how much you valued me—by supporting the cause of Milo in the Senate.

Partisan animus surely had something to do with Cato's firm defense of Clodius's killer; like Cicero, he had good reason to loathe Clodius. Freshly returned from Cyprus, Cato had been willing to sabotage his friendship with Cicero by speaking up for Clodius, even if only lukewarmly—but the question then had turned on relative technicalities. Now, on a genuine matter of life and death, common hatred of Clodius and all that he had made the two suffer came to the fore. The demon figure of Clodius had seized a dominant place in Cicero's mind—so much so that Cato's support of his killer went to great lengths to heal the friendship of these two victimized senators.

To be fair to both, the evidence coming from the survivors of the "battle" was still sketchy and conflicting, and the ambush hypothesis seemed as plausible as any other. How shocking was it, really, that a man who had lived by organized violence had also died by it?

•   •   •

The Roman riots had more than a Roman audience: They were eagerly watched in Gaul. The chafing tribes, thoroughly beaten down, saw in Rome's political crisis a last opportunity. Never, the chieftains guessed, would Caesar have such a distraction at home again. He might even return to Rome to restore order, and so be cut off from his armies. In that desperate hope, less than a month after Clodius's death, the chieftains struck their first blow. At sunrise in a rich trading town on the Loire River, they massacred a community of Roman merchants and killed the soldiers who kept Caesar's provisions. News of the uprising was shouted across Gaul: As Caesar reports, "whenever a more important and remarkable event takes place, they transmit the intelligence through their lands and districts by a yell; the others take it up in succession, and pass it to their neighbors, as happened on this occasion." By sunset of that first day, he writes, the signal for revolt had traveled more than 160 miles.

Caesar records their rallying cry: "A single and united Gaul, all of the same mind, can defy the universe." For any Roman who heard them, the shouts bore a sick echo of Mithridates' great rising in the East. It had started in just this way, with the synchronized death of Roman traders far from home.

•   •   •

March came, and still there was a skeleton government, still disarray in the Forum. Pompey bided his time—still—for a better offer from the Senate. Caesar, busy planning his answer in Gaul, sent word that he could support a government of Pompey—with conditions. And Cato's lifelong fear of Pompey seemed—a little—to be softening. More and more, it appeared that calling off the elections entirely and putting the state in Pompey's hands was the least-bad option.

Not long before, Cato had accused Pompey of sowing anarchy to win a monarchy. Now, the only questions were how the monarchy would come and how long it would last. In Cato's nightmare scenario, the warring factions of the Forum would demand that Pompey judge their claims—and having invited Pompey into the scrum, they would find that he chose to stay there, as dictator. In the East, Pompey had settled the civil wars of petty kingdoms in much the same way; what was to stop him from "settling" the Forum war in his favor? If the government was inevitably going to Pompey, Cato reasoned, it should go as a gift from the Senate. That way, at least nominally, the Senate would be able to take it back. It was, in Cato's view, "the most moderate of unconstitutional measures." Under most circumstances, for Cato, "moderate" and "unconstitutional" had no business being mentioned in the same breath. That he was suddenly prepared to parse degrees of unconstitutionality shows his estimation of the crisis and its gravity.

"Consul! Dictator!" the crowd in Pompey's garden had chanted, as if there were no distinction. But there was—a stark one. Cato and his contemporaries had only had one experience of dictatorship in their lives: the rule of Sulla, and his government by death list and charnel house. Fairly or not, any mention of dictatorship conjured up that terror from their youths. But there was also a more substantive reason to deny a dictatorship to Pompey: Dictators could never be held legally accountable for their actions. Consuls could.

With that small consolation in mind, Cato's son-in-law Bibulus rose in the Senate to make the *optimates'* final offer: Pompey would be sole consul. A consul without a colleague was supposed to be a contradiction in terms: Since the days of the kings, the very thing that distinguished a consul from a monarch was the presence of a coequal rival to check his ambition. But any debate on the measure was headed off—to many senators' shock—by Cato. His support for Pompey was grudging and laconic: "Any government is better than no government at all." Whatever opposition remained crumbled when it became clear that the unprecedented scheme had the endorsement of Rome's strictest constitutionalist. The senators need not have been so surprised: Bibulus, who often acted as his father-in-law's mouthpiece, would not have offered the consulship unless Cato had been with him from the start.

•   •   •

So—were Pompey and Cato now friends? Pompey, for his part, seemed willing to forget and forgive. One of his first official actions as consul was an invitation to Cato to join him for a parley in his gardens outside the city and its stinking tumult. Cato arrived, somewhat guardedly, to find that the man who had practically ordered him dead was all but gone, replaced by a handshaking, back-patting politician, full of thanks that Cato had finally come to his senses. Pompey begged for any advice Cato had to give on restoring order and even invited him to be his "associate in government." That ambiguous offer seemed to hold out hope that, once the Forum had quieted down, Pompey might name Cato his fellow consul.

But Cato, fresh from a painful concession, was at great pains to insist that he would answer to no one, that he would be no man's junior partner. He was not Pompey's friend—though, rather disingenuously, he added that he had never been Pompey's enemy. He was first and only a friend of the Republic. If Pompey was finally prepared to act like one as well, then they might find common ground. Did Pompey want his advice? Good: Cato was always willing to talk. In public, he would give Pompey advice whether he wanted it or not. Even at such a disadvantage, Cato would never shed the *optimates'* habitual condescension: They still regarded Pompey, at best, as a useful tool.

Cato spent the rest of the year trying to walk a thin line between influence and independence. His agility was put to the test almost immediately, as the consul moved quickly to restore order. Pompey had, by now, decided that Milo had to go. He believed rumors that Milo, feeling himself cheated out of power, was preparing an attempt on his life. More fundamentally, he knew that Milo was every bit as unpredictable as Clodius had been. By ordering the killing of Clodius, Milo had also murdered his own usefulness. Pompey had once been happy to exploit Milo's muscle; now he turned on him

199

with little compunction. The consul's first proposal was a strong law "on force"—that is, against political violence. It was written to give every retroactive justification to convict Milo, along with the Clodians who had burned down the Senate. It even created a special court to try their cases, whose jurors would be handpicked by Pompey. Though Cato and Cicero worked to shield Milo to the end, the law, offered in the wake of Pompey's clear mandate to end political violence, passed easily. Yet Cato still had a role to play. The consul wanted a clean conviction—and if the jury was going to look incorruptible, it had to include Cato.

Cicero, the natural choice to defend Milo, prepared his case. And as Rome readied for a new wave of trials—an accounting for the chaos that had gripped the city for months—Pompey brought forward a second good-government proposal: a crackdown on election buying. That year's candidates had gone to such outrageous lengths of bribery that Pompey felt justified in fast-tracking prosecutions, in ramping up penalties, and even in extending new penalties to corruption cases up to twenty years old. It looked, almost, like a law Cato might have written—if Cato hadn't grown exhausted of seeing a generation's worth of clean-election laws do so little to clean up elections. Cato knew something of failed corruption laws, and on that basis, he advised the consul that the new law would be more effective if it were less ambitious. Rather than dredge up cases from as far back as the year 70 and pack the courts with a procession of elderly witnesses, Rome would do better to focus its energy on the bribes that had yet to be handed out. Cato had a reasonable point here (one that could have applied just as well to the ex post facto law against Milo): Was it really fair to punish Romans under a law that hadn't existed when they committed their crimes?

Pompey seems to have been swayed by these arguments, and he moved to shrink his law's retroactive window—an indication that Cato, even in his standoffishness, still had a good deal of influence on the consul when he deigned to exercise it. Just as persuasive, on the same side as Cato, were Caesar's friends. Their man had dispensed plenty of electoral cash on his way to the consulship, and they weren't about to see the threat of yet another prosecution hanging over his head. Caesar—under Cato's standing threat to prosecute him for the irregularities of his consulship and his conduct in Gaul—was already in legal trouble enough.

• • •

Four days of Milo's trial passed. There was not a drink to be had in Rome. There would be a furious crowd for the finale under any circumstances, but Pompey could at least keep it from being drunk. He had ordered every tavern and wineshop in the city shuttered.

Cato and his fellow jurymen processed into a court ringed by Pompey's soldiers, weapons at the ready, and ringed again by a throng baying for Milo's head. The soldiers were on hand, officially, to protect the court from the mob; unofficially, the soldiers and the mob were on the same side. They were there, everyone understood, to manifest the consul's opinion and see that it was carried out. Milo's remaining friends understood, as well, and largely kept indoors. Pompey, surveying the scene from on high, amid his bodyguards on the steps of the Treasury, was doing what he did best: quietly lording over.

Cicero, the sole advocate for the accused, was not a physically brave man. He began his defense trembling at the armed men and the near-lynch mob. But he earned some chuckles with a little joke about the contrast between the puny lawyer and his burly client. He picked up force and confidence as he went on, mastering his fear and shouting over the crowd when it looked set to overwhelm him, shouting it down at points. By the time he was halfway through his three hours, it was clear that this was the performance of his career. By the end, as he mounted to his emotional climax, soldiers and mob and Pompey only listened in silence:

> Would that the gods had granted that Publius Clodius should not only be alive, but should even be praetor, consul, dictator, rather than I should see this sight—oh, immortal gods!—before I should see this brave man, this man who deserves to be saved by you, judges, in this plight! . . .
>
> Shall this man, born for his country, die in any other land except his country? . . . Ungrateful will this land be if it banishes him—miserable if it loses him.
>
> But I must stop. I cannot speak any longer for weeping, and this man forbids me to defend him with tears.

201

That, at least, was how Cicero imagined it, and how he recorded it for posterity. In reality, the stirring scene he wrote for himself never happened; few of those words he composed ever left his mouth.

He may have gone to court that morning with a brilliant defense of Milo in his head—but he was too frightened of the soldiers to get the words out. He spoke for a short, shaking time and broke off to seek cover once the boos (which the troops did nothing to stop) grew too loud to make himself heard.

Milo was left alone at the mercy of the jury, which overwhelmingly voted for his exile. Cato, "who had not concealed [his view] that the death of Publius Clodius had been good for the state," was one of the handful of votes for acquittal. His unintimidated support for Milo played into Pompey's hands: It made the trial look fairer than it was.

Cicero, as if somehow to undo his embarrassment, spent the next weeks polishing the text of his speech to the shine we see in it today. A brilliant piece of prose, an all-time classic of oratory, it was useless when most urgently needed. Nor could it stop Pompey from shoveling dirt on Milo's political grave. Even after the exile, the consul made sure that Milo was convicted in absentia of bribery, illegal association, and (for good measure) murder.

* * *

It was a powerful, chilling message, joined soon after by the conviction of the scribe who had incited the Forum fire, along with some of Clodius's most violent henchmen. With his trials and his troops, Pompey made the case that he was not a partisan of either side, but only of order—which was gradually finding its way back to the city. Even so, he had his share of embarrassments along the way. Pompey had, for instance, barred the irrelevance of fawning character witnesses from his trials—but when a close friend was in the dock, he broke his own law and ordered the reading of a long, praise-laden testimonial. Cato, who happened to be on the jury, was not about to let this hypocrisy go unnoticed: He theatrically put his hands over his ears (there is no record of whether he added, "I'M NOT LISTENING!") and disrupted the court until the reading was done. He was dismissed as a result, but striking such an honest man from the jury seems to have been taken as a sign of guilt. Pompey's friend was convicted.

Still, that was a sideshow: On the whole, Pompey could claim that he had efficiently carried out the Senate's mandate. He had earned his continued place at the head of the state. But he had another mandate—from Caesar.

Even as he was ordering his men to dig their way out of winter quarters and march through the snow of the Alps toward the revolt, Caesar kept an eye fixed on his future in Rome. *Imperium* and immunity would be gone at the end of 49, and Cato's vow stood: As soon as the command expired, he and the *optimates* would haul Caesar into court. Caesar could keep a trial at bay by jumping immediately into the consulship for 48—but only if he could jump directly from Gaul. As the law now read, however, he would have to campaign at Rome in person, and his commander's immunity would evaporate as soon as he entered the city. That small window—when Caesar was within the walls, without his *imperium*, and not yet consul—was all that Cato would require. And that prosecution, if it ever came, would be a struggle to make Milo's recent trial look like playacting: "He would be obliged, like Milo, to make his defense in a court hedged about by armed men." Caesar, gambler though he was, would never put himself in a position of such naked risk.

All of this had been clear to Caesar by 52, if not earlier: He had played out the game many moves in advance. When he signaled his consent to Pompey's sole consulship, he already had a condition in mind: that the law be amended to allow him to run for consul from Gaul, and so pass seamlessly from immunity to immunity. Without a word of objection, Pompey moved to give this law to Caesar.

As he had so many times before, Cato did everything in his power to prevent Rome from bending the law for a single man. He did everything in his power to ensure that Caesar would come to Rome to face justice as a private citizen. Caesar, more annoyed than angry, writes that the bill allowing him to run for consul from Gaul met "a very violent opposition from Cato, who, in his usual manner, consumed the day with a tedious harangue." But not even Cato could filibuster forever, and when he hoarsely yielded the floor, the bill still had the backing of all ten tribunes, as well as Pompey. And it still had a Senate in no position to say no to him.

On its own, the law might have kept the tenuous peace between Caesar and Pompey for a few additional years—at the price, Cato insisted to deaf ears, of the sanctity of law itself. Almost immediately, however, Pompey executed a reversal. With the ink on Caesar's exception still wet, he won passage of a second law forcing all candidates for office to nominate themselves in person. The two laws were in straightforward contradiction; did Pompey realize or care? Did he push the second law to send a message to Caesar or to pacify Cato and the *optimates*? When Caesar's friends raised a howl of objection, Pompey's answer was just as curious: He hadn't been thinking of Caesar at all. He would personally write an addendum: This law most explicitly does not apply to Gaius Julius Caesar. It was lost on no one, however, that the law was already passed and enrolled—that Pompey's assurance had no legal force and was only as good as his word.

Cato added another election reform, which he succeeded in pushing through the Senate. Not only would politicians have to campaign in person, they would have to do so alone. It was an attempt to make mandatory the austere kind of electioneering that had been Cato's nearly exclusive style: no nomenclators, no networks of friends dealing out favors, no campaign apparatus at all. It may also have been another attempt to make Caesar's life difficult. Depending on which interpretation of Pompey's laws held when the time came, Caesar might find himself running for consul from Gaul—but legally prohibited from asking friends to canvass on his behalf.

It was, at least, a fallback. But on the issue that Cato considered the single dominant problem of the day—the inhuman ambition of Julius Caesar, demagogue and war criminal—he now believed Pompey to be intolerably squishy. Pompey had proved it with his hesitant, vacillating behavior, passing laws that flatly canceled one another out, then half retreating under pressure, until no man knew where he stood. Did Pompey even know where Pompey stood? That summer, Cato attempted to force the issue by putting himself forward for consul.

But it was another of those strange, half-spirited affairs in which Cato simply would not, or could not, bring himself to behave like a man who wanted power. He had, at one point, been a forceful and fiery politician; now, a step away from the pinnacle, all that mattered was all that Cato would *not* do. He would not show off his wounds. He would not discuss his war record. He would not smile or joke with the crowd. He would not pretend to know strangers. He would not compromise what he considered his dignity, or shift his personality in the slightest. He would not put on shoes. He would not do any of the things "by which the multitude is courted and captivated." He would not be anything other than Cato; he preferred to lose on those terms.

Cato ran on the strict letter of his law and did it alone, without friends or aides. He had hoped to make the election a referendum on Caesar—but he simply couldn't interest the people. Instead, they wanted to talk about why Cato, in the name of clean government, was trying to ruin politics. Election season was the ordinary poor man's one chance to be counted and courted— the one time of year when gentlemen were beggars. Now, thanks to Cato's new law, the number of gentlemen begging favors was radically diminished. "Cato still more exasperated the common folk, in that he deprived them not only of getting money, but also of bestowing favor, and so made them at once poor and without honor." Cato never seems to have asked what the yearly spectacle looked like, or meant, from the poor man's perspective. Of the three candidates for consul, he finished last.

Where Cato had raged and refused to accept his rigged defeat for praetor, he made it clear immediately that he considered this loss a fair one and no one's fault but his own. Given how much of his Stoic self-image was tied up with his superiority to public opinion, he seems to have taken the loss as a compliment, another confirmation of his general rightness. Others, he said, might consider the consulship "the greatest of all good things"—his opponents, for instance. But not Cato. On the very morning his defeat was announced—on what would have been for an ordinary Roman a humiliating day—he made sure to be seen taking his exercise on the Field of Mars, tossing a ball with friends as if nothing had happened. That afternoon, when he should have been shut indoors moaning, he took his regular stroll through the Forum, dressed as Romulus as usual, barefoot and tunicless.

It's likely that he crossed paths that day with a friend who had once ruined his nerves and his health in pursuit of the same prize that Cato was throwing away so lightly. Cicero had endured almost half a lifetime of moral bullying from Cato, but now he had a fair accusation to make in his turn. "When affairs demanded a man like [Cato] for office, he would not exert himself nor try to win the people by kindly intercourse with them." Indeed, Cicero hit on a palpable contradiction at the heart of Cato's run—for that matter, at the heart of his career. If the Republic was in the crisis that Cato described, wasn't it worth a more-than-ordinary effort? If the stakes were as high as Cato said, wasn't it worth degrading himself with politics, just a little?

Cato's response was telling: "Since there had been no foul play in the consular elections, he saw clearly that he had given offense to the people by his manners. These, he said, no man of sense would change to please others."

Not even to check Caesar?

Seeing as he had tried and failed honestly, Cato announced, this was his last election—the end of his race in the *cursus honorum*. He was still a senator, still a pivotal man for the coming crisis, still a worshiper of the Republic (as it existed in theory)—but although he had not convinced much of Rome with his prophecies of the Republic's fall, he had thoroughly convinced himself. His bouts of resignation and indifference looked, at points, like the construction of an elaborate moral life raft. At those points, it is hard to disagree with Jaeger: "Cato had renounced the role of the savior of Rome for the salvation of his personal integrity."

• • •

Not long after, in mid-autumn, Caesar found himself in a desperate fight for a more immediate kind of salvation. The Gallic revolt had degenerated into a starvation race. Inside the besieged hill town of Alesia, eighty thousand rebels were starving. It was their last holdout. Long-haired Vercingetorix, war chief of all the Gauls, was starving along with them. Ringing the town were piles of women and children. Expelled by the rebels as useless mouths and denied passage by Caesar, they were now dead or dying in no-man's-land. Ringing the doomed women and children, Caesar's army camped, its food, too, running short. Like Janus, the army faced in two directions, encircled and encircling. For the Gauls' relief force waited beyond Caesar's wooden camp walls, probing for a weakness.

At noon on October 2, the Gauls found it: a hole in the outermost wall where a steep hill had made fortifications impossible. Sixty thousand Gauls poured into the gap. As soon as Vercingetorix saw their attack from his hilltop, he ordered his men to swarm the inner siegeworks with spears and hooks. The two hunger-weakened armies clashed beneath Alesia—but, Caesar writes, his Romans were less afraid of the warriors in front of them than of the uncertain shouting behind their backs, where their own defenses were crumbling.

At the point of crisis, attackers and defenders on the outer wall suddenly gaped in surprise: Riding down on the Gauls were six thousand Roman cavalry, led by Caesar, "his arrival being known by the color of his robe." Outnumbered as the horsemen were, ten to one, their charge was shocking enough to set off a panic among the besieging Gauls. Caesar breathlessly narrates: "The cavalry is suddenly seen in the rear of the Gauls; the other cohorts advance rapidly; the enemy turn their backs; the cavalry intercept[s] them in their flight, and a great slaughter ensues." From the heights, Vercingetorix watched as his revolt collapsed in an hour's span. He would waste no more lives: He called off the inner attack.

The next day, he offered himself to his people: dead, if they judged his head to be the best peace offering; alive, if he would be more enticing as a captive for Caesar's triumph. Alive, it was decided; he led the survivors down from Alesia to lay their arms at Caesar's feet. There were enough, Caesar writes, to award every Roman there a personal slave.

• • •

If any victory ever mandated a triumph, it was this one. Rome's long wars in Gaul were in sight of an end. Rome's ancestral fear of a Gallic invasion would be laid to rest for centuries. So much gold and plunder flowed south that Rome experienced significant inflation—to the frustration of many a rich *optimas* who found that Caesar, even from hundreds of miles' distance, still had the power to reach into a man's vaults and devalue his wealth.

It was all, as far as the Senate was concerned, too heavy a load of glory for one man. Grudgingly, the senators voted Caesar the minimum recognition they could get away with: twenty days' public thanksgiving. At Cato's urging, there would be no triumph. On this point, he spoke with Pompey's full support.

Perhaps years of warnings from Cato and the others had finally begun to bore their way into Pompey's awareness; perhaps he simply had to look north for himself. But slowly, Pompey was coming to see Caesar for what he was. He signaled as much when he married the daughter of Metellus Scipio. Cornelia was a match fit for a consul: Few women were more cultured than this aristocratic lady who could strum the lyre, quote Euclid, and hold her own with the philosophers. But just as important, the marriage meant that Pompey, once Caesar's son-in-law, now had family ties to the heart of the *optimates*. Cato may not have been overjoyed—he and Metellus Scipio had not put away their ugly rivalry—but at least Pompey was acting like a man who needed allies in the establishment. In due respect for the constitutional forms, Pompey gave up his sole consulship, naming Metellus Scipio as his consular colleague for the remainder of the year. But before leaving office at year's end, Pompey gave another sign of his growing caution: He secured himself another five years as governor of Spain, and the legions that came with it.

.   .   .

In a sense, Caesar's victory was self-defeating precisely because it was so conclusive. Caesar's stunning success gave the *optimates* a pretext for their first salvo, and it would usher in two years of posturing, escalating threats, and ultimatums, with Cato's promise to prosecute hanging over them all. One of the new consuls, Marcus Claudius Marcellus, a partisan of Pompey, rose in the Senate to declare victory in Gaul and praise the general who had made it possible. We all honor Caesar for bringing peace to Gaul, he pronounced, and no one more so than I; thanks to his accomplishments, the war is over, the army can at last disband to enjoy its spoils, and our dear Caesar can finally come home.

Dressed up in flattery as it might be, the import was unmistakable: There was no good public reason for an entire army to camp in Gaul anymore—no purpose but Caesar's own. In this view, it didn't matter that the law, forced through by Pompey himself, had given Caesar five years; commands ought to expire when their work was done, not according to some arbitrary timetable. Caesar was certainly welcome to come to Rome and run for the consulship he had done so much to earn. However, Marcellus concluded, he would do so as a private citizen, and in person—because Pompey's tacked-on amendment to the contrary had no weight.

To what extent had Pompey been warned of this polite attack? To what extent did he approve of it? It wasn't pleasant to have the force of his laws questioned so baldly—but then, Pompey was coming to see those laws as harmful. Consul or not, Pompey was still the first man in Rome, and he could have squelched Marcellus's proposal instantly, with a shake of his head. But he didn't; he let it hang in the air for almost two months, between January and March of 51, before finally swatting it down, holding on to his mantle of moderation.

In Gaul, the incident was deeply troubling. Caesar's private secretary fumed that the proposal "attacked Caesar's *dignitas*"—his authority, his worth, his honor—a word that would come to Caesar's lips again and again as the standoff mounted. Appian and Plutarch both frame Caesar's defiance even more dramatically: Brought news that the consul intended to take his command from him, the general placed a deliberate hand on his sword hilt and said, "This will give it to me."

The first open violence between Caesar and the Senate came soon after, though it came by proxy. Caesar had established a colony at the foot of the Alps, in the region of northern Italy that was reckoned a part of Gaul. As a demonstration project for Gaul's Romanization, he gave the settlers the full rights of Roman citizens. To his enemies in the Senate, this was only a flimsy excuse for Caesar to add more bodies to his political machine, and they refused to accept that the colonists were Romans. Not long after Marcellus lost the debate on Caesar's recall, a senator of the colony happened to be visiting Rome; Marcellus had him arrested and, without even bothering to offer a pretext, ordered him flogged half to death—a punishment reserved for foreigners and slaves. Standing over the visitor's broken body, the consul left him a message: "Those stripes are the mark of the alien. Go back and show them to Caesar."

With the Senate's radicals issuing such threats, with Cato denouncing Caesar almost daily—swearing oaths to prosecute him the moment he laid down his arms—Pompey could still play the statesman who held them all (barely) in check. Caesar's army, he ruled, would be off the agenda until March of 50, the earliest that a recall could be considered, under the most stringent reading of the laws. A recall in the spring of 50 was close to ideal for Pompey. Caesar might still run for consul from outside the city walls, but he would be forced to do so without provinces or troops. His physical safety would rest entirely in Pompey's hands. At the same time, the *optimates* would never rest entirely secure with any outcome short of Caesar's conviction and exile—and so they would continue to need Pompey. The consul had dreamed up a scenario that suited his ego perfectly: He would simultaneously protect Caesar from the Senate and protect the Senate from Caesar. He was, in his more magnanimous moments, willing to have Caesar as a subordinate, a client, an esteemed lieutenant—anything but an equal. And Caesar (writing in his usual third person) saw this clearly: "Pompey, incited by Caesar's enemies . . . was unwilling that any person should bear an equal degree of *dignitas*."

Pompey steered his narrow course for the remainder of 51, smiling almost always. Yet no one could silence a room like Pompey when he let the smile drop. On September 29, attending a debate on Caesar's future (the only subject that seemed to be debated anymore), Pompey was asked how the Senate could possibly enforce a decree calling Caesar back. What if Caesar simply bought a tribune and had the law vetoed?

That, Pompey answered, would be open disobedience—no different than breaking the law outright.

A senator posed the natural next question: "Suppose, then, that Caesar kept his army?"

"Suppose," Pompey shot back, "that my son took a stick to me."

That was Pompey's complacent confidence to the end. The conqueror of Gaul: a boy with a stick.

· · ·

It seems surprising that, a year before the collapse, anyone could still concern himself with triumphs and honors. But Cicero's correspondence with Cato speaks to another kind of confidence: that even as Rome was gripped by a pervasive "fear of revolution," the threats would stop short of war; that the business of politicking for honors would go on as it always had. To Cicero, a triumph for a little victory in an out-of-the-way province still mattered.

As the Senate hashed out the Caesar question, it had to make do without Cicero's eloquence. Much to his displeasure, he'd been assigned the governorship of Cilicia, a province on the southern coast of Asia Minor. He had chased down brigands and petty rebels, frightened off a Parthian raiding party, even stormed a hill fortress—not quite Alexandrian accomplishments, he joked to Atticus, but impressive for a lawyer. When his troops hailed him in the field as *imperator*, it occurred to Cicero that he could qualify for a triumph. To that end, in January of 50, he turned the full force of his flattery on Cato, who had enough influence with the Senate to give it to him.

Cato must have sensed what was coming when he opened the thick missive to read: "Your own immense prestige and my unvarying belief in your consummate virtue have convinced me of the great importance it is to me that you should be acquainted with what I have accomplished. . . ."

There followed an exhaustive accounting of all that he had accomplished, which Cato must have eagerly skimmed.

Then more gleaming flattery: "In all forms of speech, whether in the Senate or at the bar; in all kinds of writing, Greek or Latin; in fine, in all the various branches of my literary activity, I proclaimed your superiority not only to contemporaries, but also to those of whom we have heard in history."

Then, at last, the point: "After my unjust disgrace—always stigmatized by you as a disaster to the Republic, and rather an honor than a disaster to myself—I was anxious that some very signal marks of the approbation of the Senate and Roman people should be put on record." Cicero had, in other words, concluded that a triumph was the only thing that could wipe out the lingering wound of his exile—a shame that Cato understood as few others could. Cato would have understood, too, that it is easier to conquer an army than to conquer one's greed—and Cicero, who had run a clean and just administration, had done both. Finally, a rousing conclusion, delivered to a jury of one:

> I have only one last resource—Philosophy: and to make her plead for me, as though I doubted the efficacy of a mere request: Philosophy, the best friend I have ever had in all my life, the greatest gift that has been bestowed by the gods upon mankind. Yes! This common sympathy in tastes and studies—our inseparable devotion and attachment to which from boyhood have caused us to become almost unique examples of men bringing that true and ancient philosophy (which some regard as only the employment of leisure and idleness) down to the Forum, the council chamber, and the very camp itself—pleads the cause of my glory with you: And I do not think a Cato can, with a good conscience, say her nay.

It is not entirely clear how "Philosophy" endorsed a triumph for Cicero. Nor could those words make Cato forget that Cicero, when he needed to win a case, had gleefully turned Cato's Stoicism into a laughingstock. But Cicero had hit on something poignant. They were, in fact, Rome's only two philosopher-politicians. Few men of their time, and certainly no public men, took learning so seriously. One, writing purely as a hobby, left behind books of philosophy that are read to this day. The other left a lasting example of the Stoic life. But for all their "common sympathy in taste and studies," where was their common purpose? Philosophy had produced one man who did what little he could to hold back the storm, another who did all he could to urge it on; one who was preparing himself for accommodation, another for defiance; one who could write such a smooth and politic letter as that, another who could only cringe at it. Cato's reply would not be easy.

• • •

It was an offer of peace that finally brought on the war. More than a sincere compromise, it was a brilliant piece of propaganda, and the identity of the man who offered it came as a body blow to the *optimates*. Gaius Scribonius Curio had been the conservatives' shining young hope. The *optimates* loved him because few made the case against Caesar so forcefully and so intelligibly to the common man. The people loved him because, in contrast to so many of the dour men on his side, he was a partier and a gambler, "eloquent, reckless, prodigal alike of his own fortune and chastity and of those of other people, a man of the utmost cleverness in perversity." They loved him, too, because he had built them a magnificent amphitheater out of his own pocket, one whose stadium seating rotated to present instant changes of scene. They had made Curio tribune for 50—but one did not get to that point without taking on deep debts. Sometime before he took office, Curio had been approached by Caesar's people. By the time he was tribune, he was debt free, and a Caesarian.

Pompey had chosen March for a new consideration of Caesar's command. He expected Caesar, and only Caesar, to be on the agenda; he considered his own place secure. But Curio, in one stroke, took that security away from him and cast Caesar as the sensible peacemaker. Curio's presentation to the Senate sounded eminently reasonable, the words of a true independent: Caesar has an army, Pompey has an army; Caesar has provinces, Pompey has provinces. In the name of peace, they should *both* give them up. How, he asked the senators, could the Republic be secure as long as two such obvious enemies were both armed to the teeth? How could you disarm one without disarming the other? Surely the senators understood the meaning of a balance of power—a balance that had kept Rome secure for a generation.

The proposal—which surely originated with Caesar—was so inspired because Pompey was bound to resist it. It removed him from his place above the fray, as the arbiter of Caesar's fate, and cast him as one of two squabbling rivals. It also called his bluff. Pompey had stated publicly that Caesar would be tantamount to an outlaw if he bought a tribune to thwart the Senate; now Caesar had purchased his tribune. Would Pompey follow through on his threat? Then he would be not just Caesar's enemy but the enemy of the people, whose power was embodied in the tribunes. And because Pompey himself had restored the tribunes' power during his first consulship, he would be a hypocrite in the bargain. Caesar, then, had set the ideological stakes. He would fight in the name of the Roman people; Pompey would fight for his own preeminence.

In Curio's balanced words, Cato heard not a plan for peace but a justification for war. "Now," he roared, "these things are come to pass which I foretold to you! The man is at last resorting to open compulsion, using the forces that he got by deceiving and cheating the state."

There was truth to that. Caesar's command was set by law to expire; Pompey had been voted a fresh five years. What right, then, did Caesar have to treat his legions as a bargaining chip, as a counter in a game? They were soldiers of Rome, not his personal property.

But if Cato had asked the men of those legions where they put their loyalty, he might have heard differently. He might have heard that the era in which Rome's armies answered to the Senate and the people was, in all but name, coming to an end. "Outside the Senate," writes Plutarch, "Cato could accomplish nothing." Outside the Senate, Caesar appeared both a man of peace and armed protector of the people's ancient rights.

· · ·

As Pompey and the Senate groped for a response, Cato struggled to compose an answer of a different kind—a reply to Cicero that could explain, as politely as practicable, why his flattery had been a waste. Cato had refused to vote him a public thanksgiving, let alone a triumph. The thanksgiving had passed over Cato's objection, but there seemed little chance that a triumph would follow. Cicero would most likely never ride a chariot down the Sacred Way. His accomplishments, competent though they were, simply were not the stuff of which triumphs were made. For Cato, there was no other consideration: not friendship, not favor trading, not even the need to keep a valuable ally on his side as a political crisis approached. Triumphs were not to be trifled with.

Cato's answer reached Cicero in Cilicia by June; it was saved, carefully preserved along with the rest of Cicero's correspondence. It is remarkable not only because it shows a brusque and plainspoken man straining toward graciousness and almost making it—but because it is the only writing of Cato's that survives. For that reason, it is worth reproducing in full:

> I gladly obey the call of the state and of our friendship, in rejoic-ing that your virtue, integrity, and energy, already known at home in a most important crisis, when you were a civilian, should be maintained abroad with the same painstaking care now that you have military command. Therefore, what I could conscien-tiously do in setting forth in laudatory terms that the province had been defended by your wisdom; that the kingdom of Ariobarzanes [a client king whose domain bordered on Cicero's province], as well as the king himself, had been preserved; and that the feelings of the allies had been won back to loyalty to our empire—that I have done by speech and vote.
>
> That a thanksgiving was decreed I am glad, if you prefer our thanking the gods rather than giving you the credit for a success, which has been in no respect left to chance but has been secured for the Republic by your own eminent prudence and self-control. But if you think a thanksgiving to be a presumption in favor of a triumph, and therefore prefer fortune having the credit rather than yourself, let me remind you that a triumph does not always follow a thanksgiving; and that it is an honor much more brilliant than a triumph for the Senate to declare its opinion, that a prov-ince has been retained rather by the uprightness and mildness of its governor than by the strength of an army or the favor of heaven: And that is what I meant to express by my vote.
>
> And I write this to you at greater length than I usually do write, because I wish above all things that you should think of me as taking pains to convince you both that I have wished for you what I believed to be for your highest honor and am glad that you have got what you preferred to it.

Farewell: Continue to love me; and by the way you conduct your home journey, secure to the allies and the Republic the advantages of your integrity and energy.

It was an ingenious way to spin a "no" vote: Thanksgivings were meant for divine intervention, but Cicero had succeeded entirely on the strength of his own virtues (which do not make up a very martial list: integrity, self-control, and mildness). Because the credit went to the governor, not the gods, no thanksgiving was necessary—it was a higher compliment *not* to give thanks. The trick here was that Cato, literal minded as ever, took "thanksgiving" at face value—whereas, for Cicero, it was a transparently political gesture, "a very signal mark of approbation." Almost deliberately misreading Cicero's request, Cato was able to deny him all the more politely.

The deftness with which he did so is a useful corrective to the image of Cato as a bruising, inarticulate zealot. As the French classicist Gaston Boissier writes of this letter, "I would be surprised if it did not greatly astonish those who had a preconceived idea of him. There is neither roughness nor brutality, but, on the contrary, much smoothness and grace." It took years of education before one could trade flattery with Cicero. Cato's character, Boissier writes, had been "softened by the assiduous study he had made of Greek letters; he lived in the midst of an elegant world and, without meaning to, he had taken on something of it." The letter should be reread "whenever we are tempted to see him as an ill-mannered, rustic lout."

And yet, even on his best, most collegial behavior, Cato was incapable of repressing his conviction of his own moral superiority. "I have wished for you what I believed to be for your highest honor," he writes, "and am glad that you have got what you preferred to it." In other words: I know what's best for you, and I'm sorry you can't see it.

Beyond that, denying Cicero was another unforced political error in a career built on them. Cicero's allegiance in the coming conflict was still uncertain, even to himself. Cato had little to lose by backing his request and, as the face of the *optimates*, a good deal to win. But having come so far without making deals of that kind, Cato was not about to change.

A shrewder politician than either of them, Caesar was quick to exploit the opening, cheerfully reaching out to Cicero with condolences. Outwardly, Cicero would continue to be all politesse. But as he would write privately,

Cato "has been disgracefully spiteful to me. He gave his testimony to my integrity, equity, clemency, good faith—which I did not ask for. What I *did* ask, he withheld. . . . Pardon me, I cannot and will not put up with this."

●　●　●

Pompey, in the wake of Caesar's new assertiveness, was still working to recover his footing. He was shaken enough to offer a major concession: Caesar could run for consul from Gaul, as long as he was back in Rome, alone, by fall. Pompey stressed his extraordinary generosity, but it came too late: Caesar no longer wanted it. He was after equality, not dependency. Any agreement that left Caesar disarmed before the consulship, even for a matter of weeks, would render him reliant on Pompey's goodwill. There was no longer enough trust between the two to make such a thing possible.

What little trust remained vanished when the Senate demanded that each of the generals contribute a legion for a revenge expedition against the Parthians. Pompey announced that the soldiers he had loaned Caesar three years ago would count as his contribution: Caesar would sacrifice two legions, and he would lose none. Even as he continued to speak words of compromise, Pompey was using national security as an excuse to strengthen his own hand. Caesar, making a note of this bad faith, encouraged his tribune, Curio, to keep up the pressure. With the obstinacy of a Cato, he repeated his solution at every opportunity: Both must disarm.

And if not? Cato wasn't wrong to hear the threat left hanging. Much of Rome now heard it with him.

At this moment, when so much of his charm had been sapped, Pompey was blessed with a serious illness, possibly exacerbated by stress. His digestion failed, he was overcome with fever, he was confined to bed, and it looked for a time as if he would die. And in the people's building sympathy, he was no longer Pompey the sagging, wavering politician; he was Pompey the beloved, the rosy-cheeked boy-general who had gained his first triumph before his first whiskers. From his sickbed in Naples, with its soft, seaside climate, he dictated a long graceful letter to the Senate—a letter that read more like a will. He thanked Caesar for all he had done for Rome, and then recounted his own services, starting at the very beginning, in his boyhood. Through all those years, he insisted, he had never asked for armies or provinces or power for their own sake, but only for Rome's sake—only when he had been called to serve. He had always laid his power down, and now, if he lived, he would do it again. He would give up his provinces. As for his armies, "I will gladly yield them to those who wish to take them back, and will not wait for the time fixed for their expiration." *In extremis,* he returned to the role of Cincinnatus that he knew so well: He could play it in his sleep or deep in fever.

When word went out that the fever had broken and that Pompey still lived, the city of Naples flowered overnight with an outdoor feast. There were sacrifices, parades, festivals of gratitude to the gods who had spared him. Now all of Italy took up the celebration. It was more than Pompey could ever have organized; it was spontaneous and sincere. Slowly coming back into his strength, he was paraded like an idol back to Rome. His return procession from the East was reenacted, the celebrants now equal parts joyful and fearful. At each town's gates, worthies bore torches and crowns of flowers. In each town's square, tables were piled with meat and wine. The celebration climaxed with a triumphal reception in Rome; Cato was sick at the sight.

To Cato, *libertas* meant that there were no indispensable men. These demonstrations were crushing proof, if any more proof was needed, that the constituency for that view was depressingly small. The rest of the Roman world saw only the choice between two indispensables, both of whom had outgrown the state. "The Senate," writes Appian, "now had suspicions of both, but it considered Pompey the better republican of the two." It was a paltry distinction. Cato, to the detriment of his influence, had kept himself cleaner than any man of his time from complicity in what he considered evil. But as he held himself aloof from the feasting and fawning in Rome, it was clearer than ever that resisting Caesar would mean, in some way, joining in— playing his part in an evil whose face was only festive for the moment.

Pompey, restored to health, was even more his old self: more grandly lethargic, more smug. Watching the displays in every town, he was counting and calculating, and the conclusion he came to must have rung like certainty at the time: Those who came out to feast him would also come out to fight for him. He had only to stamp his foot anywhere in Italy, he said in that insouciant way of his, and armies of foot and horse would spring up out of the earth for him.

When he addressed the Senate at the celebration's end, he repeated his pledge to step down—but now with one crucial addition: Caesar would have to go first.

Except for that last caveat, Pompey had now converged on the stance of Curio and Caesar. But the caveat was crucial: It was one more way of reducing Caesar to dependency. On behalf of Caesar, and in the face of the city's pro-Pompey afterglow, Curio furiously rejected the offer. Only one answer was acceptable: Compel both of them to stand down, at the same time, or call them both outlaws. How, he demanded of the senators, can you be sure that you aren't setting up one tyrant through fear of another? The question must have cut Cato deeply—but now there was no changing course.

•   •   •

For all those who had yet to bind themselves to one of the two, the fall was a time for choosing sides. Cicero, on his journey home, received intelligence from a friend that the Senate fully backed Pompey, but that "Caesar will be joined by all whose past life gives them reason to be afraid, or their future no reason to hope." As for the *optimates,* Cicero's correspondent wrote that he "loved the cause but hated the men." We can imagine Cicero, with his irritation at Cato, reading that line with a small smile of recognition.

For months, Cicero and his prestige had been avidly courted by both sides. He still believed, with Cato, that Pompey represented the greatest chance of saving the Republic—but that didn't make the choice any less painful:

> What am I to do? I don't mean in the last resort of all—for, if it shall come to downright war, I see clearly that it is better to be beaten with the one than to conquer with the other—but as to what will be in actual debate when I arrive . . .

"Speak, Marcus Tullius."

What am I to say?

Still, neither side embraced war. Each side half believed that, if it could muster a convincing-enough show of force, war could be averted. Throughout a fall of rumors and paranoia, all the talk was of peace. There were even hopes that civil peace could come from a Parthian attack—that the Parthians would follow up on their victory and capture the attention of either Caesar or Pompey. But they proved a disappointment. Distracted by their own intrigues, the Parthians could not or would not take the fight to the Republic in any great measure. At the same time, plans for a Roman revenge expedition went nowhere.

On December 1, when the Senate took its last votes of the year on the dueling commands, it was clear that no foreign threat could be found to paper over the rift. "Lest the senators through some sense of shame or fear should vote contrary to their true opinions," they registered their votes not as individuals, but by huddling together to be counted. To the question, "Should successors be sent to Caesar?" a majority withdrew to the "aye" side of the chamber—confirmation that the Senate wanted an end to Caesar's command. To the question, "Should Pompey be deprived of his command?" a majority stayed put. But then Curio scored his greatest coup of the year: He persuaded the Senate to vote on his peace plan. By a vote of 370 to 22, both generals were ordered to lay down their arms. Cato seems to have been among the 22. One of the holdouts shouted across the chamber at Curio, "Enjoy your victory—and have Caesar for a master!"

The warning did not dampen Curio's joy. He rushed to the Forum to announce that there would be no war, and he was hailed and garlanded like a conquering athlete. The Senate, as revealed by the first two votes, was still with Pompey, but when the issue was forced, it would rather have peace.

But even in the feverish crowd cheering Curio and his escape from war, there were the first dark whispers. By the end of the day, it was news across Rome: Caesar had not waited. As the Senate was voting for peace, he was marching his legions over the border and down into Italy. He would be outside Rome in days.

In the panic that broke through the relief, a delegation of the most hardcore *optimates* made their way to Pompey's house. The crowd outside his door was not bearing the fasces this time, but an unsheathed sword. Pompey summoned all his outward gravity as he took the weapon and the commission that came with it: Defend Rome from Caesar.

There is no indication that Cato was among the sword bearers. If he was now an improbable member of Pompey's party, it was only on the most reluctant terms. The delegation, moreover, acted on its own authority, without consulting the Senate—and it is hard to imagine the legalistic Cato playing along. But with or without the leading *optimas*, the message had been sent. Pompey was ready to lead the Senate to war.

In a matter of days, the truth dawned that Caesar was not coming. He had never left; it had only been another paranoid whisper in that season of rumors. But the sword was still in Pompey's hand.

. . .

Pompey had come a long way in his estimation of Caesar. Caesar had once been a nuisance of Pompey's own creation; then he was, at worst, a junior partner, to be suffered a consulship if he would pay the proper respect. Now, by year's end, Pompey was heard to say that the consulship of Caesar, even a disarmed Caesar, would mean the destruction of the constitution. He had arrived at the position that Cato had held all along. That view of Caesar, his ambition and his danger, had once been largely powerless. Now it was mainstream and armed. After more than a decade of pounding away at the lonely warning bell, Cato could take no small share of the credit when the alarm was at last taken up and echoed.

On New Year's Day, 49, the Senate heard Caesar's final threat. Curio had carried it by hand down from Caesar's camp, just over the Gallic border. Over the shouting of the *optimates*, Caesar's tribunes succeeded in reading it out. The people of Rome are said to have loved the letter: It was not merely a final offer of Caesar's peace plan (to let the record show that he had tried) but also, presumably, a full-throated defense of the people's tribunes and their power. Did Pompey claim that Caesar was coming to wreck the constitution? Caesar insisted that he was bent on saving it. The senators had heard his offer: If they rejected it, Caesar "would come quickly and avenge his country's wrongs and his own."

Caesar's letter was greeted as a declaration of war. On the motion of Metellus Scipio, Pompey's father-in-law, the Senate passed its own ultimatum: Caesar would disband his army or he would be a public enemy. As if to underscore the utter breakdown of Roman government, the decree was immediately vetoed by Caesar's tribunes. But it was clear that neither tribunes nor senators would settle the issue. The meeting dissolved amid cruel insults and taunts. The senators left to arm themselves.

● ● ●

Three days later, they met at Pompey's villa for a last attempt at peace: Pompey; Caesar's tribunes; Cicero, struggling to play mediator; Lentulus, the fierce *optimas* consul; and Cato. In greener months, they could have looked out at gardens among the most beautiful in Rome, but little grew here in January. For two years, the men around Pompey's table had thrown threats and bluffs at one another. For as long as they could remember, the Republic that gave a shape to their ambitions and a meaning to their lives had been a fragile, faltering thing, the object of all their protective suspicions. Now, they looked across the table through a thick cloud of pride and suspicions and hates, to see if they might save the Republic without war.

Caesar, the tribunes opened, had authorized them to offer the following: He would give up the bulk of Gaul. He would give up all legions but two. He would retain immunity through the end of the year and would be consul during the year following.

Pompey and the *optimates* conferred. No: They would not trust Caesar with any troops.

Cicero, whose many gifts were not for war, offered a final compromise: one province, out of the way. One legion.

Was this acceptable to the tribunes? It was.

Was it acceptable to Pompey? A long and heavy pause. Yes. Possibly.

"You're being a fool!" shouted Cato. "You're being deceived again!"

12

POMPEY'S RING

Caesar betrayed little surprise when word came that the talks had broken down: He had planned for this. He had already sent a small contingent of his men ahead to Arminium, near the Italian border. Now, there wasn't a moment to spare. He excused himself in the middle of his own dinner party, jumped into a horse cart, and raced off to join his advance troops under cover of darkness. The forces in Arminium were a bare fraction of what he had at his disposal, but what they lacked in size he hoped to make up for in a burst of speed and surprise. If he could move quickly enough, Rome would be caught defenseless.

As it happened, the reports of Caesar's movements that reached Rome were as distorted as ever. They magnified the threat of his Arminium forces by several legions. When the Romans heard that Caesar was marching on Rome—that he had announced the die cast—they believed him to be gambling with the sum total of his army, rather than the mere five thousand troops he had on hand. As the exaggerated news spread, the city broke into an open panic. While Rome "filled with tumult, consternation, and a fear that was beyond compare," it also swelled with refugees, nearby towns emptying in advance of the devastation awaiting Italy.

Amid the noise and chaos, the city fathers turned their attention to Pompey. The *optimates* raced to their general, eager to hear his counterstrategy. But at the moment when Pompey's casual air of self-possession would have served him so well, something cracked. Asked how many troops he had at the ready, he stumbled and, "after some delay, said timidly" that he had only a handful of troops but was working to come up with the others. The assembled senators tore into him. "You've deceived us, Pompey!" cried one, demanding that he bring Caesar back to the bargaining table. Marcus Favonius, Cato's close friend, mockingly asked Pompey why he hadn't yet stamped his foot and called up all the eager troops he'd promised. Pompey had no response.

. . .

Cato, on the other hand, had no shortage of words: "If any of you had heeded what I was ever foretelling and advising, you would now neither be fearing a single man nor putting your hopes in a single man." This was the showy, preening side of Cato's moralism, the side that allowed him to gloat "I told you so" in the middle of a crisis—a crisis he himself had helped bring to a boil. On the other hand, Cato *had* told them so, ad nauseam. Self-fulfilling or not, his prophecy had at last come true. The Senate could do nothing but nod its glum agreement. Pompey too took his scolding meekly. When it came to Caesar, "Pompey acknowledged that Cato had spoken more like a prophet, while he himself had acted too much like a friend."

However the blame was divided, though, nothing could paper over the total failure to prepare for Caesar—a failure for which Cato, who had urged Pompey to war, surely bore some responsibility. But with the city imagining a sack only days away, even Cato had to concede that Pompey was the only man left to lead Rome's defense. This too Cato dressed up as a moral aphorism: "The same men who caused great evils should put a stop to them." Even as he insulted Pompey, Cato insisted that the city and the Senate rally behind him. Even as he did that, he held himself above the coming war—*in* Pompey's party, perhaps, but not *of* it.

Beneath this complex self-positioning, Cato grudgingly accepted the state of things. Caesar, fresh from victory over the invincible Gauls, was a general at the height of his power and pride. He was darting toward Rome with troops hardened by cold marches and close combat with barbarians—the Republic's best. Pompey's glory days were receding year by year, but he was still the most qualified military man left in Rome. However disappointing his recruitment efforts, no one in the Senate could command the loyalty of as many troops. In the last emergency, Cato had fought hard against a dictatorship for Pompey, to the point of backing the creation of an unprecedented office, sole consul. Now Cato advised the Senate to confer on Pompey all emergency powers needed to repel the threat. In Rome at least, Pompey was now dictator in all but name.

Pompey surely expected the appointment—but it cannot have been entirely welcome. He was struggling to fill his ranks, beset by conflicting intelligence reports of Caesar's whereabouts and strength. Now he had been named head of a city on the verge of collapse. Half of Rome's population was fleeing; the other half was battening down the hatches. The most vivid description of Rome's state of affairs, and Pompey's state of mind, comes to us from Plutarch's generally sympathetic biography:

> Since nearly all Italy was in commotion, the course of things was perplexing. For those who dwelt outside the city came rushing in hurried flight from all quarters into Rome, and those who dwelt in Rome were rushing out of it and abandoning the city, where, in such tempestuous confusion, the better element was weak, and the insubordinate element strong and hard for the magistrates to manage. For it was impossible to check the reigning fear, nor would anyone suffer Pompey to follow the dictates of his own judgment, but whatever feeling each one had, whether fear or distress or perplexity, he promptly infected Pompey's mind with this.

In a matter of days, with a handful of troops and a half-cocked plan, Caesar had managed to do what generations of invaders and insurgents couldn't: He had rattled Rome's leading men. The city was deeply spooked, and given what we know of Caesar's careful intelligence gathering, he probably knew it.

• • •

A more hardheaded general might have ignored the pleas and fears, picked a course, and pursued it single-mindedly. That Pompey wavered left a silent question to hover over his leadership: Was he too soft? Some version of the question had chased him throughout his career. Perhaps it was the unfortunate cost of owning a face of "boyish loveliness," but perhaps there was more substance to it than that.

Pompey was genuinely afraid of giving offense, of upsetting anyone by announcing firm commitments, and he rode that fear incomprehensibly far.

Before he threw in his lot with the triumvirate, he had fawned over the Senate elite for years, long after it was clear that they did not return his affections. As Caesar's partner, he had impulsively announced himself ready to defend the controversial land bill with "sword and shield"—and almost immediately had allowed friends to retract his threat and apologize on his behalf. As sole consul, he had passed laws targeting Caesar and annulled them in the next stroke. Even after it had long since become clear that he would never win Cato's respect, he continued meekly to accept Cato's abuse.

By now, his awkward unsteadiness in politics had eaten into the one part of his reputation that should have been untouchable: his achievements under arms. Had Pompey been more sure-footed in the Forum, the whispers would assuredly have died down by now, whispers that he was a "vulture," not a conqueror, that he had only stopped wringing his hands and gone after Mithridates once his subordinates had goaded him into it.

The truth of those rumors was not at issue; the issue was how they shaded perceptions of the general, and even his own perception of himself. At that moment, Pompey himself may have been searching for his killer instinct. It would explain why his next order was made in such haste and without consulting anyone but the cluster of men closest to him: Rome was to be abandoned at once. Anyone left behind was to be marked an enemy of Pompey—an enemy of the state.

• • •

Did Cato object to the plan? If he did, we have no record of it. At the time, his concerns were more immediate and personal. As war neared Rome's doorstep, his family had to be dispersed throughout Italy, his household affairs put in order. Even if Pompey hadn't made traitors of those who would choose to remain behind, Cato still had good reason to pack his family away for safekeeping: Caesar could very well use them as bait. He sent his younger son south, to the tip of Italy's boot in Bruttium. His elder son, Marcus, was to stay with him. The women of the household were put into the care of Marcia, Cato's old and new wife. Six years ago, he had given her away to Hortensius; now, with Hortensius dead and the evacuation hours away, Cato took her back.

Marcia's reappearance on the scene caused a minor scandal. Hortensius had willed every last sesterce of his estate to her, and she returned to her former husband a rich woman. Had that been Cato's plan all along? Had he married her off to the rich and aging Hortensius in the hopes of securing an inheritance? Had he acted, in effect, as Marcia's pimp? That was certainly Caesar's view, one he eagerly added to his list of Cato's hypocrisies. Plutarch passes along Caesar's explosive charge that Marcia "was set as bait for Hortensius," though he dismisses the accusation just as quickly as he brings it up. Criticizing Cato for greed, Plutarch writes, was about as absurd as calling Hercules a coward.

Yet even Plutarch concedes that something about the repeat marriage was strange. "No sooner had Cato married Marcia than he committed his household and his daughters to her care, and set out himself in pursuit of Pompey." Cato may not have been remarrying for money, but a remarriage of convenience it may still have been.

On the other hand, a truly committed partisan of Cato could make even this strange marriage into a moving set piece. The poet Lucan, composing a century after Cato's death, writes the scene as a chaste union of souls, an old man and an old woman clinging to each other in their grief:

> She came with hair disheveled, beaten breast,
> And ashes on her brow, and features worn
> With grief; thus only pleasing to the man.
> "When youth was in me and maternal power
> I did thy bidding, Cato, and received
> A second husband: now in years grown old
> Ne'er to be parted I return to thee.
> Renew our former pledges undefiled:
> Give back the name of wife: upon my tomb
> Let 'Marcia, spouse to Cato,' be engraved."
>
> Although the times were warlike and the fates
> Called to the fray, he lent a willing ear.
> Yet must they plight their faith in simple form
> Of law; their witnesses the gods alone. . . .
>   Just as she came,
> Wearing the garb of sorrow, while the wool
> Covered the purple border of her robe,
> Thus was she wedded. . . .

> *Silent both*
> *They joined in marriage, yet content, unseen*
> *By any save by Brutus. Sad and stern*
> *On Cato's lineaments the marks of grief*
> *Were still unsoftened, and the hoary hair*
> *Hung o'er his reverend visage. . . .*

That the scene is heavily embellished for pathos can be seen in the elderly bride and in Cato's "hoary hair." Cato was only in his forties, in solid middle age, and Marcia cannot have been much older, if at all. But in his poetic license, Lucan captures something that both Caesar and Plutarch overlook: the fear and uncertainty that must have hung over this wedding, as it hung over the whole emptying city. The last-minute exchange of vows was of a piece with a city under duress, a looming war, countless families rent and reconstituted. Whatever else it was, it was a grasp at stability in a rupturing world, one of the few moments of sentiment Cato ever permitted himself.

• • •

Just as war fever stood behind Cato's hasty marriage, it may have also found its way into Pompey's rash decision making. Cato and Pompey had both been young in the days of Marius and Sulla, and the great civil bloodletting of that time still haunted them, as it haunted so many of their generation. It was planted in their emotional acreage like brambles, creeping beneath everything else. What concerned Cato and Pompey at that moment was protecting themselves and their families from a recurrence of the slaughter—one in which they would not be passive observers or minor players, but the men responsible for the civic breakdown.

They were far from alone in their fears. Notes Cassius Dio: Pompey "saw that the people in the city, in fact the very members of his party, even more than the rest, shrank from the war through remembrance of the deeds of Marius and Sulla and wished to be delivered from it." Dio gives us the most vivid portrait of those who had just been asked by their recently installed commander to abandon their city:

> Such as were removing with their entire households said farewell
> to the temples and to their homes and to the soil of their ancestors,

with the feeling that these would straightway become the property of their opponents. . . . Those who were leaving behind on the spot their children and wives and all their other dearest treasures gave the impression, indeed, of having some little hope of their country, but in reality were in a much worse plight than the others, since they were being separated from all that was dearest to them and were exposing themselves to a double and most contradictory fate.

For in delivering their nearest interests to the power of their bitterest foes, they were destined, in case they played the coward, to be in danger themselves, and in case they showed zeal, to be deprived of those left behind; moreover, they would find a friend in neither rival, but an enemy in both—in Caesar because they themselves had not remained behind, and in Pompey because they had not taken everything with them. Hence they were divided in their minds, in their prayers, and in their hopes; in body they were being sundered from those nearest to them, and their souls were cleft in twain.

It was those who remained behind who had reason to be truly terrified. Few, at least at this stage, expected anything resembling mercy from Caesar. On the contrary, they were "expecting to be the first to experience the wrath and the lust of the approaching foes." Even Caesar's close friends who remained in the city were visibly on edge. They weren't sure what to expect from their friend-turned-rogue-general, and they as much as anyone depended on the city's now-fleeing leadership to maintain order.

The night before the departure became a flurry of packing and praying. At each temple in the city, clutches of family and friends could be seen crying, kissing the ground, lamenting the turn of events that had forced them to abandon the only home many of them had known. At dawn, as the first caravans began leaving the city, there were repeated holdups as families "embraced and clung to each other for a long time." Women chased after their husbands' carts, begging them to stay—or to take them along. The whole city, as Cassius Dio reports, was on hand, and "anyone who saw them would have supposed that two peoples and two cities were being made from

228

one and that the one group was being driven out and was going into exile, while the other was being left to its fate and taken captive." Rome's great men had been transformed into refugees, and the city's remaining inhabitants, largely women and children, were simply left to await an advancing army.

It was around this time that Cato adopted the appearance of a man in mourning. He refused to cut his hair or shave his beard, wore tattered clothing, and "maintained the same mien of sorrow, dejection, and heaviness of spirit." It was a strangely pessimistic posture to strike on the verge of war. Could it have been a thinly veiled critique of Pompey's strategy, a kind of preemptive funeral pose for the death of the Republic? Or was it the more personal misery of a man forced to abandon his family during wartime? There is little in the record to help us decide one way or another. But perhaps the most plausible explanation was the most obvious: The Republic that had been the cause of Cato's and his family's life was ripping apart at the seams. Under the circumstances, grief was the only emotion left.

•   •   •

Bearded, disheveled Cato set sail for Sicily. Pompey had assigned all senators a province, and the small island off the Italian coast was Cato's to defend. He made a short crossing through the Strait of Messina, then south to the capital, Syracuse. Almost immediately the news reached him that one of Caesar's men, Asinius Pollio, had touched down just north of Cato's position on the island. Cato sent a convoy demanding to know under what pretext and under whose authority the man had come to Sicily. Pollio played coy, saying he had come to Sicily (with an army) merely to inquire about what had happened in Rome. Cato wasted no time in sending a force to drive him off the island.

It was at this moment, just as Cato and other senators were settling into their assignments abroad, that Pompey took the extraordinary step of abandoning not just Rome, but Italy altogether. His argument was simple. He was the conqueror of the East, and on the eastern shore of the Adriatic and farther out, he could raise forces and funds on an unprecedented scale. To Cato, the move was the clearest sign yet that Pompey's strategy was floundering, that the cause was growing desperate before the war had even begun in earnest. (Their opponent agreed: "Caesar himself was astonished that when [Pompey] was in possession of a strong city and expected his forces from Spain and was master of the sea, he gave up and abandoned Italy.") By Pompey's own admission, Italy contained the core of his supporters. Leaving them sent a terrible signal, particularly at a moment when Caesar was busy persuading stragglers to join his cause or purchasing their loyalty outright.

By February of 49, Caesar had taken Rome without a fight, and to the Italians still on the fence, there could have been no better signal of where the balance of power on the peninsula stood. Yet Caesar's troops marched into Rome peaceably; contrary to the fears of many who remained, there had been no slaughter in the streets when the general finally arrived. But there had been sacrilege. During his brief stay in the defenseless city, Caesar ransacked the Temple of Saturn, which held the state treasury. It was a distasteful first move, and it soured some in the population who may have been willing to grant Caesar the benefit of the doubt. But Caesar's thoughts, for the moment, were on urgent needs: money, men, and materiel. Goodwill could wait.

Some substantial portion of the treasury's hoard came from Cato's fleecing of Cyprus. Would Caesar have taken pleasure in reflecting on the fact that Cato's carefully calculated extortion had, in the end, funded his enemy's army? Whether it ever crossed Caesar's mind, or Cato's, it is one of the war's darker ironies.

How could Pompey justify leaving that treasure unguarded? He could only answer that his treasure was locked up in the Eastern holdings, where his client-kings awaited his arrival. Yet the more distance Pompey put between himself and Rome, the more skeptical Cato grew. Cato, it appears, had become convinced that the war would not be settled by arms or by money, but by a more subtle battle for influence, a struggle for hearts and minds between two sides that each claimed the true mantle of the Republic. Even in this contest of soft power, though, Pompey was failing.

•   •   •

Cato was heard to remark bitterly that "there was much inconsistency and obscurity in the divine government, since Pompey had been invincible while his course was neither sound nor just, but now, when he wished to save his country and was fighting in defense of liberty, he had been deserted by his good fortune." Whatever messages the gods were sending

Pompey, Cato had one of his own, one he needed to deliver in person. He set off for Pompey's headquarters. Asinius Pollio was due to return to Sicily anyway, with a much larger army than Cato wished to face with the troops he had available. The Syracusans protested: what should we do when Asinius's forces arrive? Surrender, Cato told them. The fight against Caesar's forces, he knew, would overwhelm the meager Syracusan force and could well wreck the island in the process. Giving up would at least let them keep their families and buildings intact.

Cato's advice to Pompey was simple: pillaging wouldn't pay in this war. The wholesale destruction for which Roman forces were famous would serve them poorly in civil conflict, where the stakes were loyalty and legitimacy in the people's eyes. Pompey agreed and sent word: His soldiers were only to kill Romans on the battlefield, not off it, and under no circumstances were soldiers to pillage towns already under Rome's control. It was an unfamiliar style of warfare for Pompey's troops. Not for nothing had Pompey, in the days of Sulla, earned the reputation of a butcher. But, as he and his war council had lately recognized, this wasn't a war that could be won by grinding cities into the ground, at least not right away.

Neither side seemed to have its whole heart in the fight. Even as hostilities broke out in public, both camps were busy shuttling envoys and offering peace deals in private. Soon after Caesar crossed into Italy, Pompey sent a relative of the general to the enemy camp with an offer of terms. After he took Rome, Caesar sent an ex-officer of Pompey back with a counteroffer. But the suspicions and bad faith that had poisoned the prewar negotiations spoiled any chance for a truce. Neither man wanted to fight—but neither wanted to give the impression of being willing to concede first. And so the two generals were left in an awkward dance: sending offers of peace they wouldn't accept, and building armies they hoped never to use.

Cicero spoke for every frustrated *optimas* when he described his thoughts: "As for what is to follow, I really don't know what I am doing or going to do, I am so confounded by our crazy way of going on." He too was caught in the haze of the phony war. At the war's outbreak, he hadn't rushed to either camp, but to his country villa, where he'd hoped for more time to sort through his thoughts.

For Cato's part, Pompey was and would always be the lesser of two virtually indistinguishable evils. Cato's support for the anti-Caesar forces was conditional, colored by his belief that the two generals on opposite sides had, at one time, conspired together against the Republic. Accordingly, Cato's advice during this time can be read as thinly veiled contempt; every offer of help was made with his nose firmly held. It would have been one thing to hold these thoughts privately, but then tact had never been Cato's fashion. Where Cicero wrote long, plaintive letters to Atticus, agonizing over every move and missed opportunity, Cato simply doubled down on public mourning: When news of any Roman soldier's death reached him, whether one of Caesar's men or Pompey's, he fell into a fit of tears and wailing. It was a display that we can only assume was genuine—and that we can only assume drove Pompey mad.

• • •

However Pompey felt about Cato's teary outbursts, even he couldn't ignore the fact that Cato's advice was sound. As news of the moderated marching orders spread, more towns began pledging allegiance to Pompey, and more troops joined his ranks. As Plutarch comments, the new rules of engagement "brought to the party of Pompey a good repute and induced many to join it." The assembled forces, drawn from every corner of Rome's influence, were imposing. "His navy was simply irresistible, since he had five hundred ships of war, while the number of his light galleys and fast cruisers was immense; his cavalry numbered seven thousand, the flower of Rome and Italy, preeminent in lineage, wealth, and courage."

Pompey himself added to the allure. An uncertain strategist he may have been, but at fifty-eight, he remained vigorous and commanding on the field. He galvanized the new arrivals by taking part in every training exercise "as if he had been in the flower of his age." He could march in full armor, easily draw and sheath his sword on horseback at full gallop, and throw a javelin with deadly accuracy—farther and faster than the youngest troops in his command.

Key additions to Pompey's camp were another encouraging sign. Labienus, one of Caesar's closest lieutenants in Gaul and a brilliant cavalry commander, deserted Caesar and joined Pompey. Even Brutus, who held Pompey responsible for the murder of his father under Sulla's dictatorship and "who had never spoken to Pompey nor even saluted him before," swallowed his family loyalty and joined the republican forces.

Cicero too finally showed up. The leading voice of the moderates had made up his mind: Pompey was the true representative of the Republic. The months before his arrival had been spent in steady correspondence with Caesar and his lieutenant Mark Antony. Both eager for the Ciceronian stamp of approval, they had courted him for months. But as time passed, Caesar found it harder and harder to tolerate Cicero's waffling. In their last face-to-face meeting, he had pointedly told Cicero, "If I cannot make use of your advice, I will take it where I can find it. I will stop at nothing."

That was the final insult. At last, in early June, Cicero sailed from Italy, with his nephew Marcus and a handful of lictors. He was as nervous as ever, not just of seafaring, but of the reception that would await him at camp. He had given Pompey a loan for the war effort, but he could offer little else besides. No legions marched under his standard. What he had to bestow, however, Pompey genuinely craved: the glow of moderate respectability. Perhaps with Cicero would come the rest of the stragglers in Rome.

Pompey made sure to give Cicero warm greetings upon arrival. Yet the relief didn't last long. No sooner had he arrived than Cato asked Cicero what he was doing here. Why would he abandon Rome at such a crucial time?

An incredulous Cicero replied: Aren't *you* here? Cato's response was convoluted, even by his standards. According to Cato, it was appropriate for him to be in Pompey's camp because he had chosen to follow Pompey from the start of the war. Cicero, however, could have been of greater service to his country "if he remained at home without taking sides and accommodated himself to the issue of events."

"Accommodated himself to the issue of events"—there was nothing Cicero feared so much as irrelevance, and now Cato was prescribing precisely that. Cicero was beside himself. He had risked a great deal to join Pompey's forces. Now he was being taken to task for it? It didn't help, of course, that Pompey essentially ignored Cicero after their initial warm embrace. What good was a lawyer and orator in an army camp? Pompey and Cato prepared for battle, leaving Cicero with little to do except walk the campgrounds and offer snide remarks to anyone within earshot. He mocked his comrades, the battle plans, the general pointlessness of the whole affair.

In some abstract sense, Cato may have been right; perhaps Cicero could have been of better use as a neutral observer of events. But Cicero's name still carried weight. There was a reason, after all, that Caesar had spent months trying to talk Cicero into joining his forces. Had Cato known this? It seems likely that he knew, and yet, he still couldn't bring himself to feign appreciation at Cicero's joining him in camp—not even as one friend to another.

Could Cicero go back on his earlier decision? Whether or not he considered it, Cicero chose to sit and mope in the Pompeian camp, his pride injured and his friendship with Cato on ice again.

• • •

It was at this time that Pompey, perhaps feeling flush with money and men and the support of the elite, decided to do something previously unthinkable: The entire fleet, he declared, would report to Cato.

But then the whispers began. How loyal was Cato? And who, exactly, was he loyal to? This was the same Cato, after all, who had called Pompey a tyrant, scuttled his agenda, and ruined his political career. But the more pressing concern for the Pompeians was this: if Cato "should be made master of so large a force, the very day of Caesar's defeat would find Cato demanding that Pompey also lay down his arms and obey the laws."

Only a matter of days went by before Pompey announced that he had had a change of heart: Cato was out as commander of the fleet; the more pliable Bibulus was in.

Nothing in the sources points us to the reaction of the men in the camp, the other commanders, or even Cato. But we can imagine Cato feeling deeply offended. The same goes for the men, who couldn't have been pleased that Bibulus, a middling consul who had spent half of his consulship in hiding, was now in charge of the Republic's navy.

If there was any moment when Cato's self-control could reasonably have been expected to break, this was it. Other commanders would have left camp. Cato chose to stay. Was it another Stoic exercise, a chance to flaunt his indifference to failure? We have no sure way of knowing, but we do know that Cato remained in camp and, in the tense buildup to battle, even did his best to inspire the troops that he would no longer be leading.

• • •

Having detoured west for a rout of the Spanish legions loyal to Pompey, Caesar drove his army straight at Pompey's neck at Dyrrhachium, in what is now Albania—the first engagement of the civil war in which the generals would square off face-to-face. Forced well past the point of exhaustion, Caesar's troops seemed to have summoned up some of their commander's superhuman endurance to push themselves across a continent. Caesar wanted a quick kill, a chance to take Pompey out before the winter set in.

Pompey, though, was at the peak of his readiness. His force was well equipped and well situated for a fight, and it was three times larger than Caesar's. His army was packed with the finest soldiers and supplies the Eastern potentates could provide, as well as his own veterans from Rome. His position was strongly reinforced by a sturdy palisade and a moat. More important, he had beaten Caesar to Dyrrhachium. He held the advantageous land and naval positions, "so that every wind that blew brought Pompey grain, or troops, or money." At nine legions strong, or as many as forty thousand soldiers, Pompey had good reason to be confident.

But for the moment, what Pompey needed was inspiration. He begged his commanders to rally the troops. Ordinarily, there would have been no urgent need for high-flown words before a battle, but for many soldiers in Pompey's army, this was the first time fighting under his or Rome's standard. As Roman lined up next to Thracian next to Macedonian, it's possible that Pompey sensed some weakness in the famously resolute legionary lines.

Nothing and no one could rouse the troops. They responded "sluggishly and in silence" to every speech—until Cato's. He had a gift suited for moments like this one: the gift of absolute certainty. He could speak the stock words with unfeigned conviction:

> When Cato, after all the other speakers, had rehearsed with genuine emotion all the appropriate sentiments to be drawn from philosophy concerning freedom, virtue, death, and fame, and finally passed into an invocation of the gods as eyewitnesses of their struggle in behalf of their country, there was such a shouting and so great a stir among all the soldiers thus aroused that all the commanders were full of hope as they hastened to confront the peril.

The speaker surely carried more weight than the words. Cato was a soldier's soldier, a commander who shared in the rough treks and heavy packs.

Whatever he said, however he said it, gruff veterans were likely to stand up straighter for a man who was as close to one of their own as a senator could be. Besides, here was Cato, declaiming on behalf of the cause mere days after receiving command and then having it taken away. If he still believed, anyone could.

However earnest his convictions, there must have been some part of Cato that relished the moment as a pure snub to Pompey. Pompey could hear every word of the speech, could watch the troops cheer and celebrate Cato, could witness for himself the authority that Cato still carried. Whatever Cato actually said, what Pompey heard was this: It was I, Cato, who urged the Senate to name you commander, and now I am the one who can reach your troops where you cannot.

• • •

It was a common maxim that "the chief task of a good general is to force his enemies to give battle when he is superior to them, but not to be forced himself to do this when his forces are inferior." But Caesar—who piled up impossible debts, who upended the Roman constitution, who went to war over his *dignitas*—was ready to challenge this maxim as well. From a position of weakness, he tried to force Pompey to fight. Speaking about himself in the third person, he confessed that "the usual design of a siege is to cut off the enemy's supplies. On the contrary, Caesar, with an inferior force, was enclosing troops sound and unhurt, and who had abundance of all things." Stationing himself on the outskirts of Dyrrhachium, he orchestrated skirmish after skirmish to annoy Pompey into open battle.

The historical record is unclear on these early fights on the Adriatic coast. Plutarch has Caesar winning nearly all of them. Cassius Dio reported that Pompey's and Caesar's victories essentially canceled each other out. But both note the day on which Caesar almost lost the war entirely. On July 10, one of the melees drew in more of Caesar's troops than he had anticipated. Pompey's superior troop strength nearly wiped them out. In the disorder of the total rout, not even a commander like Caesar could keep his men from fleeing. He tried; he snatched up a fallen soldier's flag and waved it back and forth to send the men forward. But soon he too gave in and grudgingly ordered a full retreat. Two thousand of his men were dead.

This was the sort of moment that commanders dream of: a near complete victory with the opposition in full flight. Pompey had been given his chance, a rare opportunity to chase Caesar's forces down and finish them off. And had Pompey pursued Caesar as he fled the field—had he done what his commanders urged him to do—the civil war might well have ended that day. But Pompey simply could not bring himself to believe that it would be so easy. Fearing an ambush, he ordered his troops to halt. Caesar was later heard to remark: "Today victory would have been with the enemy, if they had had a victor in command." Still, Pompey had something to celebrate: a victory over Caesar, even if not total, was still a victory.

Cato, as was now his custom, remained away from the celebrations and feasting in the Pompeian camp—weeping, it was said, for the dead on both sides. If he had any other opinion about the favorable outcome of the day's battle, it is unknown to us.

● ● ●

Days passed. Pompey sent scouts to suss out an ambush and as soon as he assured there would be none, he ordered a pursuit of the fleeing Caesar, south and east into Thessaly. Unwilling to abandon his painstaking fortifications and unable to chase Caesar with all the supplies he had carefully built up, Pompey left behind some four thousand troops to hold Dyrrhachium as a supply depot and put Cato in charge.

A command at last—but it was, in essence, a way to keep Cato on the sidelines. Rather than consider his present circumstances—rather than use an able commander like Cato to maximum effect against the enemy—Pompey cast his thoughts to the post-war future. In that future, Cato could turn from uneasy ally to full-blown enemy. So Pompey kept him from the front, occupying him with supply work, denying him whatever glory might make him a force to be reckoned with further down the line. Cato made no recorded protest over the assignment—just the usual soldierly salute, outwardly correct as always, as Pompey marched off to end the war.

Others were not so pliant. Dissension had crept into Pompey's ranks. Calls went up for a quick, decisive engagement. After all, the argument went, Pompey's force still decisively outnumbered Caesar's. The recent battle was proof that Caesar was hobbled. This pressure on Pompey came from the unwieldy crew of senators, magistrates, and ex-consuls that had traveled with him from Rome. Within the exiled elite, rumor had it that Pompey was now only prolonging the war so as to prolong his dominance. Once the war ended, he would be a citizen again—without an army, without an office, without glory of any kind. Had Cato started this campaign of rumormongering? The fears certainly smack of Cato; and it is telling that many of the most vocal critics of Pompey were members of Cato's circle.

Cato's brother-in-law Ahenobarbus mocked Pompey as "Agamemnon" and "King of Kings." Cato's close friend Favonius loudly complained that the army could have been eating figs in Italy by now if Pompey had only had the nerve to finish the job. Others openly accused the general of demanding "that he might always be in office and never cease to have for his attendants and guards men who claimed to rule the world."

Chased as he was by rumors of his weakness and indecision at arms, Pompey was exceptionally sensitive to this kind of chatter. In Plutarch's judgment, he was "a slave to fame and loath to disappoint his friends." Perhaps it was fear of disappointing them, or fear of his declining reputation, that led Pompey to finally give in: he would seek a decisive battle.

We know he was not entirely at ease with the decision. He reported a dream only nights before the engagement: He saw himself at the Theater of Pompey, entering the adjoining Temple of Venus, heralded by a chorus of cheering Romans and pledging his victories and his spoils to the goddess. He awoke in a cold sweat; Venus was the legendary ancestor of Caesar. What kind of omen was this?

Perhaps Pompey's dream was only invented in retrospect, tailored to fit the facts. But perhaps, in a culture that believed devoutly in the predictive power of dreams, one went to sleep on great occasions full of self-fulfilling expectations of a prophecy. If that was the case, the prophecy was not nearly as comforting as Pompey would have hoped.

And yet, whether to prove his decisiveness to the doubters, or because he could not bear to reverse a decision on the basis of a single sleepless night, Pompey refused to change his mind. The battle would take place on the morning of August 9, on the great plain of Pharsalus in Thessaly.

•   •   •

His lines were twice the size of Caesar's, better rested and better fed. It was observed, though, that while Caesar's men waited calmly and quietly for the trumpet, Pompey's shuffled with nervous energy. Pompey himself gave the order to calm his men down: Stand stock-still and brace yourself for Caesar's charge; we'll let Caesar's men wear themselves out.

Plutarch writes:

> Now at last the signal was given on both sides and the trumpet began to call to the conflict, and of that great host every man sought to do his part; but a few Romans, the noblest, and some Greeks, men who were present without taking part in the battle, now that the dreadful crisis was near, began to reflect upon the pass to which contentiousness and greed had brought the sovereign Roman state. For with kindred arms, fraternal ranks, and common standards, the strong manhood and might of a single city in such numbers was turning its own hand against itself, showing how blind and frenzied a thing human nature is when passion reigns.

Caesar, at least as compared to Pompey, had accounted for the anxiety of his men with a simple plan: he ordered that his front line's javelins be used as spears, striking straight for the eyes, instead of thrown from a distance. It was a calculated gamble: he predicted that Pompey's frontline cavalrymen, many of them nobility, would vainly protect their faces and drop their weapons and thus their guard. The rest of the soldiers, seeing their cavalry compromised, would simply break under the pressure of Caesar's forces.

And this is precisely how the battle played itself out. The cavalry panicked and buckled; Caesar outflanked Pompey and attacked from the rear. The whole affair lasted only a few hours. Caesar lost two hundred of his own men to fifteen thousand dead and twenty-four thousand captured on Pompey's side. His camp walls breached by Caesar's forces, Pompey gathered what he could carry in his arms and fled on his horse. It was said he was too stunned to even speak.

•   •   •

Word reached Cato at Dyrrhachium. The news, it seems, came as no great shock. Cato's instructions to the troops under his command were simple and direct. If Pompey was alive, they would hold out against Caesar and await further orders. If Pompey was dead, Cato would return the army to Italy and then choose exile, saving himself from ever again looking Caesar in the eye.

While Cato responded to Pharsalus with Stoic indifference, Cicero swung between depression and gallows humor. Soon after the defeat, a senator told Cicero that there was still hope. There were seven legionary standards, or "eagles," left in Pompey's camp. Cicero shot back, "Good plan, if we were at war with jackdaws." We can imagine that his laughter was the nervous kind, the chuckles of a man who could sense that his own presence in the camp was a kind of joke.

And yet, when the remaining commanders next met, Cato nominated Cicero for commander in chief in Pompey's absence. Was that a joke? Pitting against Julius Caesar an orator who had shown up late for the war and excused himself from Pharsalus by falling conveniently sick? But as in so much else, Cato could point to the constitution to defend his decision: Cicero had been a consul; he was the highest-ranking leader remaining in the government-in-exile, and therefore the rightful commander.

Rather than put Cato's legalism to the test, Cicero made it easy on him. Just as quickly as he was given the command, he stepped down. Pompey's furious son Gnaeus cried that Cicero was a traitor and rushed at him with sword drawn. Only Cato's quick intervention saved Cicero's life. He talked Gnaeus down from his anger and shuffled Cicero through the camp to the port, for the next ship for Brundisium.

It was the last time the two would ever speak. Cicero, who set down so much else in writing, records none of his final words to Cato. Perhaps there was little said between them. Ten years before, even five, if Cato had been more politic, if Cicero had stiffened his spine—but that was past now. Cicero was on his way out of a war he had never cared to fight; Cato, to wage a war he was unlikely to win.

•   •   •

Still no word from Pompey. The best guess was that the general, if alive, had fled to Egypt or Libya. He had friends there, and perhaps he had assembled a makeshift army.

So Cato sailed for Africa. He left behind all those (and there were many) who had grown tired of civil war, of sailing, of fighting. Even the *optimates* who followed Cato south had grown weary. Africa was a reunion of losers: Afranius and Petreius, who had been defeated and pardoned by Caesar in Spain; Pompey's two sons, Gnaeus and Sextus, who had arrived separately after losing battles of their own; a handful of defeated officers from Pharsalus, who had hung around the battlefield long enough to see many of their fellows sign up with Caesar.

Sextus was the one to share the news: his father Pompey the Great was dead. After Pharsalus, he evaded the bounty hunters by making his way east across the Aegean to the island of Lesbos. There he met his wife Cornelia. Their reunion was joyful—he is said to have leaped into her arms. He was hopeful: One lost battle didn't end the war, he told his wife. He had a plan. Ptolemy XIII, the boy-king of Egypt and a client of Pompey's, possessed enough money and ships to hold off the enemy. In return, Pompey could aid him in his struggle against his sister Cleopatra.

So he set off for Alexandria. On the coast, he kissed Cornelia good-bye, setting foot in the small boat sent by the boy-king to ferry him ashore. The Egyptians in the boat greeted him as *imperator,* in both Latin and Greek. Pompey turned back to his wife and son as the boat pushed off and shared these favorite lines from Sophocles: "Whoever to a tyrant wends his way, / His slave is he, e'en though his steps be free." He tried to make small talk on the short ride to shore, but the welcoming party was strangely quiet.

The boat hit a sandbar, hard. Pompey stood and took a slave's helping hand. He couldn't have noticed the sheen from the blade that was drawn above his back. It was a Roman who had the first cut of Pompey Magnus: a certain Septimius, who had served Pompey as a tribune. The other daggers came fast, and the work was soon done. He died with all the dignity available to him, covering his face with his toga, emitting nothing more than a low groan.

Only a day before, he had celebrated his fifty-ninth birthday. His nearly six decades ended in a fishing boat off the coast of Egypt, his wife and son staring wide-eyed in horror.

•   •   •

When Caesar unwrapped Pompey's head, a gift from the Egyptians, he was heard to speak to it. He addressed it not as enemy or consul or *imperator,* but as "son-in-law." Caesar's true mind, at that moment, is impenetrable to us. But he was master enough of himself to produce what was required of him: tears.

It was not until Pompey's signet ring appeared in Rome that the people believed that their boy-faced general was dead. The ring was the only one of its kind, engraved with three trophies: the memories of three victories on three continents, three triumphs and three better days to die. Pompey, too young to shave, furious that his elephant-drawn chariot wouldn't fit through the city gate. Pompey, triumphant over Spain, stepping down from his chariot into his consulship, without even having to ask for it, Rome's favorite son. Pompey, standing in the chariot, shrouded in Alexander's cloak.

ALONE

"His course lay through deep sand, under burning heat," writes the geographer Strabo. Something in Cato seems born for a desert, for an empty and silent place, for long marches and few words, for a place where the pertinent virtues are endurance and indifference. *Apatheia*, the Stoics called it: contentment even when half dead of thirst. This was the dry landscape of Stoicism, and the place where Cato's failings ceased to matter.

Even the landscape of the war was simpler, flatter. Pompey was dead, and with him Cato's uncomfortable career as a partisan of the lesser evil. There would be no more fear of setting up a king in the name of the Republic. Plutarch writes, "No one, now that Pompey was gone, would even listen to any other commander while Cato was at hand." In Cato's mind, he and his remnant were the Republic, an exiled Republic, unmoored from Rome.

The goal, for now, was Utica, the capital of Roman Africa on the continent's northernmost tip, not far from ruined Carthage. Rendezvous with the rest of the republican forces would have required, at most times of the year, a manageable sea journey. But it was the stormy, wind-tossed season off the African coast, and the way lay across the Great Syrtis—a shallow gulf notorious for grounding ships on its muddy bottom. It would be overland, then: a desert march of some five hundred miles.

With nearly ten thousand men under arms, a contingent of North African guides claiming knowledge of all the cures and charms against snake venom, and a herd of pack asses bearing baggage and all the water that could be gathered up, Cato and his movable Republic set out from Berenice (modern-day Benghazi) in late 48. Their only consolation was that, with winter coming, it might have been hotter. Plutarch writes that they made the journey in an improbable seven days. Strabo's account seems more likely: a thirty-day trek, with staggered starts to make the best use of the sparse watering holes along the way.

Cato in the desert: none of the complications of the Forum, no objective but to walk and keep walking. It's no wonder that this month of his life was ripe for mythology. The most accomplished mythologizer was the Stoic poet Lucan, who made Cato hero of the *Pharsalia,* an epic poem of the civil war. By the time the epic was composed, a host of baroque details had made their way into the account of the march: a great sandstorm that buried an entire detachment of Cato's army; the catalog of increasingly gothic deaths by snakebite—one soldier melting into a putrescent puddle, another swelling and bloating until he burst his armor, a third spouting tears of blood. But among the horror stories, there are lines that hold true with what we know of Cato, the hardy, self-sacrificing commander:

> *Bearing his javelin, as one of them*
> *Before the troops he marched: no panting slave*
> *With bending neck, no litter bore his form.*
> *He bade them not, but showed them how to toil.*
> *Spare in his sleep, the last to sip the spring*
> *When at some rivulet to quench their thirst*
> *The eager ranks pressed onward, he alone*
> *Until the humblest follower might drink*
> *Stood motionless.*

A speech Lucan credited to Cato rings true, as well—not as literal words from his mouth, but as a deep expression of the Stoic love of fate, the faith that seemed to sustain Cato in defeat. At a bare oasis shrine of the horned god Ammon, whom the Romans identified with Jupiter, Cato is offered a chance to ask the god's oracle the outcome of the war. He refuses:

> *"Bound are we to the gods; no voice we need;*
> *They live in all our acts, although the shrine*
> *Be silent: at our birth and once for all*

244

What may be known the author of our being
Revealed; nor chose these thirsty sands to chaunt
To few his truth, whelmed in the dusty waste.
God has his dwelling in all things that be,
In earth and air and sea and starry vault,
In virtuous deeds; in all that thou can'st see,
In all thy thoughts contained. Why further, then,
Seek we our deities? Let those who doubt
And halting, tremble for their coming fates,
Go ask the oracles. No mystic words
Make sure my heart, but surely-coming Death."

Cato surely did not speak those words by the letter—but he did, at his best, live by their spirit in the time that was left to him. Others, in the months to come, would have found a great deal to tremble about; Cato was already resigned. Ragged and dusty, but largely intact, his army came within view of settlements again, of trees and cultivated land. They waited out the winter in a coastal town loyal to the Republic, possibly the old Carthaginian settlement of Leptis Magna.

* * *

By early 47, what was left of the republican cause had regrouped in Roman Africa: Cato and his legions; Pompey's young sons, Gnaeus and Sextus; Metellus Scipio and Caesar's ex-lieutenant Labienus, who had barely escaped Pharsalus alive; Publius Attius Varus, former governor of Africa, who had returned to hold it for the Pompeians; and Juba, King of Numidia. Juba, fierce and quick to anger, owed a lifelong debt to Pompey and his faction, ever since the boy-general had secured Juba's family on its throne. Juba's hatred for Caesar, however, was strictly personal. It had first sparked on a diplomatic visit to Rome, when Caesar, in a heated argument with Juba, did him the unthinkable insult of pulling his beard.

Though much was taken from them—their general, the thousands of men dead at Pharsalus—much remained. They had a friendly client king, a province that lay within striking distance of Italy and grew enough grain to feed an army, and a base of resistance that could, with luck, hold out against Caesar for years. In Africa, they could postpone open battle while they harassed Caesar with raids and recruited new legions. They might, with Cato's imprimatur, make Africa the fountainhead of anti-Caesar propaganda. They might, if all went exceedingly well, even force a negotiated settlement.

Yet Cato arrived in Utica to find the leadership of his cause in chaos. Rather than build a resistance, they had spent months squabbling over precedence. Varus had been governor here; Metellus Scipio, as ex-consul, claimed to outrank him; Juba, who held the balance of power, was happily soaking up their obsequies and playing one against the other. To Cato's immense frustration, these three rivals were arguing over who ought to sit at whose right hand, while Caesar was effortlessly handing himself consulships and dictatorships.

But the dynamic changed with the arrival of Cato, now the most recognized face of the resistance, and the thousands of soldiers loyal to him. As so often before, Cato made his feelings known with a well-timed dramatic gesture. King Juba, at his first audience with Cato and Metellus Scipio, offered the Romans chairs on either side of him, reserving for himself the center seat—the place of honor. Without a word, Cato simply picked up his chair, walked around the king and the ex-consul, and placed his chair on the other side—which gave Metellus Scipio pride of place in the center. The message did not need to be translated: Romans, even beaten and hiding Romans, did not yield precedence to a foreigner. They were, even in this reduced and sandy setting, the legitimate representatives of the Republic. In the days that followed, Cato brought order to the reeling republican cause by forcing it to settle on a chain of command. But in the other part of his gesture, there would be grave consequences: Cato had put Metellus Scipio, and not himself, at the center.

Plutarch, Cassius Dio, and Appian all agreed that Cato could have had command in Africa if he had wanted it. Metellus Scipio and Varus both offered to abandon their claims and unite behind him. Of those left on the republican side, Cato was the most competent administrator, a proven commander, the one most likely to inspire endurance in a losing cause. He backed the most plausible course for a beaten army: fortification and delay. He had too an indispensable quality for sound leadership: He didn't want it.

Metellus Scipio, by contrast, had few qualities to recommend him beyond his name. Thanks to his distant ancestor's African victory over Hannibal, the soldiers under him held the superstition that a Scipio couldn't help but succeed in Africa. But he had yet to justify their confidence; he was a proud man with little to be proud of. Nor did Cato, who had known and loathed him for a lifetime, have reason to trust him. Metellus Scipio was, by all accounts, dissolute where Cato was disciplined, and spendthrift where Cato was frugal. He was practiced in all the arbitrary uses of power that Cato detested, from oppressive taxation to summary executions. From their young manhood to their ugly campaign for the praetorship, few had hurt Cato so personally—certainly no one on his own side. Yet, in Cato's eyes, Metellus Scipio owned the only qualification that mattered: He had been consul; Cato had not. Rank was rank.

It mattered little to Cato that this was one more fruit of his poisoned relationship with Pompey. If Pompey had not stolen the election for praetor, the same election that Metellus Scipio went on to win, if Cato had not later snubbed Pompey's offer to be his "associate in government," the same role Metellus Scipio went on to fill, then Cato might have had an equal claim on the leadership. But all that was done, and to the Stoic, fate was no less fate for being unfair. Cato may have had the claim of competence and the claim of charisma, but he did not have the claim of legality. Strange as it may sound, the right of Metellus Scipio to hold command—the preeminence of a former consul over a former praetor—was squarely among the principles for which Cato believed he was fighting. Since his childhood under Sulla's rule, Cato had seen Rome's most gifted men bend the law to fit their ambition. Now he insisted that to give him command would turn the resistance into an imitation of all that it claimed to stand against. As Plutarch puts it, "He refused to break the laws in whose support they were waging war [against] one who broke them." And to enforce that principle, Cato would serve under a man he hated. He would hand over his army to an inferior commander. He would deliberately weaken his own cause.

Once again, Cato was eager to risk loss in return for purity. But the full price of his principle was not yet apparent.

• • •

Here was a place that demanded a city, and a city was put here when Rome was still unheard-of. A high, rocky headland looking down on water: a settlement. A calm bay shielded by islands from waves and weather: a harbor. Beneath the heights, low olive hills and a river plain: farmland. Utica was already old when Rome took it, and now Caesar would not take it easily. The city would be well sited, well supplied, well prepared.

But inside the walls was a population that did not much care if Caesar ruled it. Most were the descendants of the Phoenician traders who settled this land long ago. They were not citizens of the Republic, and they had little immediate stake in a factional war among their rulers. But they were—according to *The African War,* an account penned by one of Caesar's lieutenants—still grateful for unspecified "privileges" granted in Caesar's first consulship. Those who weren't Phoenicians were Roman merchants and their families, who had come for profit. They dominated the city's economic life but largely kept to their own enclave; Plutarch numbers them at three hundred households. They might give a respectful hearing when a distinguished senator from Rome lectured them on liberty, but Cato would find them a uniquely difficult audience. They had been unsentimental enough to leave their homeland and follow business to another continent, and what they wanted now, above all, was a clean end to the war and a quick return to business.

So when Metellus Scipio and Juba announced in the war council that the people of Utica were preparing to throw open their gates and harbor to Caesar, they may have had concrete proof—but they may have only had reasonable suspicions. It made sense, after all, to side with a winner. Whatever reason the generals had for their distrust, the proposed solution was brutal: They wanted to raze the city and execute its people. Plutarch suggests that Metellus Scipio backed those draconian measures to win favor with Juba. Juba, in turn, may simply have seized on a pretext to eliminate a regional rival. Yet the propaganda damage to the republicans would have been disastrous. How would it have looked for their army to bow to legal niceties when it came to choosing a commander but to wipe out an entire city without flinching? The republicans simply did not have the strength to act the part of the arrogant occupier. Cato knew that their hold on Africa would not long outlast the locals' goodwill.

With great effort and loud invocations of the gods, Cato succeeded in pressing these arguments home on the war council. Utica, thanks to his intervention, was spared the sword. And when news of these heavy deliberations became public, a delegation came to demand that—as long as the republican army was set to remain in the neighborhood—Cato be the city's governor. Now that he had saved them for the moment, the people of Utica were unwilling to trust anyone else; and, in a spirit of "it's your problem now," Cato's superior agreed.

•   •   •

In the months that followed, Utica became a bristling armed camp. High watchtowers grew on its walls. Trenches were cut through its fields. Each day began with hammers beating on the defenses and bushels of grain passing through the gates to the city's storehouses, with Cato sternly presiding over it all, hiding from no one that it would be a long siege—if the gods were willing. A long siege was Cato's only reasonable hope.

It's clear that Cato shared at least some of his colleagues' suspicions of the locals and their affinity for Caesar. As his troops moved to garrison the city, he ordered all Utican men of military age disarmed and expelled from inside the walls. Those who weren't enrolled in the army would sleep under guard among the trenches and the palisades rising in the fields. At the same time, Cato struggled to keep the peace between Romans and Uticans—and for many tense months, as the city strained for any news of Caesar, there seems to have been little violence between the communities.

While Utica readied for Caesar—and war—to land on the coast, Cato worked feverishly to equip Metellus Scipio's army, which would bear the brunt. Even the Caesarian account of the war pauses to admire Cato's industry: "Cato, who commanded in Utica, was daily enlisting freedmen, Africans, slaves, and all that were of age to bear arms, and sending them without intermission to Scipio's camp." As grain flowed into Utica, arms and men and money and whatever food could be spared flowed out to the waiting army. In sum, Plutarch writes, Cato "made the city a storehouse for the war." Within months, he had proven the practical wisdom of saving Utica. But in between the palisades and the tower work, the money raising and the troop levies, Cato's conviction was quietly growing that he was wasting all the effort of these tireless days to fortify a fool.

•   •   •

It's not clear when Cato made up his mind that he was never, not even in improbable victory, returning to Rome. Forty-eight years old and still refusing to trim his hair or shave, Cato wore his hair and beard ragged and long,

249

and now he added another sign of mourning: He no longer reclined to eat, as all free Romans did, but sat upright at his table like a slave. These have all come down to us as dignified, deliberate signs of grievance—and surely someone so skilled in the politics of gesture was eager to have it known across the Roman world that he regarded Caesar's victories as a monumental death in the family. But we also know that Cato was far from the kind of Stoic who deadened his emotions. He was capable of great rage and great grief. And he would not have been human if—after two years of loss and flight and the manifest failure of what he considered his life's work—he had not been capable of exhausted depression, as well. His unkempt hair and beard, his conversation and his dinner habits were all political signs—everything about Cato was a political sign—but they were also the marks of a deep, unfeigned sadness. We can only guess which motive weighed heavier.

Outwardly, though, the republican cause was in better health. In the spring of 47, Cicero heard from Atticus that Africa was "growing daily stronger, though rather in a way to make one hope for conditions of peace than victory." (Cicero, who by now was back in Italy and trying to make his own peace with Caesar, was inclined to doubt his friend's optimism.) In summer, with better sailing weather, the republican forces launched small raids from the African coast, striking at pro-Caesar cities on Sicily and Sardinia. Lightly defended and unwarned, the island cities were easy prey. The raiding parties sailed back to Utica with captured ships full of weapons and iron, all of which went to strengthen Metellus Scipio.

When, late in the year, there was still no sign of Caesar, the republicans felt confident enough to send the son of Pompey the Great, Gnaeus Pompey, to Spain with thirty ships, in hopes of opening up a new front. Pompey the Great had developed a deep client base in Spain, and there was reason to believe that Spain might eagerly welcome his son. *The African War* quotes Cato, at length, exhorting young Gnaeus to live up to his father's legacy under arms. There is no record of a response from Gnaeus, who had only ever been a great man's son.

•   •   •

Julius Caesar, twice consul and twice dictator, could not find an army to take to Africa. He had placed Cleopatra on the throne of Egypt and grown so enamored with her that he stopped answering letters for months. When

Mithridates' son had stirred up a new revolt in Pontus, Caesar had hurried east and disposed of him with almost casual ferocity. But through all that time, he did not think of paying his soldiers. As Cato struggled to ready Utica's defenses, he could not have known that the patience of Caesar's most trusted troops had snapped.

Caesar, in late 47, intended a brief stop in Italy to take command of the four veteran legions he'd left there and to make a quick crossing to Africa. But he arrived to find them in full mutiny. The complaint was the perpetual one: no promised discharge, no promised pay, and most of all, no land. The soldiers had crossed the northern sea for Caesar and set foot in Britain, where no Roman had ever stood. They had frozen in Gaul for Caesar and starved at Alesia. They had even killed Romans for him—and now they only demanded what was fair. Assaulting their officers, the legions marched on Rome from their camps in southern Italy, and Caesar understood that unless he won them back, he would have armed chaos at the start of his rule— and a rival government continuing to fester across the sea in Africa. Since Pharsalus, Caesar had paid his men on beautiful "indefinite promises." Now his credit, already far in excess of his cash on hand, had at last run dry.

What he did have, even at fifty-three years old, was a physical courage that was still the envy of every soldier. Alone, he appeared unannounced in the rioting camp in the Field of Mars. Suddenly ashamed to beg for land or money, the soldiers asked only for their discharge. Appian writes:

> Contrary to the expectation of all, he replied without hesitation: "I discharge you." Then, to their still greater astonishment, and while the silence was most profound, he added, "And I shall give you all that I have promised when I triumph with other soldiers."

The capstone to this shaming came when Caesar concluded by calling them "citizens," not the usual "fellow soldiers"—making it clear that they had already lost their chance and discharged themselves. After that, he turned his back in mock indecisiveness as the apologies and pleading crescendoed behind him. At the height of the grieving uproar, the Tenth Legion, which had always been Caesar's favorite, was begging for punishment: Let the commander draw lots, the soldiers shouted, and put as many of us as he pleases to the sword.

Finally, a reluctant Caesar ordered them to wipe their eyes. They would be permitted to follow him to Africa—with pay deliverable upon victory.

It was a brilliant, coldhearted bluff. If Cato was to be dealt with, Caesar needed those legions desperately. But after a lifetime of soldiering, he knew soldiers. He knew what a shock it would be to hear that they were *not* needed. He knew how much they would sacrifice to return to their commander's good grace.

Few generals understood so well or manipulated so skillfully the Roman soldier's dearly held superstitions. When Caesar learned that his troops were afraid to fight a Scipio in Africa, he found an undistinguished Scipio relative and put him on his personal staff. And when his African landfall threatened to turn into a terrible omen, Caesar was prepared for that too. On December 28, near the coastal colony of Hadrumetum, he bounded off his ship, slipped on a wet patch—and fell on his face. Rather than leaping up and brushing off his clothes, Caesar lay there and took great grabs of earth in either hand. He shouted loud enough for all to hear over the surf, "I have you now, Africa!"

$$\bullet \quad \bullet \quad \bullet$$

While he waited for transports and supplies to cross the sea, Caesar was decidedly outnumbered: "exposed, upon a foreign coast, to the mighty forces of a crafty nation, supported by an innumerable cavalry"—Juba's Numidians, who were at home in the North African wastes. And the Roman republicans were dug in and well provisioned by Cato, while Caesar's men choked on the dust and struggled even to feed their horses. On a foraging expedition only days after the landing, Caesar looked up to see dust clouds rising on the horizon: the Numidian horsemen.

Caesar, by the smallest of margins, saved his army from the encirclement that could have ended the war then and there. But in his retreat, hundreds of his men fell in a hail of darts and arrows. It was only dusk and higher ground that protected them from worse.

It was, arguably, a victory for the republicans—but it was a victory that exploded the tentative truce between their leaders. Metellus Scipio was full of plans for a decisive battle. He would seize on Caesar's weakness while it lasted. He would overcome Caesar where even Pompey had failed—and after that, he would barely let himself imagine.

ALONE

But Cato called it foolishness. No one, for many years now, had fixated on Caesar more closely, and there was respect to go along with Cato's
contempt. Not even outnumbering Caesar would Cato face him in open
battle. Cato simply advised Metellus Scipio to hold out: Avoid a rout for
long enough, and Caesar would find something to distract him, or Rome
would grow tired of him, or his army would waste away. "Trust to time,"
Cato insisted, "which withers away all the vigor that is the strength of
tyranny." But he had no power to enforce that advice: He had signed that
power away.

All that Cato got in return was a letter from Metellus Scipio, calling
him a coward who hid behind his high walls and begrudged bolder men
their glory. Was it a shouting Cato or a quietly shaking one who dictated the
response?

Coward? he wrote back. I will personally take the legions that I myself
marched to you through the desert. I will cross the sea with them to invade
Italy—tomorrow, if you see fit—and when Caesar comes back to stop me, I
will take upon myself all the force of his army so that you might have some
peace and quiet.

Metellus Scipio only laughed it off. He had other pressing matters. In
the letters from his camp, next to his plans for victory, there were long lists
of enemies and graphic pledges of revenge. The man entrusted with the last
remnants of the Republic was busily preparing a purge.

Cato regretted very little and admitted to regretting even less—but
now, in Utica, he told friends that he had made a grave error, "that there
were no good hopes for the war, owing to the inexperience and rashness of
the commanders." He had put his cause in the hands of a violent incompetent, and when and if the last loss came, he would share the guilt. But his
grief was for more than defeat. He had prepared for defeat. In the long wait
for Caesar, Cato came to see that even if every hope were borne out and he
sailed back to Rome in triumph, with Caesar in chains, there would still be
endless rows of cruel and reckless men clawing over one another, killing
and dying. Some were on Caesar's side; some were on Cato's side. In Rome,
Cato had held to the distinction like a religion, but in the heat of this new
country, it wavered and blurred. It was in Utica that Cato gave up hope for
Rome. At their strange, sitting dinners, where even swallowing food felt
unnatural, he told his friends that there was now little to choose between

253

the two camps. He told them that he had exiled himself and that he would spend whatever was left of his future far away.

. . .

The messenger rode hard up the coast for three days, his burning camp behind him, to bring Cato the news he was waiting for.

For more than three months, Metellus Scipio had fought the temptation to engage with Caesar—but at last, on April 6, 46, on what he thought was favorable ground, he succumbed to it. By afternoon, it was an even fight; by evening, a disaster. Juba had fled by land. Metellus Scipio had fled by sea. Ten thousand surrendering men had been slaughtered with their hands in the air. Wrecked camps, dying war elephants, and a few filth-covered stragglers were all that remained. "Their cause was utterly ruined." Caesar was coming.

Even in daylight there would have been blind panic, but the news came in dark of night. It was as if all Utica woke up screaming—light suddenly burning out of every window, rumor coursing down alleys, the disaster swelling at each telling, until, their eyes dazzled by the explosion of torchlight, the people could almost make out Caesar's shape at the walls, twice as tall as a man, sword in hand and pitiless.

But Cato carried himself like a man who had rehearsed this moment many times. He spent the night walking the flickering streets as though on an errand, catching passersby by the shoulders. Patience was his watchword. It might not be the end, he said into face after face. Sometimes he screamed over their cries, imploring them to remember how stories are magnified in the telling. He spoke as if he believed it. One calm man in a city could only calm so many, but by the exhausted morning, the first panic had largely fizzled out.

At dawn, Cato called together his "Senate": the three hundred Roman merchants and moneylenders of Utica and the *optimas* dignitaries who had arrived with him. Here in Africa, he finally had a Senate of his own over which to preside at a moment of crisis—but it was a pale parody of that grave body he had worshiped in Rome. Seeking safety in numbers, his senators had brought their wives and sons and daughters. Cato stood at the head of a chamber filled with screaming, squirming children. And yet, even before this Senate of near-strangers, even in a poor, provincial temple—their makeshift Senate House—Cato found the familiar pattern repeating itself. No one could light fiercer fires of inspiration; no fires burned themselves out more quickly.

For a long time, Cato said nothing but only turned the pages of the military account book he held in his hands. Once he had given this exaggerated gesture of calm enough time to sink in across the room, he spoke, thanking the three hundred for dedicating their lives to the cause of liberty during this unwilling year when they had seen their calm trading city turned into an armed camp. They had not asked for war, but war had found them, and they had lived up to it bravely. He would not lie to them: The news was very bad, and though the depth of their defeat was not yet certain, it was possible that Utica was all that was left to stand against Caesar in Africa. He would not fault them if they followed fortune to the winning side. He urged them to think it over, to deliberate as long as they would like, and to choose what they thought best for themselves and their families.

He would only add this: He knew Caesar as they did not. Caesar would not rest until he had put a bit and saddle on Rome—but to his credit, he also had a Roman's contempt for cowardice. Cato would only ask the three hundred to consider this: Imagine Caesar's contempt if he should find them fleeing with what they could carry on their backs; imagine Caesar's respect if he should come to the gates and find them standing against him as one. When that day came, they would be free to surrender. And if history might show that their enemy had risked his life and expended every breath to establish his tyranny—while the defenders of the Republic had chosen not to go quite so far—the decision was theirs. Cato could not promise them freedom. War was too fickle for that. But he could promise them, if they stood their ground, one of two most sacred things: a free life, a glorious death. And:

> if they should face the threatening evil and accept danger in defense of liberty, he would not only praise them, but would admire their valor and make himself their leader and fellow combatant, until they had fully tested the ultimate fortunes of their country; and this country was not Utica, nor Hadrumetum, but Rome.

"This is not Utica, but Rome." Cato, after a lifetime, had finally found the Rome he wanted—a Rome abstracted from place and politics, an idea entirely.

Watching him burn with that idea, though they barely shared it, was enough for the assembled Romans to give up thoughts of their safety. They shouted that they would die with Cato before they betrayed him. And to prove the newfound depths of their sacrifice, they sent up a call to free and arm every slave in Utica. For merchants who had much of their wealth tied up in slaves, a general emancipation would be a crushing blow—but this was no time to think of money.

Cato stopped them there. They were fighting for liberty, he said, and liberty meant law. If anyone was willing to free his own slaves, he was welcome to do so—but Cato was not about to seize any man's property. He left the fate of the slaves to their masters and, after taking pledges from the masters who were willing, adjourned his Senate.

·   ·   ·

Utica had been able to hold on to the possibility that the first message might have been wrong. Maybe, by the gods' grace, the defeat had been hugely overstated. But now, as more pieces of the shattered republican army crawled toward safety, it was clear that the disaster was real. Soon after the Senate meeting, more messengers came from the fled commanders: Juba was hiding in the hills; Metellus Scipio was hiding just offshore. Each promised to help Cato through a siege with what little strength was left him. But for the moment, Cato sent back no answer.

He had the war to himself now, and was at last able to defend a position of complete purity—and he was not eager to see matters complicated again. But he had a more concrete cause for concern: Only a slow dribble of slaves reported to arm themselves, far from the expected flood. For the Roman *optimates* who had come with Cato, slaves represented a small fraction of their wealth, and it was no great cost to give them up. The *optimates'* slaves were soon free and equipped. But for the rest of Utica, economic reality was slowly reasserting itself. In the hours after that grimly joyful mass meeting in the Temple of Jupiter, the drunkenness of the first shock was wearing off, and with it, the pledges to die with Cato. Overtiredness was turning to plain exhaustion. Desperation was turning to mundane fear. The three hundred, sober now, were rethinking. Were they about to bankrupt themselves? Were they about to risk their lives, when they had favored Caesar all along? Who were they to die with Cato?

Cato did not have to hear any of this to know that he was once more being admired and ignored. He had only to compare the long list of pledges from the morning with the paltry list of new soldiers. He sent word that Juba and Metellus Scipio should stay away—that Utica could not be trusted.

·   ·   ·

South on the coastal road from Utica lay the small town of Parada. It had not suffered greatly in the war. But as Cato was steeling for the siege and weighing the commitment of the three hundred, war came to Parada: a large detachment of horsemen, the remnants of Metellus Scipio's cavalry that had survived the rout. The exhausted, beaten riders demanded entrance and provisions. The town, which now sided with Caesar as the victor, refused. The horsemen broke down the gates instead and took; and when they had pillaged all they wanted, they lit a great fire in the small forum and burned what they did not care to take, the better to purge their fury at their defeat. Caesar's lieutenant writes—in what is either an authentic atrocity or war propaganda—that they "threw all the inhabitants into [the fire], without distinction of age or sex, with all their belongings." Then they rode for Utica.

They fell on the encampment of Uticans that Cato had built outside the gates. Divorced from discipline and maddened by their loss, the horsemen called it a camp of Caesar's supporters and charged its wooden walls. Even an unfair fight against unarmed civilians would save the cavalry some face. But when the Uticans put up an unexpected resistance, throwing rocks at the horses and brandishing makeshift clubs, the riders wheeled around and withdrew. As they huddled on the plain and considered their next move, they sent three envoys to the gate to demand Cato.

After some time, Cato cautiously emerged with the senators who had followed him from Rome. These rogue horsemen could be the margin of the siege, Cato knew. They could give Utica the strength to hold out, even without the three hundred and their slaves, or they could do the city grave damage before Caesar even arrived. As the senators put on a show of weeping and outstretched hands, Cato begged the cavalry to stay and fight. Beaten as they were, small as they were next to Caesar's force, they were now among the last armies loyal to the Republic. Surely they would not abandon senators of Rome, whom they would obey in any normal time; surely they could hold out on the city's promontory, behind the walls, with food and water that could last for years. But now, senators were in no position to give orders—only to trade offers. The envoys answered, blankly, that they would take Cato's offer to the men and return with a response, but it looked, they warned, as if the majority would rather ride with Juba or give up the fight altogether.

Cato and the senators sat glumly there in the dirt outside the walls and watched the three horsemen ride out of sight. Cato had sent a friend, meanwhile, to watch over the slave enlistments in the city. While they waited for the horsemen's answer, the friend came with angry word that the numbers were worse than they feared. Worse yet, some of the three hundred were starting to talk openly of surrender or flight. The envoys returned in time to see the senators absorbing the bad news and breaking into new tears. The message they brought from the cavalry was only slightly more encouraging. They were prepared to stay and hold Utica, but only if it were emptied of Uticans. The decision was clear, and quite possibly touched with shame at their sputtered attack on the camp outside the walls: "To be shut up with the people of Utica, a fickle Phoenician folk, was a fearful thing; for even though they were quiet now, whenever Caesar came up against them they would play the traitor and aid him in his attacks." Before they would stay, they required that Cato help them finish what Metellus Scipio had first demanded: to drive these budding traitors from the city or put them to death.

Cato had interceded for the Uticans a year before, when his cause was much stronger. Would he reconsider now that it was weak enough to depend on slaves? He still seems to have considered any cleansing of the civilians as "excessively barbarous," but he begged the horsemen to wait while he conferred with the city's Romans.

*   *   *

Inside Utica, the mood had changed dramatically. The same ordinary traders who not long before were shouting their defiance at Caesar now turned all their anger on Cato—this politician, practically a foreigner to them, who had imposed himself on their city and forced them into war to satisfy his own grudges, who had forced them to stake their lives because he himself wanted to die. The same accusations spilled over onto the Roman senators, the war party that was enabling Cato's recklessness. From the back of the crowd confronting Cato, there were even mutters that the senators ought to be detained as hostages for the city's safety. Whatever political order Cato had worked to build among merchants, senators, and locals in his personal Republic, whatever unanimity had arisen in the brief flare of the first news, was now in pieces.

Cato did not respond to the demands to arrest the senators. For the moment, he pretended not to hear them. But the prospect of violence within the city made retaining the cavalry even more vital. If the three hundred fell on the senators—or on Cato himself—the horsemen would be their best defense. So when lookouts brought Cato news that the horsemen, tired of waiting, were galloping away, he broke off the meeting and set off in pursuit. At the gates, he found them too far off to be called back. He mounted a horse and chased down the cavalry on the plain.

Cheers went up as he came into sight, riding hard. The horsemen hailed him as their new commander, a man who had done the sensible thing in saving himself from the doomed city. Now, together, they could take cover in the hills. But as Cato came into better view, it looked as if he were actually, unthinkably, weeping. One last time, on the exposed plain, he begged them to stay in Utica and protect Roman senators in grave danger. When they hesitated, he grabbed at their sleeves, seized hold of a horse's bridle, tried desperately to point it in the right direction, as if he could will them back to wait for the siege. But still they were immovable.

At last, Cato extracted a compromise: They would stay one more day, to protect the senators as they escaped.

· · ·

Cato rode back, with less urgency now, at the head of the horsemen. He set some to guard the gates and stationed others at the citadel. When the three hundred saw that Cato had won over these armed men, at least temporarily, they feared that their intemperate plans for the senators had been overheard and that Cato was set to punish them for their desertion of the cause. The merchants sent word that he should come and hear them out in person. To Cato's friends, and the senators who had become the flashpoint of the conflict in the city, the invitation was an obvious trap; they crowded around him and forcibly held him back. But at length he shook them off and went again, alone, to meet with the three hundred. Watching him go, the senators could only murmur among themselves that their chief had grown strangely careless of his safety.

They need not have feared so much, yet. The three hundred had no intention of detaining him, or worse. Their resolution had evaporated entirely, leaving only a residue of guilt. They wanted out: out of their commitment, out of the war. They were unanimous: They would take advantage of Caesar's mercy while it lasted, but they would be sure to pray for Cato first. And if Caesar refused clemency to Cato, then and only then would the three hundred hold out. It was the best they could offer. As they said, by way of apology, "they were not Catos."

Did that phrase strike a bitter chord in the man it was meant to flatter? Three generations ago, "we aren't Catos" was the proof that his great-grandfather had arrived. The saying had marked him as no mere ambitious "new man," but a proverb in his own lifetime. Now, "we aren't Catos" was the excuse that marked the end of Cato's cause. His Republic had been whittled down to the smallest possible point.

Cato freed the three hundred to send their surrender to Caesar. He only demanded that they ask no mercy for him:

> Prayer belonged to the conquered, and the craving of grace to those who had done wrong; but for his part he had not only been unvanquished all his life, but was actually a victor now as far as he chose to be, and a conqueror of Caesar in all that was honorable and just; Caesar was the one who was vanquished and taken; for the hostile acts against his country, which he had long denied, were now detected and proven.

For these straightforward men of business, that was nothing more than Cato's game with words, a faintly silly attempt to define his way out of defeat. For Cato, it was an article of faith.

*　　*　　*

All gates were closed, now, but the gate to the sea. The harbor was a chaos of baggage and flight, senators scrambling onto ships, haggling with captains over the cost of passage, troops and families shoving and crowding at the docks, food spilling out of carts or hoarded aboard by the armful, Cato doing all he could to keep order amid the flight and panic. He moved from ship to ship through the disarray, breaking up fights where he could, stuffing vessels full of refugees and provisions, persuading wavering friends to flee, but all the time looking back over his shoulder, waiting for the horsemen covering the retreat to grow tired of their promise.

Soon enough, before the ships were gone, the shouting from the city matched the clamor on the shore. The cavalry, considering its word to the senators kept, was leaving Utica and looting as it went. The Caesarian account records the horsemen rifling through homes for valuables, killing the civilians who stood with arms raised in their way, and raping those women they could lay hands on amid the wrecked homes—as if Utica were a conquered city. These were the conquerors whom Cato had invited in; now, at the sound of the shouts, he sprinted from the harbor up to the city to plead with the horsemen to stop and leave. Plutarch writes that he only had to snatch the plunder out of the hands of one offender before the rest, stricken with shame at the sight, dropped plates and coins, art and fine clothing, and rode away with hanging heads. But the version in *The African War* seems more plausible, more in keeping with the behavior of a pillaging cavalry with little to fight for but what it could carry: "Cato, unable to prevail with them to abstain from rapine and slaughter . . . gave each a hundred sesterces to make them quiet." Sated and bribed to go away, they rode to find Juba, and the city was alone again.

With most of the senators aboard ships, and the horsemen gone, the scene at the harbor quieted to a state of only ordinary disorder. Beneath the ships there was time for longer good-byes and embraces with friends who understood, without speaking of it, that they would not be seeing Cato again. The escape was now open to all who would take it, and late into the night Cato remained awake, supervising the loading of the ships and sending them off when they were full, even buying passage for those too poor or too ruined by the war to afford it. After a night of begging or bullying every acquaintance he could find to get on a ship, he was left with only a few of those closest to him. Among them was the son of his first marriage, Marcus, a man in his thirties who shared his father's courage and taste for drink, but not the taste for philosophy that tempered them. Cato made a token effort to convince his son to flee—but he seemed pleased when Marcus refused, pleading his duty to stand by his father.

In the dwindling crowd, the two house philosophers whom Cato had brought to Utica, Apollonides and Demetrius, remained, a Stoic and an Aristotelian retained for the pleasure of their conversation. Though they were expected to disagree on a great deal—indeed, that was the point of keeping two—it was common knowledge that a philosopher of any stripe was supposed to be above fear at a time like this. They would not be worth their reputations if they fled on a ship now, so, eagerly or not, they stayed.

And there was one of those earnest young imitators whom Cato had spent a lifetime grudgingly attracting. Statyllius, barely more than a boy, had followed Cato from Rome, burning with hatred for Caesar and tyranny. Aping Cato in everything, he refused to go when Cato intended to stay, his face a mask of studious calm, even when his idol grabbed him by the shoulder and yelled at him to drop his foolishness. Frustrated, Cato pulled aside his two philosophers and gave them clipped orders: "It is your task to reduce this man's swollen pride and restore him to conformity with his best interests."

· · ·

But another man's swollen pride was Cato's necessity. The next day, April 12, was a day for completing the evacuation. Besides that, the only glum job that remained was to settle the matter of the three hundred, who were seeking Caesar's pardon. For their envoy, Cato chose the member of his staff with the best chance of winning mercy: Lucius Caesar, Cato's quartermaster and a distant relative of Caesar's. The two spent much of the day composing a plea to be read out to Caesar, throwing the city on his clemency. Cato, with a degree of irritation we can well imagine, helped Lucius find the words most likely to soften Caesar's heart. All that was left after that was to add names to the petition. Cato gave up his son and his household to Caesar's mercy, but when Lucius offered to fall at the general's feet and plead for him, Cato would not hear of it.

There was little doubt that Caesar, for all that he despised Cato, would have saved him. Pardoning the face of the opposition would have been the surest way for Caesar to paint his regime as a new beginning for the Republic, as something more than a return to Sulla's terror. Indeed, clemency for the defeated was a central plank of Caesarian propaganda. Caesar fought under the banner of mercy. He made certain that his tears at Pompey's death were heard far and wide. He was eager to let the whole Roman world know that he bore no grudges in victory.

Cato was well aware of those stakes. The scene could become the stuff of legend in an instant, Caesar magnanimously reaching out his hands to Cato, lifting him up from the dust; it was already written in Caesar's mind. But Cato would not give Caesar the gift of his silence; he had scripted his own scene. He would not recognize a tyrant's legitimacy by accepting his power to save. As Cato saw it, Caesar broke the law even in offering pardons, because he offered them on no authority but his own. To accept forgiveness would mean conceding Caesar's right to forgive, and Cato would not concede that.

So Lucius rode south from Utica to find Caesar and recite to him Cato's words asking for the lives of all but Cato. And now, with evening coming in, Cato handed over his account books to the authorities left in the city, along with all the surplus money that remained. At last, he was free of business.

Cato, readying for his evening bath, called for his son and broke to Marcus the news of the petition. All Marcus asked was why it was right for the son to accept a pardon while the father refused. According to Cassius Dio, Cato answered, "I, who have been brought up in freedom, with the right of free speech, cannot in my old age change and learn slavery instead; but for you, who were both born and brought up amid such a condition, it is proper to serve the divinity that presides over your fortunes." He had no tenderness in him, not even now. He could only tell his son that he was, through no fault of his own, a slave, and a born slave. Cato, reflecting back, decided that freedom had left the Republic many years before and was so far gone that a degraded generation had come of age not knowing it.

Maybe this was the nostalgia of an aging man, but it was more than any common nostalgia. It was the deep pessimism of a man who believed his world was dying with him. He had little hope for Marcus: How could a generation rebuild a freedom it had only known from hearsay? With his last instructions, Cato did not set his son burning to fight on for the Republic: He forbade him from practicing politics altogether. What would politics be in the world that was coming? Wheedling the prince for scraps of favor, at best, whispering plots in corners and locked rooms; either way, for a Cato, it was a disgrace.

With those dark thoughts, Cato set out for the public bath with Apollonides, his house Stoic. But as he let his mind wander in the water, one more piece of undone business broke his calm. "Statyllius! Did you bring him down from that high purpose of his? Has he set sail without even saying good-bye?"

Apollonides sighed that he and his colleague had spent the day reasoning with him, struggling from every angle to talk him down from his resolve—but he remained unmoving. He had one answer for everything: He would do whatever Cato did.

Cato smiled in his bath. "Well, we shall see about that."

• • •

This was how you came to Stoicism: paradoxes, little sayings that were absurd enough on their face to stop you in your tracks. Virtue alone is happiness. All virtues are one and the same. All sins weigh equally heavy. All bad men are insane. If you heard and cared to ask how that could possibly be, as Cato must once have asked, you found that each was a little door opening on a vast space.

Cato was at dinner at a great table with what was left of his household, his friends, and the city magistrates, sitting upright and forcing the rest to sit up, too. When the food was cleared and the wine came in, the conversation turned to philosophy, as it always did. Cato had lived with the paradoxes for most of his life, and it must have been almost a ritual—one of Cato's few pleasures—to send them around the table, quoting, disputing, offering evidence. "The good man alone is free, and the bad are all slaves." They each took a turn with it, and when the conversation came to Demetrius, Cato's Aristotelian, he gamely made the usual objections. He must have made them hundreds of times before—but this one time, Cato shouted him down. He hit the table and shot back that Demetrius was dead wrong, "and in loud and harsh tones maintained his argument at greatest length and with astonishing earnestness."

When he paused for breath, no one spoke, no one moved. The fiction of a pleasant dinner party fell away, and it was clear across the breadth of the table that Cato had staked his life on those words. It had been unspoken; now he had all but spoken it. Cato looked from face to face and knew that they knew; and now he clumsily changed the subject to the evacuation and his fears for those at sea, but he had never known how to conceal himself, and had not learned how in the last minute, and nothing broke the tension in the room. The guests made their excuses. Cato left for a walk and filled his lungs with the night air.

•   •   •

More tightly than usual, he hugged his son and his friends good night. They swallowed their worry and kept silent. Cato shut himself in his room. They heard him calling, from inside, for a book to be brought for his bedtime reading, Plato's dialogue *On the Soul*.

We know it as the *Phaedo*. It is the story of how Socrates, condemned to death, calls his closest friends to his prison cell to watch him die; how he spends his last hours in the conversation he loves, and at length proves that the soul is immortal, and that he will live on even after he drinks poison; how the hour finally comes, and Socrates swallows his death with the composure of a king:

> He held out the cup to Socrates. He took it, and very gently . . . without trembling or changing color or expression, but looking up at the man with wide open eyes, as was his custom, said, "What do you say about pouring a libation to some deity from this cup? May I, or not?"
>
> "Socrates," said he, "we prepare only as much as we think is enough."
>
> "I understand," said Socrates, "but I may and must pray to the gods that my departure hence be a fortunate one; so I offer this prayer, and may it be granted." With these words he raised the cup to his lips and very cheerfully and quietly drained it.

Cato read to the end and began again. It was the ideal, almost the fantasy, of a perfect death. It was also, literally speaking, suicide. Socrates had scorned the mercy of the court that convicted him, and had himself put the cup to his lips. He had been forced to it, but hadn't Cato been forced? Forced from a greater distance, perhaps, but still forced to it.

Cato must have lingered long over Socrates' words on suicide. If we come to wisdom by leaving behind our bodies and all that is base, why are we not free to leave our bodies in an instant? To a friend who raises just that point, Socrates patiently answers, "It will perhaps seem strange to you that these human beings for whom it is better to die cannot without impiety do good to themselves, but must wait for some other benefactor." Most of the time, we *must* wait—because all that we are is the property of the gods, because we cannot run away from our station without their leave.

Socrates finishes the thought: "Perhaps from this point of view it is not unreasonable to say that a man must not kill himself until the god sends some necessity upon him, such as has now come upon me." Drinking the poison was, literally, suicide. But it was also obedience, because a god had sent the necessity. It was also martyrdom.

Cato had called for the book, loudly. He wanted it known that it was with him that night. He wanted to put himself beside Socrates as a philosopher-martyr, dying by his own hand only in the simplest sense— dying under necessity, for his convictions. He wanted it known that when his own sword entered him, he would not be holding it; Caesar would.

Self-serving or not, Cato's deliberate identification with Socrates—the wise man forced into suicide for his beliefs—was his last, and most lasting, political gesture. But to set himself next to Socrates, he only needed to call for the book. He did not need to read it through—certainly not, as Plutarch reported, to read it through twice. Why was the *Phaedo* worth his last thoughts? It was not only the book of dignified death. It was also the book of immortality, the best argument available that the soul lived after the body died, that all it knew of truth came from the eternal world, that it partici- pated in Plato's Form of Life, which death could not enter. Its guiding spirit was the Socrates who died with utter confidence that he was not dying.

Stoicism had brought Cato far: It had brought him here to the desert, and the point of death, shut in his lamplit room. But it could not bring him the rest of the way: Stoicism offered no assurances of another life. And Cato seems to have wanted an assurance. It did not have to be consistent, it did not have to be Stoic—but it had to be absolute. He had to believe that some- thing of him was going to live. He had to be able to say with Socrates:

I would assert as positively as anything about such matters that I am going to gods who are good masters. And therefore, so far as that is concerned, I not only do not grieve, but I have great hopes that there is something in store for the dead, and, as has been said of old, something better for the good than for the wicked.

He reached for his sword.

•   •   •

Cassius Dio and Caesar's lieutenant say that the weapon was already there with him, concealed in his room or under his pillow, and that what happened next happened in secret. But Plutarch and Appian write, plausibly, that Cato's friends and son weren't sitting passively as Cato went for his walk after dinner—that they acted on their fear for his safety and hid his sword. When Cato reached and found it gone, he called a slave to ask who had taken it. The slave mumbled that he would see, but didn't return. Cato let more time pass and turned through the book again, and then renewed his call for the sword, straining to make his voice matter-of-fact, as if he were only looking for a lost object. Still no one came.

Now he was standing up and calling for his sword more loudly. Still, as if the whole house were conspiring against him, no one answered. Now he was demanding his sword. Now he was interrogating his slaves one by one, now ordering the sword be put in his hand instantly. Now he was shouting that his household had betrayed him to Caesar, that the enemy would come and find him unarmed, defenseless—and in his sudden fury he punched an unfortunate slave in the mouth, and now he screamed in pain at his broken hand. Finally, with Cato's friends, his son came in tears to say what no one had said openly, to beg his father to live.

Cato wanted his death to himself. Even now, he would only speak of it in the most oblique words. He pulled himself up to his full height, clutching his injured right hand, and spoke to Marcus with all of the grave authority of a Roman father: "When and where, without my knowledge, have I been judged a madman?" His son was silent. Cato demanded that they argue with him like men or leave him secure in his own judgment. Did they presume that they could stop him? Could they stop him from bashing his head against the wall? Could they stop him from holding his breath? Zeno, the first Stoic, was said to have died that way, such was his remarkable will; and if Cato chose to follow him, who were they to put their judgment above his? Did they have any argument besides tears?

Only more tears. They filed sullenly out, all but Demetrius and Apollonides—and it says a great deal about Cato that he saved his last real conversation for his philosophers, not his son. He was calmer now. He spoke, or tried to speak, like a philosopher among philosophers. He asked these two silent men if they intended to sit by his bed on suicide watch all night or if they were here to change his mind. Did they have a shining new argument that made sense of Caesar, or made Caesar's mercy less bitter? "Why, then, do you not speak persuasively and convert me to this doctrine, that we may cast away those good old opinions and arguments which have been part of our very lives?"

They had nothing to say. What was there to say? What words could convince Cato that he could live another day without renouncing every other day of his forty-eight years?

The silent men filed out, and the sword at last came in. Cato shut the door, pulled the sword from its sheath, tested the blade on his hand. When he saw that it was true enough to draw blood, he was satisfied, and he lay down beside his sword to finish his book. Soon he was asleep, and snoring loud enough to be heard through the house.

Who could take a nap before suicide? What man set on dying would call, as Cato called when he started awake toward midnight, for a doctor to bandage his hand, and for a freedman to run and bring back news from the harbor? Among his friends sitting vigil, the mood was lighter now. Maybe something in Plato had changed his mind. Maybe he had tested the sword and lost the will as he felt its point. Maybe it had all been a show of pride.

Cato's swollen hand was wrapped, and his servant returned with news from the sea: The evacuation was done. All ships were gone but one, and it was hoisting sail as they spoke. But there were winds and choppy waves in the port, and a storm looked to be coming in. All those Cato had sent to sea were far gone now, beyond his help in dark water, but still, he sent his servant back one more time, to scan the harbor for any ships the storm might have driven onto the land.

Cato slept again, still beside the sword. An hour or two before dawn, with the first birds starting up, news from the harbor came back. All was still. The storm had gone elsewhere. Far out at sea, beyond their sight, it might be tossing ships and straining masts to breaking, but that was past their power now. Cato sent his freedman away and ordered the door closed, and when it was closed, he took up the sword and stabbed himself below the heart.

On another day, he might have had the strength to finish himself. But his right hand was weak and could barely grip the hilt. Bleeding but not dead, he flailed and stumbled and fell, and the house heard the crash of the overturned furniture and of his body. His son and slaves and friends burst through the door to find him moaning in his own blood and the slick rings of his intestines, eyes open and staring.

• • •

Alive still? Someone stood over him in the lamplight, bloody hands pushing his bowels back into the wound, sewing him up with needle and thread. He reached down to where the pain was, beneath the stitches and into the wound, and tore himself open.

14

CATO IN PURGATORY

He is frozen like that: twisted face, open wound, nails digging into entrails. The sword, which failed, is out of the frame. He is the man who killed himself with bare hands. This speaks to some of an inhuman courage, to others, of a subhuman ferocity. The scene will be painted, sculpted, narrated for centuries, with varying degrees of dignity and sympathy—but the first to order it painted is Caesar. He has ordered it bloody.

At the end of the dictator's quadruple triumph—over Gaul, over Egypt, over Pontus, over Africa, but not, for the record, over any Romans—it is carried high on a placard, so all the crushing crowds can see Cato ripping open the wound "like a wild beast." It is state-sanctioned news; it is the official version; it is also perhaps Caesar's way of owning at last the man he could not pardon and could not buy. But it is far too much. The crowd is too frightened to boo Caesar, but it can groan in pity for Cato, loud enough for Caesar to hear.

• • •

Now that he was buried—at Utica, by the sea, extravagantly—Cato embarked on his second life. It was, to a great extent, a life that the flesh-and-blood Cato would have hated: a life as the property of anyone with a pen and a point to grind out, a career as an object. Yet it was a life that Cato had made inevitable, all the way to his self-mythologizing death.

Caesar was self-aware enough to know that the Cato myth was, in its early days, more than gauzy nostalgia for the old Republic. It was a direct attack on his legitimacy. It was the means by which Cato's once-fringe view of Caesar's intentions, which had already spread to the inner circle of the *optimates* and then to Pompey, might be communicated to the rest of Rome. Unmaking the Cato myth was one of the consuming political challenges of the two years that remained to Caesar. Clemency would have been easiest: A Cato in dignified retirement or even as a tolerated senatorial crank would not have been able to pose as the Republic incarnate. He would have been one more ex-Pompeian who had made his peace with the new order, as his friend Cicero and his half nephew Brutus had made theirs.

When Cato effectively crumpled up and lit that possibility on fire, he forced Caesar into a new posture, that of a reasonable man rejected by a fanatic. Just as he had shed shrewd tears for Pompey, he worked hard to strike the proper attitude of manly grief when he entered Utica to find his enemy already buried. "Cato, I begrudge you your death, just as you begrudged me the chance to spare your life."

That much was well received, but it prompted the question: What kind of man chooses death to make a point? Caesar's answer was: a man like a wild beast. And there, he badly miscalculated.

At Caesar's triumphs, not a word was said about Pompey. Caesar understood that he had become a universal figure, and that the political risks of "triumphing" over such a figure—rather than over an assorted collection of foreigners—were grave. But he failed to consider that Cato, partisan as he had been in life, now belonged in the same company. Humiliating death scenes of enemies were not uncommon at Roman triumphs; Pompey's last triumph, for instance, had prominently featured the death of Mithridates. But Romans were supposed to be exempt from such shameful treatment. By broadcasting Cato's grisly death—along with the death scenes of other defeated republicans—Caesar was branding him not only an animal, but an alien. The crowd's response showed that it was not willing to follow Caesar that far, not after a war that had cost a hundred thousand lives and cut Rome's population, whether by flight or battle casualties, in half.

Was Cicero in that crowd? It is hard to imagine how he could have been absent from such a mandatory occasion of state. It's harder still to imagine his state of mind as the image of Cato passed. Here went the man he had always viewed with equal parts awe and exasperation. Here went the man who had vowed to carry on the war himself, after Cicero had surrendered and sailed away. But wasn't Cato responsible for the war in the first place? And yet he died for his beliefs, even as Cicero saved his own skin. But wasn't it just like Cato to take the showy exit and leave to others the hard work of navigating this new world?

The wisest course would have been silence. For the second time, Cicero owed Caesar for a safe return to Rome. This time, he arguably owed the dictator his life. In the new order, governed by a dictator and his handpicked men, Cicero was a sixty-year-old without place, without allies, with few friends left. He was heavily dependent on Caesar's kindness, and he worked hard to cultivate it. As Cicero later reflects, "For some reason he was extraordinarily patient where I was concerned."

For a final time, Cato held out to Cicero the possibility that all could have been otherwise, and in his frustration at his dependency, Cicero was finally willing to listen. It was bookish Brutus, at work on a life of Cato, who suggested that Cicero write his own version; Cicero's friend Atticus pushed the project, as well. As Cicero sat down to the task in the quiet of his villa, he soon found it "a problem for Archimedes." There was no praising Cato without infuriating Caesar. Yet he persisted.

He could have approached his *Cato* with the mockery of the Murena speech or with the frustration that so often found a place in his letters. He could have, if he had chosen to, painted a portrait of true nuance. Instead, Cicero painted an icon. He wrote of Cato the Stoic saint, the Roman ideal, the republican martyr. He swallowed his fear of reprisal long enough to write the definitive myth of Cato, and he brought to it all the polish of Rome's greatest prose stylist. Cicero's *Cato* is lost, but there are traces of it in all of his post-Utica praise for his friend, writings in which Cato, stripped of his irritating qualities, takes on an icon's flatness and gold-flecked colors.

Cato, among the republicans, was uniquely right to die:

> Was the case of Marcus Cato different from that of the others who surrendered to Caesar in Africa? Yet had they killed themselves, they might perhaps have been worthy of censure, because their mode of life was less severe, and their characters were more pliant; while, since nature had given Cato an incredible massiveness of character, and he himself had strengthened it by undeviating self-consistency, and had always been steadfast in the purpose once

272

conceived and the design once undertaken, it seemed fit for him to die rather than to look upon the face of a tyrant.

Cato, exactly as he had intended, was a new Socrates:

> Cato left this world in such a manner as if he were delighted that he had found an opportunity of dying; for that god who presides in us forbids our departure hence without his leave. But when the god himself has given us a just cause, as formerly he did to Socrates, and lately to Cato, and often to many others—in such a case, certainly every man of sense would gladly exchange this darkness for that light.

Cato was, in sum, a "godlike and unique man," a man whose life was sufficient proof that virtue existed.

Perhaps Cicero was chastened into this effusive attitude by his friend's death or by a survivor's guilt. Perhaps he was simply happy to have Cato as an obedient symbol, rather than an impossible man. Regardless, he wrote his *Cato* at no little risk to his position and his safety—and in that respect, writing it was among the most Catonian things he ever did.

It was also among the most influential. Cicero praised Cato as both a model Roman and a model Stoic, which would have been unthinkable in an earlier time. His *Cato* helped to end the conflict between the two, helped to complete Cato's project of Romanizing Stoicism. It was the literary expression of the crowd's groan at Caesar's triumph, turning Cato from partisan failure to national hero by owning and celebrating the death that Caesar saw as a humiliation. It was, as the historian L. R. Taylor puts it, "the foundation of the Cato legend that went down into the empire." It is a lost book with the gravitational pull of a hidden planet.

•   •   •

Completed in August, *Cato* was published in late 46, to the fury of Caesar. An unexpected personal attack, it was a distraction from a feverish period of reform. In a matter of months, Caesar had brought a wealth of new blood into the Senate, even friendly Gauls, army officers, and sons of ex-slaves. He had cut back the grain dole in the name of fiscal restraint, but he had arranged to settle some of Rome's poorest citizens in new colonies and had worked to guarantee agricultural jobs to freeborn Romans. Most lastingly, he had restructured the inaccurate Roman calendar on the model he had learned in Egypt, giving us our year of 365¼ days. These reforms were sweeping—but they hardly constituted the populist nightmare dreamed up by Caesar's enemies. Sensible, moderate, and even technocratic as they were, they should have been the best rebuttal to *Cato*. Where, Caesar demanded to know, was the tyranny in any of this? Where was the massive redistribution? Where was the end of Rome? That Cicero could see these results and still deify Cato—it was to Caesar one more sign of a broken old order blindly idealizing the broken old way of things.

Caesar ordered an immediate response from Hirtius, his personal secretary and occasional ghostwriter. But Hirtius's pamphlet was such a rushed-out, overheated piece of personal abuse that it only worked to cement Cato's heroic image and cast Caesar's faction as petty and tone-deaf. Seizing on a chance to publicize the embarrassment, Cicero actually had his own scribes churn out more copies of Hirtius's failed rebuttal.

Caesar took no action against Cicero, but as the extent of the flop became clear, he concluded that painting Cato in a truer light would require his personal attention. As had so often been the case, his attention could only be spared in short snatches, in army tents at the sore end of a day's march. In late 46 and early 45, Caesar was en route to Spain to confront the last scraps of resistance under Pompey's son. Even in the thick of the fighting in Gaul, Caesar had never been able to put Cato fully from his mind. He had found time to abuse him in his letters and war chronicles. Now, on the way to Spain, it was as if nothing had changed. Caesar was not one to forget an insult to his *dignitas*. Having gone to war over it, he could certainly spare the effort to dictate a pamphlet.

The result was mildly shocking. Caesar's *Anti-Cato* was not a careful piece of positioning, nor did it even gesture at respect for the dead. It was, instead, a rich, raw vein of insult—and every word was deeply felt. It was the most glaring exception to his policy of clemency. Though the *Anti-Cato* is also lost, its accusations were momentous enough to be preserved by a number of later writers.

Cato was terminally arrogant. He neglected his family. He was a notorious drunk. He had suspicious relations with Servilia, his own sister (and

Caesar's mistress). He prostituted his wife, Marcia: "The woman was at first set as a bait for Hortensius, and lent by Cato when she was young so that he might take her back when she was rich." And a final calumny: After the luxuriant funeral of his brother, Caepio, Cato could be found on his hands and knees beside the extinguished pyre—sifting through his brother's ashes for any trace of melted gold.

Even by the high standards of Roman political invective, this was stunning. "If ever a Roman writer allowed himself to be carried away by hatred," one historian writes, "Caesar did so in this instance." His target already dead and beaten, showing such naked anger ran directly counter to Caesar's interests. In the course of his pardons and his moderate rule, Caesar had painstakingly built the image of a mild and merciful conqueror, exactly the kind of man who was supposed to be above such gratuitous insults. In his anger at Cato—in his bewilderment at the sanctification of such a high-handed fool—Caesar missed much more promising avenues for attack. If there was ever a place to spell out the costs of Cato's absolute resistance to change or to pin him with blame for the civil war, this was it. There was no need to invent macabre stories of corpse robbing. And if Caesar had been able to distance himself from his anger, he might have seen that ridicule, not rage, was the most effective way to puncture such a self-righteous opponent.

Instead, Caesar discovered an enduring lesson for all those who wrestle with martyrs' ghosts: There is little to gain in attacking a dead man, and a great deal to lose. With his *Anti-Cato,* Caesar lost any chance to nip the Cato myth in the bud. Instead, he provoked a powerful backlash. In Taylor's judgment, "Caesar's vicious and unjust attack served only to build up Cato's reputation. It contributed to the revival of republicanism at Rome." Hardcore republicanism may have remained a minority taste, but it was alive, armed, and unified by Cato's memory.

Still, that must have seemed a far-off concern as Caesar met Gnaeus Pompey in an unexpectedly ferocious battle in March of 45. It was the only time, Caesar remarked afterward, that he felt himself to be fighting not for victory, but for his life. For a final time, Caesar's luck in war held. With the capture and execution of Gnaeus, outward opposition to Caesar was over. Yet he and Cato were still not done with each other.

•   •   •

Porcia, Cato's eldest daughter, had inherited something of her father's care-lessness for pain and something of his self-destructiveness. It was 44; the scandal of her remarriage the previous year was beginning to fade, but she would never be able to set foot in public with her new husband without keeping an ear cocked for whispers. Brutus, in a perfectly good marriage of his own, had not given a single reason for divorcing his old wife, Claudia Pulchra. When asked, he simply said that he preferred Porcia. So perhaps, the rumors went, there had been an affair, or perhaps they were actually in love, or perhaps this was Brutus's way of proving his respect for Cato, of silently showing that even as he accepted favors from Caesar, he remained a republican at heart. That was certainly how the marriage was regarded and celebrated among what was left of the old Pompeians.

But in the early spring of 44, Porcia was spending most nights sleepless next to Brutus, who had somehow taken on the habit of starting awake in a sweat. Or he would lie unmoving with open eyes, under some heavy weight. But before Porcia dared to ask, she set out to prove to her husband and her-self, in the most vivid way possible, that, should he reveal the secret of his distress, not even torture could force it from her:

> She took a little knife, such as barbers use to cut the fingernails, and after banishing all her attendants from her chamber, made a deep gash in her thigh, so that there was a copious flow of blood, and after a little while violent pains and chills and fever followed from the wound.

> Seeing that Brutus was disturbed and greatly distressed, in the height of her anguish she spoke to him thus: "Brutus, I am Cato's daughter. . . . Now I know that I am superior even to pain."

> Thus having spoken, she showed him her wound and explained her test; whereupon Brutus, amazed and lifting his hands to heaven, prayed that he might succeed in his undertaking and thus show himself a worthy husband of Porcia.

It was no coincidence that the conspiracy against Caesar gathered around Cato's family, and especially around Brutus, his nephew, his son-in-law, his assistant, and his biographer. Brutus did not initiate the conspiracy, nor was it as high-minded as he might have liked. It was the usual mix of principle and greed. The circle, which grew as wide as sixty, included its frustrated office seekers and pardoned *optimates* with grudges intact, as well as sincere republicans. But the resources contributed by Brutus were inestimable. The dictator had heavily favored Brutus with trust and offices and had even named him an heir, so Brutus's leadership of the plot against Caesar was undertaken in all apparent selflessness. Brutus's lineage too was impeccable. He traced it back to the Brutus who had driven out Rome's last king.

Most important, Brutus blessed the plot with the legacy of Cato. It was the ideology of Cato that sanctioned the conspiracy, that made it plausibly more than a naked grab at power. Murder could not be justified if Caesar were set, as he claimed, on healing the wounds of civil war, on rebalancing the constitution, on bringing the empire's administration up to date for a new world. But if Caesar were fundamentally illegitimate, as Cato had died insisting, then his death would be a patriotic sacrifice. Wasn't Caesar's death the necessary conclusion of all that Cato had believed? It was not for nothing that the circle of aristocrats around Brutus called themselves the Liberators.

But not all of Cato's old intimates were invited to the liberation. Brutus gauged their zeal over wine, under the guise of philosophical conversation, and found that some had been markedly changed by defeat. Cato's protégé, Favonius, now argued that civil war was worse than tyranny. That the two could be held up as reasonable alternatives suggests that he feared the chaos that might break loose with Caesar's death. According to Plutarch, Brutus also ruled out the participation of a certain "Statilius." Was he the same Statyllius who had vowed in Utica to imitate Cato all the way to the end? If so, his courage had failed, and the experience of defeat had left him bitter and detached. "It did not become a wise and sensible man," he lectured Brutus, "to be thrown into turmoil and peril for the sake of feeble and foolish folk." Cicero too was left in the dark. He was too cautious, it was agreed, and too old.

The rest saw Caesar's behavior as confirmation of Cato's worst fears. There was nothing egregious on the level of policy, no Sullan purges. But symbolically, Caesar showed disturbing inclinations. He was willing to be paraded through Rome like a king in the making. His face was stamped on coins like a king's. He presided over the Senate from a gilded chair suspiciously like a throne. On the Capitol, his statue stood next to the old kings.

Even more scandalously, the statue of his Egyptian mistress, Cleopatra, stood in the Temple of Venus. And Caesar made a mockery of the consulship, drawing up a list of officeholders three years in advance and tossing an ex-army officer an honorary consulship lasting all of a few hours.

In February came the culminating insult: appointment as dictator-for-life. And about a month before the end, unconscionably, the dictator-for-life refused to rise from his chair for a party of senators. All of this together amounted to Caesar's death warrant.

Cato wanted it known that the sword that ended his life was, at least figuratively, held by Caesar. By the same process—we might call it ideological action at a distance—were the daggers that killed Caesar held by Cato? One historian writes that the assassination of Caesar was, in effect, the last act of Cato's career:

> Cato had consistently maneuvered Caesar . . . into illegal or unpopular positions. His death at Utica was the apex of this policy. Not Pompey's might but Cato's *auctoritas* was most lethal to Caesar. Caesar was left struggling with a myth, not a man. . . . Ultimately [Cato's] inevitable suicide immortalized the republican cause and dealt Caesar the final blow which was consummated on the Ides of March 44.

That is arguably too pat, too symmetrical for life. A clutch of jealous elites might have murdered Caesar even if Cato had never lived or never died so spectacularly. But there is a reason why Caesar's death remains the archetypal assassination, just as Cato's death remained, for centuries, the archetypal suicide. It wasn't only the fame of the victim, but the great cause in whose name he died.

Both were killed for the Republic. And what was the Republic without Cato? It was Pompey and Crassus ambitiously racing to massacre an army of slaves. It was the quaestor Marcellus striking the debts of senators with a stroke of a pen. It was Cicero laughing his way through corruption trials. It was Catiline's men strangled in a basement cell. It was Metellus Celer going to jail to stop a land reform. It was Scaurus draining his province of silver. It was Gabinius marching on Egypt for ten thousand talents. It was Clodius's body burning with the Senate House. But the Republic also produced, as it collapsed, the man who cemented the myth of the Republic—who sanctified it into something worth dying and killing for.

• • •

Cato's two eldest children both learned something from him about the value of a memorable ending. His son Marcus took his advice to stay clear of politics and spent much of his life after Utica drinking and whoring, as if to release, in a few years, all the accumulated pressure of generations of Cato family rectitude. Cato too had lived with that burden and had no doubt spent a lifetime fending off its frustrations. The same frustrations, it seems, crushed Marcus. He lived as if he had taken his father's last instructions as an expansive permission. The satirical verses of the day, the closest thing to gossip pages in the Roman world, recorded him as a great seducer—even, in one case, of a foreign prince's young wife.

And then, at the last possible moment, Marcus clawed back his reputation. He fought in Brutus's army, against Caesar's heirs, and when the battle was lost and his line collapsed around him, he stayed rooted in place, screaming for Brutus and the Republic until he was cut down where he stood, "amazing his foes by his valor."

Porcia, when news of the defeat reached her, is said to have joined her father in suicide—as legend has it, by swallowing burning coals.

• • •

Of all the facts used to draw a contrast between Caesar and the cold-eyed emperor Augustus, his great-nephew and adopted son, who became emperor after years of civil war following Caesar's assassination, one of the most telling is also one of the least remarked on: Augustus wrote an *Anti-Cato* of his own. It was a response to Brutus, his deified father's killer. And yet, after a private reading for family and friends, Augustus filed it away. Nothing about it, save the fact of its existence, survives. It's easy to imagine an urbane sketch free of Caesar's bombast, something forgettable that played well to a small and privileged room.

It would be wrong to say that Augustus lasted four decades on the throne, to his great-uncle's two years, because of his attitude to Cato. But it would be closer to the truth to say that his attitude to Cato epitomized the strategy that kept Augustus untouchable for so long. Julius Caesar did nothing to hide the fact that he considered the Republic a relic, and he hardly hesitated in accepting a series of dictatorships—for one year, for ten years, for life. But Augustus had seen Caesar die, in large part, over the misuse of symbols. So, after an era of ruinous war, he called himself the restorer of the Republic and its virtues. He aspired to nothing more than the honor of being *princeps*, "first citizen." He was content to cobble together power out of the Republic's rusting offices; he was variously a consul, a tribune, a censor, or sometimes simply a concerned private citizen. And in the Republic's name, under cover of this immense modesty, he founded five centuries of monarchy.

Another contrast between Julius and Augustus, from Suetonius: Whenever Julius Caesar was obligated to attend the public games, he spent them reading and answering correspondence and made no secret that his time was being wasted; whenever Augustus attended, he made sure to smile and clap.

Augustus's embrace of Cato, whatever feelings he expressed behind closed doors, was his way of smiling and clapping at the spectacle of the Republic. A state visit once brought Augustus into the house where Cato had lived. A sycophant in his entourage launched into what he thought the *princeps* would want to hear, a tirade on Cato's stubbornness. Augustus cut him off: "To seek to keep the established constitution unchanged is a sign of a good citizen and a good man." In Cato's own home, Augustus summed up Cato's philosophy more succinctly than Cato ever had. He claimed it for himself, even as he took the Republic to pieces.

So when the national epic came to be written in the secure twenties, with Augustus as the outcome of the divine plan, there had to be a place for Cato. Cato became pure hero, virtue incarnate, resting at last from the complications of politics. In lines of the *Aeneid* that Virgil recited for the *princeps* and his family, lines commissioned and paid for by the ruling circle, the Roman founder Aeneas goes to battle bearing a shield lovingly crafted by a god, decorated with all of Rome's fated history. Just before that history culminates in Augustus, there is this scene of the underworld:

> *Vulcan*
> *added the house of Tartarus, the high*
> *doorways of Dis, the penalties of crime;*

> *and Catiline, you hanging on a cliff*
> *that threatens, trembling at the Furies' faces;*
> *and, set apart, the pious who receive*
> *their laws from Cato.*

Catiline and Cato, chaos and order—from the proper perspective, it was that simple. From the proper perspective, there was no more shame in being a republican. After all, the emperor was one, too.

• • •

In this plaster Republic, generations of well-off boys grew up imagining themselves as Cato, acting out his death in the schools of rhetoric, delivering high-flown lines like this one, from a handbook on public speaking: "Marcus Cato, alone the greatest model of how to live and how to die, preferred death over begging for his life." Enacting Cato was becoming a patriotic cliché, the kind of homework that certain eye-rolling boys worked hard to escape. One imperial writer of the first century CE sheepishly recalled faking an illness to get out of his class's Cato day:

> *I remember, when I was little, I used to feign sore eyes,*
> *And dab them with oil so as not to have to learn Cato's*
> *Majestic speech as he faced death, a speech praised to*
> *The skies by my mad teacher. . . .*

But of all the playacting Catos, no one imagined himself into the role more fully than Lucius Annaeus Seneca, the most powerful Stoic Rome had ever known.

By 49 CE, when he was called to tutor the future emperor, Nero (incidentally, the great-great-great-great-great-grandson of Cato the Elder, through Cato's sister), Seneca had already made and lost his fortune and his good name. He had made them as a successful investor and as an author of moralizing tracts and tragedies, and he had lost them when exiled for a sex scandal with a lady of the imperial court. Recalled to court to take charge of Nero's education, Seneca found himself almost instantly restored to his place as one of the empire's great men. It was precisely the sort of jarring, arbitrary change of fortune for which Stoicism seemed to be made. As Seneca taught, we can survive such a change with soul intact if we keep our eyes fixed on the example of a master. "Choose a Cato; or, if Cato seems too severe a model, choose . . . a gentler spirit."

For Seneca, however, no one but Cato would do. Cato was proof that the inhuman ideal of the Stoic sage could be lived out in this world, that it was attainable even in the disillusioned, mythless present:

> Cato did not grapple with wild beasts . . . he did not hunt down monsters with fire and sword, nor did he chance to live in the times when it was possible to believe that the heavens rested on one man's shoulders. In an age when the old credulity had long been thrown aside, and knowledge had attained its highest development, he came into conflict with Ambition, a monster of many shapes, with the boundless greed for power. . . .

> He stood alone against the vices of a degenerate state that was sinking to destruction beneath its very weight, and he stayed the fall of the Republic to the utmost that one man's hand could do to draw it back, until at last he was himself withdrawn and shared the downfall that he had so long averted, and the two whom heaven willed should never part were blotted out together. For Cato did not survive freedom, nor freedom Cato.

This was something more dangerous than the soft-edged, depoliticized Cato favored by Augustus, and it cannot have sat well with Seneca's royal pupil, the sixth and last ruler in Julius Caesar's line. However direct Seneca's efforts to shape an emperor in the mold of Cato, they ended in notorious failure: "While denouncing tyranny, he was making himself the teacher of a tyrant."

When Nero ascended to the throne in 54 CE, at the age of seventeen, Seneca became one of his closest advisors, but his power to hold back the emperor's excesses faded year by year. Seneca cannot have approved of Nero's growing drunkenness and his savage political purges, which culminated in the assassination of his own mother in 59. But as long as the philosopher remained on the imperial payroll, he was open to charges of complicity with the increasingly deranged regime. As the mad emperor's reign grew less tolerable and his own position less tenable, Seneca grew more and more fixated on the unattainable figure of Cato. Again and again, he narrated Cato's life—and especially his death—in letters to friends. His stand against tyranny, and the freedom he had found in suicide, had gathered a frightening new relevance:

> You see that thirst can be endured: He marched over sun-baked hills, dragging the remains of a beaten army and with no train of supplies, undergoing lack of water and wearing a heavy suit of armor; always the last to drink of the few springs that they chanced to find. You see that honor, and dishonor too, can be despised: For they report that on the very day when Cato was defeated at the elections, he played a game of ball. You see also that man can be free from fear of those above him in rank: For Cato attacked Caesar and Pompey simultaneously, at a time when none dared fall foul of the one without endeavoring to oblige the other. You see that death can be scorned as well as exile: Cato inflicted exile upon himself and finally death, and war all the while.

It's hard to believe that Seneca wasn't, first and foremost, exhorting himself. He and Cicero might have understood each other: Both were would-be philosophers unable to escape from politics, both compromised by power and wealth, both in awe of the man whom they decided had effortlessly merged the political and philosophical lives. Whether the living Cato would have measured up to that standard mattered little, a century after his death.

In 62, Seneca asked for and received permission to retire. At the same time, his nephew, Marcus Annaeus Lucanus, only twenty-two years old, was embarking on a massive poem of praise for the emperor. By the time both uncle and nephew were dead, three years later, it had turned into the most subversive document of the age.

• • •

We've already seen, in his narration of the desert march, how Lucan (as we know him) became Cato's greatest mythologizer. At first, however, his *Pharsalia* was intended to celebrate the imperial status quo. A literary prodigy,

Lucan first came to the emperor Nero's attention for his uncanny ability to extemporize verse on the spot. He repaid the emperor for his lavish gifts by beginning an epic of the civil war that pointed toward Nero as the destined savior, just as Virgil, in an earlier generation, had pointed toward Augustus. The epic's opening dedication includes these chillingly obsequious lines: "But Rome is greater by these civil wars / Because they resulted in you."

But by the time the poem turned to narrating the war, it was easier to make sense of those lines as an ironic thumb in the eye. It is not clear what turned the sparkling young poet, halfway through his poem, into a fierce republican. It is possible that he came to question Nero's rule under the influence of his uncle Seneca, though some sources paint his conversion more selfishly: In their telling, he reconsidered his politics only after he fell out of the emperor's favor. However it happened, Lucan came to imagine a civil war entirely stripped of glory, a brutal struggle between two power-mad generals. He told the story with a bloody realism that did nothing to hide the staggering cost of the Republic's fall. Where other writers had glossed over the war or ignored it entirely, Lucan looked it squarely in the face— down to the scavenger dogs and birds picking over bodies in the aftermath of Pharsalus.

What Lucan learned from Cato was the art of finding victory in defeat. There was no denying the fact that Caesar, and by extension the whole imperial line, was favored by the gods—but if that was the case, so much the worse for the gods. As the poem's most memorable epigram puts it: "The victorious cause was dear to the gods; the lost cause, to Cato." The poem places Cato and the gods on the same level, exactly parallel. And in the world of the poem, there is nothing noble about victory. It attaches itself blindly to the greedy, the brutal, the corrupt. Meditating on the bloodshed, Lucan was driven to the brink of outright atheism:

> *No guardian gods watch over us from heaven:*
> *Jove is no king; let ages whirl along*
> *In blind confusion: from his throne supreme*
> *Shall he behold such carnage and restrain*
> *His thunderbolts? . . .*
> > *Careless of men*
> *Are all the gods.*

With the old religion rendered meaningless by war, what was there to put in its place? For Lucan, the only figure worth Rome's reverence was the defeated Cato, whose desert march amounted to a triumphal procession:

> Rather would I lead
> With him his triumph through the pathless sands
> And Libya's bounds, than in Pompeius' car
> Three times ascend the Capitol. . . .
>   Rome! in him behold
> His country's father, worthiest of thy vows;
> A name by which men shall not blush to swear,
> Whom, should'st thou break the fetters from thy neck,
> Thou may'st in distant days decree divine.

Lucan took praise of Cato to its furthest extreme: He proposed him as the new god of a civic religion, as the name by which Romans would swear oaths in a restored Republic. This was more than rhetorical bluster: The call to break Rome's fetters was openly revolutionary.

In 65, for the second time, the memory of Cato loomed over a conspiracy against a Roman ruler. But the plot against Nero—an unstable alliance of republicans and partisans of a new emperor—ended in failure. A careless conspirator let the plans slip before the blow could be struck, and both Lucan and Seneca were swept up in the court's ruthless reaction, though Seneca insisted on his innocence to the end.

Both had celebrated Cato's death with an eloquence far beyond their hero's, but when it came to their own forced suicides, neither could match him. Seneca came well prepared with last words. Forbidden to write a will, he turned to his friends and announced, "I bequeath to you the only thing I still possess, yet the finest of all—the pattern of my life." He cut open the veins of his arms, and as he waited to expire, dictated more official last words to his secretaries, who waited with pens in hand. Meanwhile, the blood was barely flowing and the philosopher was hanging tediously on, so he demanded the Socratic cup of hemlock. When this too failed to speed things up, he climbed into a hot bath, after sprinkling some of the water on the nearest slaves, "as a libation to Jupiter Liberator." A combination of blood loss, poison, steam, and exhaustion eventually carried him away.

Lucan, at twenty-five, died before he could complete his poem or narrate Cato's death. In his last hours, in hopes of a pardon, he evidently incriminated his mother in the conspiracy.

•   •   •

With the Republic long gone and power fixed in an imperial bureaucracy increasingly indifferent to claims of high birth, the aristocracy's traditional avenues of glory—and even of identity—were closing. The value of a good death was never higher. As the classicist Miriam Griffin writes:

> The Roman nobility found it more difficult to live up to the example of their ancestors in acquiring military and civic fame, but they could still die noble and memorable deaths. Suicide had a particular advantage in this context, for it could be staged. One could make sure that one had an audience and that one said memorable things. (Only in opera is it usually easy to achieve this with other forms of death.)

A senator under Nero "escaped the miseries of decrepit old age by opening his veins. Because of his notorious effeminacy, no one had thought he had the courage to kill himself."

Thrasea Paetus, a Stoic senator and biographer of Cato, was condemned by Nero for setting a bad example of sobriety. When the news came, he slit his arms and held up the wounds to his audience: "You have been born into times in which it is well to fortify the spirit with examples of courage."

A Roman jurist recorded the causes of suicide: guilt, disgust with life, bad health, and "showing off, as with certain philosophers."

•   •   •

The charge of "showing off" would become the basis for the most damaging attack on Cato's memory, an attack launched not by his political enemies, but his religious enemies: the Christians.

Cato's Stoicism was part of the Christian inheritance. Many of the leaders of the early church were former Stoics, and even those who were not Stoics had come of age in a Roman intellectual culture dominated by Stoicism. It is no surprise that the early Christians borrowed much of their religious vocabulary (terms like *"Logos,"* "conscience," and even the multiple *"personae"* of God) from the Stoics; that they emphasized, like the Stoics, freedom of conscience and mastery of the passions; that they spoke, like the Stoics, of human brotherhood under a benevolent creator; that they dwelled, like the Stoics, on unshakable human sinfulness. All of this gave Christianity a familiarity and a respectability that served it well, but it also required the new religion to struggle to set itself apart as uniquely true. The pagan philosophies from which Christianity borrowed, no less than the Judaism from which it grew, became in time rivals to be conquered. So the fathers of the church felt obliged to wrestle with Cato, who had become the model of the Stoic life. Demonstrating the deficits of the Stoic life required them, in large part, to cast Cato as a moral failure, crippled by pride.

But doing so often required them to fight their own admiration of Cato. In a culture that made Cato an icon, not even Christians were immune to his appeal. Some of them used him as a cudgel against the pagan culture. For instance, Tertullian—a second-century lawyer-turned-theologian—cleverly picked up where Lucan had left off, attacking Rome for *failing* to deify Cato. He demanded, "Which of those gods of yours is worthier and wiser than Cato?"

Cato's most lasting appeal continued to lie in his suicide. Christians, who opposed suicide on all counts, pored over Cato's death with the intensity of Seneca. Rather than celebrating it, however, they were set on undermining its moral force, on exposing Cato's (typically pagan) motives as anything but heroic. Lactantius—an influential advisor to the first Christian emperor, Constantine—helped set the pattern in his fourth-century treatment of Cato and suicide, and this argument was central to his case against the vanity of pagan thought as a whole. Pagans, Lactantius argued, failed to recognize that suicide, no less than murder, is the destruction of a human life, a crime against God: "We can only withdraw from this habitation of the body, which has been appointed for us to keep, by the command of Him who placed us in this body, that we may inhabit it until He orders us to depart from it." Surprisingly, this is almost identical to the argument against suicide voiced by Socrates in the *Phaedo*, which reassured Cato before his own death. The only controversy lay in one crucial clause: "until He orders us to depart from it."

Lactantius meant those words literally—until God physically evicts us from our bodies. Cato, however, took political defeat as a sufficient order to die. Borrowing from the usual rhetoric surrounding Cato, Lactantius conceded that he "appears to have had some cause for death in his hatred of slavery." But he immediately proceeded to throw this cause into doubt. The real motive for Cato's "great crime" was nothing more than pride:

> It appears to me that Cato sought a cause for death, not so much that he might escape from Caesar, as that he might obey the decrees of the Stoics, whom he followed, and might make his name distinguished by some great action; and I do not see what evil could have happened to him if he had lived.

No evil could have come to Cato, as Lactantius saw it: not in the political sense, because Caesar would have kept his promise of clemency; not in the Stoic sense, because if he was a good man, he supposedly had everything he needed for happiness; and not in the Christian sense, because no action of Caesar could touch his immortal soul. Cato was deceived by the *Phaedo* and its promise of an easy immortality, but he was *willfully* deceived. In the final accounting, Cato was just "an imitator of Socratic vanity." At the same time, he was also "the chief of Roman wisdom," and if the wisest pagan was fooled into self-murder, it was a sad commentary on every pagan.

•   •   •

But the most sustained and most withering critique of Cato belonged to Augustine, arguably the greatest intellectual influence on the early church. Augustine, a pagan into his thirties and a professor of rhetoric at the fifth-century imperial court, was deeply immersed in the culture that idolized Cato, a culture that was turning to Cato's example of courage with renewed devotion, as the empire shook under external attack. Even after his famous conversion, Augustine held on to his inherited affection for Cato. He seems to have regarded him as a man ahead of his time in his almost-Christian humility. Turning to Sallust's comparison of Cato and Caesar, Augustine noted that Caesar was praised for seeking out war to display his talents; but

> praise of a higher kind is bestowed upon Cato, for [Sallust] says of him, "the less he sought glory, the more it followed him." We say

praise of a higher kind, for the glory with the desire of which the Romans burned is the judgment of men thinking well of men. And therefore virtue is better, which is content with no human judgment save that of one's own conscience.

Still, to Augustine's mind, Cato fell far short of real virtue. In his magnum opus, *The City of God against the Pagans*, Augustine drew a sharp contrast between the City of God, the spiritual city founded on eternal truth, and the City of Man, the human city founded on temporal ambition; and Augustine cast Cato, for all his appeal, as one who lived and died for the City of Man. Cato suffered, like the vast majority of men of his time, from the terminal illness of pagan culture, an obsession with winning praise and glory, attributes that properly belonged to God alone. Cato's case of the disease may have been less virulent than Caesar's, but the disease was fatal to both.

Augustine, more than any other Christian writer, appears to have read Plutarch's Cato biography closely. Two scenes from Cato's last day stood out to Augustine as incriminating details: Cato shouting down the friends who begged him to live, and Cato working to secure a pardon for his son. To Cato's Roman admirers, these details spoke to his brave, single-minded selflessness. But Augustine managed to turn them into proof of Cato's foolish pride:

> His example is appealed to, not because he was the only man who did so, but because he was so esteemed as a learned and excellent man, that it could plausibly be maintained that what he did was and is a good thing to do. But of this action of his, what can I say but that his own friends, enlightened men as he, prudently dissuaded him, and therefore judged his act to be that of a feeble rather than a strong spirit, and dictated not by honorable feeling forestalling shame, but by weakness shrinking from hardships?

> Indeed, Cato condemns himself by the advice he gave to his dearly loved son. For if it was a disgrace to live under Caesar's rule, why did the father urge the son to this disgrace, by encouraging him to trust absolutely to Caesar's generosity? Why did he not persuade him to die along with himself? . . . Cato, then, cannot have deemed it to be shameful to live under Caesar's rule; for had he done so,

the father's sword would have delivered his son from this disgrace. The truth is that his son, whom he both hoped and desired would be spared by Caesar, was not more loved by him than Caesar was envied the glory of pardoning him (as indeed Caesar himself is reported to have said); or if envy is too strong a word, let us say he was ashamed that this glory should be his.

Augustine believed that Cato's last actions were the utter opposite of selflessness. Had Cato really meant his high words about freedom and slavery, he would not have hoarded such a dramatic death for himself alone. The fact that he did so was proof, to Augustine, that Cato's end was not grounded in any principle higher than his own good name. To make this argument, Augustine had to ignore the claim—made by Cicero, as early as the year of Cato's death—that suicide at Utica was uniquely fitting for a man of Cato's character, but not for others. Yet even so, Augustine seems to have fixed on two facts at the core of Cato's psychology: his lifelong tending of his heroic image, and his deeply personal rivalry with Caesar.

For those who refused to accept prideful envy as the motive, Augustine argued that there was only one alternative: cowardice. Here, his attack on Cato drew on all of his rhetorical training:

> Was it, I would ask, fortitude or weakness that prompted Cato to kill himself? For he would not have done so had he not been too weak to endure Caesar's victory. Where, then, is his fortitude? It has yielded, it has succumbed, it has been so thoroughly overcome as to abandon, forsake, flee this happy life.

The high emotional pitch of this insult concealed a trap for Stoics. The natural response to the attack on Cato's cowardice would have been to deny that his life, after Caesar's victory, was worth living. But Augustine anticipated that challenge. He continued, "Was it no longer happy? Then it was miserable. How, then, were these not evils that made life miserable—a thing to be escaped from?"

Augustine, in other words, used Cato *against* Stoicism (and pagan philosophy more generally). After all, pagans claimed that happiness was possible in this life. Stoicism was built on the conviction that virtue alone was sufficient for happiness. But if the greatest exemplar of Stoic virtue concluded that life was not worth living, if he was miserable despite his philosophy, then he put the lie to the Stoic life and its possibility of unyielding happiness in this world, rather than the next. Unless, of course, Cato was a coward. The church father thus put an impossible choice to pagans: Confess the weakness of the life, or the weakness of the man.

In place of Cato, Augustine put forward a different model, one he knew would infuriate many: "Our opponents are offended at our preferring to Cato the saintly Job." He intended Job's endurance, rather than Cato's defiance, to be the model for a new world.

• • •

For almost a millennium, Cato essentially remained where Augustine left him. It was a place of conditional admiration, tempered by contempt for his suicide. "The final and complete vindication of Cato among the Christians," as one historian writes, would have to wait some nine hundred years. And the vindication only occurred when the first Christian humanists, led by the poet Dante, turned again to the writing of the ancients.

They approached the classical world in an entirely different spirit than that of the church fathers. Rather than setting the City of God *against* the pagans (as Augustine succinctly characterized the struggle for superiority), the humanists intended to revive the pagan world and set it in harmony with Christendom. Dante, working out this fusion in his epic, *The Divine Comedy*, assigned the pagan philosophers an honored and painless place in Hell and accepted Virgil as his spiritual guide. In Christian allegory, Dante transformed the most controversial moments of Cato's life—and Cato's place in that allegory was startling.

Cato's strange divorce and remarriage had brought him shame from the moment it became news, and continued to do so long after he and his wife Marcia were both dead. Dante, however, drew from Lucan's sympathetic narration of their reunion a universal drama—not the remarriage of two individual Romans, but the return of the soul to God. In his prose work on the virtues, *The Banquet*, Dante used Marcia to stand for the human soul at every stage of life and Cato for the soul's ultimate destination:

[Lucan] says that Marcia returned to Cato and begged and implored him to take her back in her old age. Here Marcia signifies the noble soul. And we may translate the figure of the allegory as follows. Marcia was a virgin, and in that state she signifies adolescence; she later married Cato, and in that state she signifies maturity; then she bore children, and they signify the virtues that are said above to be fitting for those who are young; she then left Cato and married Hortensius, signifying the departure from maturity and the onset of old age; she also bore this man's children, who signify the virtues that are said above to be fitting in old age. Hortensius died, by which is signified the end of old age; and having become a widow—which signifies senility—Marcia returned at the beginning of her widowhood to Cato, signifying that the noble soul returns to God at the beginning of senility.

Why use Marcia and Cato to stand in for the soul's journey? Why not any other couple? In answer, Dante asked, "What man on earth was more worthy to signify God than Cato? Surely none."

Cicero may have called Cato godlike; Lucan may have proposed making him the deity of a civic religion; but no one, until Dante, had proposed him as history's greatest mortal symbol for God. The allegory is especially remarkable from the mouth of a devout Christian, who had his pick of biblical heroes and saints and still left them aside.

The deep awe in which Dante held Cato also figures in *Monarchy,* a defense of secular government. In Dante's explanation of the uplifting possibilities of empire, he held the ancient Romans up as "holy, pious, and full of glory, putting aside all avarice, which is ever adverse to the general welfare, cherishing universal peace and liberty." This is far removed from the church fathers' attacks on pagan self-seeking and pride. It is also far removed from the historical facts of the avarice intimately connected with the winning and running of Rome's empire. But as an idealized picture of Rome's civilizing force, it was highly seductive—especially because it could call on the example of Cato. In the roll call of Roman heroes used to bolster Dante's claim of imperial selflessness, he saved Cato for last: "That ineffable sacrifice of Marcus Cato . . . proved what liberty meant to him, when, in order that the love of freedom might blaze up in the world, he chose rather to depart from this life a free man than abide therein without freedom."

Cato was back among the martyrs, his motives once again entirely cleaned. To the extent that his suicide mattered at all to Dante, it only heightened the praise. Rather than a victim of circumstance or envy, Cato was a man who chose, in an act of self-denial, to convert his flesh into a lasting symbol. He was, in fact, a type of Christ. For the poet, as Dante scholar Robert Hollander writes,

> Cato's suicide . . . as distinct from the suicidal sin which leads to [Hell] is to be thought of . . . as prefiguration of Christ's "suicide." . . . The historical Cato's motives are understood by Dante as implying the kind of devotion to liberty that is the mark of Christ, who sought and found true liberty for all men.

In Dante's *Divine Comedy*, then, Cato is nowhere to be found in the Inferno: not among the virtuous pagans and not among the suicides. Instead, when Dante and Virgil pass through the underworld and emerge blinking into the open air, at the foot of the mountain of Purgatory, they are face-to-face with an ancient man:

> *I saw nearby an old man on his own,*
> *deserving (from the air and look he had)*
> *of all respect a son might give his sire.*
>
> *The beard he wore was long and flecked with white,*
> *as, too, the hair that flowed down from his head,*
> *falling upon his breast in double braids.*
>
> *The rays that shot from those four holy stars*
> *adorned his brow with honor so I saw*
> *his face as clear as if the sun shone there.*

The old man, as legalistic as he ever was in life, demands to know how Dante has broken the law and come alive out of Hell: "The laws of the abyss—do these break down?" Virgil answers that they are on a divine mission:

Look kindly on his coming, if you will.
He goes in search of liberty. All know—
who gave their life for that—how dear it is.

You know yourself. For, dying in that cause,
death had, at Utica, no sting for you.
Your mortal robe, on Judgment Day, will shine.

Cato's liberty, freedom from Caesar, has become freedom from sin, the freedom of will at the heart of atonement. Because he died for freedom, Dante made Cato one of only four pagans to escape Hell. He named him keeper of Purgatory, God's holy mountain, where the saved are washed clean of their failings with suffering and sweat. On the last day, Cato too would ascend the mountain.

By now, the link between the flesh and the myth had grown so attenuated, and Cato had grown so abstracted from politics and from life, that Dante could call him saved and still place Brutus, the man who finished Cato's work, in the devil's mouth.

15

CATO THE REVOLUTIONARY

If the defining feature of Cato's afterlife through the time of Dante was a moral debate—the struggle to place him on a spectrum from heathen to holy—then the centuries that followed the publication of *The Divine Comedy* nudged Cato into a different forum. The story of the revolutionary Cato, which began in earnest in the eighteenth century, was about the man and his politics. It was a debate over secular virtues. Those moments in Cato's biography that suggested something divinely inspired were still fiercely debated, but the thinkers of the new era turned more and more to the substance of his public life, his outlook and behavior as one of Rome's leading witnesses to and shapers of the crisis of the Republic.

It remained, as it had always been, a life easily hyperbolized. The secular Cato was still treated as a sacrosanct figure. For the revolutionaries who consciously looked to republican Rome for models, there was, in the words of historian Gordon Wood, "no ancient hero like him." Yet again, Cato was enlarged in death—and he was still moral clay, shaped and reshaped to suit the purpose at hand. The result was a multitude of Catos, each buffed and polished, each carrying a particular message for a particular audience. There was Cato the model of civic virtue, Cato the virtuous death, Cato the hero of principled resistance. All were wild (if flattering) exaggerations. They grew from cherry-picked moments of Cato's life and rarely reflected the whole of it.

Taken beyond the page, onto canvas and into song, stage, and popular entertainment, Cato became a universal figure, the property of an entire culture. His death was among the best-known parables of the day. Once again, as in the early days of the Roman principate, his life was taught as a model for schoolboys. On two continents, in a multitude of languages, in a wealth of media, Cato reached the greatest audience he had ever known.

• • •

The play that made Cato a household name throughout Europe and eventually the American colonies—arguably the most popular play of the entire eighteenth century—was almost never staged at all. Joseph Addison, a twenty-seven-year-old fellow and classics star at Oxford, had written up four acts of what was to be a five-act drama exploring the final days of Cato's life. The unfinished work was circulated among his friends, including Jonathan Swift. Then politics interrupted. In 1699, at the request of prominent friends, Addison was invited on a diplomatic trip through Europe. With a stipend from King William III, he spent years crisscrossing the continent, studying foreign affairs, meeting diplomatic leaders, and dining with kings. Only fourteen years later did he at last find the time to pen his tragedy's final act. It was a slapdash effort of one week.

Cato: A Tragedy was conceived as a political weapon from the start, though not even its author could imagine its ultimate impact. Addison completed the draft under pressure from his well-connected friends, prominent liberal Whigs who needed fresh ammunition against their Tory opponents. They saw Addison's unfinished play as a potentially valuable propaganda piece. Samuel Johnson explained the Whig sentiment: "The time was now come when those who affected to think liberty in danger, affected likewise to think that a stage-play might preserve it, and Addison was importuned . . . to show his courage and zeal by finishing his design." Addison, as it happened, had the zeal to finish the play—but he lacked the courage to release it. He didn't want to risk offending the Tories, who could squash his promising career. Only at the final hour—and only after coaxing a Tory writer to pen the play's epilogue and convincing a Tory government censor to sanction its release—did Addison consent to see *Cato* staged.

As it happened, the play benefited from bipartisan approbation. Both the Tories and the Whigs gushed over it, falling over themselves to identify their party as the one who best reflected its themes. At intermission of the first performance, Henry St. John—the Viscount Bolingbroke and one of the most public faces of the Tories—made his way backstage to press fifty guineas into the hand of the actor playing Cato, as a reward for his depiction of the defense of liberty.

The broader public swooned over the play, as well. "Cato was not so much the wonder of Rome itself in his days as he is of Britain in ours," wrote Alexander Pope. Voltaire called Cato "the greatest character that was brought upon any stage." Among other successes, *Cato* was translated into six languages, copycatted across Europe, turned into a burlesque show, and cheered on the British stage for the longest theatrical run in history. By mid-century, to be educated in Europe was to have read and studied (and, ideally, memorized) the tragedy of *Cato*.

For such a resounding success, *Cato* has not aged as gracefully as might be expected. In 1960, the Scottish critic David Daiches called it "utterly lifeless." In the twenty-first century, John Miller of the *National Review* called its characters "uncomplicated mouthpieces rather than compelling personalities." Even critics closer to the tragedy's popular spell, such as Samuel Johnson, had their reservations: *Cato* had much to recommend it in the way of memorable one-liners and moving themes, but it was almost totally lacking in believable human interaction. Johnson called it "rather a poem in dialogue than a drama, rather a succession of just sentiments in elegant language, than a representation of natural affections, or of any state probable or possible in human life."

Yet, despite its faults, Johnson allowed that *Cato* made up in gravitas what it lacked in grace. And its depiction of Roman heroism was wildly welcomed. Addison knew his audience. The play debuted at a moment when mania for ancient Rome had reached new and fevered heights. Politicians humbly measured themselves against Caesar and Pompey; the Republic was the talk of parlors and dinner tables, "familiar to the schoolboy and the statesman." The philosopher Montesquieu spoke for an entire age when he insisted that "it is impossible to be tired of so agreeable a subject as ancient Rome."

Cato's theme, death in defense of liberty, was as agreeable to its audiences and as politically resonant as any theme from the ancients. As Johnson noted: "The Whigs applauded every line in which Liberty was mentioned, as a satire on the Tories; and the Tories echoed every clap, to show that the satire was unfelt." For the Whigs, the play was a not-so-subtle attack on the old

Tory aristocracy. For the Tories, the example of Cato's life was a criticism of the Whigs: Here, they noted, was the kind of incorruptible, independent man Britain needed, and precisely the opposite of the kind that the country had had during two decades of Whig leadership.

Cato, then, gave voice to the frustrations of the age. It spoke to hopes of limited government in the wake of England's Glorious Revolution. And it spoke to new fears as well. Fears of a new, moneyed elite—of the growing power of stock companies and banks—found expression in Cato's critique of the corruption brought on by wealth and empire. Cato's death, in this charged atmosphere, became a model for public selflessness, and his life a model for private restraint. A return to ancient virtues, it was held, could cure modern England's addiction to excess and luxury.

In holding up a virtuous pagan, *Cato* also spoke to the era's religious anxieties. Some of its success can surely be attributed to a poignant death scene—to which Addison, departing from Plutarch and the other ancients for propriety's sake, added a last-minute reconsideration. Here are Cato's last words as Addison imagined them:

> *Whoe'er is brave and virtuous, is a Roman—*
> *—I'm sick to death—O when shall I get loose*
> *From this vain world, th' abode of guilt and sorrow!*
> *—And yet methinks a beam of light breaks in*
> *On my departing soul. Alas! I fear*
> *I've been too hasty. O ye powers that search*
> *The heart of man, and weigh his inmost thoughts,*
> *If I have done amiss, impute it not!—*
> *The best may err, but you are good, and—oh!*
>   [Dies.]

From *Cato* to Rousseau's *Julie* and Samuel Richardson's *Clarissa,* vivid deathbed scenes were all the rage—in part because, in a climate of growing religious skepticism, they offered a vital reassurance that a virtuous life might, at the very least, guarantee a dignified end. More than that, contemplating such a scene was virtuous exercise. Responding to that sort of scene properly was proof of virtue, and such virtue was enough, as dying Cato insisted, to make one an honorary Roman.

The prologue to *Cato*, penned by Pope, made the charge explicit: "Britons, attend: be worth like this approv'd, / And show you have the virtue to be mov'd." *Cato*, in other words, was a play that invited its audience to a moral test—and by cheering it so loudly, generations of spectators convinced themselves that they had passed.

• • •

Not long after *Cato*'s successful run, its title character seemed to take on a life of his own in the British press. In 1720, a series of letters on liberty began to appear in the popular *London Journal*—all signed, simply, "Cato." This Cato spoke like an eighteenth-century Englishman, but the lessons he had to offer read as if they had come down unchanged from the last days of republican Rome. "Thus it is," Cato writes, "that liberty is almost everywhere lost: Her foes are artful, united and diligent: Her defenders are few, disunited, and inactive." And elsewhere: "This passion for liberty in men, and their possession of it, is of that efficacy and importance, that it seems the parent of all the virtues."

These dispatches, 144 of them in all, were devoured in coffeehouses across Britain and its American colonies. As a collected volume, *Cato's Letters* became the age's most influential popularization of natural rights and limited government. The letters surely borrowed some of their authority from the legacy of the historical Cato, but far more of their emotional punch came by association with *Cato*, the stage sensation. While Addison left his play's contemporary political implications in the realm of allegory, the letters' authors—two British reformers named John Trenchard and Thomas Gordon—enlisted Cato far more directly in current affairs.

We can read the influence of this Whiggish Cato in the direct line between his words and the American Declaration of Independence. Here is the Cato of *The London Journal:* "[L]iberty is the unalienable right of all mankind. All governments, under whatsoever form they are administered, ought to be administered for the good of the society; when they are otherwise administered, they cease to be government, and become usurpations." By the latter half of the century, according to one historian's estimate, copies of the volume containing those radical words appeared in private libraries throughout the American colonies. Two centuries later, the libertarian Cato Institute would choose to name itself after *Cato's Letters*.

• • •

But not all attempts to exploit Catomania proved as successful. On a drizzly night in mid-January 1728, crowds hustled into Rome's Teatro delle Dame, not far from the Forum where so much of Cato's life played out, to witness Cato transposed into Italian opera.

Catone in Utica was a lyrical, sweeping story of love and war. Its political and historical outlines were roughly the same as Addison's tragedy: Cato and Caesar, in a final standoff on the African coast, with special attention paid to Cato's suicide. But no opera would be complete without a larger-than-life love triangle—and in this case, the librettist Pietro Metastasio decided to embellish the historical narrative with a secret romance: an imagined relationship between Cato's daughter, and her father's sworn enemy, Julius Caesar.

A Roman hero for a Roman audience; a reinvention of a classic drama; a tangled love story—the opera had all the makings of a hit, and yet on opening night it flopped. The audience was willing to countenance a suicide, but apparently not one as gruesome and drawn out as the one portrayed on stage. Cato staggered and bled to death for two elaborate scenes, singing the whole time. Whether more disturbed by the brutality or the implausibility, the audience was livid. One critic's accusation summed up the view of the crowd: "Cruel Metastasio, you have reduced all the heroes of the Tiber into a drainpipe." Stung by the reaction, the librettist rewrote the final act. His new Cato died offstage and out of sight.

• • •

Reworked, translated copies of Addison's *Cato* appeared in France, Germany, Italy, the Netherlands, and as far east as Poland. But in colonial America, the play received its most passionate reception. From the moment *Cato* reached American shores, the tragedy and its themes caught fire. By any measure—theatrical run, critical acclaim, compulsive quotability—it was the play of the century, the defining drama of revolutionary America.

Performances of *Cato,* both professional and amateur, took on new force in the midst of the Stamp Act protests of 1765. *Cato* was, in fact, one of the strongest cultural threads binding together the founding generation of a new nation. And the play was not mere entertainment for America's

Founders—it was vivid political fodder. As Johnson noted, the play's weakness as a human drama was tied to its strength as a memorable, inexhaustible collection of aphorisms. These aphorisms found their way into the letters, speeches, and everyday conversation of Benjamin Franklin, Patrick Henry, John Adams, and many more. *Cato*'s words were as meaningful in private as in public. Franklin, for instance, kept a diary of his efforts toward the attainment of "moral perfection." Every time he took up this private log, he saw these words from the tragedy, which he took as a motto:

> *Here will I hold. If there's a power above us,*
> *(And that there is, all nature cries aloud*
> *Through all her works,) he must delight in virtue;*
> *And that which he delights in, must be happy.*

By all accounts, however, no one was more taken with *Cato* than George Washington, who read and reread it, constantly quoted it, staged it at Valley Forge—and set out to make himself into a latter-day Cato. The play had already been running for eighteen years when he was born, and Washington was exposed to it as a young man. From the age of sixteen, he was an avid reader of back issues of Addison's newspaper, *The Spectator*. At twenty-six, in the western woods and the French and Indian War, his mind was still on *Cato,* and he imagined playing a role in it. As he writes home to Virginia, "I should think my time more agreeable spent believe me, in playing a part in Cato."

Washington had found the Roman ideally suited to his temperament. This was the same Washington, after all, who unselfconsciously copied down the 110 *Rules of Civility & Decent Behavior in Company and Conversation* at age eleven. What better model than Rome's heroically wet blanket for a young, humorless future army officer who was enough of a fusspot to write to himself that while "In the Presence of Others Sing not to yourself with a humming Noise, nor Drum with your Fingers or Feet"?

Long before he staged the famous Valley Forge production of *Cato,* and long before his career as a revolutionary, Washington had grown enamored of Cato. Cato the man seems to have meant as much to him as Cato the symbol of liberty. This is unsurprising given what we know about Washington's other reading preferences. At seventeen, he acquired an English copy of Seneca's dialogues, which lionized Cato's Stoic virtues and left a deep impression on the future general. Biographer Ron Chernow notes that Washington would spend his life striving to make those virtues his own: "As his life progressed, Washington would adhere to the stoic creed of governing one's passions under the most adverse circumstances and facing the prospect of death with serenity."

Cato and *Cato* were Washington's comforts in times of public and private distress, and in 1778 at Valley Forge he gambled—correctly—that they could serve the same role for an entire army. At his army's soul-trying point of lowest morale, Washington's affection for Cato made a valuable difference. Its impact may not have been measurable, but the general estimated it highly enough to incur real political risk in staging a play at all. In late 1774, the Continental Congress had passed a series of nonimportation and nonconsumption agreements. As a gesture toward America's economic and cultural independence, they had outlawed "the exhibition of shews, plays, and other expensive diversions and entertainments." At a time of impending war, when the fashion was for republican frugality, theatergoing was seen as an intolerable luxury. *Cato* was especially suspect. After all, it was a British import. So while Addison's praise of liberty rang as loudly for Washington's men as it did for British Whigs at the century's start, Valley Forge was not Utica. *Cato,* in a time of war, faced new complications. One historian notes that the performance may have been "a distasteful if not unpatriotic gesture at a time when the performance of English drama remained as politically problematic . . . as the importation of silks and teas from the English Empire."

As soon as news of the Valley Forge staging of *Cato* leaked, the Continental Congress came down hard on Washington and his men. It announced that any representative of the emerging government who participated in a theater production would be removed from duty. Samuel Adams concurred with the sentiment, writing that "in humble Imitation, as it would seem, of the Example of the British army some of the officers of ours have condescended to act on the Stage while others, and one of Superior Rank were pleased to countenance Them with their presence." The "one of Superior Rank" was, no doubt, General Washington.

It was a ripe moment of irony in Cato's afterlife. The play that gave voice to the sentiments of revolution was denounced as unpatriotic. The play that portrayed Cato's Stoic hatred of luxuries was attacked as a luxury. But those attacks could not dampen for long the Founders' fascination with Cato and all he had come to represent. They could not displace Cato from the public imagination or from Washington's.

• • •

Cato was still with him at war's end. In 1783, with the revolution won, Washington's officers threatened a mutiny over undelivered pay. There were even whispers of a march on Congress to take what was theirs. It was the point at which representative government might have degenerated, as so often before and since, into rule by army. Caesar, confronted with such a crisis in his war against Cato, had responded with the winning bluff of a mass discharge. Washington responded with *Cato*. A number of historians have found an echo of the play in Washington's words to the mutinous officers. Be patient, he insisted,

> and you will, by the dignity of your Conduct, afford occasion for Posterity to say, when speaking of the glorious example you have exhibited to Mankind, "Had this day been wanting, the World had never seen the last stage of perfection to which human nature is capable of attaining."

Addison's Cato, facing rebellious troops of his own, had voiced the same thought.

But the general's greatest coup remained for the end. Unable to read his men a letter from Congress, Washington fumbled in his pocket for his glasses—and when he stood before the officers with glasses on, a sight few had ever seen, he suddenly looked far older than his fifty-one years. "Gentlemen," he remarked, "you will permit me to put on my spectacles, for I have not only grown gray but almost blind in the service of my country."

That was all that was required for the mutiny to dissolve in spontaneous tears.

Washington's line was improvised and devastating. But here too he had help—here too he was acting the part of Addison's Cato:

Which of you all suspects that he is wrong'd,
Or thinks he suffers greater ills than Cato?
Am I distinguished from you but by toils,
Superior toils, and heavier weight of cares?
Painful pre-eminence!

Cato himself might have approved of those words. And yet, just as likely, he would have been exasperated by the greatest irony perpetrated on him in his posthumous career: Cato—who had made a fashion out of his utter refusal to change or budge, who had above all advocated the preservation of an ancient system in its original form—had somehow grown to become the watchword for violent revolution.

EPILOGUE

FORGOTTEN BUT NOT GONE

On June 3, 1990, Jim Webb—former U.S. Navy secretary and future senator—stood in the shadow of a Civil War memorial in Arlington National Cemetery and offered these words in praise of the Confederate dead:

> These men, like all soldiers, made painful choices and often paid for their loyalty with their lives. . . . Duty is a constant, frozen in the context of the moment it was performed. Duty is action, taken after listening to one's leaders, and weighing risk and fear against the powerful draw of obligation to family, community, nation, and the unknown future. We, the progeny who live in that future, were among the intended beneficiaries of those frightful decisions made so long ago.

The thirty-two-foot-high Confederate Memorial at Webb's back was nearing its eightieth birthday.

Tucked into the northernmost tip of the cemetery grounds, the statue is topped by a woman, the personified South, her head crowned with olive leaves. Her left hand holds a laurel wreath, her right, a pruning hook on top of a plow stock, a reminder of Isaiah's promise of remade swords and spears. Friezes of gods and soldiers ring the statue's base.

Perhaps the least obvious, least intelligible feature of the monument appears on its front face. Underneath the Seal of the Confederacy is a Latin inscription with no translation:

The line is Lucan's, and he wrote it in reflection on a different civil war: "The victorious cause was dear to the gods; the lost cause, to Cato."

Secretary Webb had nothing to say about Cato, but he was standing in the Roman's shadow. Webb's words on duty owed no small part to the Stoicism injected by Cato into the mainstream of Western thought. And the romance of the "lost cause" also descends to our time through Cato. In Rome as in America, that romance has long held a compelling, ambiguous power. It offers the seductive proposition that victory need not imply virtue, that right does not always make might. That proposition has strengthened generations of those looking for victory in defeat; it has also cast undeserving causes in a beautiful light. It consoled those who went to war to preserve a failing Republic, and those who went to war to preserve a new republic founded on slavery.

•   •   •

If this is obscurity—an untranslated line from a little-read poem on a fairly unknown statue—perhaps it is fitting. Indeed, the history of the Republic's last days often overlooks Cato. That history is often written as a conflict between a pair of would-be strongmen: Caesar and Pompey. These two found themselves opposed on the battlefields of a civil war—but in a larger sense, they were allies. Both came to conclude that Rome demanded the rule of one man; both were willing to kill to be that man. They were playing the same game, and had Pompey played it marginally better, czars and kaisers of later ages might have styled themselves after his name, not Caesar's.

Yet Caesar's truest rival was not Pompey. It was Cato. Cato offered something other than the prospect of some other man at the head of the state: He offered a radically different vision of what that state should be. His vision rested on the myth of a pristine history, a simpler and purer past, one that he spent his life striving to embody. In its way, his goal was as ambitious as any Roman general's, and we can see his success in the reaction of his contemporaries. They saw Cato as a miracle. In a world that took decline as a natural law, Cato kindled hope that the ancient virtues were alive and well. For a ruptured present and an uncertain future, Cato incarnated Rome's founding myth—and it was contact with the myth that gave him his power. Every Roman who feared that the traditional virtues were guttering out, who saw the state's crisis as a moral crisis—as the product of terrifyingly modern avarice or ambition—looked, in time, to Cato.

Compelling as this vision was, it was also artificial: It did not entail clinging to living traditions, but resurrecting an entire imagined past, one long gone even before Cato's birth. Perhaps it was lost on Cato that the abstract principle of his project, and its implausibility, was the part of him most foreign to the ancestors he idealized. The old Romans, if they were anything, were a famously concrete-thinking people. By their hardheaded standards, Cato demonstrably failed.

Cato's vision was thrillingly simple, thrillingly clear to a people facing debt crises and imperial war and corruption and overcrowding and urban violence. The more complex the crises, the greater the appeal of a Cato—in any age, our own included. But Cato's promise of a restored past was compromised and crippled by a shallow view of the present. He went to extraordinary lengths to refine and publicize his example as an alternative to Rome's faltering politics. Yet he did precious little to reform that system's deep sources of weakness and corruption. At times, his platform amounted to little more than performance art. His Stoic charisma was enough to attract a passionate following and lend him real authority, yet he failed to use the power he won to do much more than point insistently, through himself, to the past. And he ran from power when, in his own terms, he could have done the most good.

It is hard to judge his methods of resistance as anything other than out of proportion to the danger he claimed to be resisting. Politics is founded on successful compromise and coalition building, and yet, at every turn, Cato managed to alienate the very people he needed: Cicero, whose friendship he repeatedly pressed to the breaking point, and Pompey, whom he pushed out of an alliance with the Senate when it mattered most.

"Ten Catos," writes one historian, "might have saved the Roman Republic." But "Ten Catos" is a contradiction in terms. He lived his life and practiced his politics so that there could only ever be one.

For two millennia, his suicide at Utica has stood as the image of the saintly Cato. But another image ought to be placed alongside it, in a diptych: Cato, on the brink of war, shouting that Pompey is a fool for considering peace with Caesar; Pompey, under the spell of Cato's inflexibility, giving way and settling on the war that would kill him and the Republic. Absent Cato, how much longer might the Republic have stayed whole?

• • •

Yet even in his failings, Cato remains indisputably great. He is the kind of man that every statesman aspires to be: physically tough, intellectually brave, unflinchingly principled, beloved despite his warts. In many ways, he is the model of what we say we want in a leader, though his lonely end casts a shadow on the recurring hope that a leader, no matter how singular, can transcend the dirty business of politics.

Despite his lost cause, or exactly because of it, Cato succeeded in making himself an icon. The best efforts of his personal enemies and of opponents he never knew could not shake him from the ranks of heroes. Few who have failed so spectacularly at their life's work have been revered so deeply in the postmortem. Perhaps that is because—just as Cato may have desired it—his fundamental success was personal, not political. No Roman leader, and few leaders in any age, ever came close to his standard of self-mastery and self-abnegation. Few leaders have ever put ambition so squarely in the service of principle. These were the qualities that set Cato apart from his fellows—and that made posterity take notice.

Cicero had his legendary eloquence and wit; Pompey had his organizational genius and boyish charm; Caesar, until the end, seemed blessed by the gods. Against all that, Cato made himself their equal by putting to the best possible use the least promising of weapons. His source of authority in the world was a series of dogged habits. His triumphs were accomplishments in the negative: shoes unworn, horses unridden, bribes ungiven, compromises unoffered. Through these, more than any of his contemporaries, he seamlessly united the personal and the political, his life and his work.

That was his great achievement. Surely, Cato was self-righteous, rash, often blind. He was victim of the same delusion that attached itself to Caesar and Pompey, the conviction that he, and he alone, could cure what ailed Rome. More than he ever admitted, his passions—anger, ambition, resentment—mastered him, perhaps even at the very end. His imagined past, and the inhuman fortitude he ascribed to his great ancestor, were the impossible standards he set himself. Of course he failed to meet them. But as the founders of his school taught, foolish passion is universal. All Stoics are failed Stoics. To our minds, Cato is all the more formidable for asking so much of himself and of his times.

•   •   •

Powerful as he was in life, he was never so powerful as in death. And whether Cato died in calm self-possession or in a fit of rage, what he died for ultimately mattered far less than what "the unknown future" believed he died for. Cato is at the heart of the metamorphosis from the *libertas* of Rome—a domineering, slaveholding oligarchy—to liberty as we know it. Cato's judgment was clear: He believed that he had witnessed the end of *libertas*. But it was his own powerful example that helped prove his pessimism wrong.

The challenge of studying Cato lies in grasping his sway over our era without unintentionally burdening him with its views—in understanding his power over the originators of liberal democracy without making Cato himself, through an excess of sympathy, into a modern democrat. For the elite of Cato's Rome, the state was the arena of unending competition—for wealth, for office, for political clients, for status—a competition that grew progressively fiercer and higher staked with the growth of empire. Roman *libertas* was freedom from fear that the contest would ever end. *Libertas* was hatred of autocracy, hatred of any single man dominant enough to end the competition once and for all. Liberty began its life as an aristocratic virtue, as the freedom of oligarchs from the all-excelling man. And for centuries, republican Rome was proof of that maxim: An oligarchy that clung to its *libertas* would never be overthrown.

But in the wake of Cato's death, liberty took on a strange new life. When his son-in-law Brutus led the conspiracy that murdered Caesar, the assassins' rallying cries were Cato and liberty. When political subversives stood against the emperor Nero, Cato was their watchword and secular god. When the early Christians fought for pagan hearts and minds, they took Cato's Stoic life and death as equal parts inspiration and rival. When the poet Dante built his elaborate afterworld, he plucked Cato out of Hell, taking his life as a prefiguration of Christ—because, as he asked, "What man on earth was more worthy to signify God than Cato?" And when Washington and the American Founders searched for a martyr to dignify their cause, they looked back eighteen centuries and found the Roman Republic bleeding to death in the person of Cato.

Cato became the constant companion of this evolution from *libertas* to liberty—very often the means by which it was carried out. At virtually every step, Cato was there as liberty's embodiment, as an enduring inspiration to all those who defined and redefined the word while claiming at the same time to be true to its ancient heritage. The full story of Cato is the story of his example and the many uses to which it was put—by Cato himself and by the long line of successors who felt its force and turned it to ends of their own. There is no sense in asking whether Cato would have endorsed the revolutions made, in part, in his name. He was made to endorse them; the dead are other people's property.

In January of 1941, President Franklin D. Roosevelt proposed Four Freedoms to stand in opposition to the Axis tyrannies: freedom of speech, freedom of worship, freedom from want, and freedom from fear. Shortly after, the British economist Joan Robinson commented on the rhetorical sleight of hand that enabled the president to class economic security—freedom from want—alongside its more limited neighbors. She called it "a noble pun."

Perhaps that also is how we can understand the relationship of Cato's *libertas* to Washington's liberty: a noble pun, and a world-changing one.

• • •

His whole life, Cato portrayed himself as the Republic embodied, the last repository of its ancient liberty and virtue. And whether by chance or design, he lived so as to bring this hyperbole close to reality. By the end, defeated and abandoned, he was a Republic of one—and he seems never to have been more content. It is in this sense that Cato was Rome's last citizen. Legally, the category of *civis romanus*, Roman citizen, long outlived Cato. But a great deal of its substance died with him, and waited ages to be reborn.

What successor generations found in Cato was the conviction that republican citizenship, self-governing citizenship, even citizenship of a republic as fatally flawed as Rome's, was something precious and set apart.

Even as the idea of liberty continues its contentious evolution, that conviction traces some part of its origins to the desert sands of Utica.

Cato of Utica—history's neglect has not erased him from our story. He remains there, a silent shaper of our era: firm, flawed, and full of lessons for our time.

CHRONOLOGY

BCE

234: Cato the Elder born.

202: Hannibal defeated by Roman force at Zama; Rome wins war against Carthage.

184: Cato the Elder elected censor.

149: Cato the Elder dies.

146: Rome destroys city of Carthage.

133: Tiberius Gracchus elected tribune; assassinated when he seeks reelection on platform of land reform.

122: Gaius Gracchus, social reformer and brother of Tiberius, declared enemy of the state; commits suicide to escape capture.

95: Cato the Younger born.

91: Cato's uncle and guardian Drusus murdered; outbreak of war between Rome and its Italian allies.

88: War between Rome and Italian allies comes to negotiated close; Mithridates orders massacre of eighty thousand Romans and Italians living in Asia Minor.

82: Sulla marches on Rome, seizes dictatorship, and orders political purge.

81: Sulla resigns dictatorship.

73: Spartacus launches slave revolt.

72: Cato volunteers for service in war on Spartacus.

71: Spartacus defeated by legions under command of Crassus.

70: Crassus and Pompey elected consuls.

67: Cato takes command as military tribune in Macedonia; death of his half brother, Caepio.

c. 67: Cato marries Atilia.

66: Pompey named to command war against Mithridates; Cato tours Asia Minor.

65: Cato elected quaestor.

64: Cicero elected consul.

63: Catiline's conspiracy; Cato elected tribune; Cato persuades Senate to sentence leading conspirators to death; death of Mithridates.

62: Catiline dies in battle with Roman forces; Cato, as tribune, expands grain dole; Cato and allies block bill enabling Pompey to run for consul in absentia; Pompey returns to Italy and disbands his legions.

60: Cato successfully filibusters renegotiated contracts for tax collectors; *optimates* block Pompey's political settlement of the East; Caesar elected consul alongside Cato's son-in-law Bibulus.

c. 60: Cato divorces Atilia on suspicion of adultery; takes Marcia as second wife.

59: Caesar unveils alliance with Pompey and Crassus; passes land-reform bill over Cato's objections; secures command in Gaul.

58: Cicero exiled at instigation of Clodius; Cato ordered to oversee annexation of Cyprus.

57: Cicero returns from exile.

56: Caesar, Pompey, and Crassus renew triumvirate; Cato returns to Rome; Cato attacked on Pompey's orders.

55: Cato loses first campaign for praetor; Pompey and Crassus voted governorships in Spain and Syria; Caesar's term in Gaul extended; Cato accuses Caesar of war crimes in Gaul; Cato elected praetor at end of year.

c. 55: Cato divorces Marcia, presides over her remarriage to Hortensius.

54: Cato attempts to curtail electoral bribery by serving as private election monitor and proposing corruption court; death of Julia, Caesar's daughter and Pompey's wife; Cato presides over trials of Scaurus and Gabinius.

53: Crassus defeated and killed by Parthians; violence derails Roman elections and year ends without new consuls.

52: Clodius murdered; Senate selects Pompey as sole consul with mandate to quell violence in Rome; Cato runs unsuccessfully for the consulship of the following year; Caesar wins Battle of Alesia, breaking Gallic resistance to Roman rule.

51: Early proposals for Caesar's recall from Gaul.

50: Cato rejects Cicero's request for triumph; Curio announces Caesar-backed "peace plan" requiring both Caesar and Pompey to disband legions.

49: Caesar threatens Senate with war and Pompey's allies declare Caesar an enemy of the state; Pompey, at Cato's urging, rejects final compromise attempt; Caesar crosses Rubicon; Cato and Marcia remarry; Pompey and allies flee Rome.

48: Caesar escapes Pompey's victory at Dyrrhachium, then leaves Cato behind to oversee supply depot; Caesar wins decisive victory at Pharsalus; Pompey assassinated in Egypt; Cato takes refuge in North Africa and leads remnant of republican forces across desert to Utica.

47: Cato defers command to Metellus Scipio; Cato persuades Metellus Scipio and Numidian King Juba to spare Utica from destruction, then fortifies it against Caesar; Caesar lands in Africa.

46: Caesar crushes Metellus Scipio and republican forces at Battle of Thapsus; Cato commits suicide at Utica; Cicero publishes *Cato*.

44: Caesar assassinated at hands of conspiracy led by Brutus, Cato's son-in-law.

42: Cato's son, Marcus, killed at Battle of Philippi, in which Caesar's assassins are defeated; Cato's daughter, Porcia, commits suicide on receiving news of defeat.

27: Octavian, Caesar's adopted son, awarded title of "Augustus" by Senate; consolidates power as emperor.

CE

c. 61: Lucan begins *Pharsalia,* an epic poem of the civil war, which lionizes Cato.

65: Failure of conspiracy against the emperor Nero; Lucan and Seneca both implicated and ordered to commit suicide.

c. 413: Augustine launches Christian polemical attack against Cato in *The City of God against the Pagans.*

1308: Dante begins work on *The Divine Comedy*, ultimately situating Cato as guardian of Purgatory.

1713: First performance of Addison's *Cato: A Tragedy.*

1720: Initial publication of *Cato's Letters* in defense of political liberty.

1778: Washington stages performance of *Cato* for American troops at Valley Forge.

ACKNOWLEDGMENTS

We are grateful to the many friends and colleagues who supported two first-time authors, who struggled with us through the hard stretches of this project, and who celebrated with us on the several different occasions when we thought it was finished. Of all those who helped make this book possible, we want to note a few by name.

We are fortunate that Laura Yorke, of the Carol Mann Agency, saw the value in a book about an obscure Roman senator and championed it from start to finish. Her tenacity and compassion are without equal. We're grateful to our editor, Rob Kirkpatrick, of Thomas Dunne Books, who saw promise in the book as well and worked to make it a reality. We hope we've made good on Rob and Laura's early faith in the project.

This final draft owes a great deal to the challenging and stimulating comments of Julian Harris, Katie Boyle, Trina Vargo, Wes Moore, Bronwyn Lewis, Eric Greitens, Ken Harbaugh, Allen Foster, Justin Richmond, Judith Ruderman, Claire Richardson, David Boaz, Bruce Jentleson, Bruce Payne, Dan Kimerling, Christine Bader, and Andrew Collins. Thanks also to our friend Chris Good (then of *The Atlantic*), who helped us publish a teaser piece on Cato and the filibuster.

In the same vein, we appreciate the advice and encouragement of Professors Mary Boatwright and Nancy Sherman. Our gratitude to Arianna Huffington, who embraced the project from the moment she heard of it and has been evangelizing about it ever since. Melissa Nevola was a tireless supporter at the start of this project; with patience and grace, she endured hundreds of stories about long-dead, little-known Roman figures. Our great thanks to Ryan Holiday, whose passion for Stoicism and interest in Cato—combined with an unrivaled sense of the book's audience—helped us to refine key themes in the book.

To John Montorio, our deepest appreciation: He devotedly read every page of this book, and the final draft is stronger for his keen editorial eye. David Frum and Danielle Crittenden helped push this project over the finish line; their advice and encouragement in the final stages were indispensable. Amy Lazarus was the first to read a draft in full; she was merciless, and the final product owes much to her generosity and her unwillingness to pull any punches.

We'd also like to thank Kolb Ettenger and Rebecca Katz for their assistance with fact-checking, Meg Knox and her husband, Dan Baum, for their editorial work, and Jodie Goodman for her help with translation from French. And we appreciate the diligent production- and copy-editing of Rafal Gibek and Kate Davis.

We are especially grateful to Mary Lou Hartman, Cliff Sloan, and Joel Fleishman. They supported the idea of the book when it was only an idea, read and critiqued the proposal, and encouraged us through the long march of writing the text. Mary Lou offered perhaps the best advice any young author could receive: She was our first phone call when the book sold, and she promptly told us to hang up the phone and call our mothers. Cliff's passion for the book sustained us; we wanted to finish it if only to give him the opportunity to read it. And Joel was an agent when we didn't have an agent and an editor when we didn't have an editor. This project may never have gotten off the ground without his early belief in it.

To countless colleagues at *The Huffington Post*, McKinsey and Company, the mayor's office in Washington, D.C., and the office of Rep. Steny Hoyer, thank you for indulging the Cato story and always appearing interested no matter how many times you had heard it.

The bulk of our work was done on alternating evenings at our apartments in Washington, D.C. So, last but not least, we send a special thank-you to two patient people who put up with a regular houseguest and his laptop for many months: Matt Hoffman (Jimmy's roommate as this book was written) and Ellen Goodman (Rob's wife). Thanks for keeping the noise down and the coffee warm.

A NOTE ON PLUTARCH
AND HIS SOURCES

While Cato the Younger was an evergreen subject for a wide range of historians, biographers, and moralists in the Roman world, the most detailed classical treatment of his life comes from Plutarch. Plutarch was a Greek biographer, magistrate, and priest of Apollo, who took the Roman name Lucius Mestrius Plutarchus. He flourished during the reign of the emperor Trajan and is best known today for his *Parallel Lives* of eminent Greeks and Romans, a collection that includes his life of Cato. More than a century and a half separate the deaths of Plutarch and his subject—and because of that distance, and our reliance on Plutarch for many of the surviving details of Cato's life, it is fair to ask how much historical stone we can set by his biography.

There is no doubt that Plutarch was an admirer of Cato, whom he called "the best and most illustrious man of his time." But that admiration did not stop Plutarch from judging Cato harshly where he felt it necessary (e.g., his rejection of Pompey's proposal of alliance by marriage), bluntly narrating Cato's political failures (e.g., his lackluster campaign for consul), adding facts that complicate a purely heroic portrayal of the subject (e.g., that Cato was honored on his return from Cyprus not simply because of his service there, but because one of the current consuls was his father-in-law), or citing the accusations of Cato's political enemies. Plutarch's narration of Cato's suicide is an especially strong example of this complicated attitude: *The African War*, Cassius Dio, and Appian all discuss the suicide, but only Plutarch includes so many unflattering details, such as Cato striking a slave in anger and breaking his hand in the process. In sum, there is no reason to believe that Plutarch was blinded by his respect for Cato or that he engaged in hagiography.

In writing our life of Cato, we have, though, worked to account for those instances in which Plutarch seems to be carried away by admiration. For example, how did Cato persuade the remnants of Metellus Scipio's cavalry to stop pillaging Utica? Plutarch suggests that he did it by sheer force of personality; *The African War* suggests that he paid them to go away. Plutarch's account seems less probable here, and this is one of the occasions for which we have noted as much in the text. And because Plutarch often grouped his stories thematically (e.g., Cato's relationships with women), he cannot always be relied on for chronology.

Most important, however, there is good reason to believe that Plutarch's biography is founded on eyewitness accounts of Cato's life. Joseph Michael Conant (*The Younger Cato: A Critical Life with Special Reference to Plutarch's Biography*) makes a strong case that Plutarch worked largely from two sources, now lost. One of these was likely Cicero's *Cato,* which dealt with some of the most important events in Cato's political life, from the perspective of a man who saw many of them firsthand. The other was a life of Cato by Thrasea Paetus, the Stoic senator condemned by Nero; this work, in turn, was based on the memoirs of Munatius Rufus, Cato's Stoic companion. The two most important sources for Plutarch's biography, then, appear to have been written by men who knew Cato intimately: a political ally and a close personal friend. It is certainly possible that these sources became garbled as they were passed down through Plutarch and that, as the works of men who were close to Cato, they were biased to begin with. But because Plutarch's life seems to originate in firsthand accounts, and because it contains such a wealth of detail, it is fair to agree with the classicist Robert J. Goar's judgment: Plutarch "brings us as close to the historical Cato as it is possible for us to come."

NOTES

Epigraph

xi "Whether these things": Plutarch, *Cato Major* V 6. Though Plutarch is here referring to Cato the Elder, this book is, in part, an argument that the same words characterize his great-grandson's mixture of principled stubbornness just as well.

Preface: The Dream

1 a converted bakery: see Mark Evan Bryan, " 'Slideing into Monarchical extravagance': Cato at Valley Forge and the Testimony of William Bradford Jr.," 127–29.

2 liberty or death: compare to Joseph Addison, *Cato: A Tragedy*, act II, scene 4: "It is not now time to talk of aught / But chains or conquest, liberty or death."

2 one life to give: compare to Addison, *Cato,* act IV, scene 4: "What a pity it is / That we can die but once to serve our country."

2 "not in the power": letter from George Washington to Benedict Arnold, December 5, 1775. Compare to Addison, *Cato,* act I, scene 2: " 'Tis not in mortals to command success; / But we'll do more, Sempronius, we'll deserve it."

NOTES

Chapter 1: War Games

7 "Come, beg your uncle . . . How lucky for Italy": Plutarch, *Cato Minor* II 1–4.

9 "the Italian race": Appian, *The Civil Wars* I 9.

10 "It is with lying lips": Plutarch, *Tiberius Gracchus* IX 5.

10 "the grief he had suffered": Plutarch, *Gaius Gracchus* III 2.

11 "If you give citizenship": Heinrich Meyer, ed., *Oratorum Romanorum Fragmenta* VIII 28.

11 "all the spectators": Plutarch, *Gaius Gracchus* XVII 2.

12 "Whoever wants to save the Republic": Valerius Maximus, *Factorum ac Dictorum Memorabilium* III 2.17; Velleius Paterculus, *Roman History* II 3.1–2 ; Plutarch, *Tiberius Gracchus* XIX 3–6; Appian, *The Civil Wars* I 16.

12 "he sank upon his knees": Plutarch, *Gaius Gracchus* XVI 5.

13 "A free state": Pseudo-Sallust, *Letter to Caesar* II 6.1.

13 "Drusus—your blood": Pseudo-Cicero, *Rhetorica ad Herennium* IV 21.31.

14 "the Roman name": see Adrienne Mayor, *The Poison King*, 19.

14 "the common enemy": Mithridates to his satrap Leonippus. See C. Bradford Welles, *Royal Correspondence in the Hellenistic Period*, 293.

15 "her husband": Cicero, *Pro Caelio* XIII.

15 "Cato, when he understood": Plutarch, *Cato Minor* II 6.

16 "The column split apart": Virgil, *Aeneid* V 580–93.

18 They went on strike: Plutarch, *Cato Minor* III 1.

18 "looked exactly like an Inferno": ibid. III 2.

19 "like a mulberry": Plutarch, *Sulla* II 1.

19 "At least let us know . . . I am adding to the list all of the names I can remember": ibid. XXXI 2–4.

21 "If you had put": Valerius Maximus, *Factorum ac Dictorum Memorabilium* III 1.2.

21 "Because men fear him . . . Give me a sword": Plutarch, *Cato Minor* III 3.

22 "I do think": Isocrates, *Against the Sophists*.

22 "I didn't come here": Plutarch, *Sulla* XIII 4.

23 his poor neighbor's bees: For this and other examples of rhetorical topics, see Seneca Rhetor, *Controversiae* and *Suasoriae*.

23 "There can be nothing baser": Cicero, *De Re Publica* II 26.

322

23 "If anyone kills": Cicero, *De Officiis* III 19.

23 "Do you teach rhetoric? . . . What iron bowels": Juvenal, *Saturae* VII 150–54.

24 "Men find fault . . . Only let them": Plutarch, *Cato Minor* IV 2.

Chapter 2: The Pillar

25 in defense of a pillar: Plutarch, *Cato Minor* V 1–2.

27 "I have never": Heinrich Meyer, ed., *Oratorum Romanorum Fragmenta* VIII, XLIV 173.

28 "The community suffers": Cato the Elder, *Pro Lege Oppia*, in *Oratorum Romanorum Fragmenta* XI–XII.

28 "What do you expect? We aren't Catos": Plutarch, *Cato Major* XIX 5.

29 "Romans, this is the date": Aulus Gellius, *Noctes Atticae* IV 18.3.

29 UNGRATEFUL FATHERLAND: Valerius Maximus, *Factorum ac Dictorum Memorabilium* V 3.2.

31 WHEN THE ROMAN STATE WAS TOTTERING TO ITS FALL: Plutarch, *Cato Major* XIX 3.

31 "The Carthaginians are already our enemies": Cato the Elder, *De Bello Carthaginiensi*, in *Oratorum Romanorum Fragmenta* III 195.

31 "In addition, Carthage must be destroyed": Plutarch, *Cato Major* XXVII 1.

31 "the first recorded incitement to genocide": Ben Kiernan, "The First Genocide: Carthage, 146 BC," 27.

32 "In due course": Cato the Elder, quoted in Pliny the Elder, *Naturalis Historia* XXIX 13–14.

33 "As he looks about": Virgil, *Aeneid* XII 896–902.

35 "a very remarkable fact": Pliny the Elder, *Naturalis Historia* VII 31.

37 "in agreement with nature": Zeno of Citium, quoted in Diogenes Laertius, *Lives and Opinions of Eminent Philosophers* VII 4.

37 "If I actually knew that I was fated now to be ill": Chrysippus, quoted in Arrian, *Discourses of Epictetus* II 6.9.

37 "a second-rate Greek philosophy": Edith Hamilton, *The Roman Way*, 162.

38 "to be ashamed only of what was really shameful": Plutarch, *Cato Minor* VI 3.

38 "I don't even remember": Seneca, *De Ira* II 32.

Chapter 3: "Slaves Tower Above Us"

39 his ABCs: Suetonius, *Divus Julius* LXXVII.

41 "He betook himself to iambic verse": Plutarch, *Cato Minor* VII 2.

41 "the measure in which ruthless warfare": Ovid, *Ibis* 644.

43 "Should Cato marry?": Quintilian, *Institutio Oratoria* III 5.8.

44 "We rule the world": Plutarch, *Cato Major* VIII 2.

44 "stayed up all night": Cicero, *Pro Murena* XIII.

45 "herdsmen and shepherds": Plutarch, *Crassus* IX 3.

45 "in sagacity and culture superior to his fortune": ibid. VIII 2.

46 "How our runaway slaves tower above us in largeness of spirit": Pliny the Elder, *Naturalis Historiae* XXXIII 14.

46 "the new Hannibal": Plutarch, *Sertorius* XXIII 2.

46 "like a strong wrestler": ibid. 1.

48 "Resolve your differences": Cicero, *De Legibus* I 53.

49 Cato rejected any and all decorations: Cato's refusal of military honors calls to mind these lines of a character with which he shares a great deal in common, Shakespeare's Coriolanus: "I thank you, general; / But cannot make my heart consent to take / A bribe to pay my sword. . . . / No more, I say! For that I have not wash'd / My nose that bled, or foil'd some debile wretch.— / Which, without note, here's many else have done,— / You shout me forth / In acclamations hyperbolical; / As if I loved my little should be dieted / In praises sauced with lies." (*Coriolanus*, act I, scene 9).

49 "discipline, self-control": Plutarch, *Cato Minor* VIII 1.

50 and to scorn as a pauper: see Cassius Dio, *Roman History* XL 27.3.

50 "He had demonstrated": Appian, *The Civil Wars* I 118.

51 "the Teenage Butcher": Valerius Maximus, *Factorum ac Dictorum Memorabilium* VI 2.

52 "The battle was long and bloody": Appian, *The Civil Wars* I 120.

Chapter 4: The First Command

55 "You must caress men": Quintus Tullius Cicero, *Commentariolum Petitionis* XI.

55 "It is the privilege": Cicero, *Pro Plancio* XI.

59 "It would not be wrong to describe their drills as bloodless battles": Josephus, *The Jewish War* III 5.1.

59 "He thought it a trifling and useless task": Plutarch, *Cato Minor* IX 2.

59 "those things which are within the grasp": James Stockdale, "Courage Under Fire," 7.

60 "It would be hard . . . He made himself": Plutarch, *Cato Minor* IX 3–4.

61 "We should look": Zeno of Citium, quoted in Plutarch, *On the Fortune of Alexander* 329A–B.

61 "placed in a situation of great danger": Diogenes Laertius, *Lives and Opinions of Eminent Philosophers* VII 34.

62 "Lead me, O Master": Cleanthes, quoted in Epictetus, *Enchiridion* LIII, and in Seneca, *Epistulae* CVII 1.

63 "My brother": Plutarch, *Cato Minor* III 5.

64 "Not all men": ibid. XII 5.

65 "As long as it could": Cicero, *In Verrem II*, V.

65 "Fellow citizens" Plutarch, *Crassus* XII 4.

66 "a virtual monarch": Cassius Dio, *Roman History* XXXVI 34.

67 "Oh, my endless tasks!": Plutarch, *Pompey* XXX 6.

67 In Ephesus: This outline of Cato's Asian travels follows Jane Bellemore ("Cato the Younger in the East in 66 B.C."), who notes a number of small implausibilities of place or chronology in Plutarch but concludes that "it is possible to reconstruct Cato's movements without having to do much injustice to the account of Plutarch."

67 "must render an account . . . Everyone knew": Plutarch, *Cato Minor* XIV 2–3.

Chapter 5: The Swamp

72 *Sic vivitur*: see, for example, Cicero, *Epistulae ad Familiares* II 15.

72 "surpass all Romans . . . It would be a shameful thing": Plutarch, *Cato Minor* XVI 4–5.

74 "All men hated them . . . thought that with their deaths . . . punished before men's eyes": ibid. XVII 4–5.

75 "the quaestorship with dignity of the consulship . . . It is impossible": ibid. XVII 1–XVIII 2.

Chapter 6: "Do You Not See a Storm Coming?"

79 "debauchees, adulterers, and gamblers": Sallust, *Bellum Catilinae* XIV.

79 *Tabulae Novae*: ibid. XXI.

79 "We are poor": ibid. XXXIII.

81 "Catiline has fouled himself": quoted in Asconius, *Commentaria in Ciceronis Orationes*.

81 "Who is better qualified": Cicero, *Pro Murena* L.

81 "I see two bodies": Plutarch, *Cicero* XIII 4–5.

83 "He sacrificed a boy": Cassius Dio, *Roman History* XXXVII 30.3.

84 "I have been informed that" as a catchphrase: see Anthony Everitt, *Cicero: The Life and Times of Rome's Great Politician*, 102.

84 "this lunatic criminal enterprise": Cicero, *In Catilinam* I, IV 8.

86 "Shall you seek": quoted in Cicero, *Pro Murena* LXXIV.

86 "a war against women": ibid. XXXII.

87 "I am much more afraid": ibid. LVIII. This interpretation of Cicero's strategy in the Murena trial is indebted to Christopher P. Craig's "Cato's Stoicism and the Understanding of Cicero's Speech for Murena."

87 "There once was a man . . . That no one is merciful": Cicero, *Pro Murena* LXI–LXII.

89 "By the way, why is it that you have a nomenclator": ibid. LXXVII.

89 "but our habits": ibid. LXXIV.

90 "What a witty consul": Plutarch, *Cato Minor* XXI 5.

90 "I am talking to you": Cicero, *Pro Murena* LXXXI.

91 "There was nothing": Sallust, *Bellum Catilinae* XL.

91 "Consider what your views demand": ibid. XLIV.

92 "when citizens of such eminence": ibid. XLVI.

92 "the extreme penalty": ibid. L.

92 "Their guilt": Sallust, *Bellum Catilinae* LI.

93 "every woman's man": Suetonius, *Divus Julius* LII 3.

93 "acted with wisdom . . . guilty of many acts . . . that the utmost degree of torture . . . the good and the bad . . . stay its progress . . . For certainly": Sallust, *Bellum Catilinae* LI.

95 *Rem tene, verba sequentur*: quoted in Julius Victor, *Ars Rhetorica* I.

95 "You have always valued . . . the luxury and greed . . . fall, along with ourselves . . . Other crimes": Sallust, *Bellum Catilinae* LII.

96 "Take it, you drunk!": Plutarch, *Cato Minor* XXIV 1–2.

96–97 "fair and elegant . . . mischievous and profligate friends . . . will advance upon you . . . Why do you hesitate . . . Do not suppose . . . the most inhuman of traitors . . . We are completely surrounded":

Sallust, *Bellum Catilinae* LII. Cicero took the unusual step of posting stenographers in the Senate to record the debates on the conspiracy, including Cato's speech. See Plutarch, *Cato Minor* XXIII 3 and Cicero, *Pro Sulla* XLI-XLII.

98 "Cicero—the Father of the Fatherland!": Plutarch, *Cicero* XXIII 6. Cicero reported (*In Pisonem* III 6) that the title was bestowed by Catulus; Everitt conjectures that it was voted by the Senate and announced by Cato.

99 "Their birth, age, and eloquence . . . Caesar grew eminent": Sallust, *Bellum Catilinae* LIV.

Chapter 7: Men of the People

102 "Gracchus": quoted in Cicero, *Tusculanae Disputationes* III 48.

102 "would draw the plebeians away": Cicero, *Pro Sestio* CIII.

102 about forty thousand Romans: for these estimates on the size of the Roman grain dole, see Alessandro Cristofori, "Grain Distribution in Late Republican Rome," 148–49.

103 "Of the many": Sallust, *Bellum Catilinae* LXI 8–9.

103 the king had dreamed: Mithridates' dream is noted in Plutarch, *Pompey* XXXII 4.

104 "that domestic poison": Appian, *Roman History* XII 16.111.

104 "in the person of Mithridates": Plutarch, *Pompey* XLII 1.

104 "all that was unlawful": Josephus, *Antiquitates Judaicae* XIV 4.4.

104 "vulture": Plutarch, *Pompey* XXXI 6.

106 "Great dejection and fear . . . What a bold man": Plutarch, *Cato Minor* XXVII 2–4.

108 "Nepos had to explain": Wiseman, *New Men in the Roman Senate 139 B.C.–A.D. 14*, 360.

109 "Just as, often": Virgil, *Aeneid* I 148–54.

110 his longtime wife, Mucia: Mucia was Pompey's third wife. His previous wife, Sulla's stepdaughter (as noted in chapter 3), died in childbirth in 82.

112 "Go, Munatius": Plutarch, *Cato Minor* XXX 4.

113 "If we are to judge": ibid. XXX 6.

113 THE INHABITED WORLD: Cassius Dio, *Roman History* XXXVII 21.2.

113 "How happy": Plutarch, *Pompey* XLI 1. For a vivid description of Pompey's triumph, see also Mary Beard, *The Roman Triumph*, 7–14.

Chapter 8: Creating the Monster

114 "*Dicit enim*": Cicero, *Epistulae ad Atticum* II 1.

114 "He talks like he's living": Tom Holland, *Rubicon*, 196.

115 "a scandalous affair": Cicero, *Epistulae ad Atticum* I 17.

116 "It is now three months": ibid. I 18.

117 "They were thinking": Everitt, *Cicero*, 129.

117 "dregs": Cicero, *Epistulae ad Atticum* I 19.

120 "let [the triumph] pass": Cassius Dio, *Roman History* XXXVII 54.2.

121 "even Cato": Suetonius, *Divus Julius* XIX 1.

122 "end of parliamentary government": Joseph Michael Conant, "The Younger Cato: A Critical Life with Special Reference to Plutarch's Biography," 100. See also Paul Groebe, "Die Obstruktion im römischen Senat."

123 "If he made a friend . . . It seemed to him": Cassius Dio, *Roman History* XXXVII 55.1–2.

124 "Crassus thought that he ought": ibid. 56.4.

124 "so that he seemed in a way to have included the whole world": Plutarch, *Pompey* XLV 5.

125 "Three-Headed Monster": Appian, *The Civil Wars* II 9.

126 "The swollen population": Cassius Dio, *Roman History* XXXVIII 1.2–3.

127 "a point on which he strenuously insisted": ibid. 1.7.

127 "It is, indeed, a matter for profound reflection": Cicero, *Epistulae ad Atticum* II 3.

127–28 "They suspected": Cassius Dio, *Roman History* XXXVIII 2.3.

128 "descended upon the whole city . . . Heaven was not ignorant": ibid. XXXVII 58.2–4.

129 "a woman of reputed excellence": Plutarch, *Cato Minor* XXV 1.

129 "even though no one spoke against him": ibid. XXXVIII 2.3.

130 "urged [the Senate] on general principles": ibid. XXXVIII 3.1.

130 "not of the distribution of land": ibid. XXXI 5.

130 "offered himself . . . I'd rather be in prison . . . I have made you judges": Cassius Dio, *Roman History* XXXVIII 3.2–3.

131 "that he was driven forth": Plutarch, *Caesar* XIV 3.

132 "You will have the law . . . You will not have the law . . . were not striving for any unnatural or unjust end": Cassius Dio, *Roman History* XXXVIII 4.3–6.

133 "In case any resistance . . . Yes, indeed": Plutarch, *Pompey* XLVII 4–5.

133 "an impulsive and mad speech": Plutarch, *Caesar* XIV 6.

134 "fell back": Cassius Dio, *Roman History*, XXXVIII 6.2–3.

134 "All the other senators . . . swear solemnly": Plutarch, *Cato Minor* XXXII 2–3.

135 "came into collision . . . needy and noisy . . . He therefore wished to bind him . . . He left the Forum": Plutarch, *Marius* XXVIII–XXIX.

136 "senseless and mad . . . It would be the greatest of evils": Plutarch, *Cato Minor* XXXII 4–5.

137 "elated by this success": ibid. XXXIII 1.

137 "made submissive": ibid. XXXIV 1.

138 "was overcome by the shame . . . although Cato warned the people": ibid. XXXIII 2–3.

139 "Consulship of Julius and Caesar": Suetonius, *Divus Julius* XX 2.

139 "Even when they did prevail": Plutarch, *Cato Minor* XXXIV 1.

140 "a man from the lap of Pompey": ibid. XXXIII 4.

Chapter 9: Almost Exile

141 "It is hard to imagine": Everitt, *Cicero*, 120.

143 "One might think": Cicero, *Epistulae ad Atticum* I 16.

145 "Your fury": Cicero, *De Domo Sua* XXV.

146 "to swallow any indignity": Holland, *Rubicon*, 326.

147 "he regarded Cato . . . a snare and an insult . . . Well, then, if you don't think it's a favor": Plutarch, *Cato Minor* XXXII 2–3.

148 "It must have given Cato": Muriel Jaeger, *Adventures in Living, from Cato to George Sand*, 23.

149 "He—who was always an ally": Cicero, *Pro Sestio* XXVII.

152 "The king, as if brought to his senses . . . convinced that he had slighted": Plutarch, *Cato Minor* XXXV 5.

153 "and sent men out": Cassius Dio, *Roman History* XXXIX 13.2

154 48 percent a year: Cicero discovered evidence of Brutus's moneylending practices during his service as proconsul in Cilicia (with jurisdiction that included Cyprus) in 50. See Cicero, *Epistulae ad Atticum* VI 1.

154 "a man of high principles": see Dirk Baltzly, "Stoicism," in *The Stanford Encyclopedia of Philosophy*.

156 "lavished kindness": Plutarch, *Cato Minor* XXXVII 5.

Chapter 10: Cato the Prophet

161 "heroes": Caesar, *Commentarii de Bello Gallico* II 27.

162 "He tried to reconcile them": Plutarch, *Crassus* XIV 2. The mention of Catulus seems to be inaccurate, however: He evidently died in 61.

163 "a sort of second life": Cicero, *Epistulae ad Atticum* IV 1.

163 "the greatest man": Cicero, *Post Reditum ad Quirites* VII.

163 "Since those who": Cicero, *Epistulae ad Atticum* IV 5.

164 "It was a funeral of the Republic": quoted in Cicero, *De Provinciis Consularibus* XIX. Though the individual Cicero is quoting—"a man of the highest *auctoritas* and of the greatest eloquence"—is not named, it seems clear from the context that he is referring to Cato.

165 "the only two men": Jaeger, *Adventures in Living,* 18.

165 "We shall only see": Cicero, *De Provinciis Consularibus* VIII.

165 "As for Caesar": ibid. XII.

166 Cicero wrote to Atticus to apologize: Cicero, *Epistulae ad Atticum* IV 5. Everitt concludes that Pompey was most likely vetting the speech.

166 "spent the rest of the year": Cassius Dio, *Roman History* XXXIX 30.4.

168 a lurid picture: the accusations are preserved in Pliny the Elder's *Naturalis Historiae* VII 30.113, VIII 48.196, XXIX 4.96, and XXXIV 8.92. Conant argues that Metellus's pamphlet is Pliny's most likely source for these passages.

168 Metellus Scipio was evidently among the victors: Conant argues that Metellus likely won the praetorship in this year, because he served as consul in 52 and would only have qualified if he had filled the lesser office.

170 "As if inspired from heaven": Plutarch, *Cato Minor* XLII 4.

171 "and this part of Cato's life": ibid. XXV 1.

171–72 "According to the opinion": ibid. XXV 3.

000 "Obviously it is rational": Jaeger, *Adventures in Living,* 26.

172 "Community in heirs": Plutarch, *Cato Minor* XXV 3.

174 "in order that he might be silenced": Cassius Dio, *Roman History* XXXIX 34.3.

175 "Thunder! . . . at length, by open force": Plutarch, *Cato Minor* XLIII 4.

176 "was now, without knowing it, taking Caesar upon his own shoulders": ibid. XLIII 5.

176 "Always secure": ibid. XLIII 6.

178 "As he was leaving": Valerius Maximus, *Factorum ac Dictorum Memorabilium* II 10.8. The incident is also referenced in Seneca, *Epistulae* XCVII 8, and Martial *Epigrammata* I, preface.

179 "[The Germans'] confusion being made apparent . . . granted those whom he had detained": Caesar, *Commentarii de Bello Gallico* IV 14–15.

180 "Let us sacrifice": Plutarch, *Cato Minor* LI 2.

181 "Assailing Caesar's plans": ibid. LI 3–4.

182 "the most carefully prepared": Cicero, *In Pisonem* XXXVIII.

182 the same austere way: Asconius, *Commentaria in Ciceronis Orationes* XXIX.

183 Cato drank more openly: see Plutarch, *Cato Minor* XLI 1; Pliny the Younger, *Epistulae* III 12.2; and Seneca, *De Tranquillitate Animi* XVII 4, 9.

183 interest rate doubled . . . five hundred sesterces: Cicero, *Epistulae ad Quintum Fratrem* II 14. Plutarch (*Cato Minor* XLIV 5) puts the rate at 125,000 drachmas.

183 "If the election": Cicero, *Epistulae ad Quintum Fratrem* II 14.

184 "This conduct of Cato": Plutarch, *Cato Minor* XLIV 7.

185 objections of the consul Ahenobarbus: Cassius Dio, *Roman History* XXXIX 64.1.

185 "And everywhere surging tumult": Plutarch, *Pompey* LIII 5.

185 120 Sardinians: Valerius Maximus, *Factorum ac Dictorum Memorabilium* VIII 1 absol. 10.

186 "The worthlessness of their nation": Cicero, *Pro Scauro* XXXVIII.

186 "and he greatly impressed the jury": Asconius, *Commentaria in Ciceronis Orationes* XX.

186 Cato's renewed push against public corruption: while Plutarch places Cato's Senate decree before his arrangement with the tribunician candidates, Conant argues for the opposite order, based on the contemporary evidence of Cicero's letters.

187 "I cannot praise *you*": Plutarch, *Cato Minor* XLIV 4 (our emphasis).

188 "a trafficker in provinces": Cicero, *Post Reditum in Senatu* IV.

188 ancient prophecy: a line in the ancient Sibylline books regarded as prophecy by Romans, cited in Cassius Dio, *Roman History* XXXIX 15.2. "If the king of Egypt come requesting any aid, refuse him not friendship,

nor yet succour him with any great force; else you shall have both toils and dangers."

188 "When guilty mortals": Homer, *Iliad* XVI 385 (translated by Alexander Pope, a writer to match Cicero's gentility), quoted in Cicero, *Epistulae ad Quintum Fratrem* III 7.

188 (and the jury sufficiently bought): Conant believes that Cato may have sat on the jury for Gabinius's first trial. If so, he surely voted to convict.

189 "regain control . . . adapting it": Elaine Fantham, "The Trials of Gabinius in 54 B.C.," 437–38.

190 "armies of this great size . . . using anarchy": Plutarch, *Cato Minor* XLV 3–4.

190 Pentheus: Plutarch (*Crassus* XXXIII 1–4) describes how the Parthians used Crassus's head as a prop in a performance of Euripides' *Bacchae*, which tells of the destruction of Pentheus, the king of Thebes, as a consequence of his failure to honor the god Dionysus. Cassius Dio (*Roman History* XL 27.3) describes how the Parthians mocked Crassus after his death by pouring molten gold into his mouth.

Chapter 11: Ultimatum

193 "The people went down": Plutarch, *Caesar* XXVIII 4–5.

193 "were absolutely without a government": Cassius Dio, *Roman History* XL 27.3.

193 "as was the custom": Asconius, *Commentaria in Ciceronis Orationes* XXXI.

195 "Consul!": ibid. XXXIII.

195 "He did not authorize": ibid. XXXV.

196 twenty-six slaves: ibid. XXXIV for the Clodian version.

196 "battle": Cicero, *Epistulae ad Atticum* V 13.

196 "I pass over": Cicero, *Epistulae ad Familiares* XV 4. It is unclear when Cato supported Milo in the Senate, possibly in the wake of Clodius's death, possibly during the debate on the law *de vi* ("on force") during Pompey's sole consulship.

197 "whenever a more important and remarkable event": Caesar, *Commentarii de Bello Gallico* VII 3.

197 "A single and united Gaul": ibid. 29.

198–99 "the most moderate . . . Any government": Plutarch, *Cato Minor* XLVII 2–3.

199 "associate in government": Plutarch, *Cato Minor* XLVIII 1.

200 turned on him: for Pompey's motives in abandoning Milo, see Robin Seager, *Pompey the Great: A Political Biography*, 145.

200 it had to include Cato: Cassius Dio, *Roman History* XL 52.1; Cicero, *Pro Milone* XVI; Asconius, *Commentaria in Ciceronis Orationes* XXXI.

200 a good deal of influence: see Conant, *The Younger Cato*, 152.

201 "Would that the gods": Cicero, *Pro Milone* XXXVIII.

202 "who had not concealed": Asconius, *Commentaria in Ciceronis Orationes* LIII.

203 "He would be obliged": Suetonius, *Divus Julius* XXX 3.

203 "a very violent opposition": Caesar, *Commentarii de Bello Civili* I 32. See also Plutarch, *Pompey* LVI 3 and Livy, *Periochae* CVII.

204 "by which the multitude": Plutarch, *Cato Minor* XLIX 4.

205 "Cato still more exasperated the common folk": ibid. 3.

205 "the greatest of all good things": ibid. 2.

205 "When affairs demanded . . . Since there had been no foul play": ibid. L 2–3.

206 "Cato had renounced": Jaeger, *Adventures in Living*, 21.

206–7 "his arrival being known . . . The cavalry is suddenly": Caesar, *Commentarii de Bello Gallico* VII 88.

208 "attacked Caesar's *dignitas*": *Commentarii de Bello Gallico* VIII 53 (this last book of Caesar's Commentaries was, in fact, written by Hirtius).

209 "This will give it": Appian, *The Civil Wars* II 25. See also Plutarch, *Caesar* XXIX 6 and *Pompey* LVIII 2.

209 ordered him flogged: Appian, *The Civil Wars* II 26 and Plutarch, *Caesar* XXIX 2.

209 oaths to prosecute him: Suetonius, *Divus Julius* XXX 3.

209 "Pompey, incited": Caesar, *Commentarii de Bello Civili* I 4.

210 "Suppose that my son took a stick to me": Cicero, *Epistulae ad Familiares* VIII 8.

210 "fear of revolution": Cicero, *Epistulae ad Atticum* V 21.

210–11 "Your own immense prestige . . . In all forms of speech . . . After my unjust disgrace . . . "I have only one last resource": Cicero, *Epistulae ad Familiares* XV 4.

212 "eloquent, reckless": Velleius Paterculus, *Roman History* II 48.3.

213 "Now these things are come to pass . . . Cato could accomplish nothing": Plutarch, *Cato Minor* LI 5.

214 "I gladly obey": saved among Cicero's letters, *Epistulae ad Familiares* XV 5.

215 "I would be surprised . . . softened by the assiduous study . . . whenever we are tempted": Gaston Boissier, *Cicéron et Ses Amis*, 293–94.

216 "has been disgracefully spiteful": Cicero, *Epistulae ad Atticum* VII 2.

217 "I will gladly yield": Appian, *The Civil Wars* II 28.

217 "The Senate now had suspicions of both": ibid. 29.

218 "Caesar will be joined": Marcus Caelius Rufus, saved among Cicero's letters, *Epistulae ad Familiares* VIII 14.

218 "What am I to do?": Cicero, *Epistulae ad Atticum* VII 1.

219 "Lest the senators": Cassius Dio, *Roman History* XLI 2.1.

219 among the 22: see Conant, *The Younger Cato*, 163.

219 "Enjoy your victory": Appian, *The Civil Wars* II 30.

220 destruction of the constitution: see Cicero, *Epistulae ad Atticum* VII 8.

220 "would come quickly": Appian, *The Civil Wars* II 32.

221 "You're being deceived": Plutarch, *Pompey* LIX 4.

Chapter 12: Pompey's Ring

222 "filled with tumult . . . You've deceived us": Plutarch, *Pompey* LX 3–4.

223 "If any of you . . . Pompey acknowledged . . . The same men": Plutarch, *Cato Minor* LII 2.

224 "Since nearly all Italy": Plutarch, *Pompey* LXI 1–2.

226 "was set as bait . . . No sooner had Cato": LII 4–5.

226 "She came with hair disheveled": Lucan, *Pharsalia* II 333–73.

227 "saw that the people in the city": Cassius Dio, *Roman History* XLI 5.1.

227–28 "Such as were removing with their entire households": ibid. 7.3–6.

228 "expecting to be the first": ibid. 8.5.

228 "embraced and clung . . . anyone who saw them": ibid. 9.4–6.

229 "maintained the same mien of sorrow": Plutarch, *Cato Minor* LIII 1.

229 "Caesar himself was astonished": Plutarch, *Pompey* LXIII 1.

230 "there was much inconsistency": Plutarch, *Cato Minor* LIII 2.

231 "As for what is to follow": *Epistulae ad Atticum* VII 10.

232 "brought to the party of Pompey": Plutarch, *Cato Minor* LIII 4.

232 "His navy . . . as if he had been in the flower . . . who had never spoken": Plutarch, *Pompey* LXIV 1–3.

233 "If I cannot make use": quoted in *Epistulae ad Atticum* IX 18.

233 "if he remained at home": Plutarch, *Cicero* XXXVIII 1.

234 "should be made master of so large a force": Plutarch, *Cato Minor* LIV 4.

235 "so that every wind that blew": Plutarch, *Pompey* LXV 4.

235 "sluggishly and in silence . . . When Cato": Plutarch, *Cato Minor* LIV 5.

236 "the chief task": Plutarch, *Comparison of Agesilaus and Pompey* IV 1.

236 "the usual design": Caesar, *Commentarii de Bello Civili* III 47.

237 "Today victory": Plutarch, *Pompey* LXV 5.

238 "that he might always be in office . . . a slave to fame": Plutarch, *Pompey* LXVII 2–4.

239 "Now at last the signal": ibid. LXX 1–2.

239 fifteen thousand dead: *Commentarii de Bello Civili* III 99. Pollio, on the other hand, recorded a more modest six thousand dead on Pompey's side (his history is lost, but it is cited in Appian, *The Civil Wars* II 82).

240 "Good plan, if we were at war with jackdaws": Plutarch, *Cicero* XXXVIII 7.

241 "Whoever to a tyrant": Cassius Dio, *Roman History* XLII 3.2; Appian, *The Civil Wars* II 85; Plutarch, *Pompey* LXXVIII 4.

241 "son-in-law": Cassius Dio, *Roman History* XLII 8.1.

Chapter 13: Alone

243 "His course lay": Strabo, *Geographica* XVII 20. Given that Cato's march began late in the year, Strabo may have been exaggerating the temperature.

243 "No one": Plutarch, *Cato Minor* LVI 2.

243 Great Syrtis: see Strabo, *Geographica* XVII 20. "The difficulty of navigating both [the Great Syrtis] and the Lesser Syrtis [arises from the

circumstances of] the soundings in many parts being soft mud. It sometimes happens, on the ebbing and flowing of the tide, that vessels are carried upon the shallows, settle down, and are seldom recovered."

243 five hundred miles: the approximate distance from Berenice to Leptis Magna, where the army may have wintered. A direct march to Utica would have been some eleven hundred miles.

244 seven days: Plutarch, *Cato Minor* LVI 4.

244 thirty-day trek: Strabo, *Geographica* XVII 20.

244 "Bearing his javelin": Lucan, *Pharsalia* IX 587–93.

244 "Bound are we": ibid. 573–83.

247 arbitrary uses of power: see Caesar, *Commentarii de Bello Civili* III 31–33.

247 "He refused": Plutarch, *Cato Minor* LVII 3.

247–48 Utica was already old: for the situation of Utica, see Strabo, *Geography* XVII 13.

248 "privileges": *De Bello Africo* LXXXVII.

249 disarmed and expelled: ibid. Cato, "distrusting the inhabitants of that city, on account of the privileges granted them by the Julian law, had disarmed and expelled the populace, obliging them to dwell without the warlike gate, in a small camp surrounded by a slight intrenchment, around which he had planted guards." Plutarch also notes Cato later "calling the people of Utica together *into* the city" (*Cato Minor* LXV 3, emphasis added).

249 "Cato, who commanded in Utica": *De Bello Africo* XXII.

249 "made the city a storehouse for the war": Plutarch, *Cato Minor* LVIII 3.

250 "growing daily stronger": Cicero, *Epistulae ad Atticum* XI 12.

250 a new front . . . exhorting young Gnaeus: *De Bello Africo* XXII–XXIII.

251 "indefinite promises . . . Contrary to the expectation . . . fellow soldiers": Appian, *The Civil Wars* II 92–93.

252 "I have you now": Suetonius, *Divus Julius* LIX; Cassius Dio, *The Roman History* XLII 58.3.

252 "exposed, upon a foreign coast": *De Bello Africo* X.

253 "Trust to time . . . That there were no good hopes . . . Their cause . . . if they should face": Plutarch, *Cato Minor* LVIII 4–LIX 5.

257 "threw all the inhabitants": *De Bello Africo* LXXXVII.

257 fell on the encampment: *De Bello Africo* skips directly from the horsemen's failed attack on the encampment to their pillaging in Utica, eliding over any negotiations with Cato. Plutarch (*Cato Minor* LXII–LXV) dwells on the negotiations but does not mention the attack on the camp. The account we have given here seems the most plausible way of solving the discrepancy.

258 "To be shut up . . . excessively barbarous . . . they were not Catos . . . Prayer belonged": Plutarch *Cato Minor* LXIII 2–LXIV 5.

261 "Cato, unable to prevail": *De Bello Africo* LXXXVII.

262 "It is your task": Plutarch, *Cato Minor* LXV 5.

263 "I, who have been brought up in freedom": Cassius Dio, *The Roman History* XLIII 10.5.

264 "Statyllius! Did you bring him . . . Well, we shall see": Plutarch, *Cato Minor* LXVI 4.

264 "The good man alone . . . and in loud and harsh tones": ibid. LXVII 1–2.

265 "He held out the cup": Plato, *Phaedo* 117b–c.

266 "It will perhaps seem . . . Perhaps from this point . . . I would assert": ibid. 62a–63c.

267–68 "When and where . . . Why, then": Plutarch, *Cato Minor* LXVIII 4–LXIX 2.

Chapter 14: Cato in Purgatory

270 "like a wild beast": Appian, *The Civil Wars* II 99.

271 "Cato, I begrudge": Plutarch, *Cato Minor* LXXII 2.

272 "For some reason": Cicero, *Epistulae ad Atticum* XIV 17.

272 "a problem for Archimedes": ibid. XII 4.

272–73 "Was the case": Cicero, *De Officiis* I 31.

273 "Cato left this world": Cicero, *Tusculanae Disputationes* I 30.

273 "godlike and unique": Cicero, *De Finibus* III 6.

273 "the foundation of the Cato legend": L. R. Taylor, *Party Politics in the Age of Caesar*, 170.

274 its accusations: Caesar's *Anti-Cato* appears to be paraphrased or quoted in Aulus Gellius, *Noctes Atticae* IV 16.8; Pliny the Younger, *Epistulae* III 12.2; Priscian, *Institutiones Grammaticae* VI 7.36; and Plutarch, *Cato Minor* XI 3, XXXVI 3, XLIV 7, LII 4, and LIV 2.

275 "The woman was at first set as a bait": Plutarch, *Cato Minor* LII 4.

275 "If ever a Roman writer": Robert J. Goar, *The Legend of Cato Uticensis from the First Century B.C. to the Fifth Century A.D.,* 17.

275 "Caesar's vicious and unjust attack": Taylor, *Party Politics,* 171.

276 "She took a little knife": Plutarch, *Brutus* XIII 5–11.

277 "It did not become": ibid. XII 3. Plutarch reported that the Statyllius at Utica with Cato (whether or not he is the same person referred to in the *Brutus*) died at Philippi on Brutus's side.

278 "Cato had consistently maneuvered": R. M. Russo, *Marcus Porcius Cato Uticensis: A Political Reappraisal,* 106.

279 "amazing his foes": Plutarch, *Cato Minor* LXXIII 3.

280 Another contrast: Suetonius, *Divus Augustus* XLV 1.

280 "To seek to keep": Macrobius, *Saturnalia* II 4.18.

280 "Vulcan / added the house of Tartarus": Virgil, *Aeneid* VIII 666–70.

281 "Marcus Cato, alone the greatest model": Seneca Rhetor, *Suasoria* VI 2.

281 "I remember": Persius, *Saturae* III 44–47.

281 the most powerful Stoic: until, at least, the Stoic emperor Marcus Aurelius. His writings, however, contain only a glancing reference to Cato the Younger: "From my brother Severus [I learned] . . . to love truth, and to love justice; and through him I learned to know Thrasea, Helvidius, Cato, Dion, Brutus" (Marcus Aurelius, *Meditations* I 14).

282 "Choose a Cato": Seneca, *Epistulae* XI.

282 "Cato did not grapple": Seneca, *De Constantia* II 2.

282 "While denouncing tyranny": Cassius Dio, *Roman History* LXI 9.2.

283 "You see that thirst": Seneca, *Epistulae* CIV.

284 "But Rome is greater": Lucan, *Pharsalia* I 44–45.

284 "The victorious cause": ibid. I 128.

284 "No guardian gods": ibid. VII 445–55.

285 "Rather would I lead": ibid. IX 598–604.

285 "I bequeath . . . as a libation": Tacitus, *Annales* XV 62–64.

286 "The Roman nobility": Miriam Griffin, "Philosophy, Cato, and Roman Suicide: II," 197–98.

286 "escaped the miseries": Tacitus, *Annales* XIII 30.

286 "You have been born": ibid. XVI 35.

286 "showing off": Ulpian, *Digesta* XXVIII 3.6.

287 *"personae"*: for instance, see Seneca, *Dialogi* XII 8.3: "Our sole right in the moral instincts of our own hearts . . . is the gift to us of the supreme power which shaped the universe. That power we sometimes call 'the all-ruling God,' sometimes 'the incorporeal Wisdom' which is the creator of mighty works, sometimes the 'divine spirit' which spreads through things great and small with duly strung tone." On "the Stoic strain in Christianity," see also Edward Vernon Arnold, *Roman Stoicism*, 408–36.

287 "Which of those gods": Tertullian, *Apologeticus* XI 15.

287 "We can only withdraw . . . appears to have had some cause . . . It appears to me . . . an imitator . . . the chief": Lactantius, *Divinae Institutiones* III 18.

288 "praise of a higher kind": Augustine, *De Civitate Dei contra Paganos* V 12.

289 "His example": ibid. I 23.

290 "Was it . . . Was it": ibid. XIX 4.

291 "Our opponents": ibid. I 24.

291 "The final and complete vindication": Goar, *The Legend of Cato*, 102.

292 "[Lucan] says that Marcia returned to Cato . . . What man on earth": Dante, *The Banquet* IV 28.

292 "holy, pious": Dante, *Monarchy* II 5.2.

292 "That ineffable sacrifice": ibid. II 5.11.

293 "Cato's suicide": Robert Hollander, *Allegory in Dante's* Commedia, 127–26

293 "I saw nearby": Dante, *Purgatorio* I 31–39.

294 "Look kindly": ibid. I 71–75.

Chapter 15: Cato the Revolutionary

295 "no ancient hero": Gordon S. Wood, *The Idea of America*, 50.

296 "The time was now come": Samuel Johnson, "Life of Addison," in *Lives of the Poets*, 19.

297 "Cato was not": Alexander Pope, personal letter to John Caryll, April 30, 1713. *The Works of Alexander Pope*. Volume 6, 183.

297 "the greatest character": Voltaire, *Letters on England*, Letter 18.

297 "utterly lifeless": quoted in Fredric M. Litto, "Addison's *Cato* in the Colonies." 432.

297 "uncomplicated mouthpieces": John J. Miller, "America's Greatest Play."

297 "rather a poem": Johnson, "Life of Addison," in *Lives of the Poets*, 34.

297 "familiar to the schoolboy": Edward Gibbon, *Memoirs of My Life and Writings*, 74.

297 "it is impossible": Montesquieu, *The Spirit of the Laws* XI 13.

297 "The Whigs applauded": Johnson, *Life of Addison*.

298 "Whoe'er is brave": Addison, *Cato*, act V, scene 4.

299 "Britons, attend": Prologue to *Cato*.

299 "Thus it is": John Trenchard and Thomas Gordon, *Cato's Letters*, Letter 99.

299 "This passion for liberty": Trenchard and Gordon, *Cato's Letters*, Letter 62.

299 "[L]iberty is the unalienable right": Trenchard and Gordon, *Cato's Letters*, Letter 59.

299 half of the private libraries: see Bernard Bailyn, *The Ideological Origins of the American Revolution*.

300 "Cruel Metastasio": quoted in Robert C. Ketterer, *Ancient Rome in Early Opera*, 125.

301 "Here will I hold": Addison, *Cato*, act V, scene 1.

301 "I should think": George Washington, letter to Sally Fairfax, September 25, 1758.

301 "In the Presence of Others": George Washington, *Rules of Civility and Decent Behavior in Company and Conversation*, Rule 4, Page 1.

302 "As his life progressed": Ron Chernow, *Washington: A Life*, 75.

302 "the exhibition of shews": Chauncey Worthington Ford, ed., *Journals of the Continental Congress, 1774–89*, vol. 1, 79.

302 "a distasteful if not unpatriotic": Bryan, " 'Slideing into Monarchical extravagance' " 135.

302 "in humble Imitation": Samuel Adams, letter to Samuel P. Savage, October 17, 1778.

303 A number of historians: see, e.g., Carl J. Richard, *The Founders and the Classics: Greece, Rome, and the American Enlightenment*, 58–60.

303 "and you will . . . Gentlemen": quoted in ibid., 59–60.

304 "Which of you all": Addison, *Cato*, act III, scene 5.

Epilogue: Forgotten but Not Gone
305 "These men": Jim Webb, "Speech at the Confederate Memorial."
307 "Ten Catos": Charles Oman, *Seven Roman Statesmen of the Later Republic*, 233.
310 "a noble pun": Joan Robinson, *Private Enterprise or Public Control*, 13.

A Note on Plutarch and His Sources
320 "brings us as close": Goar, *The Legend of Cato*, 72.

BIBLIOGRAPHY

Classical Sources

Appian, *Roman History* (Trans. Horace White. Loeb Classical Library, 1912)

Appian, *The Civil Wars* (Trans. Horace White. Loeb Classical Library, 1913)

Arrian, *Discourses of Epictetus* (In *The Hellenistic Philosophers*, vol. 1, ed. and trans. A. A. Long and D. N. Sedley. Cambridge: Cambridge University Press, 1987)

Asconius, *Commentaria in Ciceronis Orationes* (Trans. John Paul Adams)

Augustine, *De Civitate Dei contra Paganos* (Trans. Marcus Dods, ed. Philip Schaff. Grand Rapids, MI: Wm. B. Eerdmans, 1886)

Aulus Gellius, *Noctes Atticae* (Trans. J. C. Rolfe. Loeb Classical Library, 1927)

Caesar, *Commentarii de Bello Civili* (Trans. W. A. McDevitte and W. S. Bohn. New York: Harper and Brothers, 1869)

Caesar, *Commentarii de Bello Gallico* (Trans. W. A. McDevitte and W. S. Bohn. New York: Harper and Brothers, 1869)

Cassius Dio, *Roman History* (Trans. Earnest Cary. Loeb Classical Library, 1914–1925)

Cato the Elder, *De Agricultura*

Cicero, *De Domo Sua* (Trans. Alessandro Cristofori, in "Grain Distribution in Late Republican Rome." In *The Welfare State: Past, Present, Future*, ed. Francesca Petrucci, 141–54. Pisa: Edizioni Plus, 2002)

Cicero, *Epistulae ad Atticum* (Trans. E. O. Winstedt. Loeb Classical Library, 1912. Also trans. Frank Frost Abbott. Boston: Ginn and Company, 1897)

Cicero, *Epistulae ad Familiares* (Trans. Evelyn S. Shuckburgh. London: George Bell & Sons, 1899–1900)

Cicero, *Epistulae ad Quintum Fratrem* (Trans. Evelyn S. Shuckburgh. London: George Bell & Sons, 1900)

Cicero, *De Finibus Bonorum et Malorum*

Cicero, *De Legibus*

Cicero, *De Officiis* (Trans. Walter Miller. Loeb Classical Library, 1913)

Cicero, *De Provinciis Consularibus* (Trans. C. D. Yonge. London: George Bell & Sons, 1891)

Cicero, *De Re Publica* (Trans. Francis Barham. London: Edmund Spettigue, 1841–1842)

Cicero, *In Catilinam I–IV* (Trans. Michael Grant. New York: Penguin Books, 1969)

Cicero, *In Pisonem* (Trans. C. D. Yonge. London: George Bell & Sons, 1891)

Cicero, *In Verrem II* (Trans. T. P. Wiseman, in *Classics in Progress: Essays on Ancient Greece and Rome,* London: British Academy, 2002)

Cicero, *Paradoxa Stoicorum*

Cicero, *Post Reditum ad Quirites* (Trans. C. D. Yonge. London: George Bell & Sons, 1856)

Cicero, *Post Reditum in Senatu* (Trans. C. D. Yonge. London: George Bell & Sons, 1856)

Cicero, *Pro Caelio*

Cicero, *Pro Milone* (Trans. C. D. Yonge. London: George Bell & Sons, 1891)

Cicero, *Pro Murena* (Trans. C. D. Yonge. London: George Bell & Sons, 1856)

Cicero, *Pro Plancio* (Trans. Tom Holland, in *Rubicon*. London: Little, Brown, 2003)

Cicero, *Pro Scauro* (Trans. C. D. Yonge. London: George Bell & Sons, 1856)

Cicero, *Pro Sestio* (Trans. Alessandro Cristofori, in "Grain Distribution in Late Republican Rome." In *The Welfare State: Past, Present, Future,* ed. Francesca Petrucci, 141–54. Pisa: Edizioni Plus, 2002)

Cicero, *Tusculanae Disputationes* (Trans. C. D. Yonge. New York: Harper and Brothers, 1877)

Diogenes Laertius, *Lives and Opinions of Eminent Philosophers* (Trans. C. D. Yonge. London: George Bell & Sons, 1895).

Epictetus, *Enchiridion*

Isocrates, *Against the Sophists* (Trans. George Norlin. Loeb Classical Library, 1980)

Josephus, *Antiquitates Judaicae* (Trans. Ralph Marcus. Loeb Classical Library, 1976)

Josephus, *De Bello Judaico* (Trans. H. St. J. Thackeray, Loeb Classical Library, 1927)

Julius Victor, *Ars Rhetorica*

Juvenal, *Saturae* (Trans. G. G. Ramsay. Loeb Classical Library, 1918)

Lactantius, *Divinae Institutiones* (In *The Ante-Nicene Fathers*, vol. 7. Eds. Alexander Roberts and James Donaldson. Grand Rapids, MI: Wm. B. Eerdmans, 1886)

Lucan, *Pharsalia* (Trans. Edward Ridley. London: Longmans, Green, and Co., 1896)

Macrobius, *Saturnalia* (Trans. P. V. Davies. New York: Columbia University Press, 1969)

Marcus Aurelius, *Meditations* (Trans. George Long. London: G. Bell, 1881)

Martial, *Epigrammata*

Ovid, *Ibis* (Trans. Henry T. Riley. London: G. Bell, 1878)

Persius, *Saturae* (Trans. A. S. Kline)

Plato, *Phaedo* (Trans. Harold North Fowler. Loeb Classical Library, 1990)

Pliny the Elder, *Naturalis Historiae* (Trans. John Bostock and H. T. Riley. London: Taylor and Francis, 1855)

Pliny the Younger, *Epistulae*

Plutarch, *Caesar* (Trans. Bernadotte Perrin. Loeb Classical Library, 1919)

Plutarch, *Cato Major* (Trans. Bernadotte Perrin. Loeb Classical Library, 1914)

Plutarch, *Cato Minor* (Trans. Bernadotte Perrin. Loeb Classical Library, 1919)

Plutarch, *Cicero* (Trans. Bernadotte Perrin. Loeb Classical Library, 1919)

Plutarch, *Comparison of Agesilaus and Pompey* (Trans. Bernadotte Perrin. Loeb Classical Library, 1917)

Plutarch, *Crassus* (Trans. Bernadotte Perrin. Loeb Classical Library, 1916)

Plutarch, *On the Fortune of Alexander*

Plutarch, *On Stoic Self-Contradictions*

Plutarch, *Gaius Gracchus* (Trans. Bernadotte Perrin. Loeb Classical Library, 1921)

Plutarch, *Gaius Marius* (Trans. Bernadotte Perrin. Loeb Classical Library, 1920)

Plutarch, *Lucullus* (Trans. Bernadotte Perrin. Loeb Classical Library, 1914)

Plutarch, *Marcus Brutus* (Trans. Bernadotte Perrin. Loeb Classical Library, 1918)

Plutarch, *Pompey* (Trans. Bernadotte Perrin. Loeb Classical Library, 1917)

Plutarch, *Sertorius* (Trans. Bernadotte Perrin. Loeb Classical Library, 1919)

Plutarch, *Sulla* (Trans. Bernadotte Perrin. Loeb Classical Library, 1916)

Plutarch, *Tiberius Gracchus* (Trans. Bernadotte Perrin. Loeb Classical Library, 1921)

Priscian, *Institutiones Grammaticae*

Pseudo-Caesar, *De Bello Africo* (Trans. W. A. McDevitte and W. S. Bohn. New York: Harper and Brothers, 1869)

Pseudo-Cicero, *Rhetorica ad Herennium* (Trans. Harry Caplan. Loeb Classical Library, 1954)

Pseudo-Sallust, *Ad Caesarem Senem de Re Publica Epistula*

Quintilian, *Institutio Oratoria*

Quintus Tullius Cicero, *Commentariolum Petitionis* (Trans. Anthony Trollope, in *The Life of Cicero*, vol. 1. New York: Harper and Brothers, 1881)

Sallust, *Bellum Catilinae* (Trans. John Selby Watson. New York: Harper and Brothers, 1867)

Seneca, *De Constantia* (Trans. John W. Basore. Loeb Classical Library, 1928)

Seneca, *De Ira* (Trans. John W. Basore. Loeb Classical Library, 1928)

Seneca, *De Tranquillitate Animi* (Trans. John W. Basore. Loeb Classical Library, 1928)

Seneca, *Dialogi*

Seneca, *Epistulae* (Trans. Richard Gummere. Loeb Classical Library, 1917–1925)

Seneca Rhetor, *Controversiae*

Seneca Rhetor, *Suasoriae*

Strabo, *Geographica* (Trans. W. Falconer. London: George Bell & Sons, 1895)

Suetonius, *Divus Augustus*

Suetonius, *Divus Julius* (Trans. J. C. Rolfe. Loeb Classical Library, 1914)

Tacitus, *Annales*

Tertullian, *Apologeticus* (Trans. Alexander Souter. Cambridge: Cambridge University Press, 1917)

Ulpian, *Digesta*

Valerius Maximus, *Factorum ac Dictorum Memorabilium Libri IX* (Trans. Henry John Walker. Indianapolis, IN: Hackett, 2004)

Velleius Paterculus, *Historiae Romanae* (Trans. Frederick W. Shipley. Loeb Classical Library, 1924)

Virgil, *Aeneid* (Trans. Allen Mandelbaum. Berkeley, CA: University of California Press, 1971)

Modern Sources

Addison, Joseph. *Cato: A Tragedy*. New York: Players Press, 1996.

Alighieri, Dante. *The Banquet*. Translated by Elizabeth Price Sayers. Whitefish, MT: Kessinger, 2007.

——. *Monarchy*. Edited by Prue Shaw. Cambridge, UK: Cambridge University Press, 1996.

——. *Purgatorio*. Translated by Jean Hollander and Robert Hollander. New York: Anchor, 2004.

Arnold, Edward Vernon. *Roman Stoicism*. London: Routledge and Kegan Paul, 1958.

Astin, Alan Edgar. *Cato the Censor*. Oxford: Clarendon Press, 1978.

Ayers, Donald M. "Cato's Speech Against Murena." *Classical Journal* 49, no. 6: 245–53.

Bailyn, Bernard. *The Ideological Origins of the American Revolution*. Cambridge, MA: Belknap Press of Harvard University Press, 1967.

Balsdon, J. P. V. D. "Review: *The Idea of Liberty*." *Classical Review* 2, no.1 (1952): 43–44.

——. *Romans and Aliens*. Chapel Hill, NC: University of North Carolina Press, 1979.

Baltzly, Dirk. "Stoicism." In *The Stanford Encyclopedia of Philosophy* (Winter 2010 edition), edited by Edward N. Zalta. Available online at plato.stanford.edu/archives/win2010/entries/stoicism.

Barton, Carlin A. *Roman Honor: The Fire in the Bones*. Berkeley: University of California Press, 2001.

Beard, Mary. *The Roman Triumph*. Cambridge, MA: Belknap Press of Harvard University Press, 2007.

Bellemore, Jane. "Cato the Younger in the East in 66 B.C." *Historia* 44, no. 3 (1995): 376–79.

——. "The Quaestorship of Cato and the Tribunate of Memmius." *Historia* 45, no. 4 (1996): 504–8.

Boissier, Gaston. *Cicéron et Ses Amis*. Paris: Hachette, 1888.

Brennan, T. Corey. *The Praetorship in the Roman Republic.* Vols. 1 and 2. New York: Oxford University Press, 2001.

Brennan, Tad. *The Stoic Life: Emotions, Duties, and Fate.* Oxford, UK: Clarendon Press, 2005.

Brunt, P. A. *The Fall of the Roman Republic and Related Essays.* New York: Oxford University Press, 1988.

Bryan, Mark Evans. " 'Slideing into Monarchical extravagance': Cato at Valley Forge and the Testimony of William Bradford Jr." *William and Mary Quarterly* 67, no. 1 (2010): 123–44.

Busch, Bernhardus. "De M. Porcio Catone Uticensi quid antiqui scriptores aequales et posteriores censuerint." Diss., Münster, 1911.

Collins, John H. "Caesar and the Corruption of Power." *Historia* 4, no. 4 (1955): 445–65.

Conant, Joseph Michael. "The Younger Cato: A Critical Life with Special Reference to Plutarch's Biography." PhD diss., Columbia University, 1954.

Craig, Christopher P. "Cato's Stoicism and the Understanding of Cicero's Speech for Murena." *Transactions of the American Philological Association* 116 (1986): 229–39.

Crawford, Michael H. *The Roman Republic.* 2nd ed. Cambridge, MA: Harvard University Press, 1993.

Cristofori, Alessandro. "Grain Distribution in Late Republican Rome." In *The Welfare State: Past, Present, Future,* edited by Francesca Petrucci, 141–54. Pisa: Edizioni Plus, 2002.

Damon, Cynthia. "Sex. Cloelius, *scriba.*" *Harvard Studies in Classical Philology* 94 (1992): 227–50.

Deutsch, Monroe E. "Pompey's Three Triumphs." *Classical Philology* 19, no. 3 (1924): 277–79.

Dillon, Matthew and Linda Garland. *Ancient Rome: From the Early Republic to the Assassination of Julius Caesar.* London: Routledge, 2005.

Drumann, Wilhelm K. A., and Paul Groebe. *Geschichte Roms in seinem Übergange von der republikanischen zur monarchischen Verfassung.* Berlin: Gebrüder Bortraeger, 1899.

Edwards, Catharine. "Modeling Roman Suicide? "The Afterlife of Cato." *Economy and Society* 34, no. 2 (2005): 200–222.

Ellison, Julie. *Cato's Tears and the Making of Anglo-American Emotion.* Chicago: University of Chicago Press, 1999.

Everitt, Anthony. *Cicero: The Life and Times of Rome's Greatest Politician.* New York: Random House, 2001.

Fantham, Elaine. "The Trials of Gabinius in 54 B.C." *Historia* 24, no. 3 (1975): 425–43.

Farney, Gary D. *Ethnic Identity and Aristocratic Competition in Republican Rome.* Cambridge, UK: Cambridge University Press, 2007.

Ford, Chauncey Worthington, ed. *Journals of the Continental Congress, 1774–89,* vol. 1. Washington, D.C.: Government Printing Office, 1904.

Freeman, Philip. *Julius Caesar.* New York: Simon & Schuster, 2008.

Gelzer, Matthias. *Caesar: Politician and Statesman.* Cambridge, MA: Harvard University Press, 1968.

George, David B. "Lucan's Cato and Stoic Attitudes to the Republic." *Classical Antiquity* 10, no. 2 (1991): 237–58.

Gibbon, Edward. *Memoirs of My Life and Writings.* Teddington, UK: The Echo Library, 2007.

Griffin, Miriam. "Philosophy, Cato, and Roman Suicide: I." *Greece & Rome* 33, no. 1 (1986): 64–77.

———. "Philosophy, Cato, and Roman Suicide: II." *Greece & Rome* 33, no. 2 (1986): 192–202.

Goar, Robert J. *The Legend of Cato Uticensis from the First Century B.C. to the Fifth Century A.D.: With an Appendix on Dante and Cato.* Brussels: Latomus, 1987.

Goldsworthy, Adrian. *The Complete Roman Army.* London: Thames & Hudson, 2003.

———. *Caesar: Life of a Colossus.* New Haven, CT: Yale University Press, 2006.

Groebe, Paul. "Die Obstruktion im römischen Senat." *Klio* 5 (1905): 229–35.

Gruen, Erich S. *The Last Generation of the Roman Republic.* Berkeley: University of California Press, 1974.

———. "Pompey, the Roman Aristocracy, and the Conference of Luca." *Historia* 18 (1969): 71–108.

Haley, Shelley P. "The Five Wives of Pompey the Great." *Greece & Rome* 32, no. 1 (1985): 49–59.

Hamilton, Edith. *The Roman Way.* New York: W. W. Norton, 1932.

Hill, T. D. *Ambitiosa Mors: Suicide and Self in Roman Thought and Literature.* London: Routledge, 2004.

Holland, Tom. *Rubicon*. London: Little, Brown, 2003.

Hollander, Robert. *Allegory in Dante's* Commedia. Princeton, NJ: Princeton University Press, 1969.

Inwood, Brad. *The Cambridge Companion to the Stoics*. Cambridge, UK: Cambridge University Press, 2003.

Irvine, William Braxton. *A Guide to the Good Life: The Ancient Art of Stoic Joy*. Oxford, UK: Oxford University Press, 2009.

Jaeger, Muriel. *Adventures in Living, from Cato to George Sand*. New York: William Morrow, 1932.

Jiménez, Ramon L. *Caesar Against the Celts*. New York: Sarpedon, 1996.

Johnson, Samuel. *Lives of the Poets*. Rockville, MD: Arc Manor, 2008.

Ketterer, Robert C. *Ancient Rome in Early Opera*. Chicago: University of Illinois Press, 2008.

Kiernan, Ben. "The First Genocide: Carthage, 146 B.C." *Diogenes* 51, no. 3 (2004): 27–39.

Litto, Fredric M. "Addison's *Cato* in the Colonies." *William and Mary Quarterly* 23, no. 3 (1966): 431–49.

Long, George. *The Decline of the Roman Republic*. London: Bell and Daldy, 1866.

Marin, Pamela. *Blood in the Forum: The Struggle for the Roman Republic*. London: Continuum, 2009.

Mayor, Adrienne. *The Poison King: The Life and Legend of Mithridates, Rome's Deadliest Enemy*. Princeton, NJ: Princeton University Press, 2009.

Means, Thomas and Sheila K. Dickison. "Plutarch and the Family of Cato Minor." *The Classical Journal* 69, no. 3 (1974): 210–15.

Meyer, Heinrich, ed. *Oratorum Romanorum Fragmenta*. Zurich: Orell Füssli, 1832.

Middleton, Conyers. *The History of the Life of Marcus Tullius Cicero*. London: Innys and Manby, 1741.

Miller, John J. "America's Greatest Play." *National Review,* February 18, 2005. Available online at old.nationalreview.com/miller/miller200502180801.asp.

Montesquieu, Charles de. *The Spirit of the Laws*. Translated by Thomas Nugent. New York: Hafner, 1949.

Morstein-Marx, Robert. *Mass Oratory and Political Power in the Late Roman Republic*. Cambridge, UK: Cambridge University Press, 2004.

Nelson, Haviland. "Cato the Younger as a Stoic Orator." *The Classical Weekly* 44, no. 5 (1950): 65–69.

Oman, Charles. *Seven Roman Statesmen of the Later Republic*. Edinburgh: Ballantyne, Hanson, 1902.

Oost, Stewart Irvin. "Cato Uticensis and the Annexation of Cyprus." *Classical Philology* 50, no. 2 (1955): 98–112.

Piotrowicz, Ludwig. "De Q. Caecilii Metelli Pii Scipionis in M. Porcium Catonem Uticensem invectiva." *Eos* 18 (1912): 129–36.

Richard, Carl J. *The Founders and the Classics: Greece, Rome, and the American Enlightenment*. Cambridge, MA: Harvard University Press, 1995.

Robinson, Joan. *Private Enterprise or Public Control*. London: Association for Education in Citizenship, 1943.

Russo, Peter Mansson. "Marcus Porcius Cato Uticensis: A Political Reappraisal." PhD diss., Rutgers University, 1974.

Sanford, Eva Matthews. "The Career of Aulus Gabinius." *Transactions and Proceedings of the American Philological Association* 70 (1939): 64–92.

Schiff, Stacy. *Cleopatra: A Life*. New York: Little, Brown, 2010.

Schils, Gretchen J. *The Roman Stoics: Self, Responsibility, and Affection*. Chicago: University of Chicago Press, 2005.

Seager, Robin. *Pompey the Great: A Political Biography*. 2nd ed. Oxford, UK: Blackwell, 2002.

Sherman, Nancy. *Stoic Warriors: The Ancient Philosophy Behind the Military Mind*. New York: Oxford University Press, 2007.

Shotter, David. *The Fall of the Roman Republic*. London: Routledge, 1994.

Stem, Rex. "The First Eloquent Stoic: Cicero on Cato the Younger." *The Classical Journal* 101, no. 1 (2005): 37–49.

Stockdale, James B. *Courage Under Fire: Testing Epictetus's Doctrines in a Laboratory of Human Behavior*. Stanford, CA: Hoover Institution Press, 1993.

Swain, Simon. "Plutarch's Lives of Cicero, Cato, and Brutus." *Hermes* 118, no. 2 (1990): 192–203.

Taylor, Lily Ross. "On the Chronology of Caesar's First Consulship." *The American Journal of Philology* 72, no. 3 (1951): 254–68.

———. *Party Politics in the Age of Caesar*. 6th ed. Berkeley: University of California Press, 1971.

BIBLIOGRAPHY

Thorne, Mark Allen. "Lucan's Cato, the Defeat of Victory, the Triumph of Memory." PhD diss., University of Iowa, 2010.

Trenchard, John, and Thomas Gordon. *Cato's Letters, or Essays on Liberty, Civil and Religious, and Other Important Subjects.* Indianapolis, IN: Liberty Fund, 2010.

Trollope, Anthony. *The Life of Cicero.* London: Chapman and Hall, 1880.

Voltaire. *Letters on England.* New York: General Books, 2010.

Washington, George. *Rules of Civility and Decent Behavior in Company and Conversation.* Available online at www.foundationsmag.com/civility.html.

Webb, Jim. "Speech at the Confederate Memorial." June 3, 1990. Available online at www.jameswebb.com/speeches/speeches-confedmem.htm.

Welles, C. Bradford. *Royal Correspondence in the Hellenistic Period.* New Haven, CT: Yale University Press, 1934.

Wiseman, T. P. "Roman History and the Ideological Vacuum." In *Classics in Progress: Essays on Ancient Greece and Rome,* edited by T. P. Wiseman, 285–310. London: British Academy, 2002.

———. *Roman Political Life, 90 B.C–A.D. 69.* Exeter, UK: University of Exeter, 1985.

———. *New Men in the Roman Senate, 139 B.C.–A.D. 14.* London: Oxford University Press, 1971.

Wirszubski, C. *Libertas as Political Idea at Rome During the Late Republic and Early Principate.* Cambridge, UK: Cambridge University Press, 1950.

Wood, Gordon S. *The Idea of America.* New York: Penguin, 2011.

INDEX

INDEX